Additio

The Fight to Vote

"Waldman draws a clear picture full of amusing anecdotes of voting and voting rights over the past 228 years. He demonstrates how the political establishment, fearing change, usually has been behind the people on this question."

—*The Buffalo News*

"[An] important new book."

—E.J. Dionne Jr., *The Washington Post*

"Using a wealth of solid historical scholarship and political biography, Waldman's work makes the contemporary issues concerning the right to vote accessible to the average American. When read along with Robert E. Mutch's *Buying the Vote,* any citizen concerned about the health of America's democracy will be well informed."

—*Library Journal*

"A compelling—and disheartening—history of voting in America . . . Waldman urges citizens to find a way to celebrate democracy and reinvigorate political engagement for all. A timely contribution to the discussion of a crucial issue."

—*Kirkus Reviews*

"Michael Waldman's masterly history reminds us that 'We the People' can and must restore our experiment in constitutional freedom."

—Taylor Branch, author of *America in the King Years*

Additional Praise for

The Second Amendment: A Biography

"A smart history of guns and the U.S. . . . his calm tone and habit of taking the long view offers a refreshing tonic in this most loaded of debates."

—*Los Angeles Times*

"Rigorous, scholarly, but accessible book."

—*The New York Times*

"Waldman relates this tale in clear, unvarnished prose and it should now be considered the best narrative of its subject."

—*Publishers Weekly*

"Waldman offers historical perspective on the fierce debate. . . . A lively and engaging exploration."

—*Booklist*

"Thoughtful, accessible . . . useful to anyone arguing either side of this endlessly controversial issue."

—*Kirkus Reviews*

"Waldman's new book will not make the most zealous NRA advocates happy, but for anyone who wants his or her history of the Second Amendment straight-up, this is the most comprehensive, accessible, and compelling version of the story in print."

—Joseph J. Ellis, author of *Founding Brothers*

"Compelling."

—*The Washington Post*

"An insightful look at both the historical foundation of the Second Amendment . . . [and] a welcome re-injection of historical context into the present debate over the rightful role of guns in American culture."

—*Chicago Tribune*

"Terrific."

—Nicholas Kristof, *The New York Times*

Also by Michael Waldman

The Second Amendment: A Biography

A Return to Common Sense: Seven Bold Ways to Revitalize Democracy

My Fellow Americans: The Most Important Speeches of America's Presidents from George Washington to Barack Obama

POTUS Speaks: Finding the Words That Defined the Clinton Presidency

Who Robbed America? A Citizens' Guide to the S&L Scandal

Who Runs Congress?
(with Mark Green)

THE FIGHT TO VOTE

MICHAEL WALDMAN

SIMON & SCHUSTER PAPERBACKS
New York London Toronto Sydney New Delhi

Simon & Schuster Paperbacks
An Imprint of Simon & Schuster, Inc.
1230 Avenue of the Americas
New York, NY 10020

This Simon & Schuster trade paperback edition January 2022

SIMON & SCHUSTER PAPERBACKS and colophon are registered trademarks of Simon & Schuster, Inc.

For information about special discounts for bulk purchases, please contact Simon & Schuster Special Sales at 1-866-506-1949 or business@simonandschuster.com.

The Simon & Schuster Speakers Bureau can bring authors to your live event. For more information or to book an event, contact the Simon & Schuster Speakers Bureau at 1-866-248-3049 or visit our website at www.simonspeakers.com.

Interior design by Ellen R. Sasahara

Manufactured in the United States of America

3 5 7 9 10 8 6 4 2

Library of Congress Cataloging-in-Publication Data is available.

ISBN 978-1-9821-9893-0
ISBN 978-1-5011-1650-6 (ebook)

To Liz

CONTENTS

THE FIGHT TO VOTE

INTRODUCTION

On August 9, 1787, in a locked room at the Constitutional Convention, delegates debated the shape of America's new system of elections. A handful wanted to give state legislatures unfettered power to set the rules. But James Madison recoiled. The Virginian, architect of so much of the Constitution, was determined to give the national government authority to override the machinations of state politicians.

"It was impossible to foresee all the abuses that might be made of the discretionary power," Madison warned. He sketched out an array of ways to manipulate voting rules: "Whenever the State Legislatures had a favorite measure to carry, they would take care so to mould their regulations as to favor the candidates they wished to succeed." Madison's view carried the day.

Well over two centuries later, on June 25, 2013, the U.S. Supreme Court struck down the key provision of the Voting Rights Act, the landmark civil rights law.

Just two hours after the announcement, the State of Texas implemented new rules. Texans would now have to show a state-issued photo ID to vote. The law was mischievously crafted by the state's Republican lawmakers; voters could present a concealed-carry gun permit, for example, but not a University of Texas student card.

Instantly hundreds of thousands of citizens, disproportionately African American or Hispanic, many of whom had cast ballots for decades, were ineligible to vote.

One of them was Sammie Louise Bates. She grew up in Mississippi in the 1940s and remembered carefully counting out money so her grandmother could pay that state's notorious poll tax. Bates had voted since she was twenty-one. After living in Chicago and Detroit, she retired to Round Rock, Texas, where she lived on Social Security and little else. Now she would have to obtain her birth records from Mississippi to vote again.

Sitting at a burnished conference table in a law firm office, Bates was asked why she had not quickly procured the paperwork. "I had to put $42 where it was doing the most good. It was feeding my family," she explained. She gazed evenly at her questioner. "We couldn't eat the birth certificate."

In October 2014, persuaded by Bates's videotaped testimony, among others, a federal judge struck down Texas's voter law. In 2016 the nation's most conservative appeals court agreed.

How could this be happening now?

We Americans are proud of our democracy, the world's oldest. That system rests on the right to vote, the idea that every citizen should have an equal voice: one person, one vote. Yet today that democracy seems to be under siege, and the *right* to vote has become the *fight* to vote.

A wave of laws attempts to make it harder to vote in dozens of states for the first time since the Jim Crow era. Vast sums from a handful of donors, much of it donated secretly, dominate campaign spending. Pervasive gerrymandering ensures that most elections are not even competitive. Once again core tenets of American democracy are the subject of heated and surprising controversy.

Today's arguments are intense and consequential. But they are not new. The fight to vote has always been at the heart of our national story, and raucous debates over how to expand democracy have always been at the center of American politics. Our effort to translate ideals into the reality of representative government has been about more than process; for more than two centuries it's been raw, rowdy—a fierce and often rollicking struggle for power. At every step of the way, while some fought to gain a voice in their government, others fought just as hard to silence them.

This book looks at that full history. The fight to vote didn't start recently, or even half a century ago in Selma, Alabama. It's been under way for over 240 years, ever since the country's beginning. This book puts that battle fully in political context, for politics was never far from the concerns of those who fought for the vote. It traces the way voting rules have always entangled with broader issues of wealth, class and race, campaign finance, and political parties. In all this it illuminates some lessons from that past to provide a context for today's controversies.

Creative and controversial leaders waged these fights: some well known, others lost to obscurity. There was Benjamin Franklin, leading a workingman's movement in Pennsylvania that demanded the right to vote for those without property; Frederick Douglass, who grasped with unfiltered eloquence the idea that enfranchisement was the next great struggle after the abolition of slavery. Or creative agitators such as Inez Milholland, a young lawyer astride a white horse who led parades for voting rights for women. There were crafty politicians pressed by social movements—Martin Van Buren, Lyndon Johnson—who etched the effort into law. And there were men who worked as hard to restrict the vote as others did to expand it, such as John Randolph of Roanoke, who fought to deny the franchise to men without property, declaring, "I am an aristocrat. I love liberty. I hate equality;" John Wilkes Booth, moved to murder by Abraham Lincoln's seeming change of heart on voting; Paul Weyrich, a founder of the modern conservative movement, who mocked religious figures who "want everybody to vote" and thundered, "I don't want everybody to vote."

Through their stories this book focuses on key moments, turning points when controversy eventually yielded a lurch forward—or when the country actually moved backward. I believe we are at such an inflection point today.

At the time of the founding, as described in part I, only white men who owned property could vote. The original Constitution never mentions a right to cast a ballot. A few radicals pressed for more. But the ideas that fired the American Revolution and the crafting of the Constitution set in motion inexorable pressure to extend democratic rights more widely. "There will be no end of it," warned John Adams.

Part II tells of the propulsive rise and discouraging retreat of American democracy in the nineteenth century. First to fall was the property requirement, as a new political party, the Democrats, fought to extend the vote to white workingmen and the poor. The United States became the world's first mass democracy, with political parties driven by millions of active citizens. After the Civil War, the Republican Party extended the franchise to Black men through the Fifteenth Amendment. Former slaves voted in huge numbers and served in Congress. But racial terrorism and cynical deals effectively repealed the right to vote for African Americans in the South, a region that sank into a century of feudal repression. In the North widespread fraud prompted efforts to limit suffrage for the working class. Gilded Age inequality drained the vote of its meaning. This era, with unsettling echoes of our own, reminds us that history can retreat as well as advance.

What happened then? Part III tells of the relentless push during the twentieth century toward a more meaningful democracy in the United States. More than is commonly recognized the Progressive Era focused on political reform. Citizens won the right to vote for U.S. senators in a bid to curb corruption. An innovative protest movement led by Alice Paul and other suffragists gained the vote for women, effectively doubling the size of the electorate. At midcentury courts began to set new standards for political equality under the slogan "one person, one vote." In the 1960s the civil rights movement and its political allies won the most profound victory of all: voting rights for all Americans regardless of race or wealth. Other changes followed: extending the vote to eighteen-year-olds, giving voters the chance to choose presidential nominees, limiting the role of big money. The basic rules seemed to be in place. Put your pencils down.

But over the past fifteen years that progress seems to have jolted into reverse. Part IV describes the modern war over voting.

At some point during the Florida 2000 recount debacle—to be

honest, probably at around four in the morning that first topsy-turvy night—partisans realized anew that razor-thin margins can be turned by manipulation of voting rules. Surging turnout among minority voters began to remake the electoral map, provoking a sharp backlash. Starting in 2011 states began to enact dozens of laws that a leading conservative judge has concluded amount to "voter suppression." The U.S. Supreme Court led by John Roberts has made things worse. In *Citizens United* in 2010 the Court allowed unlimited election spending by corporations, while other courts effectively gave that right to wealthy individuals. Three years later, in *Shelby County v. Holder*, a five-justice majority struck down the key provision of the Voting Rights Act. More major rulings followed.

New chapters for this 2022 edition describe an intense new moment. Voter turnout plunged in 2014 to the lowest level in seven decades. But in 2020, despite the COVID-19 pandemic, turnout soared to the highest level since 1900. The response: Donald Trump's "Big Lie" that the election was stolen, and the insurrection at the Capitol aiming to block the Electoral College vote. The wave of new state voting restrictions driven by that lie. And the drive, at long last, for federal democracy reform legislation.

I work on these issues every day. I lead an institute, the Brennan Center for Justice at NYU School of Law, that works to reform the systems of democracy. I explored this history seeking a usable past, lessons that could illuminate today's struggles. I was surprised by much of what I learned.

To start, this debate has always been deeply, properly political. While it might exasperate readers sick of partisanship, the political parties have been the engines of expanding democracy. The greatest gains came when hard-eyed operatives realized that expanded participation was in their enlightened electoral self-interest. This is a story, then, of joyous, cynical, rambunctious politics.

From the beginning, too, Americans have wrestled with much more than the formal ability to cast a ballot. We ask not just who can vote, but how—and for what. Politics has been plagued by unfair rules, rigged election districts, and partisan shenanigans. And, yes, there is a rich history of election fraud—but not the kind pundits scream about today. Invariably it has been misconduct by politicians, not individual voters. After all, politicians have wanted to stuff the ballot box since senators wore togas.

Of course, the fight to vote has been a story of America's long, unfinished effort to ensure that racial minorities, especially Black Americans, can fully participate. But just as often this struggle has gone well beyond race, to issues of class and economic opportunity. Today, frequently, we see "voting" and "campaign finance" as separate issues, yet for most of our history they were self-evidently linked. The story of the vote is also a story of the constant struggle between a system dominated by dollars and one dominated by voters.

One final surprise, especially for those who expect to read of the Supreme Court as a heroic protector of liberties: the fight to expand the vote rarely has been won in the courtroom; most of the time the courts were absent. Only briefly during the twentieth century did judges lead the way. The people themselves have driven most constitutional change. In fact it took five separate constitutional amendments to explicitly enshrine the right to vote.

Which brings us to today, and tomorrow. The new controversies over democracy create the possibility of the next wave of reforms—improvements in the way our system works that address current problems, not those of 1905 or 1965. Out of today's fights to protect voting and campaign finance law, we're starting to see innovative reforms. They rely on technology to address some of the most stubborn and long-standing gaps in our system. As history makes clear, changes do not come from judicial fine print or technical tweaks. Rather they start with a recognition that these issues—the core issues of American democracy—once again are properly the topic for deep, engaged, contentious, often partisan debate.

The story begins at a time when Americans could barely imagine the democracy we've become: in the heat of rebellion against the world's most powerful empire.

PART I

THE FOUNDING

1

"The Consent of the Governed"

At the start of America's drive toward democracy, many thought about representation and how to give power to the people. Surprisingly few thought about the vote.

On June 11, 1776, Philadelphia pulsed with revolution. In quick succession the Continental Congress appointed three committees to prepare for the expected final break with Great Britain. One panel would explore foreign alliances; another would set terms for a confederation of the newly independent states; and the Committee of Five would write the Declaration of Independence. As that document grew in importance over the years, its authors described how it was drafted. The story got better with each retelling. John Adams claimed he had chosen the thirty-three-year-old Thomas Jefferson, just as he had tapped George Washington to lead the Continental Army. "You should do it," he remembered Jefferson insisting.

"Oh! no," Adams replied.

"Why will you not? You ought do it."

"I will not."

"Why?"

"Reasons enough."

"What can be your reasons?"

"Reason first—You are a Virginian, and a Virginian ought to appear at the head of this business. Reason second—I am obnoxious, suspected, and unpopular.—You are much otherwise. Reason third—You can write ten times better than I can."

Years later Jefferson would serenely deny such a conversation, claiming it was clear all along that he would write the Declaration. In any case, that Jefferson's hand held the quill would have echoing consequences. Adams, after all, was a fussily conservative thinker, fearful of what he called the "leveling" tendencies of democracy. The Virginian did more than draft a bill of complaints against the British Crown. His draft began with a statement of principle that became an enduring American creed.

Working on a portable desk made to order by a local carpenter and attended by a fourteen-year-old slave boy, Bob Hemmings, Jefferson consulted the "declaration of rights" drafted for the new Virginia constitution. The *Pennsylvania Gazette* had printed it in full that week. That document, written by George Mason, began by declaring that "all men are by nature equally free and independent and have certain inherent rights, of which, when they enter into a state of society, they cannot, by any compact, deprive or divest their posterity; namely, the enjoyment of life and liberty, with the means of acquiring and possessing property, and pursuing and obtaining happiness and safety." It went on to proclaim that "all power is vested in, and consequently derived from, the people; that magistrates are their trustees and servants and at all times amenable to them."

Jefferson pared, pruned, and reshaped the words into the ringing preamble of America's Declaration. "We hold these truths to be self-evident"—the last phrase Benjamin Franklin's felicitous edit—"that all men are created equal, that they are endowed by their Creator with certain unalienable Rights, that among these are Life, Liberty and the pursuit of Happiness." Jefferson's opening salvo evoked the philosophy of natural rights. Historians recently have been scrutinizing the parchment again and have concluded that the passage ended not with a period but a comma, thus driving forward to the next point:

> —That to secure these rights, Governments are instituted among Men, deriving their just powers from the consent of the governed,
> —That whenever any Form of Government becomes destructive of these ends, it is the Right of the People to alter or to abolish it, and to institute new Government, laying its foundation on such principles and organizing its powers in such form, as to them shall seem most likely to effect their Safety and Happiness.

The "consent of the governed"—consent that must be won from "all men," "created equal." It was an idea both revolutionary and "intended to be an expression of the American mind," as Jefferson put it. This ideal was far from reality at the time it was pronounced in 1776. Young America was anything but a democracy. But the fight to give life to those words was under way, even as Jefferson wrote. That creed would rebuke civic inequality from the beginning. Abolitionists declaimed the preamble in mass meetings in the 1830s. The first women's rights convention, at Seneca Falls, New York, traced its language. Abraham Lincoln, decrying the spread of slavery in 1854, called that passage "the sheet anchor of American republicanism." He paraphrased it at Gettysburg. Franklin Roosevelt borrowed it to decry "economic royalists" during the Depression. Dr. Martin Luther King Jr. cited it as "the true meaning of [our] creed." Mostly these later Americans focused on its articulation of equality. Less clear, and the basis of two centuries of battle, is the connection between equal citizenship and a government that relies on and is responsible to the people. The power of that idea would impel a movement toward democracy that would take two centuries.

"No Will of Their Own"

At the time of the Revolution, America was a traditional, stratified society. A small cluster of wealthy men led the revolt: plantation owners like Washington, attorneys like Adams, and merchants like John Hancock. Americans paid deference. The sense of social hierarchy—and the idea that political power should flow from that rank—was palpable.

The colonists inherited political ideas lauding Great Britain's "balanced" system. That approach split power between the king ("the one"), the nobles ("the few," found in the House of Lords), and the people ("the many," represented in the House of Commons). Such a system of checks, balances, and limits would protect liberty—the right, above all else, to be left alone by a potentially tyrannical government. In England representation was visibly uneven in the eighteenth century. "Rotten boroughs" in the countryside elected members of Parliament from just one family's estate. Old Sarum, a verdant but unpopulated mound in rural Salisbury, sent two men to Parliament. In effect some *buildings* had the right to vote, but not all *people*. Meanwhile the new industrial cities Manchester and Birmingham went without direct representation. The satirical painter William Hogarth parodied the state of British elections. Colorful images of bribery, drunkenness, and lechery—and a mayor passed out from eating too many oysters—spill across the canvas.

When the colonial agitators and pamphleteers of 1776 spoke of "consent of the governed," they echoed the language of the British philosopher John Locke and his notion of the social contract: the idea that rulers and people must forge an agreement for government to be legitimate and that the people have the right to overthrow an unjust state. The colonists weren't thinking about turning out incumbent officeholders, as we might today, but the much more disruptive task of overthrowing a regime. At first these arguments mostly referred not to individuals and the government but to the colonies and the mother country. Conflict first flared over the Stamp Act of 1765. The British had insisted that the colonists be satisfied with "virtual" representation in Parliament, just as most Englishmen were. Now the American colonists demanded direct representation in the halls of power. Repeated calls for representation and equal rights—calls directed by colonial Whig leaders toward England—in turn led some within the colonies to ask uncomfortable questions. Religious minorities such as Baptists and Catholics, debtors, and backwoods farmers began to direct similar demands at the governments closer to home.

Yet this debate about representation, one of these first forays toward the ideas of democracy, rarely revolved around voting itself.

In the colonies as in England, only white men with a defined amount of property could vote. The restriction dated to the Middle Ages. A British law enacted in 1430 limited voting to only those with a freehold estate producing an annual income of 40 shillings—enough to "furnish all the necessaries of life, and render the freeholder, if he pleased, an independent man." Colonists solemnly rehashed the arguments for voting limits: only men with a stake in society could be trusted with the franchise. Not just African slaves but indentured servants, tenant farmers, women, children, indebted artisans—many found themselves dependent on someone else. William Blackstone was an English jurist whose influential lectures landed in Boston and Philadelphia bookstores just a few years before the Revolution. The property limit on voting, Blackstone explained, seeks "to exclude such persons as are in so mean a situation that they are esteemed to have no will of their own." Poor people would be "tempted to dispose" of their votes—literally, to sell them. "This would give a great, an artful, or a wealthy man, a larger share in elections than is consistent with general liberty." Excluding the poor, he insisted, would actually foster greater equality among the remaining voters. His arguments echo in later claims that the poor are duped, easily induced to fraud, somehow shady—and the assertion that blocking their vote would actually help them. Even then this must have seemed something of a stretch. Palpable fears lingered not far below the surface. Give everyone a vote, and who knows what they will vote for?

Just how limited was the right to vote at the time of the American Revolution? Historians can't quite agree. The thirteen colonies were independent of one another and had varying rules. Seven restricted voting to men who owned land with specific acreage or value, others to those with specific amounts of personal property. One summary suggests that "by and large the property clauses prohibited at least a quarter—and in some states possibly as many of half—of the white male adults from voting for representatives to their state legislatures." In newly settled areas inland, cheap land meant wider ownership. There as many as 80 percent of white men could vote. But in established areas and cities that hugged the Atlantic coastline only 40 percent of white men could cast ballots. One historian claimed colonial Massachusetts was a "middle class democracy." Yet women were prohibited from voting almost everywhere; in most colonies so were Catholics and free Black men. And of course neither slaves nor Indians could vote. Of the 3 million people who lived in the thirteen colonies, only a fraction could cast ballots.

In any event, before the Revolution voting did not matter much. Royal appointees made the big decisions about taxes, appointments, and whether to take military action. Legislatures were a check on distant executive power, not the source of legitimate public authority. The sovereign was, well, sovereign. Elections were infrequent. In a brief ritualized moment of equality, members of the gentry would stoop to mingle with the public and seek support. Crowds would gather, eager to see the candidates and their families arrive by fancy coach. Office seekers would host fêtes for voters, with ample hard cider and food. Colonists called it "treating." When young George Washington ran for office in Virginia in 1755, Daniel Okrent writes, "he attributed his defeat to his failure to provide enough alcohol for the voters. When he tried again two years later, Washington floated into office partly on the 144 gallons of rum, punch, hard cider and beer his election agent handed out—roughly half a gallon for every vote he received." He gently chided his campaign agent,

"My only fear is that you spent with too sparing a hand." Politicians called it "swilling the planters with bumbo." Another, younger Virginia office seeker was more fastidious. James Madison disdained "personal solicitation" of voters and "the corrupting influence of spirituous liquors, and other treats." Madison lost. Voting was generally done viva voce (by voice). Sometimes it was done "by view," with supporters lining up to stand behind candidates. Enthusiasts with clubs would drive off their opponents' backers. Paying for votes was so common in one small colony, it became known as "Rhode Islandism." Polling places across the colonies were scattered, sometimes a full day's ride from where voters lived. Elections were marred by bribery and intimidation.

As a result few people voted, even when they had the right to do so. In a Connecticut gubernatorial election after Independence, only 5 percent of eligible voters turned out. One clergyman bemoaned the apathy. The "multitude," he complained, "will not leave the plow to have a governor of their taste." Of course poor people might be enraged or engaged for a brief time by a public issue. If they could not vote, they could engage in "mobbing"—burning an official in effigy, say, or enthusiastically rioting. The roughnecks organized by Sam Adams in his protests against British policy—throwing stones as they whooped "Liberty and Property!"—were making their voices heard (loudly) in a manner quite familiar to their countrymen.

That was America on the eve of the Revolution. A world of deference and disinterest, where a few great families were presumed to govern. In *The Radicalism of the American Revolution*, the historian Gordon S. Wood traces what happened next, how the ideas held by the colonists began to shift—rapidly, vertiginously. They thought they could replace monarchy with a republic, in which a few dispassionate men would hold power. Virtue would govern. They erected a new edifice of government that would enable those men to sift through society's competing demands. The Constitution, with its checks and balances, its tentative nods to democracy and its multiple veto points, embodied their theories. The founders discovered they had set loose political and intellectual energies that quickly overwhelmed those dreams and ideas.

"The Influence and Control of the People"

In January 1776 word arrived: King George III had rejected the "olive branch petition" sent by the Continental Congress the previous summer, refusing even to read it, denouncing those in the colonies who "openly avow their revolt, hostility, and rebellion," and vowing "the most decisive exertions" of military force to quell the uprising. The very day the Royal Address was printed in Philadelphia, Thomas Paine published *Common Sense*. Paine had arrived in the New World just two years before, escaping a failed marriage and a desultory career as a rope maker and tax collector in England. His pamphlet proved a sensation, a wild and widely bootlegged best seller with 150,000 copies in print. Paine argued for a break not just with Britain but with monarchy itself. "England since the conquest hath known some few good monarchs, but groaned beneath a much larger number of bad ones," he wrote. The Americans cast off British rule in town meetings and colonial assemblies over the coming months. In December residents of Pittsfield, Massachusetts, demanded a new state government, organized on a different basis. "If the right of nominating to office is not invested in the people," their statement read, "we are indifferent who assumes it whether any particular persons on this or on the other wide of the [wa]ter." A month later the colony's general court lauded the people for quickly establishing "a Form of Government" under the "Influence and Control of the People, and therefore more free and happy than was enjoyed by their Ancestors."

On May 10, 1776, the Continental Congress urged each colony to form a new government. Five days later it went further, pushing colonists to act so that any trace of the king's authority would be "totally suppressed." John Adams lauded the move as "an epocha, a decisive event," and enthused to a friend, "We are in the very midst of a Revolution, the most compleat, unexpected and remarkable of any in the History of Nations. . . . Every Colony must be induced to institute a perfect Government."

Across the colonies revolutionaries quickly fell to writing new constitutions to replace the royal charters. New Hampshire had already created a republic after its aristocratic royal governor escaped. Soon it enacted a law giving the vote to any man who paid taxes. It was, writes historian Marchette Chute, "the first sign that the crust which had formed in America on the subject of the franchise could crack under the pressure of war." South Carolina too had already declared its independence. There only large landowners were allowed to sit in its legislature, and they kept intact the colonial rule that only white men who owned an ample amount of property could vote.

In the newly independent states up and down the seaboard, with few models, Americans moved toward a more accountable form of government. The legislature was key, especially the lower house. John Adams wrote a treatise to share with fellow congressmen, many of whom were hurrying home to write their state charters: "The principal difficulty lies, and the greatest care should be employed, in constituting this Representative Assembly. It should be in miniature, an exact portrait of the people at large. It should think, feel, reason, and act like them." That required "equal representation," he insisted. "Great care should be taken to effect this, and to prevent unfair, partial, and corrupt elections." The legislature was balanced with an upper house, often apportioned by county rather than based on population size. These state senates represented property—not so much to enshrine wealth as to ensure that elites could tamp down the excesses of democracy. Elections now were frequent. Whigs—the political party in England that challenged the Crown—held to a basic political maxim: "Where ANNUAL ELECTION ends, TYRANNY begins." Every state except South Carolina now elected members to the state legislature every year. For the first time power came from the people—some broad group of them, at least—and the most important lawmaking body was the legislature. Gordon Wood explains that to the colonists, the role of the legislature was a startling change, the thing "that made the new governments in 1776 seem to be so much like democracies." And these legislatures were chosen by voters. America's new states considered themselves separate, independent countries. Of course they each set their own voting rules. That fact of late eighteenth-century life has significant consequences today.

Most states kept or only slightly eased colonial-era property limits on suffrage. One Virginia constitution writer reported, "It was not recollected that a hint was uttered in contravention of this principle." Jefferson had scratched out a proposed draft constitution for the state that significantly expanded suffrage. It arrived after the delegates were already done drafting and was ignored. John Jay led the writing of New York's constitution, in a small upstate town since the British occupied Manhattan. Jay believed that "the mass of men are neither wise nor good." (His son later recalled that it was "a favorite maxim with Mr. Jay, that those who own the country ought to govern it.") New York actually curbed voting rights, imposing the property requirement for the first time on residents of New York City and Albany.

But as war cascaded and Americans mobilized, a new strain of radicalism pressed for a wider democracy and demanded expanded voting rights.

A key institution in colonial America was the "well regulated militia." We know it in vestigial form through the Second Amendment. Adult men from age sixteen to sixty were required to serve and to own a military weapon. Militia members were drawn not solely from those with property, as had been the case in England, but from the full population of available men. In peaceful times militias fell into disuse. But as the break with Britain neared, they mobilized. Weapons were stockpiled, stolen from the British, and smuggled from Europe. The militias took on the coloration of a proto-political organization, partway between a tarring-and-feathering mob and the later mass political parties of empowered voters. When the Virginia aristocrat George Washington arrived at Cambridge, Massachusetts, in 1775 to take command of the scruffy continental forces, he was startled to discover that New England's soldiers elected their officers. Men who bore arms for independence grew incensed that the new political order might still prevent them from voting for legislators. Some Maryland counties simply ignored the old rules, declaring instead that "every taxable bearing arms, being an inhabitant of the county, had an undoubted right to vote for representatives at this time of political calamity."

With mounting pressure several states went further, changing the basic rules for voting. Georgia and North Carolina eliminated property requirements. Vermont, a new state that had broken away from New York and had not yet joined the union, wrote its first constitution without a property requirement, so long as residents displayed "quiet and peaceable behavior." Men who had served in the militia and the Continental Army led the fight there, most visibly the Irish immigrant Matty Lyon, a former indentured servant who would later be elected to the U.S. Congress. And those working-class militiamen who mustered in the very town where Jefferson was writing the Declaration helped produce the most radical of all state constitutions.

The Pennsylvania Revolution

Philadelphia bustled as the British Empire's second busiest port. Its streets teemed with sailors, indentured servants, shopkeepers, slaves, printers, and mechanics. A few dozen wealthy Quaker families dominated, but the colony welcomed every ethnic group and religion. Old and new worlds clashed: the same year the Continental Congress first met there, a crowd killed a woman it suspected of being a witch. Yet there were lending libraries, scientific societies, bookstores, and coffeehouses filled with debaters. In many other colonies Whig elites quietly switched sides, decorously shedding loyalty to the Crown. Not in Pennsylvania. In vibrant Philadelphia, the Revolution was recognizably revolutionary.

Its militia, according to historian Eric Foner, "was drawn most heavily from the ranks of poorer artisans and laborers and included 'a great many apprentices' and servants as well. Although Blacks were excluded by law, some may have served illegally in 1775. . . . Aristocratic Whigs described the militia privates as 'in general damn'd riff raff—dirty, mutinous, and disaffected.'" Increasingly the unkempt militiamen spoke out. First they insisted on the right to elect officers, as their New England counterparts did. Then they began to demand the right to vote for public officials as well, regardless of property qualifications. "For such men," Foner writes, "participation in the militia was the first step in the transition from crowd activity to organized politics." A Philadelphia newspaper editorialized that the vote should belong to "every man who pays his shot, and bears his lot."

Pennsylvania's insurrection boiled over on a rainy day in May. The existing state assembly had instructed its delegates to the Continental Congress to oppose independence, but Congress's plea for "suppressing" royal government checked that move. A seething crowd of four thousand gathered outside the statehouse in an open meeting to cheer Congress's call and to demand a new constitution. Authority dissolved; the assembly was rendered irrelevant. Committees of Correspondence and "associators" across Pennsylvania chose delegates to a new state constitutional convention. It first met in June at Carpenters' Hall. At the same time, a new provincial legislature formed, meeting down the hall from the Second Continental Congress in the statehouse. Three separate revolutionary conclaves worked within a few blocks of each other, with overlapping membership. The lurking presence of the nation's most energetic agitators turned up the heat even higher. Sam Adams, fresh from instigating rebellion in Boston, served as a delegate to the Continental Congress but quietly worked with the local patriots to upend their government.

The Pennsylvania constitution of 1776 was at the time the world's most democratic such document. "Every freeman of the full age of twenty-one Years," it declared, "shall enjoy the right of an elector," so long as he paid taxes. (The very poor still could not vote.) Pennsylvania would have only one legislative house, elected annually. The position of governor was eliminated; instead a committee exercised executive power. In a touch that uncomfortably prefigured twentieth-century revolutionary fanaticism, only those who swore an oath to the constitution could vote. For a time the drafters even toyed with limiting the size of personal wealth. It gave little fealty to the idea of checks and balances; popular sovereignty, accountability to the common people, would be enough. By 1787 nearly 88 percent of Pennsylvania's adult white men could vote.

The most prominent American led the way. Benjamin Franklin was now eighty-one. Philadelphia's artisans revered him and considered him their political spokesman. Franklin served on all three revolutionary bodies. He chaired the new state's constitutional convention and was credited with authorship of its charter (parenthood he never denied). He ridiculed the property requirement for voting:

> Today a man owns a jackass worth fifty dollars and he is entitled to vote; but before the next election the jackass dies. The man in the mean time has become more experienced, his knowledge of the principles of government, and his acquaintance with mankind, are more extensive, and he is therefore better qualified to make a proper selection of rulers—but the jackass is dead and the man cannot vote. Now gentlemen, pray inform me, in whom is the right of suffrage? In the man or in the jackass?

When the radical legislature hired Thomas Paine as clerk, America's most powerful polemicist joined with Franklin. Paine served as its functionary as well as a subsidized propagandist. *Common Sense* had vaguely urged that "qualified voters" be empowered to choose a new government, without saying who they might be. Paine was out of town when the new constitution was written, but now he roared support for its provisions. A property requirement for voting, he said, "makes scarce any, or no difference, in the value of the man to the community." Still, even Paine found it hard to embrace universal voting rights. He fretted that servants would be unable to break free of their masters and exercise individual will. Independence was key. (Two decades later Paine's evolution was complete. Writing from Paris during the French Revolution, he now proclaimed, "[The] right of voting for representatives is the primary right by which other rights are protected. To take away this right is to reduce a man to slavery, for slavery consists in being subject to the will of another, and he that has not a vote in the election of representatives is in this case.")

Pennsylvania's government provoked nonstop tumult. Quaker businessmen realized they were losing their grip on power. They tried repeatedly to repeal the constitution or dull its most democratic features. Over the months they staged what one historian called a "counter revolution." Dr. Benjamin Rush spoke for them when he scolded, "They call it a democracy—a mobocracy in my opinion would be more proper. All our laws breathe the spirit of town meetings and porter shops."

Conservatives tried to overturn the 1776 constitution three times. They wanted to create an upper chamber of property owners, to allow British sympathizers to vote, and to have a single man serve as governor. Franklin responded to one such effort, just months before he died, pronouncing himself opposed to any system that gave "the rich a predominancy in government." Meeting in the City Tavern, merchants and their allies mapped a grassroots campaign to elect legislators who would rewrite the charter. Ironically they found popular mobilization the key to undermining the populist constitution. Finally, in 1790 they succeeded. Pennsylvania joined the other states in creating a bicameral legislature, an elected governor, and an independent judiciary. Even so they did not dare repeal broad voting rights.

"There Will Be No End of It"

John Adams was aghast at the radicalism of Franklin's Pennsylvania constitution. He called Paine a "Disastrous Meteor." The mutual disdain between Adams and Franklin, the prig and the worldly epicurean, is one of the more engrossing subplots of the Revolution. Adams was enormously jealous of Franklin's renown. Later he would complain, "The history of our Revolution will be one continued lie from one end to the other. The essence of the whole will be that Dr. Franklin's electrical rod smote the Earth and out sprung General Washington. That Franklin electrified him with his rod—and thence forward these two conducted all the policy negotiations legislation and war." Franklin returned the sentiment. "He means well for his country," he wrote of Adams, "is always an honest man, often a wise one, but sometimes and in some things absolutely out of his senses." Here the rivalry played out as a clash of political philosophy.

Adams wrote a proposal for a new Massachusetts constitution. Ironically all men could vote in the election to choose delegates to write the state charter, but the resulting document actually narrowed suffrage, tightening property requirements from what they had been under the British.

One legislative leader wrote to Adams suggesting that suffrage be expanded to all men. Adams recoiled. "Depend upon it, sir," he replied, "it is dangerous to open so fruitful a source of controversy and altercation, as would be opened by attempting to alter the qualifications of voters. There will be no end of it. New claims will arise. Women will demand a vote. Lads from 12 to 21 will think their rights not enough attended to, and every man, who has not a farthing, will demand an equal voice with any other in all acts of state. It tends to confound and destroy all distinctions, and prostrate all ranks, to one common level."

Critics assailed the proposed charter. The town of Northampton warned that "many persons" would be disenfranchised. According to one clergyman, writing in a Boston newspaper, the exclusion of Blacks, Indians, and "mulattos" from the franchise showed white men "meant their own rights only, and not those of mankind, in their cry for liberty." Citizens rejected the Massachusetts constitution the first time they voted. It won ratification on a second round, but only because of presumed widespread voter fraud in the western part of the state.

An idea in motion, to paraphrase Isaac Newton, tends to stay in motion. The logic of the revolutionaries' argument—"the consent of the governed"—in part created pressure for a wider franchise. Americans understood, even then, that the ideals of the Declaration formed a standard by which practices would be measured and found wanting. Women began to object that they were denied the vote. A famous exchange between Abigail Adams and her husband, John, during the break with Britain wittily explained the momentum.

"I long to hear that you have declared an independancy," Abigail wrote, "and by the way in the new Code of Laws which I suppose it will be necessary for you to make I desire you would remember the ladies, and be more generous and favourable to them than your ancestors. Do not put such unlimited power into the hands of the husbands. Remember all men would be tyrants if they could. If particular care and attention is not paid to the ladies we are determined to foment a rebellion, and will not hold ourselves bound by any laws in which we have no voice, or representation."

John replied with mordant flirtatiousness: "As to your extraordinary code of laws, I cannot but laugh. We have been told that our struggle has loosened the bonds of government everywhere; that children and apprentices were disobedient; that schools and colleges were grown turbulent; that Indians slighted their guardians, and negroes grew insolent to their masters. But your letter was the first intimation that another tribe, more numerous and powerful than all the rest, were grown discontented.—This is rather too coarse a compliment but you are so saucy, I won't blot it out."

2

"Who Are to Be the Electors?"

A DECADE LATER delegates gathered once again in the statehouse in Philadelphia. Those who attended the Constitutional Convention in the spring of 1787 were less prone to flights of sentimental rhetoric than the patriots of 1776. Jefferson, a passionate if vague believer in the right of revolution, was in Paris. Adams, conservative skeptic, was in England, busy being ignored by the British court. Instead it was younger men, mostly tempered by service in the Continental Army and with experience of the failures of the Articles of Confederation in place after the Revolution, who met in secret to write an entirely new constitution.

These men focused intently on the practical political science of how to create a workable self-governing republic—something that had never been seen before on a continental scale. They were acutely aware that they had to craft a document that would win enough popular support to be ratified. Some later called their move a counterrevolution. They believed in popular sovereignty, but not too much of it.

For the first month it was far from clear that they would succeed at all. We know the details of the deliberations only because of Madison's meticulous notes, which were not made public until five decades later. Delegates clashed repeatedly over grave issues of representation. Early on they decided that "the people" should elect the House of Representatives. Only a few New Englanders warned against what Elbridge Gerry of Massachusetts called "the excess of democracy." Connecticut delegate Roger Sherman opposed direct election. The people, he said, "should have as little to do as may be about the government." George Mason of Virginia, who had written the "declaration of rights" from which Jefferson drew, heatedly objected to that view. The convention should "attend to the rights of every class of the people." Direct popular election for the House of Representatives carried, six states to two. The body was to be apportioned directly on population, an approach influenced by the radical Pennsylvania constitution.

For many weeks the delegates wrestled over the question of the Senate. The upper body was supposed to represent an aristocracy, whether of wealth or talent or wisdom. Eventually the delegates agreed that each state, large or small, would be represented by two senators, the Great Compromise we live with today. It was hardly an elevated debate. Dunning Bedford Jr. of Delaware warned that unless the big states capitulated, "the small ones will find some foreign ally of more honor and good faith, who will take them by the hand and do them justice." As the journalist Hendrik Hertzberg observes dryly, "The Senate was formed less by rational argument than by threats of treason and war." Madison furiously fought for representation by population in the Senate. His young colleague from New York, Alexander Hamilton, seconded that view. "As states are a collection of individual men," Hamilton asked, "which ought we to respect most, the rights of the people composing them, or the artificial beings resulting from that composition?" Madison could barely bring himself to defend the arrangement in the *Federalist Papers*, insisting, "[It] does not call for much discussion." Some of the framers, at least, were ruefully aware that they were creating a homegrown version of "rotten boroughs," so that today Wyoming (population 700,000) has as much representation in the U.S. Senate as California (population 38 million). Few other countries building democracies mimic this part of our system, reports political scientist Robert A. Dahl in his withering book, *How Democratic Is the American Constitution?* Dahl calculates that the level of inequality in representation in the U.S. Senate is the worst of any federalist democracy he studied, except for Argentina and Brazil. As for the vote, the delegates in Philadelphia never even considered having senators elected by the people rather than chosen by state legislators.

"Will Such Men Be the Guardians of Liberty?"

Behind closed doors the delegates clashed briefly but sharply over whether to restrict the vote to men who owned property.

On August 6 the Committee of Detail reported the first draft of the Constitution. The new country, it stated offhandedly, would be called "the United States of America." The first article established Congress. Discussing the House of Representatives, it said, "The qualifications of the electors shall be the same, from time to time, as those of the electors in the several States, of the most numerous branch of their own legislatures." In other words, a man who could vote for the lower house of the state legislature could vote to elect a member of Congress.

The next day Gouverneur Morris of New York objected and demanded a property requirement for voting, to be spelled out in the Constitution. The "rake" of the Revolution, Morris was a thirty-two-year-old sybarite who had lost a leg in an accident, supposedly fleeing a jealous husband. He was one of the few delegates who spoke out strongly against slavery. It was, he told the delegates, a "nefarious institution," "the curse of heaven on those States where it prevailed." Later he would be tasked with writing the Preamble ("We the People" and so forth) and would brag of the U.S. Constitution, "That instrument was written by the fingers which write this letter." But Morris was no fan of "the People." Describing a meeting at Fraunces Tavern during the Revolution's early days, he shivered, "The mob begin to think and reason. Poor reptiles! It is with them a vernal morning, they are struggling to cast off their winter's slough [skin], and ere noon they will bite, depend upon it." Repeatedly he spoke for the wealthy. He had helped engineer New York's narrowing of voting rights during the Revolution. Now, speaking in secret at the Philadelphia convention, Morris proposed that voting to elect House members be restricted to freeholders, that is, those men who owned land. Nine out of ten white men owned enough land to vote anyway, he claimed implausibly. If merchants "value the right," well, they could buy some property. "If not they don't deserve it."

James Wilson, a prominent Pennsylvania lawyer, quickly objected on practical grounds: "It was difficult to form any uniform rule of qualifications for all the States." Others thought such a move might imperil ratification. "The people will not readily subscribe to the National Constitution," warned one Connecticut delegate, "if it should subject them to be disfranchised." George Mason concurred: "Eight or nine States have extended the right of suffrage beyond the freeholders, what will the people there say, if they should be disfranchised."

Yet some delegates looked ahead, and shuddered. They saw a nation that would soon be populated by immigrants and city-dwellers. One Pennsylvanian urged "restriction of the right to [freeholders] as a necessary defense against the dangerous influence of those multitudes without property and without principle with which our country like all others, will in time abound." Morris rehashed Blackstone's weirdly circular arguments that voting by the poor will just hurt those without money. "Give the votes to people who have no property, and they will sell them to the rich who will be able to buy them. . . . The time is not distant when this country will abound with mechanics and manufacturers who will receive their bread from their employers. Will such men be the secure and faithful guardians of liberty?"

Madison spoke up. It was he who, more than anyone else, had set in motion the clockwork of the Constitution, its pitting of branches against each other and levels of government in conflict. His innovative focus on checks and balances does not obscure his central thrust at the time. Above all Madison pressed relentlessly for a stronger central government to forestall abuses by the states. "The right of suffrage is certainly one of the fundamental articles of republican government, and ought not to be left to be regulated by the Legislature," he began. "A gradual abridgment of this right has been the mode in which aristocracies have been built on the ruins of popular forms." He thought a national property requirement was a good idea in principle, but simply too controversial. Weeks before he had worried that "the power will slide into the hands" of those who "secretly sigh for a more equal distribution of [life's] blessings." Now he made an eloquent argument against popular democracy. "In future times," he worried, "a great majority of the people will not only be without landed, but any other sort of, property. These will either combine under the influence of their common situation; in which case, the rights of property and the public liberty will not be secure in their hands: or which is more probable, they will become the tools of opulence and ambition, in which case there will be equal danger on another side."

Finally Benjamin Franklin spoke. He did so rarely that summer; like Washington, he husbanded his status as the most eminent delegate. Franklin's interjection may have ended the debate. Madison's notes gently summarize a meandering disquisition, though perhaps the sage actually spoke with more heat than recorded. He paid homage to the patriotic zeal shown by American sailors—men without property—when captured by the British. By contrast captured English seamen quickly switched sides—a lack of commitment he ascribed to "the difference in the way the common people were treated in America and in Great Britain." Franklin "did not think that the elected"—in other words, political leaders—"had any right in any case to narrow the privileges of the electors."

Franklin would continue to swat down ideas that sought to enshrine property or birth as the basis for political power. Years before he had wryly proposed having "Hereditary Professor[s] of Mathematicks." He reacted most fiercely when John Rutledge, a South Carolina aristocrat, proposed that the states be represented in the new government based not on population but on wealth. "Property was certainly the principal object of Society," he had asserted earlier. Rutledge of course counted his slaves both as people and as property. He won either way.

Franklin replied extemporaneously on August 10, capping the week's discussion of democracy. His passion bursts through Madison's deadpan notes: no summary here, but a transcript. "Doctor Franklin expressed his dislike of every thing that tended to debase the spirit of the common people. If honesty was often the companion of wealth, and if poverty was exposed to peculiar temptation, it was not less true that the possession of property increased the desire of more property. Some of the greatest rogues he was ever acquainted with, were the richest rogues." If the Constitution "should betray a great partiality to the rich," it would even discourage the immigration that the new nation needed.

Do these musings about democracy's dangers constitute the "original intent" of the framers? Not exactly. When the time came to explain the Constitution in public, Madison embraced Franklin's egalitarian approach. It can be hard, at times, to discern what Madison actually believed. Behind the closed doors of the Constitutional Convention he found himself making assertions that might tip his listeners his way. He made different arguments during the fight for ratification, when writing anonymously; still others when speaking out in his own voice. Federalist 57 is one of the last of the remarkable articles he wrote, along with Hamilton and Jay, during the contentious fight over ratification of the Constitution. He published it in the *New York Packet* newspaper in February 1788. It responded to critics' claim—"of all the objections [to] the federal Constitution . . . perhaps the most extraordinary"—that the House of Representatives would "elevate the few at the expense of the many." Madison pointed to limited terms and frequent elections, and to the very fact of electoral democracy itself: "Who are to be the electors of the federal representatives? Not the rich, more than the poor; not the learned, more than the ignorant; not the haughty heirs of distinguished names, more than the humble sons of obscurity and unpropitious fortune. The electors are to be the great body of the people of the United States."

Madison's ringing credo has sometimes been cited in Supreme Court cases but has not received the attention it deserves. In the public debate over ratification of the Constitution, both sides—Federalists and Anti-Federalists—insisted that wide voting rights were key. The entire legitimacy of the government rested on that popular consent.

In the end the delegates rejected the idea of limiting the vote to those with property—or of including in the Constitution any particular definition of the electorate at all. The states would decide. Those that were expanding voting rights could continue to do so. This refusal to set a national standard, any standard, would have lasting consequences. It left in the hands of state governments one of the most basic elements of national citizenship. And it set the stage for continued conflict, when national effort was required to forcefully advance democracy.

"It Was Impossible to Foresee the Abuses"

If the delegates were blasé about *who* could vote, they focused intently on *how* they could vote. Madison and the others saw tremendous potential for abuse, for factions to seize control of the machinery in states and twist the rules to advantage their own allies or views. Their answer was to give Congress the power to override the states. One provision read (as slightly cleaned up in the final version), "The Times, Places and Manner of holding Elections for Senators and Representatives, shall be prescribed in each State by the Legislature thereof; but the Congress may at any time by Law make or alter such Regulations, except as to the Places of chusing Senators."

The framers focused sharply on the risks of corruption. As republicans they had come to believe legislators should mirror the interests and sentiments of their constituents. But they saw myriad ways that the system could be abused, either by wealthy and powerful interests bending the legislature or by lawmakers themselves manipulating the levers. This authority to supersede state laws was one of the few places that the new Constitution actually reached into the world of states and overrode the prerogatives of local legislators.

One reason was the concern that state legislators would simply try to strangle the new government by refusing to hold federal elections. That fear was not far-fetched. Local potentates such as Patrick Henry, who dominated the Virginia legislature, and George Clinton, who held sway in Albany as New York's governor, would prove the new Constitution's most dogged foes.

Madison's rationale went deeper. He assumed that left to their own impulses, local political factions would tilt election rules. The debate in Philadelphia did little to assuage his fears. Two delegates from South Carolina proposed deleting congressional override of state law, and for all the wrong reasons. They represented their state's elite from its coastal Tidewater region. Owners of large slave plantations near the Atlantic held power in the state through ruthless malapportionment of the legislature. To them a federal referee was unappealing. Madison replied at length. State legislatures, he noted, "will sometimes fail or refuse to consult the common interest at the expence of their local conveniency or prejudices." Congress's power to override statehouse politicians was properly quite broad—"words of great latitude." He ticked off ways a political faction could manipulate the rules to garner a favorable outcome:

> It was impossible to foresee all the abuses that might be made of the discretionary power. Whether the electors should vote by ballot or viva voce, should assemble at this place or that place; should be divided into districts or all meet at one place, should all

> vote for all the representatives; or all in a district vote for a number allotted to the district; these and many other points would depend on the Legislatures, and might materially affect the appointments. Whenever the State Legislatures had a favorite measure to carry, they would take care so to mould their regulations as to favor the candidates they wished to succeed.

Moreover unequal representation within states would reproduce itself, leading to lopsided representation in Congress. Madison prevailed, and the grant of power to the federal government stayed in the Constitution.

Modern Americans living through today's voting fights might recognize two of the great themes, in miniature, in these first secretive moments in the creation of America's government: nervousness about universal voting rights (and a clash of classes and interests prodded by those who wanted to restrict it and those who sought greater democracy) and, right alongside, a clear-eyed fear of abuse and manipulation—a recognition that the machinery of democracy would matter as much as formally articulated rights. Both views often coexisted within different coalitions and within people.

On September 17, 1787, the federal convention released its handiwork: a proposed Constitution for the United States. A roaring debate erupted. The Constitution would not take effect until nine states assented. The delegates did not want the fate of the document to rest in the hands of state legislators. Instead they specified a distinctly democratic means of ratifying it: state conventions. Twelve of the thirteen states held special elections to choose delegates. In these elections all free men could vote—even those without property. One state, Rhode Island, actually submitted the U.S. Constitution to a popular referendum. It lost. The state only joined the union when Congress threatened to treat it as a hostile foreign power.

Opponents were repelled by what they saw as the creation of a dangerous, near dictatorial central government. Dubbed "the Anti-Federalists" by the Constitution's backers, their arguments were a fervent mélange of insight and paranoia. Summoning the revolutionary spirit of 1776, they repeatedly warned that the new central government would strip power from the people.

Many objected to the clause giving Congress the authority to override state election laws. In his path-breaking study, historian Jackson Turner Main observed with mild puzzlement that this seemingly frivolous objection was "of great importance, judging from the number of times it was introduced." The Constitution's foes feared government by an aristocracy. They were easily spun up. "By altering the time," one wrote, "they may continue a representative during his whole life; by altering the manner, they may fill up the vacancies by their own votes without the consent of the people; and by altering the place, all the elections may be made at the seat of the federal government." Massachusetts's ratifying convention spent two full days chewing on the clause. Defenders said it was necessary for the House of Representatives, "the democratic branch of the national government, the branch chosen immediately by the people," to prevent the new U.S. Senate from colluding with the state legislators who chose its members. Theophilus Parsons warned the Massachusetts convention that otherwise, legislatures might "make an unequal and partial division" of congressional districts, "or they might even disqualify one third of the electors." In Pennsylvania pro-Constitution Federalists noted that without oversight, states could require voice voting or move the election to an inconvenient place. (James Wilson fretted that the polling might even take place in "Pittsburg.")

Six states urged an amendment clarifying that Congress could act only if a state failed to hold elections, perhaps because it had been invaded. Hamilton felt it necessary to publish three separate Federalist papers to rebut those criticisms, insisting rather tendentiously that the arrangement would not turn elections over to the "wealthy and well born." Few recorded voices and no proposed amendments expressed outrage over the exclusion of most Americans—everyone who was not a white man—from the vote.

Is There a Right to Vote in the Constitution?

So, did the U.S. Constitution move toward democracy?

Compared to other governments at the time, it gave greater power to the people. The House of Representatives—the body directly elected by voters—was assigned the power to originate taxes. Federal elections were frequent: every two years. Appropriations of funds for an army were limited to two years; this was designed to make sure a dictatorial president could not raise and pay a "standing army" without accountability to the voters. In a bid to avoid rotten boroughs, it established the House of Representatives, with representation based on population, and even required a census to count heads every ten years. It eschewed property requirements or other onerous burdens to serve in government. It ensured that European nobles would never be able to swoop in and assume hereditary power. State legislatures were left in place; most now held annual elections, where rowdy conflicts could unfold between gentry and poorer farmers, town and country. And the Guarantee Clause required each state to have a republican form of government. In a world ruled by kings, that commitment was no small thing.

Yet to twenty-first-century Americans the original Constitution looks unnervingly undemocratic. Citizens could not vote for U.S. senators, who were chosen by state legislators, or for the president, to be chosen by the Electoral College. While representation in the House was proportional to population, slaves were counted as three-fifths of a person—degrading the humanity of the disenfranchised slaves and simultaneously adding their weight to the size of southern congressional delegations and electoral votes. Courts imposing bankruptcy liens had sparked agrarian rebellions all along the western frontier: Federal courts too would be established and judges chosen without a popular vote and confirmed by the legislature-selected Senate, not the populist House. Women could not vote.

The document itself has posed problems for the later development of American democracy. "With respect to democratic politics," three leading legal scholars report, "the American Constitution is a curious amalgam of textual silences, astute insights into the risks and temptations of political power, archaic assumptions that subsequent developments quickly undermined, and a small number of narrowly targeted more recent amendments that reflect more modern conceptions of politics. Particularly in this arena of democratic constitutional design, the American Constitution reveals its age."

Why does it matter what the framers thought of the right to vote? Other twenty-first-century nations find these questions to be of historical interest, and little more. (Imagine British pundits today obsessing over the views of Pitt the Younger, prime minister to King George III.) After all, this was a strikingly different time. The United States had no public schools, no police forces, and no political parties. Medical care included bleeding (which would kill Washington). The founding generation's conception of human dignity and rights was in turmoil, at best. As the English writer Samuel Johnson asked the year the Revolution began, "How is it that we hear the loudest yelps for liberty among the drivers of the Negroes?"

Because of the way the United States developed over the next two centuries, what was said and thought in the founding era matters more than it would in most countries. The United States created the world's first written national constitution. No other democracy sees its judges and politicians parse so minutely the letters, aperçus, and discarded drafts of long-forgotten speeches as clues to how we should govern ourselves today.

This has been especially problematic for the law of democracy. The original Constitution's failure to guarantee a right to vote has made it far easier to deny that right in later years. Partly as a result courts have been very reluctant to read a democratic interpretation into these words. Of course Madison and his colleagues knew the country would change and assumed that the Constitution would change with it. They had less horror of amendments than later Americans did; after all, they ratified ten within the new government's first two years. But they failed to realize they had made it too hard to alter the document. As the country grew it simply became too easy for a faction in enough state legislative bodies to block an amendment. In the 1930s President Franklin D. Roosevelt considered backing a constitutional amendment to overcome the Supreme Court's decisions that overturned New Deal laws. FDR cannily noted, "Thirteen states which contain only five percent of the voting population can block ratification even though the thirty-five States with ninety-five percent of the population are in favor of it." Instead Roosevelt opted to try to pack the Court, with politically disastrous results.

Instead, in many areas of the Constitution the document has stretched and evolved through creative court decisions that reworked the understanding of what it means to accommodate the needs of a changing nation. Some hail the living Constitution; some decry it. This judicial rewriting has mostly bypassed the law of American democracy. Its controversies—the right to vote, the nature of representation, the rules that allow the majority of citizens to wield political power—rarely have been decided by major court rulings. Rather change has come, or been ratified, much as the founders themselves might have expected: by amendments. The original Constitution implied a right to vote, at least for the House of Representatives, but never declared it. But five separate amendments in the next two centuries would address that right directly: for African American men (the Fifteenth Amendment), for women (Nineteenth), for the poor without a poll tax (Twenty-fourth), for the young (Twenty-sixth). The Fourteenth Amendment at least temporarily reduced congressional representation for states that block "the right to vote." And the Seventeenth Amendment established the right to vote for U.S. senators. The original intent of the framers, the bewigged gentlemen who signed the Constitution in 1787, and the public understanding of the document at that time actually matter less than in many other areas of constitutional law.

The Federalists thought they had kept the lid on the surging democratic energy let loose by the Revolution. But John Adams knew otherwise: "There will be no end of it."

PART II

THE RISE AND FALL OF AMERICAN DEMOCRACY

3

Young America

WASHINGTON IRVING'S classic 1819 short story, "Rip Van Winkle," tells of the dramatic change that swept America in the early years of the new republic. Waking up in Sleepy Hollow after years of slumber, the easygoing protagonist notices that a tavern sign that once bore a likeness of George III now has a picture of George Washington. He looks in vain for a fondly remembered local sage who once held court outside the bar, "with his broad face, double chin, and fair long pipe, uttering clouds of tobacco-smoke." Instead, in the same spot "a lean, bilious-looking fellow, with his pockets full of handbills, was haranguing vehemently about rights of citizens—election—members of Congress—liberty—Bunker's Hill—heroes of seventy six—and other words, that were a perfect Babylonish jargon to the bewildered Van Winkle."

The pace of change—cultural, political, and legal—startled Americans. Benjamin Latrobe, the architect who designed the U.S. Capitol, hyperbolized just six years into the century, "After the adoption of the Federal Constitution, the extension of the right of suffrage in the States to a majority of all the adult male citizens, planted a germ which ha[s] gradually evolved and has spread actual and practical democracy and political equality over the whole union."

When members of the first U.S. Congress trickled into New York to hear Washington's Inaugural Address in 1789, traditional attitudes toward suffrage had seemed firm. Federalists won the elections overwhelmingly. Few voted then, but soon the surging energy loosed by the Revolution overspilled. Over the next forty years America embraced the idea of popular democracy, with wide voting rights at its core. The right to vote was extended to all white men regardless of wealth. People, not property, became the basis for self-government. Historian Sean Wilentz calls it the great "democratic rupture."

"A Candid State of Parties"

In 1788, as "Publius," James Madison wrote Federalist 10, a classic of American political theory. It condemns "faction," explaining how the new government—with its overlapping, multiple veto points—would prevent blocs from assembling a potentially abusive majority. A large republic paradoxically could block that kind of special interest domination better than a small one. Later Americans read Madison as an eloquent voice for nonpartisanship; as a Supreme Court justice wrote, citing Federalist 10, "Parties ranked high on the list of evils that the Constitution was designed to check."

Then Madison the theorist met Madison the politician—a politician quickly schooled in the rough and tumble of the new system. First, he found himself dodging the very sort of electoral shenanigans about which he had fretted at the Constitutional Convention. Former Virginia governor Patrick Henry played his tormentor. The flamboyant orator dominated Virginia's politics. Washington wrote mournfully to Madison, "The edicts of Mr. Henry are enregistered with less opposition by the majority of [the Virginia legislature] than those of the Grand Monarch are in the Parliaments of France." Henry held the floor for days at Virginia's ratifying convention, flaying the proposed Constitution. Stormy weather helped him in his histrionics; as he reached his peroration, with arms outstretched, a loud thunderclap and flashes of lightning terrified his enthralled listeners. Yet despite the drama, Madison bested Henry at the convention. Virginia ratified the Constitution, while recommending that Congress also propose a Bill of Rights. Henry would have to settle for blocking Madison's career. First, Madison sought appointment to the U.S. Senate. That, predicted Henry, would produce "rivulets of blood throughout the land." Virginia's legislators rejected Madison, so he ran for a seat in the first U.S. House of Representatives, which meant an appeal directly to voters every two years.

Henry was not finished. He carefully drew borders so that Virginia's Fifth Congressional District contained few supporters of the Constitution. Only the area around Madison's house in his hometown of Orange would be a guaranteed safe vote. Long before Elbridge Gerry signed into law an 1812 congressional district that resembled a salamander, giving the practice its name, Madison had been gerrymandered. He found himself forced to compete frenetically against his opponent, James Monroe, a charismatic war hero. The two stumped across the district. Madison pandered to voters and flip-flopped on pet issues. (To appease local Baptists he reversed course and endorsed a religious freedom amendment to the Constitution. Hence the Bill of Rights.) Campaigning in heavy snow, he got frostbite on the tip of his nose. In the end he won by 336 votes. Only 2,280 men had voted in a district of 40,000 people.

Congress convened in New York City. In those first months of American government, Madison was a blur, dashing about as Washington's de facto prime minister. He wrote the president's Inaugural Address and the House response, managed the administration's legislation, and shepherded the Bill of Rights through Congress. Quickly the bewigged gentlemen of the new government began to bicker. They divided over state debt, national finances, and the location of the new capital. The French Revolution beginning in 1789 further polarized the political class. At first most Americans warmed to the kindred republican revolution. The French enthusiast the Marquis de Lafayette sent Washington the keys seized from the Bastille prison. Soon, though, news from France divided Americans as images of the guillotine replaced liberty poles and cockades. Thomas Paine now languished in a French prison. Washington clung to neutrality between France and England. Jefferson remained enamored of the French Revolution, whose idealistic start he had witnessed. As he lost repeated policy battles within the administration, he felt pinioned as secretary of state. With Madison he traveled to New York on a nature excursion widely covered in the press; later generations might have called it a "photo opportunity." Along the way they huddled with Aaron Burr, Governor George Clinton, and other local politicians. While Jefferson posed nobly, in line with the conventions of the time, Madison got busy organizing a political party.

By 1792, just four years after he wrote Federalist 10 denouncing faction, Madison publicly changed his mind. He published a series of essays that effectively repudiated much of his masterwork. This time, still writing anonymously, he considered a "candid state of parties." Parties, he said, are "natural to most political societies." They're not bad; they're necessary and inevitable. In another essay that year he observed, "Parties are unavoidable." He proposed that their baleful impact could be minimized "by establishing political equality among all." Through them society marks its major debates: Whigs and Tories before the Revolution, and the pro-Constitution forces and their opponents. The new party, which he called the Republicans, corralled those who believe "the doctrine that mankind are capable of governing themselves." They oppose those who "are more partial to the opulent than to the other classes of society." The task of winning power, he implied, no longer was a matter of elevated thinkers cogitating together but leaders, spurring the masses of the public, building coalitions, and fighting to win.

Ironically it was a foreigner who first introduced the fermenting agent of mass politics. Twenty-nine-year-old Edmond-Charles Genêt arrived as the flamboyant ambassador to the United States from Paris's revolutionary government. "Citizen Genêt" toured the new nation as a preening hero to crowds that rapturously sang "La Marseillaise." He demanded that the United States back France in its wars, raised money, and tried to recruit privateers to harass British shipping. "Democratic-Republican Societies" formed in his wake. Eventually Washington slapped down Genêt and his attempted interference. As the tumbrels rolled in Paris, recalled home and facing certain arrest, the humbled ambassador sought asylum in the United States. He died a gentleman farmer in upstate New York.

Madison and Jefferson kept at the task of assembling the first political party out of the Genêt fan clubs. These aristocrats found themselves forced to attend to coalition building, propaganda, and the rallying of voters—quietly at first, then in open opposition to the administration of Washington and Adams.

Many of the jumbled cultural currents of American politics emerged. The Republicans were a strange mix. This primordial party combined aristocrats with a new class of uncouth, unlettered men. Matty Lyon, the Vermont militiaman who demanded a democratic constitution for the state, now served in Congress. On the House floor a Federalist congressman from Connecticut had called him a "scoundrel." Elsewhere that would have been grounds for a duel, but congressional speech was constitutionally protected. Lyon spat in his face, earning him one of the first great political nicknames: "the Spitting Lyon." His expectoration prompted Congress's first ever ethics charges. Federalist prosecutors jailed him for calling President Adams a "bully," charging him with sedition. It was the first prosecution under the Alien and Sedition Act, signed by Adams, which criminalized criticism of the government. Another politician, this one a Yale graduate, foreswore deference to "well fed, well dressed, chariot rolling, caucus keeping, levee reveling federalists." (Ivy Leaguers learned early how to rail against elitists. History does not record whether he claimed to love pork rinds, as later patrician politicians did.) Mechanics associations enlisted urban workers, while farmers formed Democratic-Republican clubs. They were just as good as the gentry, one announced, even if "they had not snored through four years at Princeton."

In the colonial era candidates "stood for office," running on character. Political parties were different: they stood for issues. They relied on newspapers, partisan instruments to denounce opponents and rally supporters. The Federalists and Republicans hastened to establish party publications, funded by wealthy supporters or by the flow of government printing contracts. Jefferson subsidized one newspaper by hiring its editor as a State Department translator.

The Federalists—now a ruling party, clinging to power—grew alarmed at the prospect of new states entering the union, states populated with small farmers and self-made men. They twisted and turned, trying to find ways to slow the trend. They began to change the rules. One early bid to stymie change came with the 1787 enactment of the Northwest Ordinance, which governed territories around the Great Lakes (from Ohio up to Minnesota). The Ordinance was significant in establishing procedures for new states to enter the union on equal footing with the original thirteen. Ohio would not be a colony. But even as the Constitutional Convention was meeting, the Confederation Congress had imposed strict property requirements to vote in new territories, rejecting a request by settlers for wider suffrage. The Alien and Sedition Acts, which cracked down on political organizing by the Democratic-Republicans, was another such bid. In effect it criminalized opposition to the Federalist Party government. As the election approached, with electoral defeat looming, the Federalists changed the rules still more nakedly. "In 1796, seven out of sixteen states relied on the popular vote," historian Jill Lepore summarizes. "But in 1800, after Republicans made a strong showing in local elections in New England, the Federalist-dominated legislatures of Massachusetts and New Hampshire repealed the popular vote, and put the selection of Electoral College delegates in their own hands. Before the year was out, seven of the sixteen states had changed their procedures for electing delegates to the Electoral College." The Federalists earned distinction as the first American ruling group, sensing demographic or political change, to try to withdraw democratic rights as an electoral tactic. The template would be used repeatedly by others. Due to the maneuvering, a smaller share of Americans voted for president in 1800 than two years before. Relatively few did so at all.

A constitutional quirk denied Jefferson an Electoral College majority, so the contest was decided after weeks of balloting in the House of Representatives. Violence was threatened, with state militias mobilizing, but none occurred. In itself that peaceful rotation of leadership marked a watershed, "the Revolution of 1800," as Jefferson called it. The election was far from democratic; it was the last one of the older, aristocratic order—and the first inkling of a newly democratic country.

"Bone, Pith, and Muscle"

Nearly 4 million people lived in the United States in 1790. Thirty years later that number had more than doubled, to almost 10 million. By 1850 it doubled again, to 23 million, as populations spread west. The colonial style of deference and formal courtesy gave way to a bumptious egalitarianism among white men. As the French writer Alexis de Tocqueville noted with surprise when he came to the United States in 1831, men no longer bowed and saluted rank as they had in colonial times. "All classes mingle incessantly, and there is not the least indication of their social position," he wrote. "Everyone shakes hands."

Out of this ethic of social equality grew a fight for political equality: a drive, over several decades, to expand the right to vote to white men who did not own property. As the new men pressed for the franchise, the existing men of power pushed back. Between 1812 and 1821 Illinois, Missouri, and four other states entered the union with universal white manhood suffrage (or close to it). Four older states in effect dropped property qualifications. Veterans of the War of 1812, including former general Andrew Jackson, helped lead the push for the vote. It was a time of boom and bust, with frequent financial panics. Economic fights over debt and banking magnified calls for democratic rights. The rising class of small farmers and businessmen embraced the natural rights idea, the vision of Jefferson's Declaration, the sense that rights adhered to individuals—and that every white man had the right to vote.

The Revolution's old lions were among those befuddled by the swirling change.

In 1821 Massachusetts held a constitutional convention to rewrite its charter. John Adams attended, alternately bitter and nostalgic. He kept up his fight against expanding the vote. The French Revolution, he said sarcastically, offered a "perfect and complete" example of universal voting's "utility and excellence." Once again Massachusetts rejected universal manhood suffrage, apportioning its upper chamber by property, not population. That would not change for three more decades.

Virginia held a convention to rewrite its constitution in 1829. Madison and Monroe, both retired from the presidency, Supreme Court Chief Justice John Marshall, and others listened quietly as younger men argued. Quoting Jefferson's Declaration Preamble and the Bill of Rights, delegates from west of the Blue Ridge Mountains demanded the vote for all white men, as well as a fair share of the state legislature. Plantation owners from the eastern part of the state resisted. Asthmatic and fading, Madison sat in front as he had in 1787. His powdered hair, short pants, hose, and buckled shoes marked him as an anachronism. He tried to craft a compromise, basing legislative representation on white male population, excluding a head count of slaves.

A vigorous foe of expanded democracy dominated the convention, someone who would begin to articulate the case against expanded voting in America. John Randolph, known as "Randolph of Roanoke," was a mesmerizing orator, at times physically violent, who dramatically declaimed in a loud falsetto. (Apparently, due to illness, he never had undergone puberty.) He named his plantation Bizarre. Randolph's best-known aphorism: "I am an aristocrat. I love liberty. I hate equality." Now, as the delegates debated the vote, he demanded, "Are we men? Met to consult about the affairs of men? Or are we, in truth, a Robin Hood society?" The founding generation had taken up arms to throw off the rule of King George. Pointing at Madison, who averted his gaze, Randolph announced, "I would not live under King Numbers. I would not be his steward—nor make him my task-master." His arguments would be echoed two decades later by John Calhoun, spokesman for the southern slaveholding elite, and in later years by many others opposed to universal suffrage. The convention voted only limited change.

Perhaps unsurprisingly the fight over suffrage was noisiest in New York. Its Revolution-era state constitution still limited voting for some offices. New Yorkers found ways to evade the rule. "Fagot" voting was widespread: property deeds were given out solely so men could vote—handed out like twigs, or "fagots"—then retrieved. Near riots were not unknown as settlers moving into the western part of the state attempted to vote.

Savvy party politicians, not a citizen movement, forced the issue in 1821. The unlikely instigator was Martin Van Buren of Kinderhook, no firebrand. A colleague once bet he could force Van Buren to give a definitive answer to a simple question. He asked "the Little Magician" whether the sun rose in the East. "As I invariably slept until after sunrise, I could not speak from my own knowledge," Van Buren replied. The suave politician assembled an aspirational coalition of what he called the "this class of men, composed of mechanics, professional men, and small landholders and constituting the bone, pith, and muscle of the population of the state." The showdown came at a constitutional convention in Albany, the capital. Chancellor James Kent, a leading law professor, made a passionate but futile defense of control of the state senate by rural landowners: "The tendency of universal suffrage, is to jeopardize the rights of property, and the principles of liberty." He warned of government by factory workers, retail clerks, and "the motley and undefinable population of crowded ports." With the vote "the indolent and profligate" can cast "the whole burdens of society upon the industrious and the virtuous." The convention broke with Kent, extending suffrage to all who paid taxes or served in the militia. Five years later New York extended the vote to nearly all white, native-born men.

The burly, tobacco-stained ranks of new voters had an ugly side. They created an idealized version of the electoral man, that hardworking backbone of society who has the right to vote. The more passionately they argued that all white men were equal and were entitled to vote, the more easily immigrants, women, Native Americans, and Blacks were shut out. New Jersey, the one state where women were allowed to vote, disenfranchised them in 1807. (In one election teams of men arrived at the polls dressed as women, an early example, hard to top, of voter fraud. The legislature, naturally, disenfranchised *women*.) The handful of states that allowed free Black men to vote also reversed course. The U.S. Constitution never limited voting to citizens; before the War of 1812, for example, Congress had encouraged settlers to move west by giving the vote to all property owners who had lived in the territory for two years, whether or not they were citizens. Nationalism stoked by war changed that. After the clash with the British in 1812, most newly admitted states limited voting to citizens.

In the South rising support for slavery magnified the push for expanded voting rights for white men. As during the Revolution, those who served in the military began to demand the franchise. Whereas northern militias had faded, a remnant of colonial times, in the South they still patrolled the plantations, looking to suppress slave rebellion. Virginia militiamen attacked the law that required citizen soldiers, who could not vote, "to patrol for the public safety, and to preserve roads and streets," while those who had the franchise "are in a great measure exempt from any participation in these duties." Extending voting rights was seen as a way to build racial solidarity and deepen support for slavery in parts of the state where few men owned slaves. A Virginia lawmaker argued, "We ought to spread wide the foundation of our government, that all white men have a direct interest in its protection."

"The Humble Members"

New voting laws and the surge of new voters combined to create a new governing coalition behind Andrew Jackson and his Democratic Party, the new name for the Democrat-Republicans. The Tennessean was the archetypal new American, quick to take offense, violent, up from nothing, proud of his success. When we look at Jackson today, we tend to focus on his racism and violence and the atrocity of his policies to remove Indians from their homes on the East Coast. Those aspects of his complex character unfortunately placed him near the center of the views of his contemporaries. At the time his fury helped drive an eruption of grassroots democracy. Jacksonian Democracy was not abstractly about rights but about power. Early historians treated Jackson principally as a figure of the American West, embodying sectional conflict against the snooty East. But more recently it has become clear that his appeal cut across the country and was rooted above all in the economic and cultural self-interest of farmers, the broad working class, and their small business allies.

In 1824 the former general won the largest share of the popular vote for president, and the most electoral votes. But the quirks of the Electoral College sent the decision to the House of Representatives. Each state cast one vote, per the Constitution. The House elected the erudite diplomat John Quincy Adams, son of the former president. Jackson's backers believed Adams had made a deal with Speaker of the House Henry Clay for his support, rewarding him with the post of secretary of state. Democrats decried the "corrupt bargain." Anger fueled organizing and the birth of the world's first truly mass political party. Jackson and his followers began to organize those ordinary men as a carefully tended and curated coalition. By 1828 all states but two had given voters—not state legislatures—the power to choose presidential electors. Four years before, turnout among white men was 27 percent; in 1828 it more than doubled, to 57 percent. That election pulled power to the people in another way. Since 1796 congressional caucuses had nominated presidential candidates; for instance, Whig lawmakers would pick the Whig standard-bearer. This seemed clubby and elitist, so Jackson's followers arranged for him to be put forward by state legislatures and statewide party conventions, raucous affairs in which thousands of voters could participate. Partisan newspapers, led by the *National Telegraph* in Washington, churned out pro-Jackson broadsheets across the country. One historian estimates that cheap postage rates and the free "franking privilege" used by members of Congress meant that $1 million was spent on the Democratic campaign (about $25 million today). New Yorker Van Buren took his organizing skills nationwide. He served as Jackson's lieutenant, eventual successor, and the manager of the mass Democratic Party. "The driving energy of Jacksonian democracy," historian Arthur M. Schlesinger Jr. wrote in his classic study, "like that of any aggressive reform movement, came from a small group of men, joined together by essential sympathies in a concerted attempt to transform the existing order." In hundreds of communities Jacksonian Democrats built political parties, established patronage systems, and organized farmers and workingmen.

Economic resentments, sharpened to a point, drove democratic engagement. The Democrats rallied new voters with denunciations of banks and "special privilege." Wider voting rights led to victory in the "war of the bank," a ferocious campaign waged by Jackson and his followers against what they saw as a citadel of entrenched economic power. The Second Bank of the United States, based in Philadelphia, was partially owned by the government but entirely controlled by private shareholders. Imagine a privately owned central bank, performing the role of today's Federal Reserve or Bank of England but without even the pretense of political accountability. Its cash flow dwarfed that of the fledgling federal government. Jackson called it "The Monster." The Bank served an important function, trying to regulate the surge and eddies of lending and default that made the frontier banking system so chaotic. But few understood its role. And the Bank's imperious president, Nicholas

Biddle, was a learned aristocrat who barely concealed his disdain for democracy. He greased support for the Bank with loans to publishers and politicians, while bullying other bankers and businessmen. "I can remove all the constitutional scruples in the District of Columbia," he bragged. "Half a dozen Presidencies—a dozen Cashierships—fifty Clerkships—a hundred Directorships—to worthy friends who have no character and no money." In 1832 Biddle gambled aggressively. He sought a renewal of the Bank's charter before Jackson ran for reelection that year, and threatened economic ruin if his demand was not met. Van Buren returned from a posting abroad and found the president alone in the White House. "The Bank, Mr. Van Buren, is trying to kill me," Jackson glowered. "*But I will kill it.*" His memorable veto message made a nakedly populist appeal to the hundreds of thousands of new voters: "It is to be regretted that the rich and powerful too often bend the acts of government to their selfish purposes." There will always be inequality, but when the law adds "artificial distinctions, to grant titles, gratuities, and exclusive privileges, to make the rich richer and the potent more powerful, the humble members of society—the farmers, mechanics, and laborers—who have neither the time nor the means of securing like favors to themselves, have a right to complain of the injustice of their Government." Otherwise, he warned, they would just watch the "rich grow richer."

Jackson went to the voters a few months later to seek reelection. The Bank veto was the central issue. Biddle spent lavishly from the Bank's coffers. He even paid to print thirty thousand copies of the veto message, thinking it would show Jackson to be a demagogue. Democratic newspapers pounced. "If the Bank, a mere monied corporation, can influence and change the results of our election at pleasure," one hollered, "nothing remains of our boasted freedom except *the skin of the immolated victim.*" Mass Democratic Party rallies hailed their hero and denounced the Bank. Voter turnout increased by 100,000 from four years before. The party swept.

Of course the demolition of the Bank was economically reckless.

It took years for the economy to recover, and for decades the country suffered from the lack of a strong central bank, until the creation of the Federal Reserve early in the twentieth century. Jackson and his contemporaries, with their diatribes against "paper money," did not realize that a reliance on gold would make it harder for small farmers and businessmen to gain credit. We can wince at their economic theories while understanding their impulses. "In Jackson's view of America," writes Wilentz, "improper activist government meant granting special privileges to unaccountable monied men on the make as well as to those already established." In crude ways the Jacksonians were trying to organize themselves against an institution, the Bank, and a man, the archetypal sneering elitist, whom they saw as challenging the nation's core egalitarian ethos. Later generations would find it necessary to decide between economic and cultural populism. Jackson's Democrats faced no such choice. Newly enfranchised social classes were experimenting with what it meant to have the vote.

Politics became a spectacle, a pageant of the common man. At Jackson's First Inaugural rowdy supporters romped through the White House, smashing furniture. This scene echoed Election Day across the country. Voting was marked by carousing, violence, and heavy drinking. (One reason given for excluding women from the vote was to shield them from the boorish behavior of men.) The way elections were conducted began to change. Previously voters had to write out their choice, even if they were voting in secret. Now parties printed ballots and passed out reams of them to their supporters. Courts upheld the practice. Illiterate voters now could participate easily, handing in preprinted "tickets." Party agents could monitor to ensure that citizens voted as they had pledged to. In the 1832 election a new movement—the country's first "third party"—briefly flared. The Anti-Masonic Party was devoted to ferreting out the influence of a secret society that supposedly ran the country. It chose its nominee in the first national political convention, another device that engaged voters. Factional newspapers, subsidized by parties and distributed by politicians through the free use of the mail, proliferated. The rules of objective journalism would be invented much later. In one article attacking Van Buren, a single paragraph flung the epithets "profligate," "dangerous," "demagogue," "corrupt," "degrade," "pervert," "prostitute," and "debauch."

Democracy became a fad. Factions proliferated; in New York alone there were Barnburners (urban radicals), Hunkers (conservatives who wanted a "hunk" of the state's money), and Renters (tenant farmers required to present chickens to their Dutch landlords on a specific day or be held in arrears). Loco Focos were primeval populists, named after the kind of match used to illuminate an early meeting when the gaslights were turned off. The democratic impulse was so strong that the Jacksonian Democrats even began to argue that judges should be elected. The reasoning, interestingly, was not just the sense that election confers the most proximate democratic legitimacy; they moved to elect judges because they also thought doing so would free jurists from the partisanship of appointment by governors and legislators. Americans of the mid-nineteenth century saw the vote as the solution to every problem.

Soon the opposition Whig Party got caught up in the new era of mass politics. A crippling depression gave the Whigs their chance. The party, backed by businessmen who supported its program of canal building and other "internal improvements," concocted a joyously gimmicky campaign. They ran their own general, William Henry Harrison. He had won the relatively minor battle of Tippecanoe twenty-nine years before, triumphing over armies loyal to the Shawnee chief Tecumseh (on a day when the chief was away). For more than a decade Harrison had lived in retirement. The Whigs stressed his humble origins, dubbing their effort the "Log Cabin and Hard Cider" campaign. Log cabin trinkets, parade floats, and rallies proliferated. Historian Ted Widmer notes that "a new word entered the American vocabulary" when the E. C. Booz Distillery of Philadelphia began to ship "Old

Cabin Whiskey." Otherwise dignified politicians joined in. Henry Clay of Kentucky told voters they faced a choice between "the log cabin and the palace, between hard cider and champagne." A widely sung campaign song, "Tippecanoe and Tyler Too," included the general's vice presidential pick, John Tyler, for good measure. ("With them we'll beat little Van, Van, Van / For he's a used up man.") Massive parades, torchlight assemblies, and partisan newspapers dueled, and Van Buren was defeated. Turnout soared to 80 percent of eligible voters.

4

"Sheet Anchor"

THE 1840S were a moment of democratic pride and bombast, when the ideals of Jefferson's Declaration were ascendant and the subject of partisan adulation. "Consent of the governed." "All men are created equal." These sentiments, predating the Constitution, became venerated as a civic creed. But they began to serve as a reproach as well. Other groups began to measure current realities against those ideals and insist their promises extend to them. The rise of mass democracy had been pioneered in the United States. These novel claims were a more unsettling development.

America's democratic ferment fascinated the Old World, where some countries were just beginning to grope toward democracy. Britain was convulsed by a long drive to pass the great Reform Act of 1832, which haltingly began to expand the franchise and to equalize representation between city and country in Parliament. English reform proponents found it necessary to reassure that they were not propounding subversive "American" ideas. Alexis de Tocqueville was a precocious thirty-year-old when he arrived in the United States, supposedly to study prisons. He filled notebooks with observations about the new nation, which became the best-selling series of books, *Democracy in America*. What struck the

French nobleman was the fact of social equality—the jumbling and erasure of classes that made political democracy possible. Added to that, Americans were joiners. "Americans use associations to give fêtes, to found seminaries, to build inns, to raise churches, to distribute books, to send missionaries to the antipodes; in this manner they create hospitals, prisons, schools," he reported. "Everywhere that, at the head of a new undertaking, you see the government in France and a great lord in England, count on it that you will perceive an association in the United States." The Democrats, the Whigs, and their offshoots grew out of the same self-help soil.

Tocqueville was describing a politics waged with passionate intensity. Exuberant, raucous, vocal, and often inebriated, Americans treated elections the way today we treat local football games. The historian Richard Franklin Bensel conducted an illuminating examination of records from disputed elections across the country. Voting little resembled today's politics of television commercials and quiet mail-in ballots. In cities voting took place in saloons. In the West balloting might be held in a distant farmhouse, moved by one party or another from place to place, often without public announcement. In most places local officials knew voters by sight. All over the country men from an ethnic or religious group would arrive at the polls en masse to display tribal loyalty and neighborhood sentiment. In 1856, in the period known as "Bleeding Kansas," two sides engaged in violent struggle over whether the incoming state would allow slavery or bar it. Battles over access to the polling place prefigured the coming civil war.

Even in a less insurrectionist environment, voting was what later generations would call a contact sport. To hand in his ballot a voter had to push through a throng of partisans, some eager to keep him from reaching his destination. Some level of violence seems to have been viewed as the norm. When Abraham Lincoln voted in 1860 in Springfield, Illinois, newspapermen covered his appearance. Meanwhile, at the same polling place, a Republican lawyer enthusiastically caned a Democratic editor in a dispute over fake ballots. Evidently a reasonable level of background mayhem was not deemed particularly newsworthy.

The fight for voting rights even provoked a miniature civil war in tiny Rhode Island. A Royal Charter signed by King Charles in 1663 still governed the state. Only property owners and their sons could vote, disenfranchising as many as six of ten white men. Thomas Dorr, a Harvard-educated son of a mill owner, was fired by idealism and his image of himself as a beloved leader of a suffrage movement. In 1841 the People's Convention wrote a new constitution. Disregarding the property-owning requirement, voters flooded the polls and elected Dorr governor, along with a new legislature that met in an abandoned factory. Inconveniently Rhode Island already had a governor. The incumbent promptly proclaimed himself the leader of a "Law and Order" party. Things got more complicated. Dorr's plan excluded Black voters; this drew the involvement of Frederick Douglass, the former slave and spell-binding speaker becoming known as the "fugitive Othello." He visited the state in his first foray out of Massachusetts and tried to address the People's Convention. Rebuffed, Douglass led a campaign against Dorr. The "Law and Order" party, in turn, passed a statute temporarily allowing militia members to vote, even if they did not own property. The soldiers hid, feasting and drinking, and emerged to cast ballots in an Election Day surprise.

In May 1841 "Governor" Dorr dashed off to Washington, seeking federal troops. Across the country newspapers and political clubs took sides. Former presidents Jackson and Van Buren urged support. One editorial hailed the "oppressed peoples" of Rhode Island. At the White House President John Tyler of less-than-democratic Virginia rebuffed the request. Despondent, Dorr stopped in New York City. There he was hailed by theatergoers and the Tammany Hall Democratic Party organization. His spirits revived, Dorr arrived at the train station in Providence, brandishing a sword and vowing to fight. The next day his followers dragged stolen Revolutionary War cannons across cobblestoned streets and stormed the state arsenal. In a light rain the artillery flashed but did not fire. State militiamen routed the Dorrites and occupied Providence. Eventually Dorr was jailed for treason against Rhode Island.

The comic-opera rebellion in Providence yielded a significant U.S. Supreme Court decision, *Luther v. Borden*. During martial law government agents burst into the home of a leading Dorrite, named (what else?) Martin Luther. He sued for damages, insisting the state's government violated the U.S. Constitution's clause guaranteeing a "republican" form of government. The justices shrank from deciding which governor really ruled Rhode Island. Could the state's voters replace their government? Had they properly voted to do so? These were "political questions" for the other branches to decide. The justices had no stomach for sifting through election returns. The case gave rise to a "political question" doctrine that would dominate the constitutional law of democracy for the next 120 years. Not until the late twentieth century would judges be willing to wade into the challenging question of enforcing individual rights to meaningful electoral participation.

"All Men and Women"

Democratic rights for white men exposed remaining gaps. Some historians look at the history of voting in America as principally a scramble for advantage, but in this moment, at least, the intense rallying behind the Declaration and its nascent democratic ideals proved powerful. That was evident at Seneca Falls in 1848. The small convention held there on behalf of women's rights would take on the quality of legend. Eight years before, at a World Anti-Slavery Convention in London, New Yorkers Lucretia Mott and Elizabeth Cady Stanton were forced to sit quietly in the gallery as the men pontificated below on the evils of bondage. The two women walked the streets of London and discussed their disenfranchisement and the silences imposed on them. They reconvened in upstate New York several years later. Together with three other women, they sat around a mahogany table (now in the Smithsonian) and wrote a call for a convention. Stanton began to read aloud from the Declaration of Independence, and the group rewrote it to embrace women. Her husband declared he would leave town if the document were presented to the convention. Few men offered any encouragement. One did: the abolitionist Douglass let it be known he would attend. Mott, a Quaker, warned Stanton, "Thou will make us ridiculous. We must go slowly." Three hundred attendees, including forty men, heard the thirty-three-year-old Stanton make her maiden speech: "I should feel exceedingly diffident to appear before you at this time, having never before spoken in public, were I not nerved by a sense of right and duty, did I not feel that the time had come for the question of woman's wrongs to be laid before the public, did I not believe that woman herself must do this work; for woman alone can understand the height, the depth, the length and the breadth of her degradation."

The convention voted narrowly to endorse a demand for women's suffrage. A third of those present signed a Declaration of Principles, which paraphrased Jefferson's Preamble: "We hold these truths to be self-evident: that all men and women are created equal; that they are endowed by their Creator with certain inalienable rights; that among these are life, liberty, and the pursuit of happiness; that to secure these rights governments are instituted, deriving their just powers from the consent of the governed."

As democratic sentiment rose, those who resisted its pull began to hone their arguments as well. The property-based assertions made by Randolph of Roanoke had lost their legitimacy. Jefferson trumped Blackstone. But his successors adopted and rephrased Randolph's elitist arguments. John Calhoun, the "Marx of the Master Class" in historian Richard Hofstadter's phrase, saw the oncoming industrial economy in the North and urged property owners there to make common cause with slave owners in the South. Calhoun had started his national career as an orthodox politician and served as vice president under both John Quincy

Adams and Jackson. Eventually he engineered a breach, as South Carolina's legislature declared it could nullify federal law. At an 1830 dinner honoring the Declaration of Independence, Jackson stood, raised a glass, and glowered at Calhoun: "Our union—it must be preserved." Calhoun rose to respond: "The Union—next to our liberty the most dear." Calhoun was a humorless, abstract thinker. Contemporaries joked that he once tried to write a poem; it began, "Whereas." He saw the natural rights approach embodied in the Declaration of Independence—and by universal suffrage—as sentimentalism at best. (He could wax rather obsessive on the subject, declaring that all men are not "born free and equal": "Taking the proposition literally . . . all men are not born. Infants are born." And so on.) He warned that emancipation of the slaves would lead to their gaining the right to vote, with "political and social equality with their former owners" the result.

Calhoun was the theorist for a new vision of states' rights, born in South Carolina, that was devoted to deflecting any possibility that the national government would interfere with slavery. His skepticism about romanticized notions of equality and democracy, carried forward from the earliest days but curdled with racial hatred, would develop into a parallel narrative, one that constantly nourished efforts to restrict the vote over time, long after Calhoun was gone.

"The Electric Cord"

The emotional adoration of the idea that "all men are created equal" was at its peak in the mid-nineteenth century. The greatest exception to it, of course, came from American slavery.

Abraham Lincoln did not start his political career as an advocate of extending suffrage to Black Americans. In his first term in the Illinois legislature in 1835, he voted to resolve "that the elective franchise should be kept pure from contamination by the admission of colored votes." As a young politician on the make he even attacked Van Buren for being insufficiently hostile to voting by Black men earlier in his career.

But the turmoil of the 1850s awakened Lincoln. The expansion of slavery, and the threat it posed to the workingmen of the North, consumed him. Illinois's Democratic senator Stephen Douglas proposed that newly admitted states Kansas and Nebraska have the power to choose whether they would allow slavery. Lincoln denounced that suggestion in a classic speech in Peoria in 1854. "What I do say is, that no man is good enough to govern another man, *without the other's consent.* I say this is the leading principle—the sheet anchor of American republicanism." Slaves are governed by masters without consent. "Allow ALL the governed an equal voice in the government, and that, and that only is self-government."

He campaigned against Douglas for the U.S. Senate seat in 1858, when legislators, not voters, chose senators. Lincoln broke new ground by announcing his candidacy five months before Election Day. The state legislative contest became a de facto election for senator, a referendum on the spread of slavery, and a choice between two men. The incumbent "Little Giant" charged Lincoln with supporting equality. Before twelve thousand people in Charleston, Illinois, Lincoln forcefully rebutted the allegation. "I am not, nor have ever been, in favor of bringing about in any way the social and political equality of the white and Black races," he declared to applause, adding, "I am not nor have ever been in favor of making voters or jurors of negroes, nor qualifying them to hold office, nor intermarry with white people." Yet at the same time, Lincoln became a passionate advocate for the idea that the Declaration of Independence, with its assertions of equality and freedom, revered as a sacred text, predated the Constitution. The issue of immigration sharpened his view, even before slavery came to consume his passions.

In Ireland a devastating potato famine that began in 1845 killed a million people. A million more emigrated to the United States, crowding into New York, Boston, and other East Coast cities. German refugees began to pour into the country in great numbers after the liberal revolutions of 1848 were crushed throughout Europe. They moved inland, many settling in rural Illinois. In just a few years' time 3 million immigrants swelled a country of 20 million people. Notions of citizenship were fluid: the Constitution never defined what it meant until after the Civil War. The United States had no quotas for immigrants and of course depended on the flood of new people to settle the country and expand the population. Practices varied, but at some point or another, twenty-two states and territories allowed noncitizens to vote, some even for federal offices.

Most of the arrivals in the overwhelmingly Protestant country were Catholic. A nativist backlash—not the last—recoiled from the new, strange, threatening immigrant population. An angry Order of the Star Spangled Banner warned of the immigrant threat. When challenged, the secret society's members invariably murmured, "I know nothing." Derisively dubbed the Know Nothings, its ranks grew large enough to form a new political party that nominated a former president, the otherwise trivia-question-worthy Millard Fillmore, in 1856. The "American Party" was a better brand than "know nothing." It did not try to block immigration, just to prevent new Americans from voting. In 1855 Lincoln's friend Joshua Speed wrote him to ask where he would land politically as the Whig Party broke apart. Not as a Know Nothing, Lincoln replied. "As a nation, we began by declaring that '*all men are created equal.*' We now practically read it '*all men are created equal, except negroes.*' When the Know-Nothings get control, it will read 'all men are created equal, except negroes, and foreigners, and catholics.' When it comes to this I should prefer emigrating to some country where they make no pretence of loving liberty—to Russia, for instance, where despotism can be taken pure, and without the base alloy of hypocracy [*sic*]."

Recent German immigrants could vote in Illinois. They abhorred slavery, were a much sought-after constituency, and spoke little English.

Lincoln secretly invested in a German-language newspaper, the *Illinois Staats Anzeiger*, as he prepared to run for president. Giving a speech in Chicago in 1858 he noted that his audience, mostly immigrants, might feel little connection of blood to the founders and their "glorious epoch." What holds this growing, diverse country together? Look, he said, to the statement, "All men are created equal." Using a striking image, he concluded to applause, "That is the electric cord in that Declaration that links the hearts of patriotic and liberty-loving men together, that will link those patriotic hearts as long as the love of freedom exists in the minds of men throughout the world."

Here was the overwhelming polemical power of the American idea, extended to its next logical limit. Lincoln had been a Whig but pledged fealty to the ideals of the Democrats' favorite founder. "All honor to Jefferson," he wrote in 1859, "to the man who, in the concrete pressure of a struggle for national independence by a single people, had the coolness, forecast, and capacity to introduce into a merely revolutionary document, an abstract truth, applicable to all men and all times, and so to embalm it there, that to-day, and in all coming days, it shall be a rebuke and a stumbling-block to the very harbingers of re-appearing tyranny and oppression."

Frederick Douglass saw the same Declaration very differently. In 1852 in Rochester, New York, the abolitionist leader was asked to toast Independence Day. He declined to offer sentimentality: "What, to the American slave, is your 4th of July? I answer; a day that reveals to him, more than all other days in the year, the gross injustice and cruelty to which he is the constant victim."

5

"The Bullet and the Ballot"

In early April 1865 two speeches, days apart, augured hope for the next great expansion of American democracy: the grant of the vote to African Americans.

Frederick Douglass ended the Civil War as a prized recruiter for the U.S. Army. Black men accounted for one in ten Union soldiers. As the war drew near an end, Douglass had already begun to map the next phase in his fight. Shortly before Congress endorsed the Thirteenth Amendment, which would end slavery, he had unveiled a new campaign to Boston abolitionists. "I have had but one idea for the last three years to present to the American people, and the phraseology in which I clothe it is the old abolition phraseology," he declared. "I am for the 'immediate, unconditional, and universal' enfranchisement of the Black man, in every State in the Union." Loud applause was his answer. "Without this, his liberty is a mockery; without this, you might as well almost retain the old name of slavery for his condition; for in fact, if he is not the slave of the individual master, he is the slave of society, and holds his liberty as a privilege, not as a right. He is at the mercy of the mob, and has no means of protecting himself."

Douglass repeated his arguments with new urgency on April 4, 1865. That day word came of the fall of the Confederate capital, Richmond.

He spoke to a jubilant crowd at Boston's Faneuil Hall: "It is not your intention to bring to your bosom these men, who with bloody hands have been seeking the life of this nation, and invest them with the right to vote, and turn away the Negro, who has fought to uphold that flag. Shall we enfranchise our enemies and disenfranchise our friends?"

The other speech came a week later.

Lincoln sought to steer a wobbly middle course when it came to the reconstruction of the South, which he regarded as "the greatest question ever presented to practical statesmanship." After the Emancipation Proclamation in 1862 he had proposed the "Ten Percent Plan": rebel states would be readmitted to the Union if one in ten white men in the state swore loyalty. Abolitionist Wendell Phillips attacked the absence of Black suffrage in Lincoln's plan, which he said "frees the slave and ignores the negro." In 1864 congressional Radical Republicans, as they were known, passed a bill to impose harsher terms for the readmission of Southern states, but at the last minute they removed a provision for Black voting. Lincoln refused to sign it anyway, reasoning that all voting rules were a matter for the states. At the same time Congress took steps to make sure that African Americans could not vote in the newly organized Montana territory.

Lincoln's brilliant Second Inaugural Address in March 1865 set out a general approach of flexibility and reconciliation, an intention to "bind up the nation's wounds." He seemed to be articulating a cautious approach to reconstruction. Moved by its beauty and its portrayal of the war as divine punishment for the sin of slavery, Douglass told Lincoln his address was a "sacred effort." On voting, Lincoln's views were continuing to change.

On the evening of April 9, 1865, word came of Robert E. Lee's surrender to Ulysses S. Grant. Washington erupted the next day. "Guns are firing—bells ringing, flags flying, men laughing, children cheering—and all jubilant," recorded Lincoln's navy secretary. Two days later a large crowd gathered outside the White House. Lincoln rarely spoke in public, but now, by the light of a candle held by an aide, he delivered an address from a second-floor White House window. He did not give the bellicose speech of a victor. No "Mission Accomplished." Instead he read a dense state paper, setting out a detailed postwar vision.

He continued to embrace the Louisiana government, where his Ten Percent Plan was undergoing its first test as a postwar government. But close listeners heard a surprise: for the first time Lincoln endorsed extending voting rights to Black men. "It is also unsatisfactory to some that the elective franchise [in Louisiana] is not given to the colored man," he said. He now agreed with these critics. "I would myself prefer that it were now conferred on the very intelligent, and on those who serve our cause as soldiers."

At least one in the audience caught the significance of Lincoln's shift on voting rights. John Wilkes Booth was a Southern sympathizer and an acrid white supremacist. "That means nigger citizenship," Booth growled. "That is the last speech he will ever make." He tried to persuade a friend to shoot Lincoln on the spot, but the man refused. Booth swore, "By God, I'll put him through."

Meeting with his cabinet three days later, Lincoln gave them reason to think he would go even further to support full voting rights for all men. That night, at Ford's Theater, Booth made good on his vow.

Voting Rights Enter the Constitution

The story of Reconstruction is now well understood, as is the story of its ignominious end.

The extension of voting rights to African American men arose from a combination of partisan calculus, intermittent idealism, and a profound democratic awakening. War hastened reform; 180,000 Black men had fought for the Union. African Americans, many in uniform, filled out much of the crowd that heard Lincoln's Second Inaugural Address. General William Tecumseh Sherman—no idealist—spoke for many when he said, "When the fight is over the hand that drops the musket cannot be denied the ballot."

But the right to vote carried such power, was such proof of full citizenship, that Black suffrage was hard for most white Americans to swallow. First steps toward enfranchisement stumbled. The Thirteenth Amendment ended slavery in 1865; now the slaves were freed but could not vote, thus still bloating Southern numbers according to the 1787 Constitution, which counted African Americans as three-fifths of a person for the purpose of congressional apportionment. Secretary of State William Seward lamented "a great oversight" in the drafting of the amendment: "A clause was not coupled with it, adjusting the rules of representation." Eventually the South and its Democratic voters would return to the Union, and the same reactionary forces that had provoked the war would regain national power. Already the former Confederacy convulsed with violence directed at former slaves and their political aspirations. In Louisiana in July 1866 the pro-Union governor called a convention to discuss voting rights; a white political militia known as "The Thugs" stormed the meeting, killing forty-seven Black men and injuring 116 more.

National outrage over the massacre helped produce the Fourteenth Amendment. The Amendment has come to be seen as a second Founding, effectively creating a new constitutional order. Section 1 wrote Lincoln's "new birth of freedom" into the nation's organic law. Much of American constitutional development has mulled its grand but vague phrases, which prohibit states from depriving "any person of life, liberty, or property, without due process of law" and preventing denial of "the equal protection of the laws." Section 2 had a more immediate impact on voting: a state would lose representation to the degree it denied voting rights—a deterrent, possibly, or at least a shift in the math.

The 1866 midterm election turned on voter views of the proposed Fourteenth Amendment. President Andrew Johnson, the dyspeptic Democrat who succeeded Lincoln, made an unprecedented "swing around the circle." He denounced Black rights and the congressional Republicans before heckling crowds in key districts. Such promiscuous presidential speechmaking was deemed constitutionally suspect. As one article of impeachment brought against him charged, not only did he make "intemperate, inflammatory and scandalous harangues," but he did so in a "loud voice." (Perhaps this was a euphemism for Johnson's having hit the cider before mounting the rostrum.) Radical Republicans won the elections overwhelmingly, and their ranks in Congress swelled. But the idea of Black suffrage remained jarringly unpopular among white voters in the North. In 1865 five jurisdictions had ballot initiatives on whether to give Black men the vote—and in five it lost. In Colorado, seeking admission as a state, it lost by a 10–1 margin.

Yet quickly partisan math and principle meshed to make voting rights a central Republican goal. After the 1866 election Congress seized control of Reconstruction from the president, in effect giving power to the Radical Republicans. Just weeks after the midterm lawmakers passed a law enfranchising Blacks in Washington, D.C., federal territory, Johnson angrily vetoed it. Another measure extended universal manhood suffrage to the territories. Douglass and other community leaders visited the White House. "Your noble and humane predecessor placed in our hands the sword to assist in saving the nation, and we do hope that you, his able successor, will favorably regard the placing in our hands, the ballot with which to save ourselves," he intoned to a skeptical president. "Those damned sons of bitches thought they had me in a trap!" Johnson fumed to an aide. "I know that damned Douglass. He's just like any nigger, and he would sooner cut a white man's throat than not."

The First Reconstruction Act, passed over Johnson's veto, required the Southern states to grant voting rights to former slaves as well as ratify the Fourteenth Amendment as a condition of readmission. It also barred many Southern whites from voting unless they could swear they never supported the Confederacy or served in its army. Johnson fulminated. He warned a visiting editor that "the people of the South, poor, quiet, unoffending, harmless, were to be trodden under foot 'to protect niggers.'" But Johnson was unable to control the concerted drive of the Republican Congress. Lawmakers divided the South into federal districts, governed by the U.S. military. Rights now would be enforced by bayonet. Many nations ended slavery in the nineteenth century, but, as historian Eric Foner points out, the United States was the only one that granted full citizenship and political rights so soon after emancipation.

Though they had embraced the Fourteenth Amendment, Northern voters would not go further. The next year, running for president, the Union general Ulysses S. Grant fuzzed his position on voting rights. But political operatives were reminded forcefully that they needed to move. In the presidential race of 1868 Southern Blacks cast 450,000 votes, greater than Grant's slim 300,000 popular vote plurality. In the occupied South, Union troops ensured a strong Republican tally, while fraud and violence kept many others away.

Within weeks of the presidential election, and with little notice, Congress moved to pass a constitutional amendment to secure Black voting rights—what later generations would winkingly call a "December surprise." Motives were mixed. Some Republicans suddenly realized that Black voters might provide the margin of victory—not in the South but in the North. "We must establish the doctrine of National jurisdiction over all the States in State matters of the Franchise, or we shall finally be ruined," wrote Thaddeus Stevens, the forceful congressman who led the Radicals. "We must thus bridle Pennsylvania, Indiana, etc., or the South, being in, we shall drift into [Democratic Party rule]." With cloudy powers of prediction, the Radicals thought the Southern vote by former slaves to be secure.

Months of stalemate between House and Senate produced the language of the Fifteenth Amendment:

> **Section 1.** The right of citizens of the United States to vote shall not be denied or abridged by the United States or by any state on account of race, color, or previous condition of servitude.
>
> **Section 2.** The Congress shall have power to enforce this article by appropriate legislation.

Even at the time proponents realized the amendment was garnished with loopholes. It failed to explicitly address barriers to the franchise not "on account of race." At one point the Senate voted to bar all discrimination in voting or holding office because of "race, color, nativity, property, education, or religious belief." That would have cemented an affirmative right to vote for all Americans. Other Republicans recoiled. The *Nation* magazine defended literacy tests for voting, decrying the idea that "it will be taken as a solemn national declaration, made by the most progressive people in the world, that intelligence is of no importance in politics, and that a 'brute vote' [ought] to count for as much as a human one." For a time the sweeping language looked as if it would sink the bill. A call for compromise came from an unexpected quarter. The abolitionist Wendell Phillips editorialized, "For the first time in our lives we beseech them to be a little more *politicians*—and a little less reformers." Phillips's article swung the Senate toward the more timid version of the amendment. "It was one of the ironies of Reconstruction," according to the Civil War historian James McPherson, "that the nation's greatest radical and equalitarian was partly responsible for the adoption of a Fifteenth Amendment whose loopholes later allowed southern states to disenfranchise their Negroes."

Yet it can be too easy to dwell on the amendment's weaknesses. It enshrined in the Constitution an explicit recognition of "the right of citizens of the United States to vote." It made clear that racial motivations were impermissible, even as it grew a bit vague on what that might mean. Significantly it gave *Congress* "the power to enforce this article." It was just a decade after the notorious *Dred Scott* decision, in which the Supreme Court had overturned slavery compromises and declared that Black men could never be citizens. That decision had helped push the country into war. The Fifteenth Amendment made politicians, not judges, the principal guardians of the right to vote. That broad grant of power to the national government applied to races for state and local office, as well as federal contests. It upended the traditional deference to state control.

Ratification was far from assured. Twenty states out of thirty-seven already allowed Blacks to vote, but that was not enough to ratify. Both parties knew an enfranchised Northern Black vote could tip many election results. Border states rejected the amendment. Northern states ratified it, often with slim Republican majorities. Strange cross-currents tugged. California rejected it, not out of fear of Black men voting but to forestall voting by Chinese immigrants (who accounted for one in ten Californians).

The Fifteenth Amendment fight fractured a long alliance. Women's rights advocates were aghast that Black enfranchisement had leaped the queue. They had tolerated the Fourteenth Amendment's reference to "male" voters (the first explicit reference to gender in the Constitution), but they were appalled by the wording of the Fifteenth, which prohibited racial discrimination but left male-only voting in place. At the annual meeting of the American Equal Rights Association in New York City, Susan B. Anthony and Elizabeth Cady Stanton urged defeat of the Fifteenth Amendment. Stanton decried the idea that the "lower orders of Chinese, Africans, Germans and Irish" would represent women and their daughters. "Think of Patrick and Sambo and Hans and Ung Tung," she wrote, "who do not know the difference between a Monarchy and a Republic, who never read the Declaration of Independence . . . making laws for [feminist leaders] Lydia Maria Child, Lucretia Mott, or Fanny Kemble."

Frederick Douglass long had campaigned for women's voting rights. He responded heatedly at the meeting, "I must say I do not see how anyone can pretend that there is the same urgency in giving the ballot to woman as to the negro. With us, the matter is a question of life and death, at least, in fifteen States of the Union." Anthony and Stanton organized a new group, the National Women Suffrage Association, and insisted that Blacks should not be able to vote before women did. Mocking laughter met their efforts. Stanton testified before New York's Committee on Suffrage in 1867, where publisher Horace Greeley, noting that "the bullet and the ballot go together," asked if the women were "ready to fight." "We are ready to fight, sir, just as you fought in the late war," Stanton parried, "by sending our substitutes." (To dodge the draft, wealthy New Yorkers could pay another man to serve.) In the end the Fifteenth Amendment was ratified in 1870.

A False Spring

In the decade after 1867 Black Americans mobilized, learned politics, voted in large numbers, and elected representatives throughout the South. It was a small revolution. One former slave minister recalled, "Politics got in our midst and our revival or religious work began to wane." Union League Clubs were formed across the South, uniting freedmen, Confederate deserters, and white Unionists. Meetings featured a copy of the Declaration of Independence, a Bible, and a symbol of labor, such as an anvil. In Richmond, Virginia, tobacco factories closed because so many Black workers were attending the Republican state convention. A plantation manager complained in 1873, "Every tenth negro [is] a candidate for some office." A white Alabaman observed, "It is the hardest thing in the world to keep a negro away from the polls, that is the one thing he will do, to vote." Black voter turnout approached 90 percent. Blacks worked in coalition with "scalawags" (white Union supporters) and dominated state constitutional conventions and legislatures. The

U.S. Army guarded polling places, an implicit armed force for the Republican Party.

Although white candidates still dominated in most places, in the decade of Reconstruction between 264 and 324 Black men were elected to Congress and state legislatures in the former Confederate states, about one out of six lawmakers. In the South Carolina legislature Black men served as speaker of the house and led its committees. Eighteen Black men won statewide office throughout the South. P. B. S. Pinchback served as governor of Louisiana. Six Black men served as their state's lieutenant governor. Sixteen Blacks served in Congress. In 1870 Hiram Revels began his term in the U.S. Senate representing Mississippi.

This brief moment of democratic possibility was quickly covered up. Years later, after white southerners had clubbed their way back to power, a narrative was energetically advanced about Reconstruction. Politicized Blacks were derided as the puppets of carpetbaggers, white northerners supposedly bent on plunder. The film *Birth of a Nation*, described by President Woodrow Wilson on its release as "history written in lightning," portrayed the story as generations of white Americans learned it: Black voters are shown stuffing the ballot box, while U.S. Army troops with bayonets turn away white voters. Claude Bowers, a Columbia University professor, offered an only slightly less sensationalized view in his 1929 book, *The Tragic Era*.

The reaction to the new order came in what Foner calls a "wave of counterrevolutionary terror." The Ku Klux Klan and similar groups—the Knights of the White Camelia, the White Brotherhood—served as the terrorist arm of the Democratic Party. Thousands were killed. The story of the 1870 massacre in Eutaw, Alabama, still provokes particular horror. At the town courthouse a crowd of white Democrats surrounded an audience of two thousand Black Republicans who had gathered to hear speeches from state politicians. A fusillade of shots poured from the building. According to U.S. Senator Willard Warner, Klansmen "fired upon that fleeing crowd of colored men as though they had been a gang of wolves or hyenas. They stood there emptying their pistols into the backs of those people." The vigilantes killed two African Americans and wounded thirty. "Negro hunts" pursued Black voters throughout the South. For the first time the federal government stepped in. Pressed by President Grant, Congress passed new federal statutes to try to protect the voters and stanch the violence. The Enforcement Act of 1870 made it a federal crime to deny the civil or political rights of any American. Federal agents supervised elections and prosecuted those who tried to block voting. In 1873 alone they brought more than one thousand prosecutions.

When white violence surged again, the national response was more feeble. By 1876 the North was suffering from compassion fatigue. The presidential election ended the experiment with radical political reform. After years of Republican dominance, the Democrats were ready to return to the White House. On Election Day, Democrat Samuel J. Tilden appeared a close winner. Quick-thinking operatives for Republican Rutherford B. Hayes declared victory too. The Electoral College votes of several states magically slid back and forth. Democrats howled. Republicans charged wide intimidation of Black voters in the South. In one Louisiana parish where 1,700 Republican votes were counted in the previous election, the GOP this time received one vote. White rifle clubs, testimony showed, had marched through the Louisiana farmland. As they marched, they sang:

> A charge to keep I have, a God to glorify.
> *If a nigger don't vote with us, he shall forever die.*

In the end the contest turned on recounts and challenges in, yes, Florida, with the decision ultimately made by, yes, a Supreme Court justice. A recount flipped the state to a decisive Republican win. A commission was impaneled to settle the election; a high court justice chaired it and provided the swing vote. Secret negotiations unfolded at the Wormley

Hotel in Washington, ironically owned by a free Black man. Hayes's representative arrived to find the deal already settled: the Republicans would keep the White House, and the troops would be withdrawn from the South. He sanctimoniously declared he could not support anything that would seem "a political bargain," then put on his hat and left.

Piety aside, the bargain held. Reconstruction was over. So was the effort to protect Black voting rights.

6

The Gilded Age

What is the chief end of man?

A: To get rich.

In what way?

A: Dishonestly if we can; honestly if we must.

Who is God, the one only and true?

A: Money is God. Gold and greenbacks and stock—father, son, and the ghost of the same—three persons in one: these are the true and only God, mighty and supreme; and William Tweed is his prophet.

MARK TWAIN, "The Revised Catechism," 1871

DURING THE first century that followed independence, American democracy had expanded as the right to vote became a core element of national identity. The next decades reversed that trend. By the end of the nineteenth century American democracy was reeling in retreat.

In the wake of the Civil War the adolescent country grew astoundingly in size and strength. That growth came with a cost. Millions of immigrants arrived, creating the mass working class that so many of the founders feared. At first electoral competition was tight and turnout remained high, with razor-close margins despite the minor differences between the political parties. But over time wrenching economic and social changes undermined the power of the vote. Class conflict produced brutal repression. Inequality soared as a handful of industrialists and financiers came to dominate the economy and government. Amid this economic change, American democracy eroded. In the North flagrant corruption prevailed. In the South the promise of Reconstruction was replaced with grinding repression of Black citizens. The 1890s saw a breaking point with systematized disenfranchisement of millions of Americans and a newly dominant role for big money.

The North: Corruption and Disenfranchisement

Meet the iconic Boss Tweed. As a strapping, charismatic teen in the 1820s, William Magear Tweed was the foreman of a neighborhood fire company on Cherry Street. In those days in New York City, firefighting was a matter for private initiative. Tweed's "Big Six" company was a gang of toughs. Proudly wearing red uniforms, they would race to a blaze pulling their flashy wagon with a tiger painted on its side (later the emblem of New York's Democratic Party machine). Tweed's firefighting posse became his political base, as he watched the Democratic Party stuff ballot boxes and inflate vote totals. He began a quick ascent. By 1858 Boss Tweed dominated New York government. His power base was the New York County Democratic Committee, known as Tammany Hall. Over the years Tweed's Ring pocketed $45 million in inflated billings and kickbacks, though recent accounts have suggested that this number is far higher—perhaps as much as $200 million.

Tweed's blunt power came from Tammany's ability to organize, enlist, and mobilize the votes of hundreds of thousands, mostly Irish immigrants. Cartoonist Thomas Nast drew the caricatures that helped galvanize belated opposition. In one of Nast's most famous pen-and-ink drawings,

Tweed slouches arrogantly against a ballot box, cigar smoke billowing. The caption reads, "BOSS TWEED: As long as I count the Votes, what are you going to do about it? say?" (Tweed never actually said "What are you going to do about it?" Nast repeated the catchphrase in cartoon after cartoon, to the point that reporters would taunt the Boss himself with the question. Sarah Palin never said, "I can see Russia from my house," either.)

The urban Democratic Party ran on the support of new voters. Far from a broad ideological movement (as some earlier parties had been), Tammany and the other political machines were ethnic enclaves, focused on protecting constituents from a hostile Yankee world. Waves of immigrants had begun to reach the United States. As Federalists such as Gouverneur Morris and Chancellor James Kent had feared, immigration changed America. Irish Americans filled New York, Boston, and other East Coast cities. (Voting Democratic, they feared African American competition for jobs. Irish immigrants staged the draft riots in New York during the Civil War and were among the most fiercely opposed to Black suffrage.) Later in the century Italians, Poles, Russians, and other Europeans surged through the newly built immigration center at Ellis Island. Most were Catholic or Jewish. In all, 25 million immigrants arrived in the United States between the Civil War and World War I.

Urban political life became heavily transactional and marred by fraud. When the radical reformer Henry George ran for mayor of New York in 1886, Tammany Hall not only stuffed ballot boxes but threw many in the river. Before reform laws were enacted at the turn of the twentieth century, Philadelphians dryly observed that "all of the signers of the Declaration of Independence were still regularly vot[ing] in that city." Chicanery was not limited to the East Coast cities; according to a definitive early twentieth-century study, "In a contested election case in Colorado in 1904 one witness testified under oath that he voted 125 times in the city of Denver, and then quit work because the [party] organization cut the price [per vote] from one dollar to fifty cents."

These tales of fraud are lurid and colorful—and not entirely reliable.

Many were retailed by scandalized bluebloods or rural Protestants who were at least partly unnerved by the throngs of Catholic immigrants voting. City political machines provided services and power for a marginalized community. Beneficence repaid loyal votes. It was not pretty, but it helped produce heavy turnout (even factoring in the number of fraudulent votes).

Backlash ensued. Whether because they were appalled by the prospect of immigrants coming to power or the corruption that accompanied political life, members of the Protestant elite in the North recoiled. Many concluded that perhaps democracy was not such a good idea, after all.

Francis Parkman was a leading public intellectual; historians still bestow an annual award in his name. In 1878 Parkman published a widely read essay in the *North American Review*, "The Failure of Universal Suffrage," in which he wrote:

> A New England village of the olden time—that is to say, of some forty years ago—would have been safely and well governed by the votes of every man in it; but, now that the village has grown into a populous city, with its factories and workshops, its acres of tenement-houses, and thousands and ten thousands of restless workmen, foreigners for the most part, to whom liberty means license and politics means plunder, to whom the public good is nothing and their own most trivial interests everything, who love the country for what they can get out of it, and whose ears are open to the promptings of every rascally agitator, the case is completely changed, and universal suffrage becomes a questionable blessing.

Parkman seethed over the "invasion of peasants" who now governed northern cities: "If the voter has a conscience, he votes it away. . . . Witness the municipal corruptions of New York, and the monstrosities of negro rule in South Carolina." American democracy rested on social equality, public virtue, and self-restraint. He bemoaned rule by "an ignorant proletariat and a half-taught plutocracy."

Parkman's views were widely shared among the "best men," a phrase that was used without evident irony. John Adams's great-grandson warned that "universal suffrage can only mean in Plain English the government of ignorance and vice—it means a European, and especially Celtic, proletariat on the Atlantic coast; an African proletariat on the shores of the Gulf; and a Chinese proletariat on the Pacific." E. L. Godkin was editor of the not-yet-left-wing *Nation* magazine. He proposed treating New York City as a corporation and letting only "shareholders" vote. Even Walt Whitman, looking "our times and lands searchingly in the face, like a physician diagnosing some deep disease," could not "gloss over the appalling dangers of universal suffrage": the "savage, wolfish parties," the "half brained nominees," the governments "saturated in corruption, bribery, falsehood, maladministration."

In his magisterial book *The Right to Vote*, the historian Alexander Keyssar outlines how laws were changed to make it harder for Catholics and other working-class immigrants to vote. Likening this method to the repression of voting rights in the old Confederacy, he calls it the "Redemption of the North." For starters, reformers tried to reimpose a form of property requirement, targeted at big-city voters. Boss Tweed was in prison. The man who prosecuted him, Democratic governor Samuel J. Tilden, appointed a commission to draft reforms to clean up City Hall. He packed it with men such as the voting rights foe Godkin. In 1877 the panel recommended that a board of finance take over the job of governing New York City. Only those who owned considerable property or paid a high rent would be eligible to vote for its commissioners. One committee member explained that the city's propertied elite "would no longer find themselves in contest with the loafer element, which would eventually outnumber and beat them." The Chamber of Commerce, the Board of Trade, and the city's newspapers mobilized in support. One publisher warned that "ignorant voters" were "as dangerous to the interest of society as the communists of France." The *New York World* editorialized that the "uncivilized classes in Brooklyn are quite as murderous as the savage in Montana." Gleeful upstate Republican legislators voted for Tilden's measure. Tammany orators denounced the plan to disenfranchise their voters as a "menace to the rights of the people" that would "set up an oligarchy of wealth." Machine Democrats swept back into power the next year and blocked the plan from final enactment. Similar bids to disenfranchise working-class urban voters succeeded in smaller cities throughout the country.

Other states expanded the rules that barred "paupers" from voting. The term was elastic, but generally it referred to anyone receiving government assistance. According to Keyssar, pauper exclusions prevented thousands, perhaps hundreds of thousands, from voting. The curb affected the intense labor conflicts of the time. In New Bedford, Massachusetts, striking textile workers were told that if they received relief from local government, they would lose their right to vote.

The "best men" also cracked down on voting by recent arrivals. Through the first half of the nineteenth century many states allowed immigrants and noncitizens to vote; after all, they wanted settlers. Those immigrants were farmers, and mostly Protestants. The Supreme Court had blessed this approach, noting in one case that suffrage was not a privilege of citizenship—and not, therefore, limited to citizens. The traditional link between military service and voting had frayed during the Civil War. In 1863 the first nationwide draft law summoned nonnaturalized citizens to military service. President Lincoln gave immigrants two months to renounce their intention to stay in the United States, but any man who had already voted had to serve in the military. The law kindled draft riots on the streets of Manhattan, and immigrants burned much of the business district and targeted Black residents, killing at least 120. Lawsuits unsuccessfully challenged Lincoln's draft rule. "Under our complex system of government there may be a citizen of a state who is not a citizen of the United States in the full sense of the term," the Wisconsin

Supreme Court ruled unanimously in rejecting a plea to avoid the draft. "This result would seem to follow unavoidably from the nature of the two systems of government."

Anti-immigrant sentiment rose after the war. Fears mingled improbably: of Catholic bloc voting secretly controlled by the pope, or of Jewish financial domination somehow exercised at the ballot box, or of political radicalism, or of all together.

States that had allowed "alien suffrage" began to repeal it. In some parts of the country the limits were nakedly racist. California's 1879 constitution declared that "no native of China" could ever vote. That did not violate the Fifteenth Amendment, it was argued, because the state's rule did not specify race, just place of birth. Courts agreed. Other states claimed concern about voter fraud and began to apply new barriers to voting targeted especially at working-class immigrants. Some states required residents to show their naturalization papers to register or even to vote. As with later requirements to show identification, on first blush this might have seemed unobjectionable. But it offered opportunities for partisans to challenge and intimidate voters, putting tremendous power in the hands of local election officials. When New Jersey prepared to institute the requirement, the *New York Herald* pointed out a "sad feature" of the law: "Many persons will be deprived of their vote, as their papers are either worn out, lost, or mislaid."

Other states imposed literacy tests. These gained greatest notoriety in the South, where it had been illegal just a few years before even to teach a slave to read. They gave registrars near dictatorial authority over who could vote. They chilled voting in the North as well, in neighborhoods teeming with immigrants, where coat cutters or streetcar drivers spoke Italian, French, Yiddish, Polish, German, or Russian—the new class of garment workers, factory hands, and steelworkers. Some native-born men still struggled with the tests. Labor unions and immigrant groups resisted, but by the 1920s thirteen states in the West and North excluded the illiterate from voting.

Paradox of Reform

The quiet disenfranchisement continued with two new rules that live on today. Modern readers assume they are part of the way an accurate, clean election system runs, but the motives that inspired them were mixed.

Prior to the Civil War, when the population of towns and even city precincts was low, election officials knew the voters, often personally, so there was no need for formal voter registration. Massachusetts was the only state that required it. But after the war every state but North Dakota adopted some form of voter registration requirement. Often, as in New York State, a Republican-dominated legislature would impose the change only on a balky, Democratic big city. Suburban and rural areas, dominated by Protestant Republicans, were exempt. Initially voters who registered had to do so for each election. "Permanent" registration created a list that was updated by police surveys of homes and rooming houses (where landlords were asked if a registered voter was really a resident). According to one sympathetic chronicler, "After registration was put in place, voting and registration plummeted in the neighborhoods where fraud was suspected." Other historians believe that registration simply made it harder for immigrants to vote. In Chicago the new system featured tiny precincts. (Thus voters fell off the rolls when they moved even within a neighborhood.) Chicagoans had only two days per year in which they could sign up, and a voter who found himself challenged and placed on a "suspected list" was obliged to produce proof of eligibility. The tony Union League Club declared, "The foundations for honest elections were now firmly laid." The details mattered, for the new registration system offered myriad opportunities for electoral microaggression. In New York City in 1908 Democrats tried to hold down the Socialist vote by holding registration on the Jewish holy day of Yom Kippur. Writing two years later, the muckraking journalist Ray Stannard Baker concluded, "Our registration and ballot laws eliminate hundreds of thousands of voters."

Another change upended the way Americans cast their votes: the

"Australian ballot," or secret ballot. We take it so for granted that it can be hard to understand its significance or imagine any negative impact from its adoption. Recall that in the country's early days, voting took place in public, usually by voice, and in the robust party era leading up to the Civil War, ballots were used, but voters could walk into the polling place carrying preprinted party sheets. With these, voters who spoke little English or could barely read still could vote the straight party ticket, and election operatives could check to make sure the right papers were being inserted in the ballot box. One Tammany Hall leader perfumed the party tickets "so that they might be tracked by scent." Voters who expected to be paid could prove services rendered.

In England election reform had been the subject of a strong working-class movement for much of the nineteenth century. The 1832 People's Charter demanded a secret ballot, along with expanded voting rights and equal representation in Parliament. By the time the innovation came to the United States in the late 1800s, it was known as the "Australian ballot." Its elements would be familiar to modern Americans. Balloting was done in secret, usually by putting a slip of paper in a ballot box. That much was not new. What was new was this: the government printed the names of all eligible candidates, and the voter marked his choice. Ballots were distributed only on Election Day, and only at the polling place.

Ironically, at first this made it easier to stuff the ballot box; party operatives merely had to add as many new votes as proved necessary. In addition it served as a kind of literacy test, since voters had to read and mark votes on a printed ballot. They had to decipher names and obscure job titles ("County Assessor"), not just point at a picture of an elephant or a donkey. Yet at the same time, the secret ballot served to focus the act of voting on the individual, the aggregation of millions of private choices made in secret. In the 1800s splinters and start-ups frequently competed and won office: the Greenback Party, the Know Nothings, various eruptions calling themselves the People's Party. Now, because the government printed the ballot, it had to create rules for who could be listed. The number of third parties and "fusion" tickets backed by more than one party sharply declined. Today, of course, the sanctity of the secret ballot is central to our understanding of a fair electoral system.

Mass rallies, parades, giant floats, and illuminations—the boisterous ways that ordinary people showed their electoral choice—dwindled in the first decade of the twentieth century. Newspapers previously had been overtly partisan, continuing a tradition of vituperative exhortation common since colonial times. Parties started them and paid for them. Now newspapers tried to be neutral. The *New York Times* proclaimed its objectivity, pledging to present the news "without fear or favor." In some ways the tamping down of partisan effusion made newspapers less interesting. It also meant that campaigns seeking to get their message to voters unfiltered had to rely on paid advertising, starting with newspaper ads. Bit by bit the professionalization and purification of politics—which brought undeniable improvements in the tenor of governance—dimmed public enthusiasm. And it made money, and those who had it, increasingly important in politics.

What happened in the North was often subtle, a disenfranchisement of working people clothed in the noblest of rationales. Not so in the South.

The Mississippi Plan

Many wrongly assume that southern democracy collapsed as soon as the North pulled back its military forces in 1877. In fact, three years after the U.S. Army left, two-thirds of Black men still voted; even in the 1890s half of them still voted in high-profile governor races in the former states of the Confederacy. To be sure, it was not a fair fight. Fraud, ballot-box stuffing, and violent intimidation spread. In one Tennessee district with a large Black population, Democrats challenged the legitimacy of Republican voters, changed polling places without notice, and enlisted a vigilante group to "maintain order." In Louisiana the governor swore to follow the state's election law, a statute he summarized as intending "to make it the duty of the governor to treat the law as a formality and count in the Democrats." Throughout the South sheriffs controlled polling places. If they sensed an unexpected uptick in Republican votes, they could stealthily move the ballot boxes to somewhere new. Republicans would spend Election Day hunting through the countryside looking for a place to vote.

Much of this disenfranchisement was haphazard. But two developments persuaded southern elites to get systematic. The first was the renewed threat of national action. Republicans regained control of Congress as well as the White House in 1890. The party still spoke for Black equality; its 1888 platform declared "unswerving devotion" to "the supreme and sovereign right of every lawful citizen, rich or poor, native or foreign born, white or Black, to cast one free ballot in public elections, and to have that ballot duly counted." Congressional investigations exposed abuses in the South. Twenty times in the final two decades of the nineteenth century, the House rejected Democratic "winners" and seated Republican or Populist candidates because of fraud or abuse directed at African American voters. Then, in 1890, Boston Brahmin congressman Henry Cabot Lodge proposed legislation to federally supervise southern elections, aimed at securing equal voting rights. Opponents dubbed the mild measure the "Lodge Force Bill" and panicked. The bill passed the House, but a thirty-three-day filibuster blocked it in the Senate. This was the first successful southern filibuster of a federal civil rights bill: a cherished tradition began. The idea behind the Force Bill would reappear in the 1960s as the Voting Rights Act.

Southern white leaders also feared the rising Populist movement. Populism lives in the public imagination as a dimly remembered uprising of angry farmers, prone to simplistic sloganeering and railing against cultural elites. In fact it was a fleeting moment of democratic promise. In the 1870s and 1880s the economy soared and crashed, with farmers across the Midwest and South sinking deep into debt. They responded by organizing cooperatives, clubs, and political groups. In the South the

Farmers Alliance began to win elections in the late 1880s. It challenged economic aristocracy and demanded inflation (through the abandonment of the gold standard, to help creditors), regulation of railroad rates, and other economic policies. Frequently white farmers allied with Black political forces, especially in Texas. The People's Party elected Black men to state executive committees throughout the South. Especially as the economy plunged into depression in the 1890s, Democratic Party leaders saw a potent threat. They moved to reorder southern politics: to disenfranchise Black voters, and poorer whites while they were at it, and recast the region's politics around race, not class.

Mississippi moved first. In 1890 Black voters still outnumbered white voters in that state. Wealthy white political leaders from the state's "Black Belt," counties with a majority-Black population, demanded a new state constitution. It imposed an array of changes designed to disenfranchise Blacks while appearing racially neutral on their face. The state instituted a voter registration system, with local registrars empowered to exclude voters. It imposed a literacy test, again granting officials wide leeway to bar Black voters deemed insufficiently educated. And it enacted a poll tax, which also affected poor white voters. A Mississippi congressman later explained that the state had "disenfranchised not only the ignorant and vicious Black, but the ignorant and vicious white as well, and the electorate in Mississippi is now confined to those, and to those alone, who are qualified by intelligence and character for the proper and patriotic exercise of this great franchise."

Mississippi's plan was a widely hailed success. Over the next eighteen years seven other southern states changed their constitutions. Virginia's convention met in 1901 and 1902. A young journalist and state senator named Carter Glass was a delegate. He fought for progressive measures, including new state power to regulate railroads. He also fought to export the Mississippi Plan to Virginia, through a poll tax, a literacy test, and voter registration. Virginia also incorporated a lifetime ban on voting for former felons, a ban still in effect in 2016.

To raucous cheers Glass declared to the delegates, "This plan will eliminate the darkey as a political factor in this state in less than five years." The state constitution "does not necessarily deprive a single white man of the ballot, but will inevitably cut from the existing electorate four-fifths of the Negro voters."

Another delegate challenged him: "Will it not be done by fraud and discrimination?"

"By fraud, no. By discrimination, yes," Glass scoffed. "Discrimination! Why, that is precisely what we propose. That, exactly, is what this Convention was elected for—to discriminate to the very extremity of permissible action under the limitations of the Federal Constitution, with a view to the elimination of every negro voter who can be gotten rid of, legally, without materially impairing the numerical strength of the white electorate."

The convention decided not to submit the new constitution to the state's voters. It took effect without public ratification.

"Declaration in the Air"

In desperation Black activists turned to the courts. Here we are reminded of a perverse fact: throughout most of American history judges have been of little help in advancing democracy. Already the U.S. Supreme Court had undone much of the force of the Reconstruction amendments. In the *Slaughter-House* cases it neutralized the Fourteenth Amendment's protection of the "privileges and immunities" of citizenship. Another case, *United States v. Cruikshank*, arose out of the notorious 1873 Colfax massacre, in which Democratic vigilantes slaughtered African American Republicans in a small Louisiana town named after President Grant's vice president. In that case the justices ruled that the amendment protected only against discriminatory actions by government—private citizens were not covered. Now the justices proved unwilling to act to protect voting rights. Because the new disenfranchising rules did not overtly apply only to Black voters, they did not violate the Fifteenth Amendment. On a series of cases upholding Mississippi's constitution, a historian wrote in 1918 with gloriously mixed metaphors, "Thus the first of the modern reactionary constitutions passed the acid test with flying colors."

The most important Supreme Court showdown on the new voting rules came in 1903. Previously the Court had upheld Mississippi's literacy tests and poll taxes, concluding that they did not violate the Fifteenth Amendment because they did not explicitly discriminate based on race. The ruling in *Giles v. Harris* was broader, more cynical, and more troubling. *Giles* is not widely known in the canon of major constitutional cases, let alone notorious ones (such as *Plessy v. Ferguson*, which upheld racial segregation in 1896). However, its impact lasted longer. Legal scholar Richard Pildes considers it "the decisive turning point" in the Supreme Court's "removing democracy from the agenda of constitutional law."

Alabama previously had one of the most democratically robust systems in the country, including universal male suffrage and a bar against gerrymandering. But its new Jim Crow constitution gave county registrars great discretion in barring African American voters. White men could vote without anyone attesting to their good character, but Black men required the recommendation of a white voter. As a result Black voting rates fell from 180,000 to fewer than 3,000 between 1900 and 1903. Jackson Giles, president of the Colored Men's Suffrage Association of Alabama, sued the state on behalf of five thousand voters demanding to be registered. The lawsuit was secretly organized and financed by none other than Booker T. Washington, the African American leader who had publicly made his peace with segregation. Mass meetings at the Brooklyn Academy of Music and other packed venues cheered the case, along with another challenging Virginia's constitution. In April 1903 eighty-three-year-old Susan B. Anthony addressed a protest in Rochester, New York. "We women are in the same boat as the disenfranchised negroes," she declared. But shortly before the meeting began, fragmentary word came of the Supreme Court's ruling. When the opinion was published a week later, the rout became apparent.

Justice Oliver Wendell Holmes Jr., who had fought for the North in the Civil War and had been newly named to the Court, wrote for a six-vote majority. Holmes eventually would prove one of the greatest justices. His terse opinion, however, is painful to read. He acknowledged that federal courts had the power to decide the case, but to remedy the wrong the Court would need to act, not merely make a "declaration in the air." Holmes's logic twisted into a sneer. Giles had called Alabama's law a fraud on the U.S. Constitution. Holmes responded, "How can we make the court a party to the unlawful scheme by accepting it and adding another voter to its fraudulent lists?" Finally he reached his real point: the Supreme Court had no power to stop the shredding of democratic rights. The suit charged "that the great mass of the white population intends to keep the Blacks from voting. . . . Unless we are prepared to supervise the voting in that State by officers of the court, it seems to us that all that the plaintiff could get . . . would be an empty form. Apart from damages to the individual, relief from a great political wrong, if done, as alleged, by the people of a State and the State itself, must be given by them or by the legislative and political department of the government of the United States."

The opinion was rendered at a time when judges were indeed activists, striking down state laws with gusto. These laws generally protected workers, women, children, and others against industrial capitalism. This judicial period is known as the "*Lochner* era," named after a notorious case in which the Court struck down a ten-hour-a-day limitation on the hours worked by bakers because it interfered with their "liberty of contract." Holmes and other Progressive judges who followed him spoke for judicial minimalism. "If my fellow citizens want to go to Hell I will help them," Holmes later wrote a friend. "It's my job."

The Court's reluctance to rule against Alabama in *Giles* had an even deeper, more disquieting basis. Only massive federal oversight could enforce the Constitution, Holmes wrote. That would require ongoing judicial involvement, a takeover of state governments, perhaps troops. (All those proved necessary in the 1960s.) No, the courts would stay out of the fray. One despondent African American novelist wrote to Booker T. Washington, "By the decision of the Supreme Court in the Alabama case, the Negro in the South has no rights which the government, as constituted, can compel Southern white men to respect."

The Solid South

The southern bid to fully disenfranchise Republicans and Blacks hardened into fact. Even in Alabama the disenfranchising constitution had passed a public referendum with support from barely half of white voters. Remove fraud from the equation, and the constitution likely would have lost. Within years memory of that debate was erased in Alabama and other states.

Historian Alexander Keyssar reports on the consequences of these laws. "In Mississippi after 1890, less than 9,000 out of 147,000 voting age Blacks were registered to vote; in Louisiana, where more than 130,000 Blacks had been registered to vote in 1896, the figure dropped to a bleak 1,342 by 1904." In 1965, on the eve of the Voting Rights Act, just 6.7 percent of Mississippi's eligible Black voters were registered. Participation plunged for white voters as well. In the 1870s in Mississippi, marked by robust if violent political competition, turnout neared 70 percent; by the early twentieth century it scraped near 15 percent.

The victory for white supremacists scarred the South and shifted its politics. Tom Watson of Georgia had been a Farmers' Alliance leader, a congressman, and then the People's Party's vice presidential candidate in 1896. Watson campaigned against large corporations, railroads, and the debt that crushed farmers. He zealously appealed to both white and Black voters. "Now the People's Party says to these two men, 'You are kept apart that you may be separately fleeced of your earnings,'" he wrote. "'You are made to hate each other because upon that hatred is rested the arch of financial despotism which enslaves you both. You are deceived and blinded that you may not see how this race antagonism perpetuates a monetary system which beggars both.'" When the Populists were crushed and Black voters disenfranchised, Watson shifted his target, now railing against Blacks, as well as Catholics and Jews. (He waged war against "popery" and warned that Woodrow Wilson employed "a Romanist as private secretary!") By the end of his career he had become a bitter, bigoted demagogue. In 1920 Georgia's white voters elected him to the U.S. Senate.

Carter Glass, who had exulted over the end of voting by "darkeys," cut a suave, powerful figure in Washington over the next four decades. He was elected to Congress, ultimately becoming chair of the House Banking Committee, and then was named secretary of the Treasury. He played a lead role in the creation of the Federal Reserve, which brought the United States in line with other countries by instituting a central bank with at least some independence from private finance, though Glass worked to give banks more say in its structure. As a U.S. senator during the Great Depression, he cosponsored the Glass-Steagall Act, which created federal deposit insurance, strong regulation of banks, and a divorce between commercial banking and riskier investment banking. Throughout he was an implacable segregationist. Franklin Roosevelt called him "the unreconstructed rebel." Glass served into the late 1940s as chair of the powerful Appropriations Committee, dominating even as a recluse who never left his hotel suite.

That the South—the "Solid South"—guaranteed votes for Democrats was the central fact in American governance for much of the twentieth century. Southern politicians, now immune from challenge, began to accumulate seniority, then the coin of power in Congress. By 1908 most standing committees of the Senate were chaired by southerners. That situation would continue up through the 1960s. As Robert A. Caro notes, in his epic series on Lyndon Johnson's ascent, racist southerners still controlled five of the eight most powerful committees in the U.S. Senate when Johnson served as Majority Leader. The organized state violence and judicial wordplay of the 1890s disproportionately shaped American politics for six decades.

"The First Is Money"

In 1880, in a small town in upstate New York, a troubled man named Charles Guiteau delivered a speech in support of the Republican presidential candidate James Garfield. Convinced that his printed oration had won Garfield the election, Guiteau demanded an appointment as consul general to France. Rebuffed after weeks of pressing his claim, he purchased a revolver, choosing one that would look good on display in the State Department library, and tried to tour the jail where he expected to be held. Then, on July 2, 1881, at a train station, he shot and fatally wounded the president.

The assassination, seemingly random, by an imbalanced would-be office seeker set off a chain of events that was to introduce a new element into elections in America—organized money. The rising role for those with funds, and the shrinking role for people-powered campaigning, became another obstacle to the meaningful vote.

Throughout most of the nineteenth century the spoils system rewarded party stalwarts with government jobs. Those government employees, in turn, were expected to pay some of their salaries to the party that sponsored them. President Garfield, an earnest former general, had urged civil service reform in his inaugural address. Government workers would be hired on merit, not party loyalty. In an intraparty détente, Garfield's vice president was a notorious practitioner of the spoils system. Chester A. Arthur had been fired as overseer of the New York Customhouse when he refused to implement civil service reform there. Now Arthur was president. Flummoxing some, he backed civil service reform in honor of his slain predecessor. After the Civil War the federal government had remained swollen in size, but jobs were still given out to party stalwarts—what one political scientist has called America's "clientelist" period. The Pendleton Civil Service Act began to create the corps of nonpolitical professional government employees who would be chosen for jobs based on test results and other qualifications. Federal patronage began to shrink. The law also prohibited federal employees from making campaign contributions and dried up the traditional source of funds.

The political system turned for its fuel to the rising source of power in the country, what historian H. W. Brands has described as the "American colossus," the new class of monopolists and wealthy businessmen. The late nineteenth century was a time of propulsive economic growth and brutal consolidation of industry. Between 1880 and 1900 crude oil production in the United States more than doubled, to 60 million barrels per year. Railroad revenues more than tripled, to $16.2 billion. If the democracy envisioned by Jefferson, admired by Tocqueville, and lionized by Lincoln depended in some measure on equality of conditions, at least among white men, the lurch toward concentrated wealth risked a repudiation of that vision. By World War I the wealthiest 1 percent of Americans owned around one fifth of the income of the United States and the United Kingdom combined. Government at all levels often seemed an afterthought to the surging forces of markets and the rising ranks of businessmen. "What do I care about the law?" bellowed the railroad magnate Cornelius Vanderbilt. "Hain't I got the power?"

The controversial new reality came to the fore in 1884. In the last week of the presidential campaign, Republican presidential nominee James G. Blaine, a Maine politician reputed to be thoroughly corrupt, seemed headed for victory. He dined at Delmonico's restaurant in New York City with his key funders: speculator Jay Gould, railroad owner Russell Sage, telegraph mogul Cyrus W. Field, fur scion John Jacob Astor, and an array of other new and old money men. The meal was supposed to be kept secret, but Joseph Pulitzer's *New York World* got hold of every detail. Across the top of its front page the next morning, the paper blazoned a cartoon captioned "The Royal Feast of Belshazzaar Blaine and the Money Kings." The candidate and his backers were shown hungrily tucking into "Gould Pie," "Lobby Pudding," and the somewhat less appetizing "Navy Contract." Blaine was having a bad day. Before dinner he had spoken to a group of ministers but had sat quietly as a Protestant clergyman declared the Democrats to be the party of "rum, Romanism and rebellion." A furious Catholic backlash tipped the presidential election to Democrat Grover Cleveland. One senator groused, "If Blaine had eaten a few more swell dinners and had a few more ministers call on him, we should not have carried a Northern state."

All the money now flooding into the political system: what was it being used for? At that time expensive campaign advertising was not in much evidence, but money was still needed for a cruder purpose: to pay voters. Robert Mutch, the leading historian of American campaign finance, notes that by the late 1800s Americans saw "an alarming merger of an old problem, vote buying, and a new one, corporate contributions." That gave fuel to the fight for the secret ballot, which was instituted nearly everywhere by the early 1890s. In New York City ballot reform was coupled with "publicity," or disclosure of campaign spending, in 1890. The point, explained voting rights foe E. L. Godkin of the *Nation*, was to expose "the corrupt use of large sums of money."

The new era of campaign financing came into focus in one of the most epochal elections in American history, the presidential contest of 1896. William Jennings Bryan was an obscure Nebraska congressman when he addressed the Democratic convention in support of a party plank supporting the "free silver" movement (a plea for inflation, by coining money based on silver as well as gold). "You shall not press down upon the brow of labor this crown of thorns," he called out, and stretched his arms wide, holding them in a Christ-like pose, "you shall not crucify mankind upon a cross of gold." Amid pandemonium, he was nominated the next day. The People's Party nominated Bryan as well. The thirty-six-year-old plunged into a cross-country campaign by train, a first, ultimately giving at least 250 speeches to 5 million people.

Mark Hanna organized the Republican response. Hanna was an industrialist from the booming metropolis of Cleveland, who had groomed his easygoing friend William McKinley, an Ohio congressman, for greater things. In 1896 Hanna brilliantly created much of modern politics. His possibly apocryphal quip is still frequently quoted: "There are two things that are important in politics. The first is money, and I can't remember what the second is." His admiring biographer, the Progressive journalist Herbert Croly, explained, "Mr. Hanna always did his best to convert the practice from a matter of political begging on the one side and donating on the other into a matter of systematic assessment according to the means of the individual and the institution." Banks were dunned to donate one quarter of 1 percent of their capital to McKinley's campaign. John D. Rockefeller's Standard Oil gave $250,000. In all, McKinley raised ten times as much money as Bryan. The campaign astounded with its sweep and sophistication. McKinley stayed at home, waging a "front porch campaign." Hanna paid 1,400 speakers to flood swing states. The campaign printed 120 million pieces of literature, produced brochures in nine languages, erected forests of signs and billboards, and hired film cameramen to show McKinley at home, the first campaign commercial. Theodore Roosevelt complained of Hanna, "He has advertised McKinley as if he were a patent medicine." On Election Day what seemed a close race became a rout; McKinley won by fewer than 1 million popular votes but dominated outside the South. Republicans would control American presidential politics for the next thirty-six years, except when the party split, until the Great Depression. Now firmly the party of business, they had less need for Black votes after what political scientists call the Realignment of 1896.

* * *

By the end of the nineteenth century the surge of American democracy—the tide that had seemed so strong—had ebbed. The South had returned to a condition in some ways arguably even less democratic than before the Civil War, as poor whites now joined Blacks in exclusion from the franchise and elections converted into squabbles within the Democratic Party. By 1908 every southern state had enacted a disenfranchising law in one form or another. In the North a more antiseptic politics developed, with fewer voters and eventually greater reliance on modern marketing. Strict "good government" laws further reduced turnout, especially in the urban North. The federal civil service system was accompanied by an attack on patronage hiring in local government. A movement for civil service reform challenged the power of party machines and pressed for professionalization of government services. And the rising power of business and corporate money had systematized the corruption already rife in the system. The Democrats were uncontested in the South, and in large parts of the North the Republicans effectively had little opposition. The political scientist Walter Dean Burnham named the political alignment "the System of 1896." It dominated American politics for four decades, and its impact lasted for most of a century.

An inevitable but little noticed result: turnout began to decline. It had peaked in 1896 at 79.6 percent. In 1900 it was 73.7 percent and fell to just 49 percent by the 1920s.

PART III

THE TWENTIETH CENTURY

7

The Age of Reform

DO POLITICAL assassinations matter? The murder of an Austrian archduke in Sarajevo triggered World War I, of course, but Europe's great powers were straining for conflict anyway. Debate still simmers over whether John F. Kennedy would have turned away from Vietnam had he lived. One can imagine Israeli premier Yitzhak Rabin would have finished the task of making peace with the Palestinians. Lincoln followed by Johnson, Garfield by Arthur: we've seen how those steered the history of voting. We think less about the shooting that marked the start of the Progressive Era. Stolid William McKinley, sold as the "advance agent of prosperity," was president at the turn of the twentieth century. Visiting the Pan American Exposition in Buffalo in September 1901, he was shot, and died a week later. His successor was Theodore Roosevelt. During his two noisy years as governor of New York, he had denounced the "invisible empire" of campaign contributors who dominated the legislature. Party bosses kicked him upstairs—and safely out of state—figuring he could do less harm as vice president. TR's gusting energy personified a time of mobilization to reform governmental and social institutions. It is hard to imagine the era of reform without his catalytic involvement and occasional encouragement.

The Progressive Era is again coming sharply into focus as a turning point in American history. In the wake of the roaring rise to global power, the growth of cities, and massive concentration of wealth, Americans felt that their institutions were under siege, inadequate to the changing economy. There was, as Roosevelt described it, a "fierce discontent" among educated city dwellers as well as beaten-down farmers. Progressive reform bubbled up from local communities and movements across the country, engaging millions. In so many ways modern America came into focus in these decades. The challenges feel uncannily like our own.

Later preoccupations tend to color assessments. Current notions of left and right had not yet hardened. We know how Roosevelt and then Wilson created the strong presidency. "The President is at liberty," Wilson wrote, "both in law and conscience, to be as big a man as he can." They won the first federal responses to modern industrial capitalism: pure food and drug laws, workplace safety rules, the creation of the Federal Reserve. For many years the era was viewed as a mere dress rehearsal for the liberalism of the New Deal. More recently, as American liberals relabeled themselves "progressives," conservatives have taken to branding the politics of the time incipiently fascist. Glenn Beck and other modern television hosts decry Roosevelt and Wilson as the precursors of Mussolini and Hitler, proto-strongmen for the twentieth century.

Less understood is the extent to which Americans of the Progressive Era understood that restoring and expanding the institutions of American democracy were central to their mission. Buffeted by economic change and facing a once-unimagined concentration of wealth, they turned to the vote. In less than a decade's time they produced two constitutional amendments to expand suffrage and its impact. And they linked reforms to the vote with broader efforts to curb the role of money in politics. They saw the fight for reform as a fight for democracy. An archetypal figure was Boston's "People's Lawyer," Louis D. Brandeis. He warned, "We can have democracy in this country, or we can have great wealth concentrated in the hands of a few, but we can't have both."

This produced a progressive paradox: many of the same crusaders who wanted to expand the vote believed in government by experts. Just as government was built up to regulate railroad rates and organize urban public schools, the conduct of American democracy too became systematized, professionalized, and subject to government control. Many of the changes appear to have produced a political system that was cleaner, more focused on the individual, and less robustly participatory—less demonstrably democratic.

The first break came from a now-forgotten campaign finance scandal. At the time, it was huge—a combination of Watergate, with its political misdeeds, and the business conflagration of Enron. It revealed to turn-of-the-century Americans how the power of their vote was being diluted by new money.

"Day of Atonement"

On February 1, 1905, newspaper readers goggled at reports of a lavish costume ball at Sherry's Hotel in Manhattan. Its theme was "eighteenth century France"—Versailles. A fleet of bewigged waiters, costumed by the Metropolitan Opera, attended six hundred guests (including President Roosevelt's young cousin Franklin). The debonair host was James Hyde, executive vice president of the Equitable Life Assurance Society. Hyde was the firm's heir apparent, preparing to assume its presidency on his thirtieth birthday. At the turn of the century three life insurance companies—the Equitable, Mutual, and New York Life—loomed large in the economy, and in the public mind. Wall Street financial firms were remote, mysterious. J. P. Morgan was a name in the newspaper. But life insurers relied on millions of policyholders who paid premiums out of their meager wages. Middle-class Americans were shocked at rumors that company funds paid for the bacchanalian party. The cost, newspapers reported, was $200,000 (some $4 million in today's dollars). Further revelations showed that policyholders' money was funneled into speculative investments controlled by insiders and board members. Newspaper stories competed to show that the insurer, far from a prudent steward, had edged close to fraud.

The leaks from the Equitable came about as part of a boardroom struggle, in which some directors (including a U.S. senator) were trying to oust the dissolute scion before he took over the presidency of the firm. Hyde turned to the flamboyant railroad owner E. H. Harriman for help. Revelations poured out of the company in a primitive spin war.

Days before the 1904 election, newspapers had charged that Roosevelt's election campaign was bankrolled by the very business interests he otherwise zestfully denounced. According to the tabloid *New York World*, the firms were seeking to curry favor with the great trustbuster, hoping to avoid antitrust prosecution. As it happens, the charge was true. A jittery Roosevelt had indeed gone to business leaders shortly before the election to beg for campaign funds. He quickly regretted it. The attorney general happened upon the president dictating a letter returning campaign funds from John D. Rockefeller's Standard Oil trust. "Why Mr. President," he blurted, "the money has been spent." Roosevelt shrugged: "Well, the letter will look well on the record, anyhow." The industrialist Henry Clay Frick later complained, "We bought the son of a bitch, but he wouldn't stay bought." TR was elected to a full term.

Now news of the "après moi, le deluge" fête at Sherry's Hotel was a leak too far. Public indignation rose high enough that the New York State legislature felt compelled to organize an investigation. State legislative committees, then as now, rarely sparkled. This one was different. It hired as its chief counsel an ambitious Wall Street lawyer, Charles Evans Hughes. He was a Republican, but on the outskirts of power. In later decades, as Chief Justice of the United States, his pointed white whiskers made him look like Jehovah; in 1905 his hair was still a radical red. (Roosevelt called him the "bearded iceberg.") Commanding the hearing room in the Aldermanic Chamber of New York's City Hall, he focused on a mysterious check for $48,702 from the New York Life Insurance Company that had been sent to the banker J. P. Morgan. The star witness was George Perkins, Morgan's top aide, his political fixer. Hughes tried without much success to pin Perkins down. The financier stalled for time, pacing around the committee room, hoping to avoid questions. Finally Perkins warned his interrogator, "Mr. Hughes, you're handling dynamite. . . . You want to think very carefully before you put that [check] into evidence. You can't tell what may come of it."

The panel would break for lunch, Hughes replied sternly. After that, he wanted a "candid answer."

When the committee reassembled, the chamber was jammed with reporters and curious Wall Street executives. Perkins, fuming, confirmed that the money had been sent to the Republican National Committee for Roosevelt's race. That was nothing special, he asserted. New York Life had done the same in 1896 and 1900 as well. Photographers jostled, the crowd murmured, reporters raced for their phones. Hard to believe now, but this was explosive information, confirming longtime rumors. "Life Insurance Campaign Gifts," gasped the *New York Times* across three front-page columns. Newspapers soon reported more revelations: other companies contributed too. And they all gave to both parties.

The campaign finance scandal sparked sweeping change. One historian describes it as "a key moment in the development of progressivism as a national phenomenon." Cascading investigations at the local and national level led to strict controls on insurance and regulation of railroads, utilities, and other powerful industries. It made careers as well. Hughes became governor of New York just a year later, then a Supreme Court justice, the Republican presidential nominee, and eventually Chief Justice of the United States. Up in Boston, Brandeis formed one of the first modern citizens groups to fight for legislation that would let savings banks compete by offering life insurance. His crusade brought him to the attention of Wilson and other Progressive leaders, and eventually to a seat on the U.S. Supreme Court. Prosecutors arrested Perkins.

The scandal also led to federal legislation, the first modern campaign finance law that banned corporate gifts to federal candidates. Roosevelt thrashed about, denouncing his accusers and bemoaning the smudge on his integrity. Before getting caught himself, he had told a reporter, "Sooner or later, unless there is a readjustment, there will come a riotous, wicked, murderous day of atonement." Stung by scandal, he began to crusade for reform. For the first time an effective outside citizens group drove the effort. William Chandler, a former Radical Republican serving as senator from New Hampshire, had first proposed the reform in 1901. The senator angered the railroads that controlled the state government, and the legislature did not return him to Washington. In the months before his term ended he introduced a sweeping bill banning corporate gifts and requiring disclosure. Now involuntarily a private citizen, Chandler formed the National Publicity Bill Organization. He enlisted university presidents, civic leaders, and prominent business executives. Pressure built not from the sweatshops but from the gentlemen's clubs. Progressive state governments began to enact reform. Wisconsin, Nebraska, Florida, Missouri, and Tennessee banned corporate contributions. In Congress, though, Chandler could not find a Republican to introduce the bill, so he turned to a Democrat, one of the country's most virulent racists: Senator "Pitchfork Ben" Tillman of South Carolina. Tillman had organized the Red Shirts terrorists to drive Blacks away from the polls after the Civil War, and as governor he backed new controls on corporations. As Tillman's biographer put it, he posed as "the advocate of both mob violence and corporate regulation." The Tillman Act passed the Senate and House with little controversy in 1907. Newspapers overwhelmingly supported it. Congressional debate focused on the use of campaign funds to pay voters, a practice far less prevalent since the introduction of the secret ballot a decade before.

This first federal campaign finance statute is still cited today by backers and foes of laws to control big money in American politics. Senators John McCain (Republican) and Russell Feingold (Democrat) claimed TR's mantle when they pushed legislation in 2003, appearing before his New York City home. One month after the 2010 *Citizens United* case that negated corporate spending prohibitions, Justice Clarence Thomas explained his rationale to a Florida audience. "Go back and read why Tillman introduced that legislation," Thomas said. "Tillman was from South Carolina, and as I hear the story he was concerned that the corporations, Republican corporations, were favorable toward Blacks and he felt that there was a need to regulate them."

In fact, his self-pitying complaints aside, TR appears to have done little to push the bill, other than a perfunctory mention in his State of the Union address. Tillman was the sponsor, but Republicans dominated the Congress. It was the urgent need of that party's leaders to move something—anything—in the wake of the insurance company scandal that led to its smooth enactment. But what was novel, and noteworthy, was the rise of a new force: an independent citizens group, not firmly entrenched within either major party. In the twentieth century such citizen-powered pressure groups would prove increasingly influential in driving democracy reform that did not merely serve the political needs of one of the major parties. As Tocqueville had observed, Americans were joiners; clubs, associations, and civic groups abounded. The new ingredient was the upsurge in such groups that had a policy goal. Organizations pushed for worker safety legislation, for consumer protection, for environmental stewardship. They relied not only on numbers but also on expertise and the ability to garner press attention. These groups—new in the United States and rare in the world—would eventually play the role that breakaway third parties played in political systems that relied on proportional representation. By their nature—their antipolitical affect, their nonpartisan airs, even, eventually, their treatment by the tax code, which allowed deductions for donations to groups that shed a partisan label—they pushed policies that supplanted parties as the traditional engine of representation and partisanship.

Roosevelt, for his part, continued to evolve. In December 1907, after the Tillman Act became law, he was the first to propose what he called "a very radical measure," public financing of campaigns, which would be put into law only seven decades later. "The need for collecting large campaign funds," he wrote, "would vanish if Congress provided an appropriation for the proper and legitimate expenses of each of the great national parties, an appropriation ample enough to meet the necessity for thorough organization and machinery, which requires a large expenditure of money. Then the stipulation should be made that no party receiving campaign funds from the Treasury should accept more than a fixed amount from any individual subscriber or donor; and the necessary publicity for receipts and expenditures could without difficulty be provided."

After four years out of office, in 1912 Roosevelt decided to run again for president; he sought the Republican nomination but was blocked by party mandarins. So he bolted and ran as the candidate of the Progressive Party. The threats to American democracy were at the heart of his message. "To destroy this invisible government, to dissolve the unholy alliance between corrupt business and corrupt politics is the first task of the statesmanship of the day," thundered the party platform, adopted in Chicago. At that convention Roosevelt bellowed to the activists, "We stand at Armageddon and we battle for the Lord!"

Standing alongside Roosevelt in his crusade were other renegade Republicans and stray members of the old money elite. One drew raised eyebrows. Organizing and funding the effort was George Perkins—the J. P. Morgan crony. Charges were dropped a year after his arrest, and by 1912 Perkins had emerged as executive secretary of the Progressive Party, running TR's radical campaign.

The 1912 campaign was one of history's most remarkable, a moment when Americans explicitly tried to measure their current institutions against founding ideals. It was a four-way race. Wilson called the Declaration of Independence and its insistence on the ability to change governments "the central doctrine . . . the ancient vision of America." Socialist Eugene V. Debs urged socialism as the embodiment of Jefferson's ideals. "I like the Fourth of July," he said. "It breathes the spirit of revolution. On this day we affirm the ultimate triumph of Socialism."

President William Howard Taft clung to the most traditional concepts of constitutional government. Roosevelt was most emphatic in seeking to yoke his dramatic ideas to the revolutionary impulse. He called for a "New Declaration of Independence," and his Progressive platform offered the clearest distillation of the idea that the moment demanded a fundamental recasting of American democracy.

Roosevelt went beyond questions of expanded suffrage. As a central strategy he championed the wave of direct democracy—the use of citizen ballot initiatives, giving voters the chance to pass laws—then under way in the states. In 1898 South Dakota became the first state, followed promptly by Utah and Oregon, to allow citizens to vote to pass laws directly through a ballot measure. Roosevelt's platform demanded the referendum as well as voters' ability to recall elected officials. He even urged that federal judges lose their lifetime appointment and that citizens be given the power to vote to overturn judicial decisions. But Roosevelt's ultimate version of Progressivism took the institutional impulse too far for voters; they recoiled from his attack on the judiciary and voted for Wilson. Roosevelt set the debate, but the scholarly New Jersey governor prevailed. Historian Sidney Milkis concludes, "TR's crusade made universal use of the direct primary a celebrated cause, assaulted traditional partisan loyalties, took advantage of the centrality of the newly emergent mass media, and convened an energetic but uneasy coalition of self-styled public advocacy groups. All these features of the Progressive Party campaign make the election of 1912 look more like that of 2008 than that of 1908."

"The Treason of the Senate"

The great compromise over representation at the Constitutional Convention had given the power to choose senators not to the people but to state legislatures. With this the framers intended two things. They established the Senate as a buffer against democracy, to ensure a "select appointment," as Madison put it, a public-spirited and disinterested class of legislator. And they empowered the states. Madison considered the compromise so noncontroversial he deemed it "unnecessary to dilate upon" since it was "congenial with public opinion."

Over the years, however, the system had stopped working even on its own terms. The task of choosing a senator could paralyze a statehouse, crowding out other responsibilities. In the 1890s alone, legislatures left fourteen Senate seats vacant because they could not resolve party squabbles. In Kentucky in 1896 the governor felt compelled to call out the militia, and troops enforcing martial law surrounded the legislators as they met to elect a senator. In Colorado in 1903 Democratic lawmakers demanding their senate choice were backed by the Denver police, while Republicans relied on state troopers.

But the real problem with having state legislatures pick senators was the legislatures themselves: the new industrial robber barons found them easy to buy. According to one 1906 study, in seven states in the previous fifteen years "charges of corruption have been put forward with enough presumptive evidence to make them a national scandal." State legislators chose U.S. senators who doubled as industry representatives. Montana's senators represented copper; Pennsylvania's, steel; New York's, Wall Street. As the Progressive journalist George Henry Haynes observed, "In one of the North Pacific States, a subsidized continental railway company without any serious shock of surprise presently discovered both members of the firm of its recent attorneys in the United States Senate." In a *McClure's* magazine profile of Senator Nelson Aldrich of Rhode Island, the father-in-law of John D. Rockefeller Jr., journalist Lincoln Steffens charged that Rhode Island was a "state for sale." Voters there insisted on being paid, for having to miss work if nothing else. Often the senators were wealthy themselves, leading the upper chamber to be called the "Millionaire's Club."

Consider the fragrant example of Pennsylvania. Simon Cameron, Lincoln's first secretary of war, was the founding father of the state's

Gilded Age political machine. "That his reputation was not spotless was not altogether a negative" when Lincoln chose him, notes historian David Herbert Donald. Perhaps he would know how to get things done. But Cameron proved *too* corrupt. Lincoln fired him and sent him to Siberia, or the next best thing, Moscow (as ambassador). To Cameron is attributed the much recycled quip, "An honest politician is one who, when he is bought, stays bought." Cameron returned from Russia and built the Republican Party in Pennsylvania. It was saturated with oil money. In 1881 the journalist Henry Demarest Lloyd wrote that Standard Oil "has done everything with the Pennsylvania legislature, except refine it."

The state's legislators sent to Washington a legend of excess: Boies Penrose. One awed waiter remembered the lawmaker digging into "a dozen raw oysters, chicken gumbo, a terrapin stew, two canvas back ducks, mashed potatoes, lima beans, macaroni, asparagus, cole slaw and stewed corn, one hot mince pie, and a quart of coffee." Earlier the well-born Philadelphia lawyer had engineered the legislature's selection of his patron, Matthew Quay, to the U.S. Senate. To mark that festive moment, Penrose threw a party that lasted two days, pausing only when the legislators had to vote. Unfortunately Quay took bribes the old-fashioned way. Penrose "regarded Quay's grafting as cheap pocket-picking," his biographer wrote. Penrose himself relied instead on "squeeze bills": his lieutenants would introduce legislation aimed at industries such as railroads, banks, and public utilities. "Then, for a large campaign contribution, Penrose would ensure that the bills never became law." Eventually the legislators sent Penrose himself to Washington as senator. He candidly explained his theory of politics to his business supporters: "I believe in the division of labor in this business of politics. You send us to Congress; we pass laws under the operation and protection of which you make money . . . and out of your profits, you further contribute to our campaign fund to send us back again to pass more laws to enable you to make more money." Of the legislature's choice of a senator, Penrose bragged to an associate, "There isn't going to be any selection. There's going to be an auction."

In 1906 two U.S. senators were convicted of taking fees to represent corporate interests. The ravenously ambitious newspaper publisher William Randolph Hearst was then serving in the House of Representatives. He commissioned a well-known novelist, David Graham Phillips, to write a nine-part series for *Cosmopolitan Magazine*. (Yes, that *Cosmo*. Alas, no sex tips.) "The Treason of the Senate" doubled the magazine's circulation. "Politics does not determine prosperity. But in this day of concentrations, politics does determine *the distribution of prosperity*," Phillips wrote. His bombastic language seared: "The Senate is a traitor to you. . . . The senators are not elected by the people; they are elected by the 'interests.'" The series was a sensation. Senators Joseph Benson Foraker, Henry Cabot Lodge, and some others became reviled household names. Theodore Roosevelt recoiled at the attack on his congressional allies. Speaking at the white-tie Gridiron dinner in Washington, he likened investigative journalists to the character in *Pilgrim's Progress* who could only look down. "The men with the muck rakes are often indispensable to the well being of society; but only if they know when to stop raking the muck, and to look upward to the celestial crown above them, to the crown of worthy endeavor," he warned.

Muckraking journalism—practitioners promptly wore the epithet as a badge—was not enough. Progressives turned to structural reform. Their solution was to wrest the power to choose senators from the legislators and give it to the people by direct election. That would require a constitutional amendment. The Omaha convention that formed the People's Party—the Populists—had first demanded it in 1892, along with government ownership of the railroads and free coinage of silver. (It also demanded a single term for presidents.) Already creative ferment and informal political innovation had given voters a role, of sorts, in choosing senators. The 1858 Lincoln-Douglas contest—two candidates, going to the voters, months before ballots were cast—was a rare type. Other innovations spread more widely. In some states, party caucuses and conventions dictated the choice to legislators. In others legislative candidates would run newspaper ads declaring their pick for U.S. Senate in a "public canvass."

In 1904 Oregon instituted "direct primaries," in which voters could choose party nominees for Senate. When the legislature convened to make the final pick, one newspaperman marveled, "on the first ballot, in 20 minutes, we elected two Senators without boodle, or booze, or even a cigar!" The "Oregon Plan" spread throughout the country, with up to two dozen states holding primaries to narrow the field of party nominees for senator by the end of the first decade of the twentieth century. By 1911 about half of new senators had been designated at some stage of their selection by popular vote. Some citizens demanded an even greater say in how their government was chosen. Illinois voters backed direct election by a more than 4 to 1 margin.

Congress resisted, so reformers found another way to rattle Capitol Hill—the never-used trigger to summon a new constitutional convention. Article V of the Constitution sets out two ways the charter can be changed. One was familiar: with a two-thirds vote from each house, Congress can send a proposed amendment to the states. (Three-quarters of the states must then ratify.) That's how all amendments have been added. Article V also provides that "on the Application of the Legislatures of two thirds of the several States, [Congress] shall call a Convention for proposing Amendments," thus forcing action by federal lawmakers. In 1893 Nebraska petitioned for an Article V convention. In the first decade of the new century, twenty-five states joined the call—not quite enough to bring it into being but more than enough to scare lawmakers and prod for action. The chief justice of the North Carolina Supreme Court expressed doubt that "the great corporations which control a majority of the U.S. Senate will ever voluntarily transfer to the people their profitable and secure hold upon supreme power. . . . It is high time we had a Constitutional Convention." These demands were incendiary, since it was unclear whether there was any way to restrict the scope of such a convention to Senate election rules. After all, the 1787 Constitutional Convention was supposed to propose changes to the Articles of Confederation, but it had been a "runaway."

In 1911 Congress itself took up the proposal for a constitutional amendment for direct elections. Progressive Idaho senator William Borah inveighed, "The legislature is the arena, narrow and confined, wherein selfish and corrupt influences can successfully operate. . . . Why give selfish and corrupt influences such strategic advantage? Why not send the fight to the open forum upon which beats the fierce light of public opinion?" Wisconsin's Robert LaFollette denounced bribes paid that resulted in the election of an Illinois senator, who was then expelled. "I have sinned," he quoted one corrupted Springfield legislator. "I took the money." Old Guard senators fought furiously to stymie the popular vote. They warned of centralization and loss of state power. Boies Penrose himself proposed an amendment to give extra representation to larger states (a provision that would have poisoned the chances for ratification). The men whom voters had sent to Washington spoke most aggressively for change. Southern Democrats once had supported popular voting but now feared federal involvement would lead to enfranchising more African Americans. Politicians from urban machines—the colorful, cigar-chomping bosses derided by Progressive good government "goo goos" in their home territory—provided the key votes instead. Catholic and Jewish voters drove support for direct senate elections.

As ratified, the Seventeenth Amendment declares simply:

> The Senate of the United States shall be composed of two Senators from each state, elected by the people thereof, for six years; and each Senator shall have one vote. The electors in each state shall have the qualifications requisite for electors of the most numerous branch of the state legislatures.

Governors can make appointments to fill vacancies, though the legislature can set a date for a new election.

By enacting the amendment Progressive Era Americans saw themselves as extending forward Jefferson's foundational notion of the "consent of the governed." In fact they were doing more: faced with the new power of private money in elections, they wagered that the power of voters could be expanded to reduce the sway of trusts and corporations. The most lavish hopes for the amendment were dashed, however. Among other things, statewide campaigns cost money; it could be cheaper to buy the favor of a state legislature than of the electorate at large. Giving voters a say did not magically reset the power relationships in American life. The amendment and its roots would recede into history, more a subject for high school history class memorization than active contention. Then, a century later, it suddenly became the focus of renewed political debate, as Tea Party conservatives urged a repeal of citizen voting for U.S. senators, arguing that it had been a power grab by the federal government—a contention at odds with historical fact, for it was the states that forced Congress to extend the vote, not the other way around.

The Seventeenth Amendment was joined by other political reforms during the Progressive Era. In the first decade of the twentieth century, states began to adopt direct democracy. In some, citizens had the power of initiative, to vote for new laws, and in others, the power of referendum to repeal a law passed by legislators. Popular legislating swept through the West, ushered in by new states as they entered the Union. South Dakota gave citizens this power first, in 1898, followed by Utah and Oregon four years later. By 1920 in roughly half the states citizens could vote for legislation or constitutional changes.

American direct democracy has had decidedly mixed results. The mechanisms are largely credited with having given more power to the average citizen, yet at times they slipped into the control of corporate interests or demagogic appeals to slash taxes or prices. Later in the twentieth century the profusion of ballot measures reduced some state governments to incoherence. Proposition 13 launched the national "tax revolt" when passed by California's voters in 1978. It cut property taxes so severely that the state's government was paralyzed for nearly forty years, until later ballot measures began to peel back its provisions. One critic bemoaned four competing ballot measures in Oregon in 1988 dealing with auto insurance rates. He found they embodied the worst of direct democracy: "poorly designed policies, obscene amounts of money, highly technical measures, unanticipated consequences, and confused voters." Ballot measures proved far more valuable when they curbed the entrenched power of legislators—when the subject of direct democracy was, directly, democracy itself. Voters themselves voted to establish primary elections, to repeal the poll tax in Washington State, to list candidates for office by name rather than party in Ohio, even to require voting machines rather than fraud-prone hand ballots in Arkansas. In the early twenty-first century, at a time of distorted partisan gerrymandering, voters in Arizona, California, and Florida enacted measures to take the power of drawing district lines out of the hands of legislators.

Why this focus on democracy in the Progressive Era? Most broadly, its reforms augmented the first stabs at economic regulation and tentative steps toward building a modern state. Government could not be strong enough to wrestle with the untamed market unless it were a more effective, and less corrupt, reflection of the public will. Better processes, a purer expression of citizen consent, all seemed a natural part of the institutional revival sought by Progressives. Franklin Delano Roosevelt, then a young state legislator, explained, "From the ruins of the political machines, we will reconstruct something more nearly conforming to a democratic government." Later liberals often looked askance at the Progressives' focus on democracy reform and the power of the vote. Compared to subsequent reform movements, as Richard Hofstadter and other historians have argued, the Progressives distrusted much economic change, gazing suspiciously at the world through a moral lens. The New Deal in particular did not focus on expanded political rights; rather it enhanced democracy by building economic power—not only social programs such as Social Security but also the Wagner Act, which encouraged the organizing of labor unions, and the assembling of a new political coalition. The New Deal's approach to governance was far from scientific: it was chaotic, compromised, and ultimately transient. *Liberalism* would come to mean something more than just a new label pasted over *progressivism*; it focused on growing the size and strength of government as a driver of economic demand and countervailing power to the heft of business. An explicit effort to democratize America's electoral system would not come again until seven decades into the twentieth century, in the wake of the civil rights movement.

Reformers' efforts returned power to the hands of the voters, but this did not translate into expanded turnout. Quite the opposite. Reformers won changes in many state laws to require primary elections to choose candidates. This formally gave more power to the people than in nearly any other country. But the very mechanism by which reformers pursued change—by attacking traditional party organizations—contributed to a decrease in voting rates. The same Progressives who systematized voting took away the patronage jobs that had won allegiance from many voters. Often moralistic professionals, they sternly sought to end the wielding of government power by the less educated. George Washington Plunkitt, a leader of Tammany Hall, held forth from his seat atop the bootblack stand at the New York County Courthouse at the turn of the century. "I ain't up on sillygisms, but I can give you some arguments that nobody can answer," he proclaimed. "First, this great and glorious country was built up by political parties; second, parties can't hold together if their workers don't get offices when they win; third, if the parties go to pieces, the government they built up must go to pieces, too; fourth, then there'll be hell to pay." Whereas parties had traditionally provided ballots for voters, now individual polling stations took on this role. This and other measures, such as the establishment of direct primaries, weakened the party's ability to mobilize voters. The Progressives tried to replace the politics of machine and corruption with a government-administered, less partisan, cleaner, and expanded democracy. For all its merits, though, fewer voters participated in it.

8

Silent Sentinels

On January 20, 1910, Alice Paul returned to the United States. The twenty-five-year-old graduate student had spent two years in England, where she had plunged into the frenzied suffragist movement. Once, dressed as a maid, Paul had infiltrated a speech given by the lord mayor at the Guild Hall in London; she slipped in early in the morning and hid in the balcony all day. When the mayor rose to speak, she and a colleague broke stained-glass windows and threw shoes, loudly calling for "votes for women." Repeatedly arrested, she conducted a hunger strike during one of her sentences. Her jailers force-fed her, brutally inserting a five-foot-long tube into her stomach. British officials were glad to see her go. American journalists were fascinated, swarming her arrival at the dock in Philadelphia. Within months she jolted into new life the moribund movement for women's suffrage, and within years it achieved an improbable victory. Paul and a clutch of other young women galvanized a sophisticated, passionate mass movement for constitutional change.

The fight had gone slowly since the Seneca Falls declaration in 1848. When Elizabeth Cady Stanton and the other signers, quoting the Declaration of Independence, resolved "that it is the duty of the women of this country to secure to themselves their sacred right to the elective franchise," they could not have imagined how difficult it would be or how long it would take. Other conventions around the country issued similar pleas. During the Civil War, Stanton urged women "to avail ourselves of the strong arm and the blue uniform of the Black soldier to walk in by his side." But when the Fifteenth Amendment enfranchised Black men, women's groups leaders attacked it, and the long alliance between women activists and Black men was sundered. Over the coming decades, as political elites in the North and South lost their taste for democracy, that emphatically included rights for women. Activists called these decades "the doldrums." Congress considered a constitutional amendment granting women the vote, but it never came close to passage. By 1887 Congress had stopped doing even that. For the centennial of the Declaration of Independence in Philadelphia on July 4, 1876, Susan B. Anthony and other militants drafted an indictment of men for denying them the vote, in violation of the founding spirit. They had hoped to read it from the speakers' platform. Instead, as the audience rose to greet the emperor of Brazil, they leapt up on the rostrum, handed it to a startled U.S. senator and strode offstage, tossing out dozens of copies as they hustled away. Newspapers buried or ignored the incident.

The judiciary refused to help. Anthony and thirteen other Rochester women illegally voted in the 1872 presidential election. The federal government prosecuted Anthony in a widely publicized trial, with a U.S. Supreme Court justice presiding. He directed the jury to convict Anthony. She denounced the proceedings. "My natural rights, my civil rights, my political rights, my judicial rights," she told the court, "are all alike ignored." The judge declined to jail her, so a hoped-for appeal to the Supreme Court never happened. Instead, in *Minor v. Happersett* the next year, the justices ruled that the Fourteenth Amendment did not guarantee women the right to vote—or anyone else, for that matter. Virginia Minor had argued that the amendment's clause recognizing the "privileges and immunities" of citizenship gave her the right of an elector in Missouri. UCLA law professor Adam Winkler notes that this idea was one of the first instances of "the living Constitution," an attempt to tease new interpretations of rights out of the document's broadly expressed principles. The justices unanimously swatted down that idea. The Constitution did not grant a right to vote, they ruled, because that was a privilege set by states. "Certainly, if the courts can consider any question settled, this is one," the justices wrote. "For nearly ninety years the people have acted upon the idea that the Constitution, when it conferred citizenship, did not necessarily confer the right of suffrage." The case was an early marker in the Supreme Court's systematic narrowing of the Reconstruction amendments. The Court nearly nullified the Privileges and Immunities Clause altogether two years later. Judges would cite *Minor* up until the 1960s to uphold voting laws that discriminated against minorities, immigrants, and others.

Still, things had begun to stir slightly before Paul and another expatriate suffragist, Lucy Burns, returned from England. In the nineteenth century upper-class Republican women had dominated the movement, with a sensibility reflected in the argument that uneducated brutes should not be allowed to vote. Many other women opposed suffrage, thinking it would cost them the law's special protection. Rippling progressive energies began to shift that. Women long had dominated many reform movements, especially those demanding prohibition of alcohol. Now women's groups began to organize around economic issues as well, including child labor and workplace safety. The Triangle Shirtwaist Factory fire in early 1911, which killed dozens of young women working in a garment factory in New York City, spurred months of agitation for workplace protections. Labor unions became increasingly supportive. Democratic Party machines in the northern cities began to swing toward support of women's voting rights. As western states entered the union, some of them enfranchised women from the start. The open frontier produced a more expansive approach—as did the need to attract women settlers. Old ways were left behind in the east.

The National American Woman Suffrage Association, known as "the

National," led efforts around the country. In December 1912 its leaders gave Paul and Burns what was considered a forlorn assignment: to chair the group's Congressional Committee, responsible for seeing that a proposed "Susan B. Anthony Amendment" to the Constitution would be introduced in each session of Congress, typically to expire without hearings or debate. The proposed change mirrored the language of the Fifteenth Amendment. "The right of citizens of the United States to vote shall not be denied or abridged by the United States or by any state on account of sex," it read, and gave Congress "power to enforce this article by appropriate legislation." Rather than accept another session of being ignored by Congress, Paul and Burns aimed for something audacious—to actually pass the measure. They hit on a provocative new tactic: a high-profile march for voting rights at the most visible place and time.

"Where Are All the People?"

On March 3, 1913, the eve of his presidential inauguration, Woodrow Wilson arrived in Washington in triumph. The former professor and university president had served just two years as governor of New Jersey. Women's suffrage was one of the issues dividing the parties in that singular four-way campaign for president. Roosevelt's Progressives ardently backed it. Jane Addams, a prominent social worker who led Chicago's Hull House, seconded TR's nomination at the fervent party convention. Then there was Taft, the incumbent Republican president; he had supported voting rights for women, though in notably tepid fashion. Socialist Debs was a strong supporter. But Wilson was silent. Democrats were in thrall to their southern wing, which saw a constitutional amendment as a threat to states' rights.

When Wilson stepped off the train that day, some Princeton students belted out a greeting song, but there were few other supporters. The *New York Times* consolingly wrote, "'Small but vociferous' and 'made up in noise what they lacked in numbers' are the conventional terms that might be applied." An aide asked, "Where are all the people?" Wilson's greeters admitted that most were lining Pennsylvania Avenue, site of an unprecedented march for women's suffrage.

Paul and a small circle of young women had organized a pageant rich with symbolism. Leading the Women Suffrage Procession was a hallucinatory sight: a beautiful twenty-seven-year-old woman, wearing a crown and the flowing white cape of a Greek goddess, on a white steed, carrying a banner that read, "Forward Out of Error, Leave Behind the Night, Forward through the Darkness, Forward into Light." The apparition was Inez Milholland, a New York University School of Law graduate active in the Women's Trade Union League. Rows of women marched behind her. Draped on the side of a wagon, a large gold banner read, "We Demand an Amendment to the United States Constitution Enfranchising Women." Eighty floats, marching bands, and horse-drawn tableaux followed the display of the "great demand." Paul and other students marched in graduation gowns. Nurses marched in uniform. Others wore aprons and bonnets, supposedly the national garb of countries where women could vote. The parade reflected the movement's conflicted nature. Paul worried to an editor, "As far as I can see, we must have a white procession, or a Negro procession, or no procession at all." Eventually parade organizers assigned white women to march first, then white men. Black women were told to walk last. The pioneering Black journalist Ida B. Wells ignored the choreography and joined the main parade, jumping into the line with the Illinois delegation halfway down the avenue.

A throng of perhaps 100,000 men lined Pennsylvania Avenue, many of them inebriated after inaugural festivities. They heckled, spat, threw objects, and eventually broke through the meager police lines. One newspaper reported that the women "practically fought their way by foot up Pennsylvania Avenue." Over one hundred women were hospitalized. Milholland steered her steed Grey Dawn into the bowler-hatted crowd to force it back. The marchers pressed on, dragging themselves along the route to the end. Americans were fascinated by the spectacle and appalled by the violence directed at the young women. Washington's police chief lost his job. Foreshadowing the confrontation a half-century later in Selma, Alabama, the news scandalized the country and swung sympathy sharply toward suffrage.

Six months after the parade a movement for a federal constitutional amendment was fully galvanized, and Paul's committee presented Congress with a petition with 200,000 signatures. But the militants clashed with older activists, who wanted to focus on winning a referendum in New York State. The amendment backers, pushed from their positions in the traditional group, formed the National Women's Party to press for its adoption. The new visibility began to win political converts outside Washington. Using the flashiest new technology, California suffragists organized an automobile pilgrimage that motored from San Francisco to the nation's capital. Gradually women in seventeen states, mostly in the West, won the right to vote in presidential elections.

In 1915 another petition to Congress had 2 million signatures. The politicians could no longer ignore the issue: the Susan B. Anthony Amendment granting women the vote was sent to both chambers. It lost in both the House and, earlier, the Senate. That year voters went to the polls in referenda on women's suffrage in four large states. All four bids lost.

But the Democratic president, now halfway through his first term, remained silent. Wilson wanted to protect white supremacy in the South. He was, he told one suffragist delegation, "tied to a conviction, which I have had all my life, that changes of this sort ought to be brought about state by state."

The movement pursued divergent approaches. Carrie Chapman Catt, the new leader of the traditionalist National, worked the inside strategy. Focused on Democrats, she kept lines open to the White House. Some politicians worried that suffrage would pass and they would be exposed as having opposed it. Wilson spoke at the group's convention in 1916 and managed to win applause without actually embracing its position. Paul's supporters, in turn, disrupted Wilson's State of the Union address, unfurling a banner from the House of Representatives balcony before being hustled off. Charles Evans Hughes—the lawyer who had led the campaign finance probe a decade before—was now the Republican Party's nominee for president, and he backed a suffrage amendment. In the twelve states where women could vote for president, the National Women's Party opposed the incumbent.

Picketing the White House

Inez Milholland was the movement's most colorful public face, its archetypal independent New Woman. Because of her resemblance to a Gibson Girl (the ideal of modern beauty), she was frequently enlisted to ride at the head of parades, belying the notion that suffrage was at odds with femininity. She was in the thick of Greenwich Village radical political circles and had a novelistic life. Milholland had a passionate affair with the journalist Max Eastman, editor of the *Masses*, and was briefly engaged to Guglielmo Marconi, the inventor of radio. After World War I started in August 1914, she rushed alone to Europe as a journalist to cover the Allied cause. On board the ship to England she proposed marriage to another passenger. Expelled from Italy, she returned to the United States and drove herself ceaselessly, undertaking a speaking tour of the western states. She collapsed during a speech in California in 1916 and died a month later. Her last words: "Mr. President, how long must women wait for liberty?" Alice Paul arranged for a memorial service in the U.S. Capitol's Statuary Hall on Christmas Day. A widely printed poster, emblazoned "She Died for the Freedom of Women," showed her astride her white horse. The movement had a martyr.

Wilson ran for reelection on the slogan "He Kept Us Out of War," but within months Germany's unrestricted submarine attacks against

U.S. shipping drew the United States in. Wilson went before Congress and proclaimed, "The world must be made safe for democracy. Its peace must be planted upon the tested foundations of political liberty."

In previous military conflicts, men who bore arms gained an extra claim on suffrage. That did not happen in World War I, precisely. More broadly, war wrests people from private concerns. National political goals rise in importance, if briefly. Amid the tension and patriotism of the run-up to war, Paul landed on another new strategy. On January 9, 1917, three hundred women met with Wilson to present resolutions adopted after Milholland's capitol memorial service. Wilson stalked out. The next day, women began to picket the White House, standing mutely by its Pennsylvania Avenue entrance. Day and night they stood there, holding signs quoting Wilson's idealistic speeches and demanding the vote. They were called the "Silent Sentinels." Eventually five thousand women picketed over two years. Borrowing from labor union tactics, this was the first high-visibility nonviolent civil disobedience in American history—an innovation adopted before its wide use by Gandhi in India, let alone the later civil rights movement.

Police routinely arrested the Sentinels, charging them with "obstructing traffic." In October 1917 Paul herself was arrested. She stunned a judge by refusing to heed his authority, saying, "As members of the disenfranchised class, we do not recognize the court established by a police officer from whose election women were excluded. We do not admit the authority of the court, and we shall take no part in the court's proceedings." Compounding the provocation, the women refused to rise. "We are being imprisoned, not because we obstructed traffic, but because we pointed out to the President the fact that he was obstructing the cause of democracy at home, while Americans were fighting for it abroad," Paul told reporters as she was led off to serve a seven-month sentence in the District of Columbia jail. There she began a hunger strike and was confined to a psychiatric ward, where, as had happened in England, a physician force-fed her through a tube thrust down her throat.

Eventually she was freed, having visibly sacrificed herself for the vote.

Meanwhile Catt's mainstream group organized war work: staffing infirmaries, rolling bandages, selling savings bonds, and opening a military hospital in France. As Wilson's rhetoric grew ever more messianic on the subject of spreading democracy, the exclusion of women glared more visibly, for they now flooded the workforce, taking over the jobs left by men gone to war. The night before the House would again consider the Susan B. Anthony Amendment, Wilson told wavering congressmen in a White House meeting that he now favored its passage. "The President has succumbed to the pickets," reported the *Baltimore Sun*. With an eye toward the 1918 midterm election, lawmakers tumbled into support of the vote. The Nineteenth Amendment passed the House, 274 to 136, precisely the two-thirds vote needed. Hundreds in the galleries sang hymns in celebration.

"Put the 'Rat' in Ratification"

The singing was short-lived. It took nearly two years for the Senate to match the House and send the measure to the states. Southerners resisted, clinging to states' rights and fearful of the new rhetoric of enfranchisement and democracy. Wilson's aides fretted that a defeat would hurt the Democrats. A president has no formal role in the consideration of a constitutional amendment; unlike standard legislation, he can neither sign nor veto it. Wilson broke precedent and went to the Senate to address the lawmakers while they were in the middle of a contentious debate. (To give perspective on the novelty of his talk, the last president to address just the Senate was . . . Woodrow Wilson.) On September 30, 1918, with only a half hour's notice, Wilson motored to Capitol Hill. "This is a people's war," he told the senators, "and the people's thinking constitutes its atmosphere and morale. . . . I tell you plainly that this measure which I urge upon you is vital to the winning of the war and to the energies alike of preparation and battle." (He also insisted, implausibly, "The voices of intemperate and foolish agitators do not reach me at all.") Debate ground on for months. Finally, on June 4, 1919, the Senate approved the amendment.

Ratification raced through Illinois, Indiana, Michigan, and the western states, where women could already vote. With support from Tammany Hall and other urban machines, it passed in the northern states as well, despite quiet opposition from beer brewers and liquor distillers, who long had worried women supported Prohibition. But eight southern states voted against the amendment. Ratification was stuck at thirty-five states, needing one more. The last to vote was Tennessee. Thousands of activists on both sides thronged the state capital. Debate lasted weeks. Repeated tallies showed a tie: 48 to 48. On August 18, 1920, legislative leaders called for a final vote, to the dismay of the sashed suffragists crowding the galleries. A continued deadlock would mean no ratification, and no amendment.

Harry Burn was a twenty-four-year-old East Tennessee state representative and the youngest legislator. On his lapel he wore a red rose, signifying opposition to woman suffrage. (Proponents wore a yellow rose.) He was sure his constituents fiercely opposed it. That day, though, he had received a letter from his mother. Phoebe Ensminger Burn, known as Miss Febb, was a farm wife who read avidly while churning butter and sewing clothes. Frozen at his desk in the chamber, Burn repeatedly read his mother's words: "Dear Son: Hurrah and vote for suffrage. Don't keep them in doubt . . . be a good boy and help Mrs. Catt put the 'rat' in ratification."

The roll call reached Burn seven votes in. This time he called out loudly, "Aye." The tie was broken, Tennessee ratified, and the Nineteenth Amendment entered the Constitution. With that "Aye," 27 million women won the right to vote. Burn had to flee to the state capitol's attic to avoid an angry crowd of antisuffrage men.

9

"One Person, One Vote"

After the jolts of the Progressive Era—securing the vote for women, extending citizens the right to vote for U.S. senators, the wave of reform at the local and national level that sharply diminished the role of corrupt political machines—the shape of American democracy settled into a stalemate for the next half century. The entropy was finally shaken not by parties, as in previous eras, or by popular movements—but by courts. For the first time in the country's history the judicial branch stepped ahead of the public in the expansion of political equality and a meaningful vote.

Of course the twentieth century—called the American Century—was the time when the United States rose to world power. Government itself grew, becoming modernized and professionalized. The party realignment set by the epic election of 1896 held for decades, combining Republican domination with an enclave of Democratic control in the South. Another party realignment took place in the 1930s. Franklin Roosevelt's New Deal melded northern urban voters with the traditional "solid South" of white southern Democrats. It was an inherently unstable compound. For a brief moment during the 1930s, with labor unions mobilizing and great issues at stake, voter turnout and public participation spiked. Politics again turned on galvanizing new voters.

(A few years later Roosevelt memorialized this rare turn in American politics. Asked to approve of Harry Truman as his vice president during the 1944 party convention, FDR absentmindedly replied, "Clear it with Sidney"—meaning Sidney Hillman, the socialist leader of the clothing workers union.) The government and the political parties seemed more egalitarian, more open to upward mobility, than they had in a century.

Yet below the level of national politics, long-ignored satrapies and fiefdoms pockmarked American politics.

Robert A. Caro's sweeping chronicle of Lyndon Johnson's rise to power offers a textured portrayal of how the game was played in Texas in the 1940s. Johnson was a junior congressman, seen as a New Dealer, who achieved some national influence by steering oil funds to the national party through the Democratic Congressional Campaign Committee. He ran for the U.S. Senate in 1941. Caro vividly describes the political culture of "the Valley," the Texas border counties dominated by a few brutal political bosses: "On Election Day, Mexican-Americans were herded to the polls by armed *pistoleros*, sometimes appointed 'deputy sheriffs' for the day; each voter was handed a receipt showing he had paid his poll tax (usually these taxes had been purchased by the *jefes* months before and kept in their safes to . . . 'insure discipline and orderly procedure'). In some precincts, these voters were also handed ballots that had already been marked." Johnson appeared to have won the Democratic primary. The next day his chief rival—W. Lee "Pappy" O'Daniel, the former country music radio host and flour pitchman then serving as governor—produced votes from rural counties that vaulted him into the lead. Johnson frantically pressed for "corrected" vote totals from his allies. The political "duke" of Duval County rebuffed him. "Lyndon, I've been to the federal penitentiary, and I'm not going back for you," he told the congressman. Johnson had let down his guard and lost.

He would not make that mistake seven years later. When Johnson ran for the Senate again, in the 1948 Democratic primary, the counting of the votes swung between Johnson and former governor Coke Stevenson.

The election turned on the results of Precinct 13 in Alice, Texas. Originally it reported 765 votes for Johnson. His supporters in Alice insisted that was a transcription error: LBJ had received *965*, enough for a statewide win. After the balloting Stevenson and Johnson waged a court battle over who had really won. Testimony showed that the additional two hundred names had been written in pen, all in the same handwriting. Apparently these two hundred people voted in alphabetical order as well, and all for Johnson. As Johnson's career teetered, a federal court validated his win. "Landslide Lyndon" went to Washington.

Still, despite the rakishness and occasional outright theft, party machines weakened. Government, not party bosses, became the source of benefits. Labor unions, radical parties, and others competed to mobilize working-class voters. Occasional reform mayors, such as Fiorello La Guardia, a Republican-Labor fusion candidate in New York City, interrupted Democratic Party rule in urban areas. Reports of fraud dwindled too. Ever more outlandish contests were considered charming, a droll reminder of days of yore. Earl Long, the governor of Louisiana, among others, is alleged to have quipped, "When I die, bury me in Louisiana. I want to stay active in politics." Rumors claimed John F. Kennedy owed his 1960 presidential victory in Illinois to fraud by Mayor Richard J. Daley's machine in Chicago. "With a little bit of luck," Daley told the candidate, "and the help of a few close friends, you're going to carry Illinois." It's a potent historical myth. Republican nominee Richard Nixon won kudos for statesmanship in declining to challenge the result. In the Oliver Stone movie *Nixon*, an aide consoles the despondent candidate, saying, "You gotta swallow this one. They stole it fair and square." Less remembered: after Republican lawsuits, multiple state and federal investigations and recounts confirmed Kennedy's victory and found no massive fraud that could have swung the election. Kennedy himself later joked about the allegations. After speaking at a party dinner in Chicago in 1962, he went down to the basement to talk with precinct workers. "They said terrible things about you, but I never believed it. . . . I hope

Mayor Daley will keep you locked up here until November 6, then turn you loose." JFK's witticism was almost the last political speech before World War III. The next day he "caught a cold," a pretext for canceling the rest of his political trip so he could return to Washington to deal with the Cuban Missile Crisis.

Midcentury suburban America was cleaner than in the past and its politics less corrupt, if more dull. But built-in basic inequities and distortions worsened throughout the decades. As populations shifted and social pressures built, existing political power brokers proved impervious to change, then resistant to it. Not only urban voters but newly growing suburban communities demanded a louder voice.

In large parts of the country, though, especially in the South, democracy remained illusory. Voter turnout stayed low, with poor whites marginally engaged and Blacks nearly entirely disenfranchised. In Georgia in 1942, for example, only 3.4 percent of the electorate voted. It was then that William Faulkner wrote, "The past is never dead. It's not even past." Most southern states were governed not only by whites, of course, but by a very particular coalition of white elites. In the Black Belt a small fraction of wealthy property owners dominated. They made common cause with business leaders in the rapidly industrializing southern cities, mill towns such as Birmingham, Alabama, and Raleigh, North Carolina.

The one-party South controlled the U.S. Congress as well, as its lawmakers rose inexorably through the seniority system. Except for a brief period from 1933 to 1937, when the swollen majorities and economic emergency gave Roosevelt enough support to push through the New Deal measures, a coalition of Republicans and conservative southerners managed to block nearly all legislative action on major social reforms. Even those programs bore the mark of the South's "redemption." To steer legislation through Congress, the New Deal's social programs often were crafted to omit the very people who needed them most. Thus domestic workers and those who worked in agriculture—maids, nannies, sharecroppers—were excluded from the minimum wage, workers' compensation, Social Security, and unemployment insurance.

"The Silent Gerrymander"

American democracy's most visible mid-twentieth-century failure came in one of its most basic functions: representation. From the time of the framers, obsessed as they were that the legislature be a "mirror" of the people, urban and rural forces contended against each other. Throughout the twentieth century, to a surprising degree, a handful of small-town residents controlled state governments all across the country. Because legislatures draw the electoral lines for congressional seats, they controlled House representation as well. Even the framers' design was not a perfect mirror since each state had at least one seat regardless of population. The Senate, of course, was apportioned differently, with two seats per state. As larger states grew in size, the undemocratic nature of the Senate magnified.

The Constitution requires a census every ten years and specifies that congressional seats be apportioned by population. Changing demographics unnerved the powers that dominated Congress. Between 1900 and 1910 more than 9 million immigrants arrived in the United States. They came mostly from southern and eastern Europe, not Anglo-Saxon stock like prior immigrants. And they moved not to the frontier to farm but to industrial cities to fill factory jobs and tenements. During the decade after 1910, driven by industrialization and World War I, even more people flooded into northern cities, many from within the United States. The 1920 census found that, for the first time, only a minority of Americans lived in rural areas. That year Republicans won control of the presidency and Congress, with Warren G. Harding pledging a "return to normalcy." They spoke for a traditional America, lampooned in the fiction of the era as complacent "Babbitry." The Republican majority, pressured by Prohibitionists who feared the influence of alcohol-tolerant cities, chose a novel way to address its uncomfortable dilemma: for the first and so far only time, it simply refused to reapportion, leaving the congressional district lines and allocation per state exactly where they were in 1911. (The excuse: not enough chairs in the U.S. House to expand the size of the Congress.) In 1929 Congress finally reassigned congressional seats but repealed the federal law requiring congressmen to be elected from districts of roughly equal population that were "compact and contiguous." The imbalances compounded over time. By 1960, reports legal historian J. Douglas Smith, "in nineteen states, the largest district had more than twice the number of residents as the smallest. . . . The largest district in Texas contained four times the number of residents as the smallest district."

State legislatures were even less balanced. In the wake of the Civil War most had been apportioned on the basis of population. But beginning in the 1890s states increasingly moved to a "federal system" that apportioned one house based on counties or other geographic units. As cities like Milwaukee, Saint Louis, Kansas City, Atlanta, and Birmingham grew, their relative political voice shrank. In the most extreme example, by 1960 nearly 40 percent of the population of California lived in Los Angeles County, but under California's constitution that county was entitled to just one of forty state senators.

Rotten boroughs abounded. "Opting for what became known as the 'silent gerrymander,' they allowed district boundaries to remain fixed for decades," Smith writes. "Only eighteen of forty-eight states redrew boundaries in the wake of the 1940 census. Legislators in Oregon ignored their obligations for a half century after 1907. Illinois established districts in 1910 that remained in place until 1955. . . . A town of 38 residents in Vermont constituted the smallest legislative district in the United States and elected the same number of representatives—one—as the state capital, Burlington, population 33,000. In New Jersey, the state's twenty-one senators represented as few as 48,555 people or as many as 923,545."

Political control by small-town conservatives mattered enormously. Budgets, tax laws, and social policy all were bent. For example, in 1956, faced with Supreme Court rulings ordering school desegregation, the Virginia legislature voted to shut down all public schools. The majority of legislators who voted to shutter the schools represented a distinct minority of the state's population.

In the mid-twentieth century a new force entered the picture: the courts. A series of startling judicial decisions, especially from federal judges, began to blow past the obstacles that had kept representation frozen and unequal.

Entering the "Political Thicket"

From the country's earliest days the courts had largely been absent from the fight to expand democracy. Beginning with the "Dorr War" case, *Luther v. Borden* in 1849, judges steered far clear of adjudicating political rights and declined to strike down even the most imbalanced law or practice. At times the courts played a malign role: the Supreme Court winked at Jim Crow, ruling that poll taxes, grandfather clauses, and other manipulations did not violate the Fifteenth Amendment, and lower courts declined to find individual rights to be violated by political arrangements.

Of course, until the mid-twentieth century that failure to protect rights was not limited to the law of democracy. The U.S. Supreme Court rarely found much of anything to be in violation of the Constitution. The Civil War amendments—especially the Fourteenth, with its guarantee of "equal protection" and "due process of law"—were designed to restrain conduct in the states. But the Court had neutered much of the power of those amendments. By the end of the nineteenth century they effectively protected corporations but not African Americans. The Bill of Rights was deemed to restrain only the actions of Congress. That began to change, incrementally, in the 1920s. Through a process of "incorporation," the protections of the Bill of Rights were deemed to apply to states, starting with parts of the First Amendment in 1925.

The New Deal justices crafted a new approach to judicial intervention. In a series of rulings, the Court had struck down many key New Deal laws. Roosevelt's bid to expand the Court and pack it with sympathetic judges was defeated and wounded his presidency. But the majority of justices began to uphold economic regulation, the notorious "switch in time that saved nine." Soon new justices formed a majority.

The new approach was articulated in a famous footnote to an otherwise obscure regulatory case. The Carolene Products company was accused of selling "filled milk," mixing skim milk with oil. It challenged its conviction, saying that the Constitution's clause giving Congress power to regulate interstate commerce did not apply. In *United States v. Carolene Products*, the Court allowed the prosecution—and articulated a rationale for stepping back from its role in stopping economic regulation. The Court would not strictly scrutinize such rules, but "there may be narrower scope for operation of the presumption of constitutionality when legislation appears on its face to be within a specific prohibition of the Constitution, such as those of the first ten amendments." The Court signaled it would be far more skeptical of "legislation which restricts those political processes which can ordinarily be expected to bring about repeal of undesirable legislation," including the right to vote. The justices would also give special scrutiny to laws that hurt "discrete and insular minorities." The Court was out of the business of imposing laissez-faire economics on the Constitution, but it was now emphatically in the business of protecting individual rights—and making sure that the political system itself did not block changes to the political system.

Yet the justices did not follow that path in a straight line. Felix Frankfurter was a close friend of President Roosevelt, and a trusted advisor. He had represented Sacco and Vanzetti, the anarchists whose death sentence was a cause célèbre in the 1920s, and helped found the American Civil Liberties Union. The Harvard professor was a consummate political operator (and courtier). He placed his protégés—Frankfurter's "happy hot dogs"—in key jobs where they drafted New Deal laws and staffed proliferating regulatory agencies. Justice Louis D. Brandeis even paid him secretly to lobby for shared liberal causes. Frankfurter had come of age when Progressives dreaded judicial intervention designed to block activist government. Roosevelt nominated him to serve as an associate justice in 1938. Scarred by the battles between Roosevelt and the Court, Frankfurter fought for—even fetishized—judicial restraint. In 1946 he wrote for a six-vote majority in a case addressing the malapportionment of the day. A group of Illinois voters challenged that state's flagrantly unrepresentative congressional lines. The state's smallest congressional district had less than one-eighth the population of the largest. That may be so, Frankfurter explained, but the Court had no "competence" to do anything about it. "To sustain this action would cut very deep into the very being of Congress," he wrote. "Courts ought not to enter this political thicket." The answer is politics—vote for better state legislatures. This was circular reasoning, for the political branches were themselves the obstacle, complicit in the behavior being challenged.

The "political thicket": a deftly turned phrase that memorably summed up a century's reluctance to police the politicians. It was also a last gasp. As the civil rights movement began to press for change in the 1950s, the racial dimension of misrepresentation drew more attention. In 1960 the Supreme Court heard another redistricting case, this one from Tuskegee, Alabama. Segregationist legislators redrew the city's boundaries from a square shape to a peculiar twenty-eight-sided figure that managed to exclude all but four or five Black voters, while keeping all its white residents. Tuskegee was a storied town, where Booker T. Washington had founded the Tuskegee Institute. Its professors had little to do with the overalls-clad farmers and janitors of the surrounding region. Now a faculty member, Clarence Gomillion, found himself unable to vote for city government. "We were shocked into the recognition that we were still Negroes, with all the disabilities attached thereto in the sovereign state of Alabama," he told a reporter. "The country people found our comeuppance rather amusing and, I think, subtly satisfying." Gomillion and the other professors made common cause with their poorer neighbors and sued. This time the Court invalidated the lines, finding they were designed to disenfranchise Black voters. Frankfurter wrote the opinion, making clear he was relying on the explicit prohibitions on racial discrimination found in the Fifteenth Amendment.

The turmoil of the civil rights movement spurred more lawsuits. In *Baker v. Carr* the Supreme Court launched what law professors call the "reapportionment revolution." The case concerned the legislative district lines in Tennessee. Like many other states, its constitution required a redrawing of the maps every ten years, and like some others, it had not done so since 1901. Charles Baker was a Republican resident of Memphis, where the legislative district had ten times the population of some districts in rural areas. Memphis boasted an organized Black legal and business community, and they put pressure on the new Kennedy administration to back the suit. One month into Kennedy's New Frontier civic leaders met for much of a day with Solicitor General Archibald Cox, the bow-tied, crew-cut Harvard professor who would present the federal government's views to the justices. Cox then told Attorney General Robert F. Kennedy that he wanted to back the suit. Kennedy asked, "Well, are you going to win?" Cox replied, "No, I don't think so, but it would be a lot of fun anyway." The city itself backed the case, now joined by the federal government.

When the justices convened in private after hearing the arguments, Frankfurter harangued his colleagues for hours, demanding they refrain from asserting federal court jurisdiction over the topic. The pressure provoked a nervous breakdown from one justice, who resigned before deciding how to vote. Lawyers argued the case a second time. Finally, in March 1962, almost a year after the first oral arguments, the justices issued their ruling. Justice William J. Brennan Jr. wrote the opinion. Brennan was the master strategist of the Warren Court, its "playmaker." When new clerks arrived to work for him, he would slyly show them the jurisprudential rule that truly governed: he would hold up five fingers.

Baker does not expound quotably on equality and democracy. Brennan proposed no new theory of voting rights; instead, in dry-as-dust analysis, the opinion held that the courts, in fact, could step into the "political thicket" to protect individual political rights. The courts had jurisdiction, relying on the Fourteenth Amendment's guarantee of "equal protection of the law" to all citizens. The opinion set out some principles for what kinds of questions are too political for it to address, most notably when the Constitution gives another branch the assignment of deciding a matter or when there is "a lack of judicially discoverable and manageable standards for resolving it." That would prove an increasingly difficult challenge over the years.

The justices ordered the lower court judge to oversee a new apportionment for Tennessee, without specifying how to do it. The ruling was an invitation to the nation to redraw all the political maps. City governments and others seeking a louder voice challenged the apportionment schemes in thirty-four states. Within one year of the decision nineteen state legislatures were reapportioned, many for the first time in decades. Chief Justice Earl Warren would call *Baker* "the most important case of my tenure on the Court."

"The African Cry"

Two years later, in 1964, the Supreme Court embraced the profound concept of "one person, one vote": the political equality of all citizens. The idea seems self-evident to modern Americans. Of course the words appear nowhere in the Constitution.

Where did this phrase, hallowed as an encapsulation of democracy, come from? "One man, one vote" had been used over the years, especially in Great Britain, where it described Prime Minister William Gladstone's proposal to end "plural voting," in which wealthy property owners trekked from estate to estate, voting in each place. Gladstone's reform—one man, *only* one vote—took nearly seventy years to enact. The phrase had rarely been used in the United States.

Remarkably it made its way to the Supreme Court from Africa—from, among others, Nelson Mandela himself. The South African lawyer had been using it for years in his fight against apartheid. While the Freedom Charter of the African National Congress did not embrace it in 1955, in the early 1960s Mandela argued publicly for it. In a television interview in 1961, on the run from the Pretoria government, he said, "The Africans require, want, the franchise on the basis of one man, one vote. They want political independence." According to newspaper reports that year, crowds in neighboring Rhodesia (now Zimbabwe) chanted "Freedom" and "one man, one vote" as they protested white domination in a continent that was shedding colonial rule.

The slogan entered American parlance at a dramatic moment in the civil rights struggle: the August 1963 March on Washington. John Lewis was a leader of the Student Nonviolent Coordinating Committee, the group of young activists who organized integrated groups to ride on Greyhound and Trailways buses through the South on "Freedom Rides." SNCC's militant voice rebuked the tactical silences required of its elders. Lewis prepared the March's most vehement speech. When movement leaders saw his prepared text, they threatened to bar him from speaking for fear of alienating the Kennedy administration. As the day's orations rumbled across the Mall, Lewis and his elders, including Martin Luther King Jr., wrestled over wording in a tense editing session held in a guard booth behind Lincoln's statue. Among other lines, they struck his pledge to "march through the South, through the heart of Dixie, the way [General] Sherman did," albeit this time "nonviolently." But even with the editing, Lewis gave the day's angriest address to the 250,000 marchers. He spoke with authenticity and passion, the day's only speaker to refer to "the Black masses" rather than "Negroes." Criticizing the civil rights bill then before Congress, Lewis declared, "One man, one vote is the African cry. It is ours too. It must be ours." He vowed to keep marching "until the revolution of 1776 is complete."

The phrase had first been brought before the Supreme Court during a reapportionment case argued earlier that year, in an intervention for the U.S. government by Attorney General Kennedy. By tradition the attorney general appears in at least one case before the high court, and Kennedy chose this intensely political one. (In appointing his thirty-five-year-old brother President Kennedy had joked, "I don't know why people are so mad at me for making Bobby Attorney General. I just wanted to give him some legal experience before he practiced.") In *Gray v. Sanders* the federal government mostly supported a challenge to Georgia's "county unit" rule, a complex system giving rural voters extra weight in state Democratic primaries. Attorney General Kennedy drew laughs when he likened Georgia's system to the saying once common in Boston, "Vote early and vote often." Georgia's lawyer insisted that the American political system drew from sturdy British ideas of limiting the power of majorities. Equality, he said, was a notion borrowed from Jean-Jacques Rousseau. It was *French*. The attorney general responded by urging the Court to embrace equality: "In this case that is what the ideal is, one man, one vote." Just three months later, in an eloquent opinion, the Court embraced that vision. "The conception of political equality from the Declaration of Independence, to Lincoln's Gettysburg Address, to the Fifteenth, Seventeenth, and Nineteenth Amendments can mean only one thing—one person, one vote," it ruled.

The Supreme Court completed its redistricting revolution in 1964. In *Wesberry v. Sanders* it struck down Georgia's congressional map, finding that districts of members of the U.S. House of Representatives should have roughly equal population. And in *Reynolds v. Sims* the justices specified for the first time that state legislatures too must be governed by the idea of "one person, one vote." That case arose as a sideshow to the roiling protests that had earlier transformed Birmingham. Alabama had not reapportioned its legislature since the turn of the century. Birmingham's business leaders, known as "the Big Mules," long had made common cause with the rural white politicians of the state's Black Belt to fight labor unions, keep taxes low, and prevent racial progress. During a temporary feud between the factions, the Big Mules backed a lawsuit to challenge the state's reapportionment. In 1963, however, they withdrew their support for the case as civil rights protests led by Dr. King wracked the city, though a handful of lawyers continued to press for reapportionment (even as violent threats drove one of them out of town).

At their standing meeting on Fridays, after the week's arguments, Supreme Court justices cast preliminary votes and decide who will write a case's opinion. On Friday, November 22, 1963, Chief Justice Warren assigned himself the task of writing for the majority in *Reynolds*. Then his secretary burst in with the awful news from Dallas: President Kennedy had been assassinated. Warren would soon find himself dragooned into chairing the commission to investigate the murder. For several weeks his judicial clerks doubled as his commission staff. They juggled the task of writing the *Reynolds* opinion while sifting the evidence from Dallas. Warren himself shuttled back and forth between the committee's office across the street and the marble Supreme Court building. With his attention focused on the assassination, his legal clerk wrote the opinion based on the justice's comments in conference and handwritten thoughts, jotted on note cards.

Reynolds v. Sims was the most far-reaching of all the apportionment cases. The majority held that legislative apportionment must be based on population. A system that gives property extra weight or rural counties formal strength in legislatures violates that principle: "Legislators represent people, not trees or acres. Legislators are elected by voters, not farms or cities or economic interests. The right to vote freely for the candidate of one's choice is of the essence of a democratic society, and any restrictions on that right strike at the heart of representative government.

And the right of suffrage can be denied by a debasement or dilution of the weight of a citizen's vote just as effectively as by wholly prohibiting the free exercise of the franchise." The Court found that equal districts with equal population must be the basis for both houses of a state legislature. To achieve representative government, "each and every citizen has an inalienable right to full and effective participation in the political processes of his State's legislative bodies. Most citizens can achieve this participation only as qualified voters through the election of legislators to represent them. Full and effective participation by all citizens in state government requires, therefore, that each citizen have an equally effective voice in the election of members of his state legislature." This profound and even radically democratic sentiment—"an equally effective voice"—pointed to a vision of constitutional law rooted in democratic equality.

By 1968 ninety-three of ninety-nine state legislative chambers would be redrawn to comply with the court's ruling.

"Let the People Decide"

The Supreme Court's rulings provoked a backlash—one that is surprising, even hard to imagine today, when the concept of "one person, one vote" is deeply ingrained. Briefly the fight threatened to flare into a constitutional crisis.

Republican Everett Dirksen, the Senate minority leader, made a crusade out of overturning the Court's rulings. He warned, "The six million citizens of the Chicago area would [now] hold sway in the Illinois Legislature without consideration of the problems of their four million fellows who are scattered in one hundred other counties. Under the Court's new decree, California could be dominated by Los Angeles and San Francisco; Michigan by Detroit." Dirksen crafted legislation to delay state compliance; liberals blocked it with a filibuster. He then brought a proposed constitutional amendment to the floor in 1965 and 1966. Under its terms states could draw lines based on factors other than population, if a citizen referendum endorsed the practice. Each time it fell short of the required votes.

The fight then spilled out into the states. Dirksen worked with an early, sophisticated political consulting firm, Whittaker & Baxter, to create a business group that would push for an amendment. The Committee for Government of the People proved a potent fundraising operation. Instead of "One person, one vote," its slogan was "Let the people decide." State legislatures quietly began to use the process outlined in Article V of the Constitution, demanding a constitutional convention. By 1969, by most counts, thirty-three states had issued the call—just two shy of the needed amount. The nonpartisan League of Women Voters tried to monitor and oppose the move. Suddenly the national media and Congress realized the country had edged toward an unexpected crisis. The last time such a convention had been called was in 1787, itself a "runaway." A convention would be unmapped terrain. Who would chair it? Who would set the rules? Other questions were more specific to the "one person, one vote" subject. Some U.S. senators insisted that the call for a convention would be invalid if it were issued by legislatures that were themselves unconstitutionally chosen. In the end the last two states didn't join the call, and the issue faded away. Within a few years, as legislators who had been chosen by the reapportioned voters took their seats, the controversy subsided.

The well-funded, skilled drive to "let the people decide" was an early omen of political trends in coming decades. Business lobbying had been a quiet affair, a matter of whispered suggestions in the halls of state capitols. The campaign for a constitutional convention was one of the first times the business community mobilized on broad, ideological grounds. At the time publicity campaigns denounced "activist judges," but few even remember the constitutional convention that nearly was. The backlash against "one person, one vote" augured the broader response to expanded democratic rights that eventually became a central political tenet.

10

Walls of Jericho

> We are not on our knees begging for the ballot. We are demanding the ballot. . . . We will bring a voting bill into being on the streets of Selma!
>
> DR. MARTIN LUTHER KING JR., January 2, 1965

THE IMAGE is indelible, one of the great moments in the long history of American democracy: a thin line of people walking single file across Jefferson Davis Highway on the march from Selma to Montgomery, Alabama. At the safe remove of half a century, it is easy to sentimentalize. What modern recounting, even films, don't show fully is the sheer terror of the marchers, and what it took to keep going.

Modern American democracy began in a hail of police batons and kicks on the Edmund Pettus Bridge in Selma. This fight was not won by lawyers; the Voting Rights Act was born of a complex encounter between organized protest and backroom politics. Once again a mix of passion, party politics, and inspired leadership led to a major expansion of American democracy. This one was not capped by a constitutional amendment, but its impact was as profound.

Progress was visible, just barely, in states at the periphery of the Confederacy, such as Texas, Florida, and Tennessee. But in the Deep South violence, official discrimination, and retaliation continued to prevent nearly all African Americans from voting. South Carolina wiped all election laws off its books to avoid government imprimatur for its purely "voluntary" white primary.

The U.S. Commission on Civil Rights examined the true state of democracy in 1961. In one hundred counties in seven states, it found, voting rights were systematically denied to Black citizens. Blacks attempting to vote were asked to calculate their age to the day or were required to have another voter "vouch" for them—impossible when there were no other African American "vouchers." One county in Louisiana required Blacks to produce two "vouchers." The state explained that this was necessary "since it is difficult for most registrars, who are white, to differentiate between persons of the Negro race." In thirteen counties in Georgia, Alabama, Mississippi, and Louisiana—jurisdictions where Black citizens were the majority—*no African Americans* were registered to vote.

The literacy test administered in Selma in 1965 asked Black voters increasingly arcane questions:

> If a person charged with treason denies his guilt, how many persons must testify against him before he is convicted?
>
> At what time of day on January 20th each four years does the term of the President of the United States end?
>
> If the president does not wish to sign a bill, how many days is he allowed in which to return it to Congress for reconsideration?

Still, this was positively straightforward compared to some tests. In Louisiana Black voters were asked to complete a nonsensical set of thirty questions, within ten minutes, with any mistake disqualifying. For example, Question 29 directed, "Write every other word in this first line and print every third word in the same line, (original type smaller and first line ended at comma) but capitalize the fifth word that you write." Other registrars asked Black applicants to count the number of bubbles in a soap bar, to recount the news in a recent *Peking Daily* newspaper, and to define Latin legal terms.

In theory white voters faced these obstacles as well. In practice local registrars had almost complete writ to exclude Black citizens. A young African American military veteran named Jewell Wade described a typical encounter when he tried to register in Jackson Parish, Mississippi. The registrar returned his voter registration card to him, saying he had made a mistake. He checked it repeatedly but could see none. He got up to leave, asking, "Ma'am, would you do one thing for me?"

"What is that?"

"Will you tell me the mistake I made?"

"Oh, sure; you underlined 'Mr.' when you should have circled it."

As is well known, the civil rights movement swept across the South and the country in the decade after 1955. But the compelling stories and morality plays of that time yielded little new progress for voting rights. The turmoil did produce the 1957 Civil Rights Act, muscled through the Senate by Majority Leader Lyndon Johnson. It created a Civil Rights Division in the Justice Department and gave federal prosecutors power to seek court injunctions to prevent interference with the right to vote. Another civil rights law, enacted in 1960, gave courts the power to appoint monitors to supervise voting. None of these efforts had much impact; they relied on arduous, case-by-case prosecution after the fact, with little systemic consequence even when there were victories. In the spring of 1963 the Birmingham desegregation campaign honed a template to win national victories. Peaceful protest was met by bilious and violent overreaction from local white authorities. National outrage (and an awareness of international opprobrium) led President Kennedy to abruptly schedule a national television address. "We are confronted primarily with a moral issue," Kennedy declared. "It is as old as the scriptures and is as clear as the American Constitution." He barely mentioned voting rights. Johnson, elevated to the presidency after the assassination, capitalized on national mourning and revulsion to make passage of the civil rights law the memorial to the slain president. A relentless drive by churches, labor unions, and other civil rights lobbyists overcame a filibuster. But the landmark Civil Rights Act of 1964 touched only in minor ways on voting.

The wary dance between King and Johnson, two viscerally skilled southern political leaders, defined the final push for voting rights. As the historian Taylor Branch has observed, "Kennedy had charmed King while keeping him at a safe distance." Johnson, on the other hand, "was intensely personal but unpredictable—treating King variously to a Texas bear hug of shared dreams or a towering, wounded snit."

In December 1964 Johnson met with King, who had just returned from Norway, where he had been awarded the Nobel Prize for Peace. Johnson held forth on his "War on Poverty" programs to provide benefits, education, and housing for the poor. King pressed the continued need for voting rights legislation. Johnson replied, "Martin, you're right about that. I'm going to do it eventually, but I can't get a voting rights bill through in this session of Congress." Less than six months after the filibuster was broken to enact the Civil Rights Act, Johnson needed the support of southern congressional committee chairmen if he were to pass his Great Society measures. King left crestfallen.

A month later Johnson and King spoke again, this time by phone. King lobbied Johnson to appoint an African American to the cabinet. In a breathless monologue Johnson rattled off the bills he wanted to squeeze through Congress in its first months: on education, poverty, and the creation of Medicare. "We've got to get them passed before the vicious forces concentrate and get them a coalition that can block them." Again he explained why voting rights must be delayed. Then Johnson began to speak with mounting bombast and enthusiasm. A voting rights law, he told King, would dwarf the Civil Rights Act in importance: "That will answer seventy percent of your problems." King was reduced to interjections of "That's right" and "Yeah." Johnson urged King to "find the worst condition that you run into in Alabama, Mississippi, or Louisiana, or South Carolina"—such as a case where the leader of the Tuskegee Institute was denied the right to vote. "If you just take that one illustration and get it on radio, and get it on television, and get it on . . . in the pulpits, and get it in the meetings, get it every place you can, pretty soon the fellow that didn't do anything but follow—drive a tractor, he'll say, 'Well, that's not right, that's not fair.'" King, for his part, talked about Black voting rates and how a surge in voting for Democrats could lead to a "new South." "Landslide Lyndon" felt compelled to describe his soaring vision; the moral leader felt compelled to demonstrate his savvy political chops.

Johnson never told King that he had asked the Justice Department to secretly draft a voting rights bill, despite fears that a strong law would be found unconstitutional. "Get me some things you'd be proud of," he told Attorney General Nicholas Katzenbach, "to show your boy, and say, 'Here is what your daddy put through in nineteen sixty-four-five-six-seven.'" And King never mentioned to Johnson that he was already working to stage a public drama in one of the worst spots for Blacks in the South.

Selma

Selma was a small city, about thirty thousand people. Fifty-seven percent of the population was African American; about 99 percent of the voters were white. The Justice Department filed its first voting rights suit there, and had brought three since, all to little effect. SNCC had spent the better part of a year there, trying to organize voters, without success; it was preparing to give up. King and his lieutenants arrived in the town, chosen because of the expected brutality of local officials and the severity of poverty and disenfranchisement.

At a packed, raucous mass meeting, King announced a drive for voting rights: "Our cry to the state of Alabama is a simple one, 'Give us the ballot!'" The audience shouted encouragement. "When we get the right to vote we will send to the statehouse not men who will stand in the doorways of universities to keep Negroes out, but men who will uphold the cause of justice: Give us the ballot!"

Over the weeks King led treks to the courthouse, seeking to register voters. Schoolteachers marched. Citizens lined up for hours, only to be turned away. For two months King and his colleagues tried to get the country's attention, producing images of nonviolence confronted by aggressive hate. Every time it appeared their efforts were flagging, another atrocity gave the movement new life. Sheriff Jim Clark got into a fistfight with Annie Lee Cooper, who was waiting to register. She was arrested. King and his deputy, Ralph Abernathy, went to jail as well. Still, efforts seemed futile: too many local officials produced a blandly noncooperative face. Then, on February 18, in the nearby town of Marion, police burst into a restaurant after assaulting protesters. They shot a young man, Jimmie Lee Jackson, as he sought to shield his mother. King vowed to organize a march from Selma to the state capital, Montgomery, fifty-four miles away, in part as a memorial to Jackson, in part to dramatize the conflict.

While the mayhem unfolded in Selma, the White House was secretly crafting a national law to protect voting rights. Johnson had waxed and waned on the topic. He pressed the Justice Department to draft a bill, but Attorney General Katzenbach resisted, fearing it would be found unconstitutional and pleading staff overwork enforcing earlier civil rights laws. The liberal attorney general pressed instead for a constitutional amendment that would guarantee a broad right to vote for all Americans—a path not taken, one that would have been easier to block but in some ways have a longer lasting impact. But Johnson didn't want to wait for an amendment to be ratified. Eventually, under presidential prodding, the Justice Department rejected the notion of seeking a constitutional change. Instead there would be a new law, one that thrust the federal government into the role of supervising voting in large parts of the country to protect African Americans' right to vote, a duty it had not assumed since Reconstruction. A basic agreement was reached on March 1, 1965. Its key provisions survived to become the Voting Rights Act, on the books for a half century now.

To pass such a measure, Johnson believed, he must again parlay with Senate Republican leader Dirksen, who had been lionized for his role in passing the civil rights bill the previous year. Dirksen was known as the "Wizard of Ooze." His ego required constant attention. The *New York Times* drama critic likened his deep, theatrical voice to "the froth on a warm pail of milk just extracted from a fat Jersey cow." According to chronicler Todd Purdum, "He kept his vocal cords lubricated with a daily gargle of Pond's cold cream and water (which he swallowed) and subsisted on a diet of Sanka, cigarettes, Maalox, and bourbon whiskey." At a table in Dirksen's office, Attorney General Katzenbach, Democratic Senate leaders, and the "Wizard of Ooze" hammered out revisions to the draft bill. The coalition of Republicans and northern Democrats would be enough, they thought, to win passage—eventually.

History was preparing to unfold, but the protagonists kept their own counsel. That evening King again visited Johnson, who talked vaguely of his desire to submit a bill but never mentioned negotiations. King seems not to have stressed the plan to begin marching two days hence.

Bloody Sunday

SNCC opposed the march from Selma to Montgomery, which had been rescheduled more than once. By phone from Atlanta King finally gave the assent to move, and on Sunday, March 7, a small group set out.

John Lewis and King's colleague Hosea Williams led the procession. The marchers wore sober suits and dresses, some coming from church, some wearing heels. Lewis recounts that the march felt funereal, even at the start. As they rounded the crest of the Edmund Pettus Bridge, they saw a solid line of state troopers sent by Alabama's governor, George Wallace. Behind them, on horseback, were volunteers carrying whips. A crowd of white onlookers, waving Confederate flags, flanked the lawmen. A small cluster of journalists and Black residents looked on. Lewis, Williams, and the marchers stopped fifty feet before the troopers.

"Mr. Major, I would like to have a word," Williams called out.

"There is no word to be had," a state trooper replied.

The *New York Times* reporter on the scene narrated what happened next:

> The troopers rushed forward, their blue uniforms and white helmets blurring into a flying wedge as they moved.
>
> The wedge moved with such force that it seemed almost to pass over the waiting column instead of through it.
>
> The first 10 or 20 Negroes were swept to the ground screaming, arms and legs flying, and packs and bags went skittering across the grassy divider strip and on to the pavement on both sides.
>
> Those still on their feet retreated.
>
> The troopers continued pushing, using both the force of their bodies and the prodding of their nightsticks.
>
> A cheer went up from the white spectators lining the south side of the highway.
>
> The mounted possemen spurred their horses and rode at a run into the retreating mass. The Negroes cried out as they crowded together for protection, and the whites on the sidelines whooped and cheered.

The Negroes paused in their retreat for perhaps a minute, still screaming and huddling together.

Suddenly there was a report like a gunshot and a grey cloud spewed over the troopers and the Negroes.

"Tear gas!" someone yelled.

The cloud began covering the highway. Newsmen, who were confined by four troopers to a corner 100 yards away, began to lose sight of the action.

Before the cloud finally hid the scene, fifteen or twenty nightsticks could be seen through the gas, flailing at the heads of the marchers.

That night ABC television was premiering the movie *Judgment at Nuremberg*, in which Spencer Tracy plays an American attorney prosecuting Nazi war crimes after World War II. He was questioning an ordinary German family who insisted they bore no culpability for the regime's atrocities, when a news bulletin broke into the scene. For fifteen minutes, uninterrupted, ABC showed film footage from Selma. The voice of Sheriff Clark could be heard, shouting, "Get those goddamn niggers! And get those goddamned *white* niggers!" Television, now ubiquitous in American homes, showed it could rivet the attention of an unprecedentedly broad public, as it had over the prior sixteen months reporting on the Kennedy assassination (and even the Beatles' first performance on *The Ed Sullivan Show*).

At a mass meeting after the attack Lewis, dazed and still covered in dried blood, spoke: "I don't see how President Johnson can send troops to Vietnam . . . and he can't send troops to Selma, Alabama." Lewis finally consented to go to a hospital; he had suffered a fractured skull. That night King put out a call to clergy from across the country, pleading with them to come to Selma.

"We Shall Overcome"

The next week's drama has been recounted in movies, memoirs, and histories. Hundreds of ministers, priests, rabbis, and ordinary citizens poured into Selma from around the country. As they prepared to march again, a federal judge issued an injunction barring the protest until he could hear testimony. (The jurist, Frank Johnson, was widely respected and a friend to the civil rights movement. Governor Wallace had once denounced him as an "integrating, carpetbagging, scalawagging, race-mixing, bald-faced liar.") King agonized over whether to defy the judge; obedience to federal court orders was, after all, a central tenet of the movement. In a complex deal negotiated with the state government and the White House, King and the marchers crossed the bridge, prayed, and turned around. King's leadership was shaken by the embarrassing, dispiriting compromise. Then, that night, hatred did its job: James Reeb, a white Unitarian minister from Boston in town to join the march, was clubbed on the street. He lingered for two days before dying.

Just as extraordinary was what happened outside Selma that week. "Rarely in history has public opinion reacted so spontaneously and with such fury," narrated *Time* magazine. Students held a sit-in at the base of the Liberty Bell in Philadelphia. Michigan's Republican governor George Romney led a march of ten thousand people through Detroit in support of voting rights. John Lewis rushed to Harlem to recount the beatings. Protesters ringed the White House. A group of students on a tour there staged a sit-in. Other demonstrators occupied the office of the attorney general. A spontaneous mass movement had arisen, demanding full democratic rights.

Johnson felt trapped. Lady Bird, his wife, confided to a taped diary that he bore a "heavy load of tension and this fog of depression." Tapes of his endless worried phone calls to allies and staff members reflect his hesitancy. He let the pressure build to the point where Wallace had to turn to the federal government for help—and look to the president himself for action.

On Saturday Wallace came to the White House. He had first run for office as a populist and a racial moderate. When he lost he vowed, "No other son-of-a-bitch will ever out-nigger me again." In his inaugural address as governor he had declared, "I draw the line in the dust and toss the gauntlet before the feet of tyranny, and I say segregation now, segregation tomorrow, segregation forever." His swagger faded in the Oval Office. Richard Goodwin, a Johnson speechwriter who sat in on the meeting, recalls:

> The six foot four Johnson sat in the rocking chair and leaned toward the semi-recumbent Wallace, his towering figure inclined downward until their noses almost touched.
>
> "Well, Governor, you wanted to see me."
>
> For two hours, Wallace insisted that he could do little to persuade local officials to register Black voters. Johnson pounded on him. "Don't shit me about your persuasive power, George." Wallace slowly retreated. Suddenly, Johnson sat upright.
>
> "Now listen, George, don't think about 1968; you think about 1988. You and me, we'll be dead and gone then, George. Now you've got a lot of poor people down there in Alabama, a lot of ignorant people. You can do a lot for them, George. Your president will help you. What do you want left after you when you die? Do you want a Great . . . Big . . . Marble monument that reads, 'George Wallace—He Built'? . . . Or do you want a little piece of scrawny pine board lying across that harsh, caliche soil, that reads, 'George Wallace—He Hated'?"

With that, Johnson pulled a rattled Wallace out into a hallway crammed with three hundred reporters. A few minutes later, Johnson strode to the Rose Garden and announced that he would be sending a proposed Voting Rights Act to the Congress within days. (Wallace exclaimed later, "Hell, if I'd stayed in there much longer, he'd have had me coming out for civil rights.")

Now Johnson was energized, driven. The next day, a week after Bloody Sunday, he met with the congressional leadership. Through misdirection and probably prearrangement, he managed to get himself invited to Congress to present the voting rights bill. This would be the first address to Congress on a single domestic topic in nineteen years.

The next morning, still in bed, Johnson asked his devoted aide, Jack Valenti, how the speech draft was coming. Valenti didn't know; he had assigned the task to a longtime assistant. Johnson erupted: "The hell you did. Don't you know a liberal Jew has his hand on the pulse of America? And you assign the most important speech of my life to a Texas public relations man? Get Dick [Goodwin] to do it. And now!" When Goodwin arrived at work, bleary after a night of drinking, he found a nervous Valenti in his office. He told the speechwriter to prepare the address to Congress—to be delivered that evening. Goodwin worked in a fever all day. As each page was typed, a secretary would take it to the president. There were no second drafts.

Johnson phoned Goodwin only once. The president reminded the writer of a story Goodwin had heard Johnson tell before: that one of his first jobs had been teaching young Mexican American children in Cotulla, Texas. He had poured himself into that job, spending half his salary on sports equipment for the students, then going door to door to talk with their parents. "I thought you might want to put in a reference to it," Johnson said. Then he gently hung up.

After a motorcade past pickets and protesters, Johnson spoke in the well of the House while 70 million Americans watched on television. He began slowly, to rapt silence. "At times history and fate meet at a single time in a single place to shape a turning point in man's unending search for freedom. So it was at Lexington and Concord. So it was a century ago at Appomattox. So it was last week in Selma, Alabama." He drew from Jefferson's Preamble to frame the moment:

> This was the first nation in the history of the world to be founded with a purpose. The great phrases of that purpose still sound in every American heart, North and South: "All men are created equal"—"government by consent of the governed"—"give me liberty or give me death." . . . Our fathers believed that if this noble view of the rights of man was to flourish, it must be rooted in democracy. The most basic right of all was the right to choose your own leaders. The history of this country, in large measure, is the history of the expansion of that right to all of our people.

Johnson was interrupted repeatedly by applause. He outlined the voting rights bill, declaring it "wrong—deadly wrong—to deny any of your fellow Americans the right to vote in this country."

Then he astonished his listeners: "What happened in Selma is part of a far larger movement which reaches into every section and State of America. It is the effort of American Negroes to secure for themselves the full blessings of American life. Their cause must be our cause too. Because it is not just Negroes, but really it is all of us, who must overcome the crippling legacy of bigotry and injustice." He gripped the lectern, leaned forward. "And—we—shall—overcome."

Stunned silence greeted the southern president, who had just appropriated the civil rights movement's hymn of protest. The oldest member of the House then jumped to his feet, cheering wildly. Lawmakers began applauding, pounding their desks. The Senate majority leader was in tears. Southern senators slumped and glowered. In a Selma living room, watching with other marchers on a small television, Martin Luther King Jr. wept.

Johnson concluded his speech, in a quieter, more personal voice:

My first job after college was as a teacher in Cotulla, Tex., in a small Mexican-American school. Few of them could speak English, and I couldn't speak much Spanish. My students were poor and they often came to class without breakfast, hungry. They knew even in their youth the pain of prejudice. They never seemed to know why people disliked them. But they knew it was so, because I saw it in their eyes. I often walked home late in the afternoon, after the classes were finished, wishing there was more that I could do. But all I knew was to teach them the little that I knew, hoping that it might help them against the hardships that lay ahead.

Somehow you never forget what poverty and hatred can do when you see its scars on the hopeful face of a young child.

I never thought then, in 1928, that I would be standing here in 1965. It never even occurred to me in my fondest dreams that I might have the chance to help the sons and daughters of those students and to help people like them all over this country.

But now I do have that chance—and I'll let you in on a secret—I mean to use it.

Two days later federal judge Frank Johnson issued a ruling to allow the march to proceed. The state asked the federal government to protect the protesters. On March 21 they set out again for Montgomery. This time U.S. Army helicopters hovered overhead, and federalized National Guard troops lined the highway. As they passed through Klan territory, desolate farmland, danger lurked in the darkness. The marchers camped in tents surrounded by guardsmen. Near Montgomery, their numbers grew. By the time they reached the state capitol, twenty-five thousand people were there to hear speakers, musicians, and movie stars, a version in miniature of the March on Washington. Wallace could be seen peeking through the drawn blinds of the statehouse windows.

King spoke last. Exhausted, exhilarated, he gave one of his most powerful addresses. Veering from his written text, he took listeners through the true story of Reconstruction, how the threat of a populist coalition between white and Black voters had led to the passage of the disenfranchising laws seven decades before: "The threat of the free exercise of the ballot by the Negro and the white masses alike resulted in the establishing of a segregated society. They segregated southern money from the poor whites; they segregated southern mores from the rich whites; they segregated southern churches from Christianity; they segregated southern minds from honest thinking, and they segregated the Negro from everything."

Summoning "the Old Negro spiritual," he likened the marchers to "the mighty men of Joshua [who] merely walked about the walled city of Jericho and the barriers to freedom came tumbling down." King's cadences finally soared, his eyes gleaming and his arm extended, as others on the stage egged him on, and the audience, mesmerized, responded as if in church.

> I know you are asking today, "How long will it take?" . . . I come to say to you this afternoon, however difficult the moment, however frustrating the hour, it will not be long, because truth pressed to earth will rise again.
>
> How long? Not long, because no lie can live forever.
>
> How long? Not long, because you shall reap what you sow.
>
> How long? Not long—"Truth forever on the scaffold, Wrong forever on the throne,— / Yet that scaffold sways the future, and, behind the dim unknown / Standeth God within the shadow, keeping watch above his own."
>
> How long? Not long, because the arc of the moral universe is long, but it bends toward justice.
>
> How long? Not long, 'cause mine eyes have seen the glory of the coming of the Lord. He is trampling out the vineyard where the

grapes of wrath are stored. He has loosed the fateful lightning of
his terrible swift sword. His truth is marching on.*

In the wake of the great march the federal legislation moved swiftly. Dirksen intoned, "How then shall there be government by the people if some of the people cannot speak? How obtain the consent of the governed when a segment of those governed cannot express themselves?" On the Senate floor the southern demagogues who had successfully filibustered nearly every other major piece of civil rights legislation were outnumbered and resigned to defeat. In fact the most significant risk to the bill came from liberals who wanted to strengthen it, thus potentially upending bipartisan accord.

The sweeping legislation brought federal oversight and protection to voting throughout the South. Section 2 declared, "No voting qualification or prerequisite to voting, or standard, practice, or procedure shall be imposed or applied by any State or political subdivision to deny or abridge the right of any citizen of the United States to vote on account of race or color." Other sections banned literacy tests as a qualification for voting. In effect the statute gave the attorney general and private individuals the right to sue to uphold its provisions. In the past, southern judges, appointed with the approval of segregationist senators, often would not enforce such after-the-fact lawsuits, a chief weakness of earlier civil rights laws. Hence the most transformative part of the law: under Section 5 states with literacy tests and a history of discrimination and low turnout could not change voting laws without approval from the Justice Department or a federal court in Washington.

The legislation did not, however, prohibit poll taxes. A constitutional amendment had already been ratified to ban them in federal contests; now Senator Edward M. Kennedy of Massachusetts fought for an

*President Barack Obama has the speech's most famous line, "the arc of the moral universe," stitched into the rug in the Oval Office.

amendment barring the practice in state elections as well. In response Dirksen threatened to pull support for the bill. Kennedy's proposal lost in the Senate, but the House version of the legislation included it. A conference committee established to reconcile the two versions deadlocked; even now, despite all the pressure, long-standing congressional inertia threatened to take hold. Finally anxious lawmakers brokered a compromise: the bill would not bar poll taxes but would order the Justice Department to sue those southern states that still used them.

A century before, lawmakers turned to the abolitionist Wendell Phillips to bless the weakened Fifteenth Amendment. Now Johnson's aides recruited King. He abhorred the poll tax but worried that the entire bill could collapse—the practical politician trumping the voice of moral witness—so he wrote a letter endorsing the compromise. The liberals too agreed to the weaker bill. The Voting Rights Act passed the House 328 to 74 and passed the Senate 79 to 18. Immediately and unpredictably it began to transform the lives and politics of millions.

John Lewis had a remarkable conversation with Johnson the day he signed the bill into law. Decades later, by then a senior congressman, Lewis recounted his wide-eyed encounter as a twenty-two-year-old. "Now John," Johnson told the activist, "you've got to go back and get all those folks registered. You've got to go back and get those boys by the *balls*. Just like a bull gets on top of a cow. You've got to get 'em by the balls and you've got to *squeeze*, squeeze 'em til they *hurt*."

The year before, in the registration drive known as Freedom Summer, activists tried to sign up Black voters in Mississippi and were met with violence from white residents. Now civil rights groups registered African American voters under federal supervision, with immediate success. In Mississippi, African American registration leaped from 6.7 percent in 1964 to 59.3 percent four years later and 71 percent by 1998. Similar levels of Black civic participation were found across the South. The Second Reconstruction took root.

Yet if the extension of the vote to African Americans helped produce epochal political change, it was not solely of the sort that Johnson and Lewis had imagined. The previous year, in 1964, Johnson had signed the Civil Rights Act. His press secretary Bill Moyers recalled, "When he signed the act he was euphoric, but late that very night I found him in a melancholy mood as he lay in bed reading the bulldog edition of the *Washington Post* with headlines celebrating the day. I asked him what was troubling him. 'I think we just delivered the South to the Republican party for a long time to come,' he said." The 1964 Republican presidential nominee, Barry Goldwater, had opposed the Civil Rights Act. Running for president in 1968 Richard Nixon, who as vice president had been an NAACP favorite, embraced a "southern strategy" to pull white voters to the GOP. By the new century voting in the South had polarized. Over several decades, the white Solid South switched party labels—first in its votes for president, then in its votes for Congress, and finally for local office. In Mississippi in 2004, for example, 85 percent of white voters backed George W. Bush for president, while 90 percent of Black voters supported John Kerry. This polarization thus was evident well before Barack Obama became president.

The Voting Rights Act became a touchstone of consensus between Democrats and Republicans. Perhaps this is because its partisan impact was unclear; perhaps it is because the act created the first substantial bloc of Black officeholders, while allowing white Republicans to make overall gains. Congress reauthorized it in 1970, 1975, 1982, and 2006. Over the years its coverage was broadened, especially to eliminate barriers to voting by non-English speakers. It was generally regarded as the most effective civil rights law ever enacted, until the U.S. Supreme Court eviscerated it in 2013.

"Polltaxia"

Two constitutional amendments hastened the trend of broadening the base of voters and marked the fourth and fifth time that the phrase "the right to vote" was added to the Constitution.

The Twenty-fourth Amendment, ratified the year before the Voting Rights Act in 1964, banned the poll tax in federal elections. This was the provision that exerted such a pull in the congressional debate over the statute. It seems counterintuitive that a constitutional amendment—a permanent change—would come *before* legislation on the same topic. The reason illuminates how politics, advocacy, class, and race intersect in the fight for free and fair elections.

The poll tax was riveted into place starting in the 1890s as part of the disenfranchising laws and constitutions. By 1904 every ex-Confederate state had adopted it. The tax kept poor Black and white citizens from voting. In 1900, when three-quarters of the population in those states had an average annual income of $55 to $64, the poll tax was typically a hefty $1. Frequently the tax would be assessed retroactively, so that voters were charged for the previous year's unpaid assessment. As a way of marshaling support, labor unions or party bosses sometimes paid the poll tax of a voter.

The first attempt to dismantle the tax came from the New Dealers of the 1930s, who emphasized class and economic fairness rather than race. They spoke for "the forgotten man at the bottom of the economic pyramid," as Roosevelt put it. Three southern states eliminated the poll tax by the end of the 1930s. North Carolina was first, in 1920. Then Huey Long, the populist demagogue who ruled Louisiana as governor and then, long distance, as senator, fought hard to repeal the tax in 1934. His opponents labeled a repeal "an entering wedge for Negro suffrage," but Long pointed out that the state's white primary would keep that from happening. His biographer T. Harry Williams writes, "[The] only effect of the poll tax was to keep 250,000 white men and women from voting, he claimed, charging that this was the real reason the conservatives wanted to retain it." Reassured voters overwhelmingly approved a state constitutional amendment repealing the tax. In Florida the liberal firebrand Senator Claude Pepper had won repeal of the poll tax in 1937. Pepper rightly claimed the repeal "contributed to my very large majority" among white voters.

Roosevelt was endlessly timid when it came to challenging the South's caste system, neither lion nor fox. But in 1938, with his program stymied by southern reactionaries in the Senate, he launched what became known as "the purge," a bid to oust conservative Democrats in primaries. FDR privately wrote to the southern liberal Aubrey Williams, "I think the South agrees with you and me. One difficulty is that three-quarters of the whites in the South cannot vote—poll tax etc." He began to edge toward speaking out. The poll tax was a "remnant of the period of the time of the Revolution," he told reporters, and he wrote an Arkansas activist that it was "inevitably contrary to fundamental democracy and its representative form of government in which we believe." FDR's purge failed spectacularly. Challengers lost in Georgia and South Carolina. A chastened Roosevelt retreated. "At no time and in no manner did I ever suggest federal legislation of any kind to deprive states of their rights directly or indirectly to impose the poll tax," he assured one bristling southern senator.

But the issue had become a central plank in the national liberal agenda. In 1940 voter turnout nationwide neared 60 percent; in Alabama, Mississippi, South Carolina, and Georgia it reached no higher than 20 percent. Progressives joined Republicans to derisively label the region "Polltaxia." In 1942, with strong support from First Lady Eleanor Roosevelt, Congress passed a nationwide Soldier Voting Act, which allowed servicemen to vote absentee in federal elections without paying the tax. The NAACP joined with a new coalition of churches, schools, the YMCA and YWCA and other groups, called the Southern Conference for Human Welfare, to mount a national campaign. That in turn spawned the National Committee to Abolish the Poll Tax. National legislation was brought to the floor of Congress and filibustered by southerners. By 1953 all but the Deep South states had repealed the tax. Eventually an end to the poll tax became the safest civil rights measure a politician could advance.

In fact a constitutional amendment to repeal the tax was proposed by

Florida senator Spessard Holland, a staunch defender of white supremacy. Strikingly, the NAACP opposed it. "It is a travesty," civil rights advocates blared, "to call a constitutional amendment a civil rights measure when Congress has the constitutional power to abolish the poll tax by legislation." They worried an amendment would set a pattern for delay. Despite their opposition, President Kennedy and the Democrats, looking for a chance to show some progress on civil rights in the era before King's great triumphs, moved it through Congress. Slipping past a southern filibuster, they brought to the Senate floor a bill to declare Alexander Hamilton's house a national monument—and then replaced all the text with a constitutional amendment repealing the poll tax. Congress sent it to the states in 1962. Of note, the repeal boosted white voting rates immediately; it did not markedly do so for Black voters, whose participation rates stayed low until the Voting Rights Act the next year.

The story has one more twist. The amendment barred poll taxes only in federal elections. When the Justice Department brought the suits ordered by the Voting Rights Act, the Supreme Court struck down the remaining state laws. But it was an odd opinion, the height of judicial hubris. The justices never mentioned the newly minted constitutional amendment or the clear vote of Congress. Instead, as law professors Bruce Ackerman and Jennifer Nou explain, Justice William O. Douglas relied on the Court's own interpretation of the Bill of Rights—consigning the public's constitution-making to a footnote.

"Youth in Its Protest Must Be Heard"

One more constitutional change expanded the right to vote, the second in less than a decade. The Twenty-sixth Amendment lowered the voting age around the country to eighteen. As with some previous advances of the vote, this grew out of military conflict—but with a twist. Voting was not seen as a reward for service but as a diversion for those angrily opposed to the Vietnam War.

The United States first imposed a peacetime draft in September 1940, just months after Paris fell to Hitler's armies and weeks before the presidential election. At first "only those twenty-one or older" were drafted. But in 1943, as the country readied for the invasion of Europe, the draft age was lowered to eighteen. Once again a large number of men who could not vote were asked to bear arms. The draft continued after Japan surrendered, as the Cold War between the United States and the Soviet Union settled into place. Ongoing conscription was new for the United States, a factor in the unprecedented national cohesion and common identity frequently evident during the Cold War. It lasted for nearly three decades.

Only fitfully, though, did it produce a demand to give eighteen-year-olds the right to vote. The first proposal was introduced in Congress shortly after the draft age was lowered. Republicans tended to be more enthusiastic than Democrats (as they had been about the Fifteenth and Nineteenth Amendments), and Dwight Eisenhower endorsed the idea when he ran for president. States' rights still dominated Democrats' wary views on voting law changes. The proposal gained little traction. The stereotypically quiescent young people of the early postwar era posed little political threat.

Once again war, this time the Vietnam War, forced the issue, but in an unexpected way. In previous conflicts the heroic stance of young men fighting bravely in a stirringly rendered cause lent moral weight to the demand for suffrage. "The bullet and the ballot go together," as was said after the Civil War.

As has been widely chronicled (by Baby Boomers themselves, of course, endlessly), teenagers and young adults had swelled to the largest ever share of the population. "Youth" dominated not just music and fashion but the popular imagination. *Time* magazine named "25 and Under" its iconic "Man of the Year" in 1966. And starting in 1967 a movement against the Vietnam War staged increasingly visible protests. Politicians began to fret over the young like the confused suburban parents in *The*

Graduate. Within the Democratic Party it was called the New Politics. When Minnesota senator Eugene McCarthy challenged incumbent Lyndon Johnson in 1968, college students hitchhiked to starchy New Hampshire to canvass for him in the first-in-the-nation primary. Told to shave, get haircuts, and put on proper clothes, the students went "clean for Gene." When Robert F. Kennedy entered the race after McCarthy's unexpected strong showing, he began by touring college campuses, challenging students in an existential campaign of personal authenticity. Journalists noted that for all the enthusiasm demonstrated in packed gymnasiums, most of RFK's rapturous listeners could not vote. That summer angry clashes between young protesters and the Chicago police wrecked the Democratic National Convention. In 1969, after a year of quiescence, the antiwar movement rallied again, with the massive November Mobilization—this time enlisting a wide swath of moderate young people, as well as their elders.

Politicians began to urge, practically to plead, for a lower voting age. Representative Ken Hechler from West Virginia was a former speechwriter for Harry Truman. He wondered "whether the violence, animal energy, and nihilistic attacks on the 'Establishment' could not be tempered and directed into useful channels if opportunities for expression were afforded at the ballot box." Another congressman insisted, "In these troubled times, [lowering the voting age] will give us the opportunity to bridge the 'generation gap' by reaching out to the youth of the Nation." One senator consoled colleagues that the radicals "probably feel that the system that they want to overthrow is, in their mind, so bad that they would not even participate anyway." A national commission on the causes of violence urged giving the vote to eighteen-year-olds as a way to prevent crime and urban rioting. Not everyone agreed: the day after President Nixon gave his speech in 1969 calling on the "silent majority" of Americans to stand up against protesters, New Jersey voters went to the polls and defeated a proposal to lower the voting age. Some good-government groups and college organizations lobbied. One adopted the groovy name L.U.V. (Let Us Vote). Its leader promoted it on *The Dating Game* and other television shows. Student organizers teamed up with teachers unions to urge action, in an earnest but not earth-shaking drive. (One West Virginia senator warned them that they needed to "overcome the image of demonstrators and beatniks.")

Senator Edward M. Kennedy of Massachusetts and Majority Leader Mike Mansfield of Montana saw a legislative opportunity. The Voting Rights Act would expire in June 1970. Southerners put aside plans for a filibuster, hoping to speed a favored nominee for the Supreme Court. Kennedy and Mansfield announced an effort to attach a legislative rider lowering the voting age to eighteen, in time for the 1972 presidential election. Momentum faltered. The Senate passed the measure with the provision included. On April 28, 1970, the president opposed the move, arguing—with much justification—that only a constitutional amendment could lower the age nationwide.

Then, two days later, Nixon surprised the nation with a prime-time televised address from the Oval Office. Gravely pointing at a map of Indochina, he announced that the United States had invaded Cambodia in an effort to clear out North Vietnamese troops. Campuses exploded in protest. At Kent State University in Ohio, students burned down the ROTC building. On May 4 a rally of one thousand undergraduates gathered on the college green. Ohio National Guard troops, the same age as the students, mostly working class, ordered them to disperse. Amid taunts and a hail of rocks, the guardsmen opened fire, killing four students and wounding nine. Within days undergraduates went on strike at roughly 750 college campuses across the country. One million students protested that month. Interior Secretary Walter Hickel wrote the president a quickly leaked letter of dissent, insisting, "Youth in its protest must be heard." As many as 100,000 demonstrators poured into Washington, massing on the Mall.

Nixon was stretched taut. He held an agitated televised press conference at the White House as army troops slipped into hidden positions to defend the building. Into the early hours he made phone call after phone call, forty-seven in all. At 4:35 a.m., with his valet in tow, he set off for a predawn visit to the Lincoln Memorial. After viewing the statue, he encountered a handful of startled protestors on the Memorial's marble steps. "I know that probably most of you think I'm an S.O.B., but I want you to know that I understand just how you feel." He bantered with them on the war, dissent, surfing, and college football. Then he led a growing entourage to the deserted Capitol building, where he chatted with the overnight staff, signed a Bible for a cleaning woman, and sat at his old House desk. His chief of staff, H. R. Haldeman, confided in his diary that it had been the "weirdest day so far."

The killings at Kent State and their aftermath, Mansfield and Kennedy now insisted, compelled action. The day after Nixon's surreal nocturnal visit, Mansfield threatened a filibuster if the voting age provision were not passed. "There will either be an 18-year-old vote this year," he told reporters, "or there won't be an extension of the Voting Rights Act." House opposition crumbled. Nixon wrote to his aide John Erlichman, "Give someone direct orders and responsibility to stop this: highest priority." But he knew he had to sign the bill. Little more than a month after Kent State, Nixon signed the Voting Rights Act extension. He urged a quick Court test of its constitutionality.

That did not take long. In December 1970, in *Oregon v. Mitchell*, the Supreme Court confirmed that the president had been right: Congress can set the voting age for federal elections, but only states could do so for state races. Now panicked election officials weighed in. With the presidential contest approaching, they faced the nightmarish task of keeping two sets of books and registering two sets of voters. Chaos could overtake elections if Congress did not pass a constitutional amendment, and quickly. In March the Senate voted for the amendment 94 to 0, and the House with only a few dissenting votes. It met success in state after state, and in July it was ratified.

It was widely assumed that eighteen-year-olds would vote Democratic, becoming part of the New Politics coalition. "As of now, the nation's newest voters would defeat Nixon," wrote political scientist Samuel Lubell in *Look* magazine. In *Rolling Stone* the gonzo journalist Hunter S. Thompson enthused, "Surely the 25 million baby boomers between the ages of 18 and 25 would jam the polls, elect [antiwar senator George] McGovern and end the war. . . . Think of it: Only 10 percent! Enough, even according to Nixon's own wizards—to swing almost any election."

Actually, many more young people were conservative than was recognized. Most were traditional, did not attend college, or felt alienated by their more radical cohort. According to historian Rick Perlstein, Nixon came to see the amendment as a wedge to split the Democrats: "The people most terrified of the 18 year old vote were Old Politics Democrats afraid of New Politics primary challenges." The presumed coalition of the young, minorities, and the college-educated simply was not large enough—and in fact would alienate more voters than it attracted. Nixon won a majority of the youth vote in 1972. That imaginary winning liberal coalition would not achieve enough demographic heft to prevail until thirty-six years later, when Barack Obama ran for president.

The Age of Democracy

The Voting Rights Act, coupled with the Supreme Court's briefly aggressive jurisprudence, broke open the possibilities of American democracy. Over the next decade an array of new laws changed the way elections worked.

Political parties faced sweeping change. Primaries had been used intermittently around the country. After the 1968 election—in which Hubert Humphrey won the Democratic presidential nomination without directly winning any primaries—the Democratic Party rewrote its rules. Primaries would now determine the presidential nominee (with scattered remnants of caucus systems) and become near universal for lower offices. The results were profound and not always edifying. Voters had a greater say. It became easier to stage a popular insurgency against party leaders, as unhappiness over the Vietnam War gave moral force to the push for primaries. Over time, however, primaries would distort American politics. They favored self-nominated, often wealthy individuals willing to invest in purchasing positive name recognition through television advertising. Eventually they pulled the parties to their ideological extremes, as low-turnout electorates focused on philosophical loyalty rather than general election opportunities. But primaries also became seen as a sign of responsiveness and a driver of participation. The mesmerizing campaign for the Democratic nomination in 2008, which pitted a man who would be the first Black president against a candidate to be the first woman chief executive—all played out for months in public—validated the virtues of the voter-based nominating system. (The optics were slightly spurious, since Obama ultimately prevailed by eking out delegate victories in states with low-turnout caucuses.) Primaries are one of the only aspects of the American electoral system that other countries have begun to replicate, in part because of their populist sheen. In many democracies it continues to be a slur to describe a political innovation—such as the arrival of political consultants and the new focus on candidate personality rather than party ideology—as "American." The use of primaries and direct votes are now seen as a way to pierce the anomie and indifference slowly overtaking politics even in countries with greater turnout. They may also destabilize party leadership, as they have in the United States.

Other laws followed. In 1974, during Watergate, Congress enacted campaign finance contribution limits and public financing for presidential campaigns. In 1993, recognizing that voter registration rates remained too low—they had actually fallen from 1972 to 1992, with registration among the poorest one-fifth of voters falling by a third during that time—a ragtag group of activists and academic experts persuaded Congress to pass the National Voter Registration Act, known colloquially as

"Motor Voter." President Bill Clinton, calling it "our newest civil rights law," happily signed the measure. It required state departments of motor vehicles and social welfare agencies to make registration forms available. It also allowed citizens nationwide to register to vote by mail. At first it was markedly successful, and registration rates increased, especially among the poor. Registration remained high at motor vehicle offices. Few social service offices complied with the law, though, and Republican governors proved reluctant to enforce it. The overall impact, while positive, remained murky.

In the 1970s, 1980s and 1990s, American democracy won a formal openness unprecedented in its history. How far we had come from the earliest days, when only white men with property could vote: working men, then Black men, then women, the poor, the young—all won the right to vote. All won the ability to participate meaningfully.

Yet something was not right. Turnout began to fall, inexorably. In 1964, with the nation convulsed by the civil rights movement and reeling from the Kennedy assassination, 63 percent of eligible voters cast ballots. By 1996, with Democrat Clinton coasting to victory over Republican Bob Dole, while the Republicans retained control of Congress, turnout barely scraped past 50 percent. Half of eligible voters stayed home. Politics had increasingly become a spectator sport. Political parties now were bank accounts through which candidates could funnel funds for what mattered to them most: thirty-second television advertisements. As voting dropped, campaign costs continued to soar.

The stasis of American politics seemed to reach its peak as the 2000 election approached, when two candidates seemed headed for a close finish in the race for the presidency.

PART IV

THE MODERN FIGHT TO VOTE

11

Lost Decade

AMERICAN DEMOCRACY is once again under significant pressure, facing trends it has not seen in decades. The cracks first began to show in the antic days of the recount in Florida.

At 3:00 a.m. on November 8, 2000, Vice President Al Gore phoned Texas governor George W. Bush. It was, as the *Washington Post* called it, "perhaps the strangest phone call in American political history." Earlier that night television networks had called the pivotal state of Florida first for Gore, then for Bush. The vice president was minutes from delivering his concession speech when aides intercepted him.

"Circumstances have changed dramatically since I first called you," Gore told Bush. "The state of Florida is too close to call."

"Are you saying what I think you're saying? Let me make sure I understand. You're calling back to retract that concession?"

"Don't get snippy about it," Gore replied.

Bush blurted out a response that revealed much: "My little brother says it's over." Jeb Bush was serving his first term as Florida's governor.

"With all due respect to your little brother," Gore replied, "he is not the final arbiter of who wins Florida."

Through the following weeks of recount, court fights, street theater, and Supreme Court intervention, Governor Jeb Bush's control of the election machinery proved decisive. The recount fiasco surely was an extraordinary occurrence, the only time since 1876 that a presidential election had drawn so close (and the first time since 1888 that the winner of the popular vote would lose the Electoral College). But it also revealed something much more mundane. Florida's election system had rotted as if touched by the state's humidity: at every level it was rife with error and prone to abuse. The narrow margin signaled to partisans just how important it was to control those mechanisms of elections. As politicians from Boss Tweed to Lyndon Johnson to Richard Daley might have understood, the counting was as important as the voting. For the first time since television advertising began to dominate American politics in the 1960s, turning out the vote (and not just winning over a handful of moderate "swing voters") became a principal goal of campaigns. That meant tremendous partisan advantage could be obtained not only by mobilizing supporters to vote but also by blocking opponents' opportunity to vote.

Party politics provided the energy, just as it had at other periods of American history. In the early 1800s the Democrats fought to expand the franchise. Then, in the wake of the Civil War, Democrats fought to restrict the vote in the South, and Republicans to widen it there while limiting it in the North. In the twentieth century Democrats fought for civil rights, but Republicans such as Everett Dirksen joined them. Now, unambiguously, it was the Republican Party that took on a sharply partisan role: driving not to expand the vote but to contract it.

537 Votes

With pained fascination Americans watched the slapdash Florida recount as it pinballed among local election boards, courtrooms in Tallahassee, and two trips to the U.S. Supreme Court. The nation learned to distinguish a "hanging chad" (when the voter partially punched through the ballot to mark a vote) from a "dimpled chad" (an attempt that never broke through). In a reverse Selma, Republican congressional staff members and lobbyists from Washington descended on Florida to stop the counting. A raucous demonstration disrupted one election board session. The protesters pounded on windows, bellowing "Stop the fraud," and prevented the Miami-Dade board from continuing its count. It became known as "the Brooks Brothers Riot."

A recount ordered by the Florida Supreme Court at last was under way when the U.S. Supreme Court halted it. On December 11, 2000, by a vote of 5 to 4, the justices effectively handed the presidency to Bush. The Court reasoned that different counties' varying standards for conducting recounts and tallying votes violated the Fourteenth Amendment's Equal Protection Clause. It was implausible enough that the conservative justices used such a novel, elastic interpretation. After all, states, not the federal government, have plenary power over the method of voting for president. If differences among counties are unconstitutional, what about gaps between states? Even more jarring, the Court majority stressed that its ruling "is limited to the present circumstances, for the problem of equal protection in election processes generally presents many complexities." Some were reminded of the tape recorder in the television show *Mission Impossible*, which self-destructed in a puff of smoke after giving its instructions. Legally, the justices insisted, their ruling had no value as precedent. No high court opinion would cite it since. Bush's victory margin was 537 votes, out of almost 6 million cast in the state. Nationally Gore won a half million more popular votes than his rival, but Bush won the vote that counted: the Electoral College, 271 to 266. For years afterward Justice Antonin Scalia, when challenged about the ruling, would merrily reply, "Get over it!"

Harder to get over were the fissures exposed in the way America runs elections.

To begin, before the election state officials had struck from the rolls thousands of eligible Floridians. In 1997 Miami's mayoral election was overturned because of fraudulent absentee ballots; to prevent further mischief, the legislature ordered a purge of improper names from voter registration rolls. Florida's secretary of state hired a private company, Database Technologies (later part of ChoicePoint), to cull the state's rolls. The vendor compiled a list of 82,389 "possible" and "probable" felons. A month before the 2000 election the two lists were sent to county officials, compilations that totaled 1 percent of the electorate (and 3 percent of Black voters). The tallies were wildly inaccurate. The search used primitive methods, such as identifying voters who shared a common name and birth date with someone who had a criminal record. Reporters for *Vanity Fair* explained, "Middle initials didn't need to be the same; suffixes, such as Jr. and Sr., were ignored. Willie D. Whiting Jr., pastor, was caught because Willie J. Whiting was a felon. First and middle names could be switched around: Deborah Ann, Ann Deborah—same thing. Nicknames were fine—Robert, Bob, Bobby. The spelling of the last name didn't have to be exact, either. The only thing Willie Steen was guilty of was having a name similar to that of a felon named Willie O'Steen." A *Palm Beach Post* computer analysis found "at least 1,100 eligible voters wrongly purged from the rolls." Other investigations were even more alarming. One county checked each of the 694 names on the culled list provided by the state; it could confirm only thirty-four as former felons.

This Keystone Kops purge magnified a problem dating to the disenfranchising constitution that followed the Civil War: In November 2000 Florida was one of nine states that permanently barred from voting anyone convicted of a felony, unless the government decided to restore the person's rights. The practice of denying the vote to ex-felons has long-standing constitutional provenance. The Fourteenth Amendment authorizes it. But the Jim Crow constitutions crafted provisions to target African Americans, who could be stripped of voting rights due to elastic and ill-defined offenses. States' rules varied greatly. In Florida possession of one ounce of marijuana could have meant a lifetime bar on voting, while in Maine first-degree murderers could vote. The silent disenfranchisement magnified as the size of America's criminal justice system expanded. The state and federal prison population in the United States more than quadrupled from 1980 to 2000, and the ranks of those without voting rights swelled. By the time of the contest between Bush and Gore, 827,000 Floridians were disenfranchised, or about 7.5 percent of the state's voting-age citizens. Most were on parole or probation or had finished their sentences altogether. Nationwide, as of 2010 nearly 6 million otherwise eligible Americans were barred from voting due to a past criminal conviction.

In Florida as in other states, the voter registration rolls were a sloppy mess. The names were kept by individual counties, with no statewide database. Some had computers; others kept the rolls on scraps of paper stored in boxes. The tallies were filled with duplications, errors, and names of people who had moved away or died. Here Florida's problems were not markedly worse than in other states.

Then there was the porous and partisan nature of election administration itself. Part-time, poorly trained officials made key decisions in the state's sixty-seven counties. Some were harshly partisan, but most were simply overwhelmed. In West Palm Beach an earnest local official designed a "butterfly ballot" that spread the candidates' names across a page. She hoped it would help the area's elderly voters. Instead it confused them; many tried to vote for Gore but ended up punching their ballot for independent candidate Patrick Buchanan. The former Nixon speechwriter and Ronald Reagan aide had controversially quipped that Capitol Hill is "Israeli occupied territory," while denouncing the prosecution of a concentration camp guard. West Palm Beach's elderly Jewish voters were unlikely to have kvelled over his candidacy. Bush campaign spokesman Ari Fleischer gamely insisted that Palm Beach County was a "Buchanan stronghold." Even Buchanan's campaign stoutly acknowledged that was "nonsense."

Florida's chief legal officer, Attorney General Robert Butterworth, served as Gore's state campaign chair. Its secretary of state, Katherine Harris, supervised both the election and the recount while serving as Bush's campaign cochair. Privately she compared herself to the Old Testament's Queen Esther, who sacrificed herself to save the Jewish people. "If I perish, I perish," she told her staff as the recount ground on. Harris would soon ride her celebrity to a seat in Congress. Florida was far from unique in having elections run by a partisan. In thirty states that year the public elected the senior election official, usually the secretary of state, meaning that adherents of one party or another controlled the machinery of elections.

Troubling racial patterns also marred the 2000 election in Florida. According to an investigation by the U.S. Commission on Civil Rights, officials rejected a total of 180,000 ballots in the state for one reason or another, but African American voters were nearly ten times more likely than white voters to have their ballots turned away. American University Professor Allan Lichtman conducted the statistical study for the commission. He calculates that if ballots cast by Black voters were accepted at around the rate of those cast by white voters, Gore would have won Florida by forty thousand votes.

Florida 2000 quickly passed into memory as an oddity, a quirk of the Electoral College and of the state's swampy politics. Like the "Y2K bug" that some feared would crash the world's computers at the stroke of millennial midnight earlier that year, it was soon overshadowed by the terrorist attacks and wars in Afghanistan and Iraq. If remembered, it was seen as a somewhat amusing artifact of more innocent times. Americans "got over it."

Partisans drew a different lesson. Turnout now mattered more than ever, and suppressing that turnout could provide the margin of victory.

The Ramshackle Election System

As the Florida debacle showed, the machinery of American elections had grown rickety. The voting machines used in New York offered a fit symbol. In the nineteenth century ballot boxes could be seen floating in the river on Election Day, tossed into the current by Democrats or

Republicans. At the turn of the twentieth century, as local lore has it, a technological solution was deemed wise. The fix called for voting machines that were *too heavy* to throw into the river. A century later those machines were still in use and still too heavy to throw in the river, but they broke regularly, miscounted votes, and were easy to manipulate. The manufacturer had long since gone out of business. Many voters loved the old machines and the ritual of drawing the curtain closed, flicking levers, and pulling a bar to record the vote. But they didn't work.

In many ways the entire voting system was just as decrepit.

A nationwide analysis by MIT and the California Institute of Technology found that "between four and six million presidential votes were lost in the 2000 election. These are qualified voters who wanted to vote but could not or were not counted." Of those, as many as 3 million votes were lost because of voter registration problems, such as when citizens who are legitimately registered show up on Election Day to find that they are not on the rolls. Antiquated and paper-based, the voter registration rolls were full of mistakes, names of the deceased, double entries, and more. In much of the country many more people were registered than lived in the area where they were supposed to vote.

Fitfully, in the wake of the Florida recount, efforts began to fix voter registration. In 2002 Congress passed the Help America Vote Act, requiring states to create a computerized statewide database of registered voters and to try to ensure that only eligible, living people were on it. But implementation created another set of problems. Many states charged forward with flawed purges that would have erased eligible voters. Others set up a system that would block women who had changed their name at marriage or voters whose names contained a typographical error and thus did not match their driver's license file. Church groups and voter registration advocates sued, and federal courts blocked what was called "disenfranchisement by typo." By the decade's end most states had culled their rolls and created a digital master file, though some big states lagged. Oddly California, home of Silicon Valley, was the last to create a workable list, getting one ready only for the 2016 election.

Many of these problems were long unsolved. A decade after the recount the Pew Center on the States reported that one of every eight names on the voter rolls was no longer valid or was significantly inaccurate. Nearly 2 million dead people were still registered, though there is no evidence that they are enthusiastically voting. And 2.75 million people had registrations in more than one state. Officials at times can be overwhelmed, as when sixty million paper registration forms swamped the states in just two years.

Yet 51 million eligible voters—nearly one in four—were not on the rolls at all. One in four people mistakenly believed their registration automatically updates when they move. Twenty-six million voting-age Americans move every year; when they do, many of them fall off the rolls. A study by a Harvard political scientist, Thomas Patterson, concluded that one-third of unregistered voters were people "who had moved and hadn't re-registered." A 2001 commission chaired by former presidents Jimmy Carter and Gerald Ford concluded, "The registration laws in force throughout the United States are among the world's most demanding . . . [and are] one reason why voter turnout in the United States is near the bottom of the developed world."

In fact the United States is one of the few democracies in which the onus of registration rests overwhelmingly with the individual. It falls to private actors—political parties and nonpartisan voter registration groups—to gather millions of names for voter rolls. In 2008, hindered by errors committed by private voter registration efforts, one third of the names submitted did not result in a new registration or address change. Often citizens submitted their names without realizing that they were already registered. In many states voter registration forms must be turned in to the government even if the organization gathering them believes them to be duplicates or doubts their veracity.

The saga of the Association of Community Organizations for Reform Now (ACORN) demonstrates the perils of relying on low-paid voter registration workers. The antipoverty group was one of the country's most potent forces for registering poor people, and its successes drew controversy. In Florida, for example, after the group won a minimum wage increase by ballot initiative, the legislature began to crack down on its voter registration work. Eventually ACORN entangled itself in snafus. In some states it paid registration workers by the number of names gathered. Controls were inadequate; not surprisingly many sign-ups were dubious. The group vetted the names and tried to flag questionable entries, but unsympathetic officials responded harshly. In 2007, for example, three temporary ACORN canvassers pleaded guilty to submitting 1,800 fake names. The names of professional football players were falsely submitted, as was "Jive Turkey." The bogus names did not make it onto the voter rolls, though—and certainly there is no evidence they voted. "Mickey Mouse" never showed up to vote—even in Orlando, where he lives. In a presidential debate in 2008 Senator John McCain blustered that ACORN "is now on the verge of maybe perpetrating one of the greatest frauds in voter history in this country, maybe destroying the fabric of democracy." The ACORN controversy, as the scholar Rick Hasen notes, was a "gift from heaven" to those alleging voter fraud. Soon after the 2008 election Congress pulled grant money for low-income housing built by the organization, and ACORN quickly collapsed. Registration of the poor took a measurable hit.

Then there were the machines. Once considered space-age technology, the Votomatic device produced a punch card for every vote, which it then recorded. However, error rates were high. So, in addition to its fitful attempt to improve voter registration, the 2002 federal law pushed a technological fix: it required the wholesale adoption of electronic voting machines.

The computerized systems prompted intense skepticism, especially among Democrats, who feared that the machines could be hacked and reprogrammed to benefit Republicans. It didn't help when the CEO of

Diebold, one of the few firms that manufacture electronic voting devices, avowed his commitment "to helping Ohio deliver its electoral votes to the President." Among progressive activists heated conspiracy speculations drew guaranteed applause. Even four years later the Fox cartoon *The Simpsons* was spoofing the fears of and the potential for fraud. Homer Simpson enters a voting booth: "Ooh, one of those electronic voting dealies." He taps the screen for Obama, and the machine purrs, "One vote for McCain. Thank you."

"No, I wanna vote for Obama." He taps again.

"Two votes for McCain."

"C'mon! It's time for a change!" He jabs at the screen again.

"Three votes for McCain."

"No! No! No!"

"Six votes . . . for *President* McCain."

As a vacuum sucks Homer into the machine, he gasps his last words: "This doesn't happen in America. Maybe in Ohio!" (He still gets an "I voted" sticker.)

There is little actual evidence of manipulation of the machines, though the new devices were not without risk. A task force of top computer scientists and election security experts examined the devices and concluded that they could, in fact, be hacked with a PalmPilot. (Cutting-edge! It was 2006, after all.) But security can be greatly enhanced if the machines produce an "audit trail," such as paper records, which are then randomly checked and can serve as the basis of a recount. Ballot security activists won those changes in three quarters of the states, and the voting machine scare receded, a rare quiet victory in the voting fights.

Overall, however, the electoral system began to show its age. Election administration varies widely among states, counties, and towns. The United States has inherited state control and local autonomy—a system that grows out of the fact that the thirteen independent states had varying voting rules at the time of the Revolution. No unified election administration was conceivable as long as the slave South would be at risk of federal oversight. So the states reigned supreme in election administration and in turn handed the job down to local government control. Three thousand counties run our elections, with nearly 180,000 precincts and 114,000 separate polling places. No national standards govern matters such as how many voting machines there should be in each location.

So, yes, there was much work to be done in the decade after Florida. But that's not what happened.

Hunting for Fraud

Instead conservative activists focused on one thing that *hadn't* occurred: voter fraud, specifically voter impersonation at the polls. The remedies sought for this phantom threat have a very tangible consequence: they make it harder to vote, in ways that especially affect Democrats.

Of course American history offers ample evidence of *election* fraud—that is, misconduct organized by party officials or other political operatives designed to sway results. In the nineteenth century they might have stuffed a ballot box; in the twentieth century there might have been an attempt to manipulate absentee ballots (for example, by filling them out for patients at a nursing home). Purportedly independent political committees with names that obscure funding sources also pose the risk of illegality. But *voter* fraud—especially impersonation at the polling place—remains exceedingly rare. After all, the candidate who benefits gains little from one more vote, but the costs to the voter, if caught, are high. In Wisconsin, where a single improper vote can bring a $10,000 fine and three years in prison, a federal judge tartly noted that "a person would have to be insane to commit voter impersonation fraud." As for the fear that noncitizens and undocumented immigrants are voting in droves, that too poses a logical problem; few individuals would trek from home, find their way across the border, evade capture, then march into a government office and declare their name and address. Justin Levitt of Loyola University writes, "Voter fraud, in particular, has the feel of a bank heist caper: roundly condemned but technically fascinating, and sufficiently lurid to grab and hold headlines." It is also like a bank robbery in another way: such heists, once common, are no longer a significant problem. Technology has improved the security of vaults, and bank robbers now routinely get caught. Facing the cost-benefit analysis, would-be Bonnie and Clydes no longer try their luck. (In contrast electronic theft from financial institutions is sky high.)

The focus on fraud has deep roots in founding-era worries that the poor would sell their votes and in Gilded Age fears expressed by Protestants about immigrant voters. Today it is embedded within the modern conservative movement.

Elements on the right long had arched eyebrows at the unruly passions of the masses. During the 1950s Russell Kirk invoked the long-forgotten figure of John Randolph of Roanoke ("I am an aristocrat. I hate equality. I love liberty") as a patron for conservative thinkers. Kirk gave the nascent New Right intellectual heft. His volume on Randolph makes jarring reading, as Kirk praises him for his devotion to freehold suffrage for property owners and opposition to "one man, one vote." The white southerners who moved en masse to the Republican Party after civil rights legislation brought a harsh edge to the call for states' rights. Those concerns melded with the idea that, somehow, the wrong people were being allowed to vote, that a bloated, profligate welfare state was being kept aloft by millions of new voters.

Conservative skepticism about voting hardened in response to Jimmy Carter's first major policy proposal as president in 1977. Noting that voter participation in the United States ranked twenty-first among democracies, Carter proposed a nationwide system that would allow people to register on Election Day. He also urged public financing for congressional campaigns and an end to the Electoral College. At first, key Republican leaders warmed to the voting plan (the party chair called it "a Republican concept"). Within weeks, however, pressed by state party officials and conservative activists, the GOP set itself against the bill. The Republican National Committee magazine warned about "Fraud and Carter's Voter Registration Scheme." That November, Ohio voters overwhelmingly repealed that state's same-day registration law. Carter's plan never came for a vote before Congress.

A key moment in the conservative political alignment that dominated American politics for three decades came in Dallas in August 1980, just after the Republican convention at which Ronald Reagan became the party's presidential nominee. Evangelical voters had once been a bedrock Democratic Party constituency, but after the social upheavals of the 1960s and 1970s political activists organized churchgoers as a potent conservative force. The Religious Roundtable's National Affairs Briefing gathered fifteen thousand people, mostly ministers, to hear Reagan speak. He consecrated a nontraditional political marriage between the Republican Party and the ascendant religious right, telling the crowd, "I know you can't endorse me, because this is a nonpartisan meeting—but I endorse you." The week's most controversial remark was made by the leader of the Southern Baptist Convention, who declared, "It is interesting at great political rallies how you have to have a Protestant to pray, a Catholic to pray, and then you have a Jew to pray. With all due respect to those dear people, my friends, God Almighty does not hear the prayer of a Jew." Badgered by reporters, Reagan found it necessary to disavow his backer's statement.

Far less attention was paid to what New Right organizer Paul Weyrich had said to warm up the crowd. "How many of our Christians have what I call the 'goo goo' syndrome—*good government*," he mocked. "They want *everybody* to vote. I don't want everybody to vote. Elections are not won by a majority of people. They never have been from the beginning of our country, and they are not now. As a matter of fact, our leverage in the elections quite candidly goes up as the voting populace goes down." Weyrich was a prolific founder of organizations and built an infrastructure of groups that lasted decades. One was the American

Legislative Exchange Council (ALEC), a business-backed outfit that drafted proposals to be introduced by conservative state legislators. The organization principally focused on deregulation and corporate concerns but later drew notice for embracing a model "stand your ground" law pushed by the National Rifle Association. (Someone who felt threatened no longer had to try to retreat but could use a firearm in self-defense. It became notorious after a volunteer "neighborhood watchman" killed an unarmed Black teenager, Trayvon Martin, though in the end he did not cite the law.) In 2009 ALEC drafted model voter identification bills, which were introduced in statehouses across the country. Weyrich also cofounded the Heritage Foundation, an activist conservative think tank that would become a potent popularizer of the specter of voter impersonation.

After the 2000 election Missouri became the epicenter of lurid rumors. John Ashcroft lost his U.S. Senate race even though his opponent, Mel Carnahan, had died three weeks earlier in a plane crash. (The popular but deceased Democratic candidate's name remained on the ballot. After he posthumously won, his widow was appointed to the seat.) Dead candidates, and dead voters, swirled in the imagination. Senator Kit Bond decried a Saint Louis court order that allowed polling places to stay open two hours later to accommodate voters, charging that the election had been stolen by "a major criminal enterprise designed to defraud voters." That year Saint Louis election officials alleged that thousands of people had voted despite listing vacant lots as their home. The *Post-Dispatch* investigated and found that all but a few of the lots did have homes on them. In all, in 2000 and 2002 there were only four substantiated cases of double voting in the state, an overall fraud rate of 0.0003 percent.

In fact every thorough study of voter impersonation has found it to be exceedingly rare. Lorraine Minnite of Barnard College notes that in 2005, at the peak of a federal crackdown, "federal prosecutors indicted far more people for violations of the nation's migratory-bird laws than for election fraud." A comprehensive national study by the Walter Cronkite

School of Journalism at Arizona State University scrutinized thousands of allegations; it found *ten* examples of in-person voter impersonation over a dozen years. A draft study for the federal Election Assistance Commission conducted by Democratic and Republican experts concluded, "There is widespread but not unanimous agreement that there is little polling place fraud, or at least much less than claimed, including voter impersonation, 'dead' voters, noncitizen voting and felon voters." Justin Levitt calculated that statistically "it is more likely that an individual will be struck by lightning than that he will impersonate another voter at the polls."

Ashcroft recovered nicely from his unexpected defeat. George W. Bush nominated him to be Attorney General in 2001. He formally made combating voter fraud a priority for the Justice Department, demanding that "all components of the Department place a high priority on the investigation and prosecution of election fraud." Dozens of probes produced little, though an effort was made to spin the results; a press release in 2005 summing up the department's work nationwide, for example, breathlessly announced that three individuals had been convicted of fraudulent voting in both Missouri and Kansas. Nationwide from 2002 to 2005 only twenty-four people were convicted of illegal voting in federal elections and no one was charged with voter impersonation; by 2007 only 120 people had been charged and eighty-six convicted. "Many of those charged by the Justice Department appear to have mistakenly filled out registration forms or misunderstood eligibility rules," a journalistic analysis concluded.

Then why the clamor? An energetic band of partisan activists produced much of the noise, many of them clustered around Ashcroft:

Bradley Schlozman, a thirty-two-year-old lawyer, swept through the Voting Rights section of the Department's Civil Rights Division, ignoring hiring rules: he pushed out civil servants and tried to hire fellow members of the Federalist Society, the conservative legal network. A report by the department's independent inspector general revealed Schlozman's approach. "I too get to work with mold spores," he wrote to a colleague, "but here in Civil Rights, we call them Voting Section attorneys." He continued, "My tentative plans are to gerrymander all of those crazy libs right out of the section." Schlozman eventually became the acting chief of the Civil Rights Division. The inspector general concluded that he lied about his personnel practices. His lawyer denied the charge.

Mark "Thor" Hearne was a top counsel for the Bush reelection campaign in 2004, after which he and a party official created the American Center for Voting Rights; its "headquarters" appeared to be a post office box in a Texas strip mall. Four days after it materialized on the Internet, the group testified before Congress as sage nonpartisan experts. Two years later Hearne's group vanished as abruptly as it had appeared. Hearne even declined to mention it in his law firm biography.

Hans von Spakovsky had served as a local party official in Georgia. Moving to the Justice Department's Civil Rights Division, he overruled the career lawyers who wanted to object to Georgia's new voter identification law. It turned out that he had already written a law review article, using the grandly Madisonian pseudonym Publius, strongly backing the ID idea. President George W. Bush installed him on the Federal Election Commission without a Senate vote as a recess appointee. Senator Barack Obama blocked his confirmation. Eventually von Spakovsky moved to the Heritage Foundation, where he wrote dozens of articles and cowrote a book, *Who's Counting? How Fraudsters and Bureaucrats Put Your Vote at Risk.* In a typical essay for Fox News, he warned, "One doesn't have to look far to find instances of fraudulent ballots cast in actual elections by 'voters' who were the figments of active imaginations." The most recent example the 2008 article cited came from the mid-1990s. Most were at least two decades old.

A former *Wall Street Journal* editorial writer, **John Fund**, now at *National Review*, also rang alarms. Fund's books include the heated *Stealing Elections: How Voter Fraud Threatens Our Democracy*. He focuses on Democrats, he explains in that book, not for partisan reasons but because "Republican base voters are middle-class and not easily induced to commit fraud." Fund claims that eight of the nineteen hijackers on September 11, 2001, were registered to vote, but he offers no corroborating evidence, and a later study found the claim highly unlikely. Fund's book does include some genuine examples of election misconduct. Generally these involve absentee ballots—the most susceptible to manipulation by candidates or their backers. Rarely do they involve in-person impersonation.

Rounding out the squad was a talented lawyer named **Kris Kobach**, who worked with von Spakovsky in Ashcroft's orbit. Busy Kobach helped draft the 2010 Arizona law that required police to check the immigration status of drivers and passengers during traffic stops if the officer thinks there is a "reasonable suspicion" that they are here illegally. Eventually Kobach was elected to be the secretary of state of Kansas. (He lost a 2018 run for governor.)

Panic over improper voting became a recurring riff on the right. Fox News, the conservative-leaning cable network, set up a "Voter Fraud Watch." Former House majority leader Dick Armey, head of the organization FreedomWorks, declared preposterously that 3 percent of all ballots were fraudulent votes cast by Democrats. Using coded language he told Fox News that the problem "is pinpointed to the major urban areas, to the inner cities." Dick Morris, the Bill Clinton advisor turned conservative pundit, and his wife, Eileen McGann, made a telling slip.

Describing poor voters headed early to the polls in Ohio, they warned, "Photo IDs are necessary to combat this rampant voter fraud," presumably defined as poor people voting. Such imagery tapped unspoken racial fears. A University of Delaware study surveyed white voters on whether identification should be required to vote. When a photo of a Black man voting accompanied the question, support for voter ID jumped 6 percent over responses to the question illustrated by a photo of a white voter.

Hints emerged that at least some activists knew better, even as they pursued voting law changes. Royal Masset, political director of the Republican Party of Texas, was unnervingly frank in an interview with the *Houston Chronicle*: "Among Republicans, it is an 'article of religious faith that voter fraud is causing us to lose elections,' Masset said. He doesn't agree with that, but does believe that requiring photo IDs could cause enough of a drop-off in legitimate Democratic voting to add 3 percent to the Republican vote."

"You Can't Handle the Truth"

The hunt for imaginary voter fraud led to a real-life scandal, albeit one that was quickly forgotten.

In George W. Bush's second term former White House counsel Alberto Gonzales replaced Ashcroft as attorney general. Republican activists grew increasingly frustrated that the Justice Department could not find the immense voter fraud that party followers had been assured was afoot. The president grumbled to Gonzales and to Karl Rove, his political advisor, about reports he had received from party members. "We did hear complaints and concerns about U.S. attorneys," Bush later confirmed. "Some complained about the lack of vigorous prosecution of election fraud cases, while others had concerns about immigration cases not being prosecuted." Bush's aides pressed those concerns on the Justice Department. At one point Rove and other White House officials contemplated asking for resignations from all ninety-three U.S.

attorneys, the lead federal prosecutors in each region. In the end political officials at the Justice Department and the White House settled on a smaller list.

By December 2006 nine U.S. attorneys had been dismissed or asked to resign. The purge, scattered across the country, drew little notice. Still these are coveted posts, and the resignation of a U.S. attorney in the middle of a presidential term is unusual. Joshua Micah Marshall noticed the pattern and asked readers of his blog, Talking Points Memo, to forward information about the departures of the top prosecutors. Such sleuthing drew eye-rolling from reporters at some traditional magazines and newspapers. *Time* magazine's Washington bureau chief Jay Carney scoffed at the notion of snooping for "broad partisan conspiracies where none likely exist." He added, "Of course! It all makes perfect conspiratorial sense!" (Carney later became White House press secretary for Obama and acknowledged that he had missed the story.)

The scandal exploded in the spring of 2007. At least some of the prosecutors, it seems, were dismissed because they had *not* brought charges when they believed there were none to be brought.

The firings were mini morality plays. David Iglesias served as the U.S. attorney in New Mexico. He was a conservative Republican, the model for the righteous military lawyer played by Tom Cruise in the film *A Few Good Men*. (Jack Nicholson snarled his famous line at Iglesias's doppelgänger: "You can't handle the truth!") Iglesias received stellar reviews for his work as a prosecutor, but local Republicans were angry that he refused to bring corruption cases against Democrats. One wrote to Iglesias's office, "The voter fraud wars continue. Any indictment of the ACORN woman [in a local voting controversy] would be appreciated." Iglesias had convened a voter fraud task force, heard one hundred allegations, found only one that might be prosecutable, and in the end decided not to proceed. Shortly after the 2004 election he was dismissed. "What the critics, who don't have any experience as prosecutors, have asserted is reprehensible—namely that I should have proceeded without having proof beyond a reasonable doubt," he argued. Justice Department notes indicate that a Republican U.S. senator had demanded Iglesias's dismissal: "[Pete] Domenici says he doesn't move cases." "There was an illegitimate basis for their effort to remove me," the prosecutor fumed. "It was political." Iglesias ultimately summed up his experience: "First would come the spurious allegations of voter fraud, then unvarnished legal manipulations to sway elections, followed by a rigorous insistence on unquestioned and absolute obedience, and, finally, a phone call from out of the blue."

In Washington State it had taken three recounts to decide the 2004 governor's race; eventually the Democratic candidate won by 129 votes. Republicans, again, charged illegal voting. U.S. Attorney John McKay investigated but declined to bring voter fraud charges. Summoned to the White House for an interview about becoming a federal judge, McKay found himself questioned by presidential counsel Harriet Miers about why party activists believed he had "mishandled" the election. Instead of becoming a judge, McKay was fired. "There was no evidence [to merit prosecution], and I am not going to drag innocent people in front of a grand jury," he later told reporters.

The politicized prosecutions reached a nadir in Missouri. There U.S. Attorney Todd Graves clashed with Ashcroft's Justice Department when he refused to approve a lawsuit demanding a purge of state voter lists. Graves resigned. Using a provision in the Patriot Act designed to smooth the replacement of prosecutors after a devastating terrorist attack, Ashcroft slipped Bradley Schlozman into the post without a Senate vote. As acting head of the department's Civil Rights Division, Schlozman had instigated the very same sketchy lawsuit Graves had refused to bring. A federal court dismissed the suit, but five days before a close U.S. Senate election Schlozman indicted four Democratic voter registration workers for submitting false forms. The hasty charges, which misspelled the name of one of the defendants, broke the department's own rules by coming so close to an election.

Prodded by Marshall's Talking Points Memo and other bloggers, and investigations by Senator Charles Schumer of New York and his tenacious lawyer, Preet Bharara, major newspapers at last began to probe the mass firing of U.S. attorneys. News of the scandal spread. After all, firing a prosecutor for failing to find voter fraud is like firing a park ranger for failing to find Sasquatch. Congressional hearings grilled Gonzales and other officials, seeking to determine who had ordered the purge. At one session the attorney general answered "I don't recall" or some variant sixty-four times. (An audience member put down his sign protesting the Iraq war and replaced it with a running "I don't recall" tally.) In August 2007, after his top aides quit or had been fired, Gonzales resigned. It was the first time since Watergate that an attorney general had stepped down amid scandal.

The Courts Shrug

The roar about voter fraud had one significant consequence: it made it seem to be a real problem. If not, why was everyone talking about it? The broad notion began to percolate into judicial opinions, and in 2004 the U.S. Supreme Court allowed an Arizona voter identification law to go into effect. It was too close to the election to block the law, the justices unanimously held; revising the rules would sow confusion. The opinion in *Purcell v. Gonzalez* reached even further: "Voter fraud drives honest citizens out of the democratic process and breeds distrust of our government. Voters who fear their legitimate votes will be outweighed by fraudulent ones will feel disenfranchised." The historian Alex Keyssar reacted with scorn: "*Feel* disenfranchised? Is that the same as 'being disenfranchised'? So if I might 'feel' disenfranchised, I have a right to make it harder for you to vote?"

The Court's learned shrug continued with the next major case, this one addressing one of the first markedly strict new voter identification laws. Indiana had enacted a statute requiring voters to show a driver's license or other specified form of government identification. The local American Civil Liberties Union chapter and Democratic Party challenged the law as written (a "facial" challenge), a tactical mistake because it was too soon to show harm. The appeals court opinion upholding Indiana's law was written by Richard Posner. This was no anonymous scribbler; Posner was one of the nation's most respected judges and the most frequently cited legal scholar of the twentieth century, according to the *Journal of Legal Studies*. (He was also one of the nation's preeminent public intellectuals, according to a list compiled by Richard Posner.) He is also a leading conservative and a pioneer in the use of cost-benefit analysis. Posner wrote a cursory, rather dismissive opinion: "A great many people who are eligible to vote don't bother to do so. . . . The benefits of voting to the individual voter are elusive." He noted scant evidence of in-person voter impersonation. "But," he asserted, "the absence of prosecutions is explained by the endemic underenforcement of minor criminal laws (minor as they appear to the public and prosecutors, at all events) and by the extreme difficulty of apprehending a voter impersonator." Laws such as Indiana's merely impose "ordinary and widespread burdens" as part of election administration.

The U.S. Supreme Court affirmed Posner's ruling. In *Crawford v. Marion County*, Justice John Paul Stevens, the senior member of the Court's liberal bloc, observed that the type of fraud the statute protected against was solely "in person voter impersonation." "The record contains no evidence of any such fraud actually occurring in Indiana at any time in its history." The jurist cited only two examples: one from 1868 (where voters allegedly shaved off mustaches and beards in order to vote multiple times) and another in which someone in Washington State voted illegally in 2005. But Stevens chided the law's challengers for bringing forward such slim proof of actual harm done. The Court rejected the challenge to the law's constitutionality "on its face" but never addressed its impact on narrower groups of excluded voters. Significantly the Court declined to apply the most stringent "strict scrutiny" to what appeared to the justices to be a bland, technical state law designed to uphold "the integrity and reliability of the electoral process." That phrase—*electoral integrity*—would come to play an increasingly significant role in the constitutional law of democracy in the coming decade. The fear of fraud was enough to allow strict measures, even if it meant possible disenfranchisement of real voters.

The Emerging Majority

Eight years after the Florida recount, that was where things stood: a wide fear of shady practices, stirred by partisans; a continuing mess in election administration, with incremental improvements; a raft of proposals targeted at minority and other Democratic constituencies.

Through it all, demographic pressure built, with the electorate changing dramatically. In 1968 Richard M. Nixon's aide Kevin Phillips had presciently forecast "the emerging Republican majority," premised on backlash among white ethnic voters against civil rights gains. Millions of white working-class voters voted Republican in 1980, eventually becoming known as Reagan Democrats. For a generation they were the fulcrum of American politics. But they were an aging cohort. In 2002 John Judis and Ruy Teixiera predicted an emerging Democratic majority composed of minority, younger, and college-educated voters. By 2008, 5 million more voters had gone to the polls than had done so four years earlier. And while the number of white voters remained unchanged, 2 million more African Americans and over 2 million more Hispanics cast ballots. For the first time Black Americans voted at nearly the same rate as whites. The sheer numbers were growing too. In the dozen years after 2000, the share of the electorate made up of white voters fell from 81 percent to 74 percent. This upended political assumptions. To assemble two electoral vote majorities in the 1990s, Bill Clinton wooed disaffected white working-class voters, hoping to stitch them together with core Democratic urban supporters. In 2008 Barack Obama began to construct a different Democratic presidential majority, based on a "rising American electorate." His historic candidacy spurred huge excitement among young voters and in communities of color. Obama was the first Democrat to win a majority of the popular vote since 1976, a feat he achieved twice—even though he lost among older voters.

To some, Obama's election seemed inexplicable and certainly unnerving. Demographic panic appeared to lurk behind much of the anxiety, for in three decades whites would no longer be the majority in the United States. As journalist Jonathan Chait observes, a party that seeks to restrict turnout likely represents an electorate rooted in the past. Weeks before Obama's election, the bankruptcy of Lehman Brothers tipped the financial system into crisis. Within a matter of days the insurance giant AIG, Merrill Lynch, and other firms required huge infusions of funds. The Treasury Department asked Congress to pass a $700 billion bailout, the Troubled Asset Relief Program (TARP); the proposal was only three pages long. Stock markets swooned as the House of Representatives at first rejected the plan; John McCain suspended his presidential campaign; and unemployment began to soar. To many voters the epochal events seemed utterly out of the blue, as inexplicable as the electoral result a few weeks later. One poll showed that *half* of Republican voters believed that Obama had won the election thanks to voter fraud engineered by ACORN. Financial bailouts without accountability, phony voting, all stoked by Fox News and other ideological news sources, stirred deep fears among some Americans. Fears of voter fraud echoed worries about lost American identity.

Eventually some activists and politicians began to challenge basic, long-standing tenets of American democracy. They echoed Paul Weyrich's 1980 call for fewer voters. Now when the conservative columnist Matthew Vadum wrote that "registering the poor to vote . . . is like handing out burglary tools to criminals," it caused barely a stir. Tea Party conservatives consciously styled themselves on the Founding Fathers. Representative Steve King of Iowa mused, "There was a time in

American history when you had to be a male property owner in order to vote. The reason for that was, because [the founders] wanted the people who voted—that set the public policy, that decided on the taxes and the spending—to have some skin in the game. Now we have data out there that shows that 47 percent of American households don't pay taxes. . . . But many of them are voting. And when they vote, they vote for more government benefits." In his successful run for Congress in 2012, Minnesota Republican Ted Yoho slyly told supporters, "I've had some radical ideas about voting and it's probably not a good time to tell them, but you used to have to be a property owner to vote." The president of the Tea Party Nation claimed that "the Founding Fathers" imposed a property requirement on voting. "And that makes a lot of sense, because if you're a property owner you actually have a vested stake in the community," he told his radio audience. "If you're not a property owner, you know, I'm sorry but property owners have a little bit more of a vested interest in the community than non–property owners."

Perhaps most surprisingly some political leaders began to assail the Seventeenth Amendment and urged a revocation of citizens' right to vote for U.S. senator. Texas governor Rick Perry, campaigning for the Republican presidential nomination in 2012, declared that the amendment had been foisted on the country by Progressives "favoring centralization" as a way to deal "another blow to the ability of states to assert influence on the federal government." Mike Lee of Utah, considered one of the Senate's brightest constitutional thinkers, called the Seventeenth Amendment "a mistake." During a speech at Texas Tech University School of Law in 2010 Justice Antonin Scalia declared the original Constitution "providential" and called for a repeal: "I would change it back to what they wrote, in some respects. The Seventeenth Amendment has changed things enormously. We changed that in a burst of progressivism in 1913, and you can trace the decline of so-called states' rights throughout the rest of the twentieth century. So, don't mess with the Constitution." Senator Ted Cruz, who had argued eight cases before the U.S. Supreme

Court, told members of the business lobbying organization ALEC, "Prior to the Seventeenth Amendment, the state legislatures' ability and authority to select senators was a powerful check on the federal government coming and intruding on the prerogatives of the state. Because if you have the ability to hire and fire me, I'm a lot less likely to break into your house and steal your television." They all cast their arguments as a defense of states' rights, yet the historical record demonstrates that, far from a congressional power grab, the amendment was pressed on an unwilling Senate *by the states*. Regardless, repeal would have been the most significant revocation of voting rights in the country's history.

American elections began to seem a struggle over an expanded or constricted electorate, as had been the case in earlier eras of rapid demographic or political change. The emerging Democratic majority in presidential contests failed to appear in midterm elections. Turnout dropped then, as it always does when the presidency is not at stake, and skewed older, whiter, and wealthier. In 2008, 56.9 percent of the voting-age population cast ballots. In 2010, with control of Congress and statehouses at stake, only 37.8 percent voted. Voters returned control of the House of Representatives to Republicans. More consequential for the future of the vote was the story in the states. Republicans seized eighteen legislative chambers from Democrats, giving them unified control of legislatures in twenty-five states. In all but five a Republican served as governor as well. This would prove momentous when redistricting took place in the year following the election. And it would be enormously significant for a new wave of laws aimed at restricting the vote.

12

Marching Backward

May 18, 2011, Madison, Wisconsin, 1 a.m. In a raucous session in the legislative chamber, Democratic state senator Fred Risser, the nation's longest serving legislator, heatedly denounces the proposed voter identification bill now hurtling toward passage. A call for a final vote cuts him off. "In my fifty years" in office, Risser sputters, "I've never had anyone cut me off!" The meeting dissolves in chaos as spectators shout "Shame!" and "Recall!" Amid the din the bill passes 19 to 5 along party lines. Many Democrats refuse to vote at all. Others claim they tried to vote but were not counted. The new law requires citizens to produce a driver's license, passport, or other specified government document in order to vote. A government-issued student identification card from the University of Wisconsin will not suffice. According to the state's Legislative Fiscal Bureau, 20 percent of Wisconsin adults do not have the relevant government ID. Yet identification seems like a simple requirement. As a Republican senator notes, citizens must produce an ID to buy liquor and cigarettes; surely it will not be so hard to procure one in order to vote. Contention spills into the capitol's marble hallways as protestors and rival lawmakers overrun a celebratory press conference. Governor Scott Walker signs the bill days later, calling it a "common sense reform" that will "go a long way to protecting the integrity of elections in Wisconsin."

This was Wisconsin's winter and spring of discontent, as Walker also sought to limit collective bargaining rights for many public unions. He would face a recall election the next year. Attention on the new voting law faded. Outside the state the fight drew little notice.

Similar scenes could be found in Austin, Raleigh, Tallahassee, Harrisburg, and other state capitals in early 2011, though most of them were less noisy. Republicans had swept the legislative elections, a public rebuke to President Obama and a protest against the deep recession. This shift would quickly prove consequential as, across the country, a huge volume of new laws suddenly cut back on access to the most basic of democratic rights.

All told, nineteen states passed twenty-five laws to make it harder to vote. Republican legislators in forty-one states introduced 180 bills with a similar goal. The laws took many shapes. In Maine the legislature repealed the statute that allowed voters to register on Election Day. Florida and two other states curbed voter registration drives, which are especially valuable for lower income citizens. Florida also imposed potential financial penalties for mistakes by volunteers so severe that the League of Women Voters (hardly a Trotskyist sect!) felt compelled to shut down its registration operation. Ohio cut back on early voting on the days most frequently used by Democrats and minority voters. Three states required voters to produce documentary proof of citizenship—a passport, birth certificate, or naturalization papers—to register to vote; 7 percent of eligible voters and 12 percent of the poor do not have those papers, and one out of three women does not have proof of citizenship with her current married name. In Texas, Mississippi, Alabama, Wisconsin, Tennessee, and Pennsylvania strict new voter identification laws, which had been blocked by Democrats, swiftly passed. Texas's law drew particular mockery because of its provisions that did not recognize a student ID, but did recognize a gun license. "Texas, you know, is a big handgun state," explained the bill's sponsor, "so everybody has almost got a concealed handgun license over 21." The bills often appeared routine and technical and made scant national news, yet this was the first time since the Jim Crow era that states moved as a group to restrict voting. An observer from the National Conference of State Legislatures called it "remarkable."

A Republican Party strategy was evident. Of the eleven states with the highest African American turnout in 2008, seven made it harder to vote. Nine of the twelve states with the largest Hispanic population growth imposed new restrictions. These groups favored Democrats. Young people too were viewed as an increasingly strong Democratic constituency. New Hampshire House speaker William O'Brien was guilelessly frank in explaining a new law that stripped eligibility from most of the state's college students. "Voting as a liberal, that's what kids do," he told a Tea Party group. "They don't have life experience [and] . . . just vote their feelings." The Dartmouth College Republicans as well as the College Democrats objected, and the bill was withdrawn. Pennsylvania's house majority leader Mike Turzai seemed tipsy on truth serum when he appeared before the Republican State Committee in June 2012. He bragged about his state's recently enacted "pro Second Amendment" and "pro-life" laws and "Voter ID, which is gonna allow Governor [Mitt] Romney to win the state of Pennsylvania, *done*."

At first blush many of the new laws seemed unobjectionable. The public broadly supported the idea of requiring identification: certainly voters must be who they say they are, and it is not unreasonable for them to have to prove it. Many forms of ID do not disenfranchise. Under the Help America Vote Act, for example, citizens who have registered by mail must show identification when they turn up to vote for the first time. Acceptable documents include a driver's license or state ID card; passport; student, military, or employee identification card; utility bills, bank statements, or paychecks. Michigan required voters to show a government identification card but let them sign a sworn affidavit if they did not have one. In 2011 Rhode Island required voters to show one of several forms of government identification. No wide disenfranchisement resulted. Broadly speaking, these kinds of voter ID laws can make sense.

What was new was the requirement that citizens show ID that many of them *simply did not have*. About 11 percent of eligible voters do not have a current driver's license or other state government photo identification, especially the poor (less likely to own cars) and the elderly. Minorities were hit especially hard. Black voters were nearly three times as likely as white voters to lack a photo ID. Some states promised to make ID cards available for free, but only after citizens proved their identity by providing specific forms of documentation, which could be costly or hard to locate. Birth certificates can cost between $8 and $25. Marriage licenses, required for married women who have changed their names, can cost between $8 and $20. In the most extreme example, for someone who has misplaced citizenship papers, it costs $345 to obtain a replacement proof of naturalization. By contrast, the poll tax was $1.50 when it was declared unconstitutional in 1966, about $11 in today's dollars.

In several states the most contentious issue revolved around early voting. The practice had become increasingly popular. Election Day falls on the first Tuesday after the first Monday in November, but that is not stipulated in the Constitution. Rather it comes from a statute enacted in 1845; Congress set a uniform day for federal elections in order to prevent voters from moving from state to state and casting ballots in each place. (The practice was known as "pipelaying.") Why Tuesday? Sunday was out: the Sabbath. Wednesday was market day. Citizens needed a day to travel to and from the polling place, by horse or on foot. On the first Monday of the month judges held court at the county seat. Hence the first Tuesday after the first Monday, all for the convenience of farmers in the 1840s. In today's workaholic era, when men and women have jobs and can find it hard to go to the polls on Election Day, early voting is a matter of customer service. Oregon abandoned polling places altogether in favor of mail-in voting; Washington State did the same, save in Spokane and Seattle. In 2006 about one in five voters cast ballots in person or by mail before Election Day, but in 2008 that number jumped to one in three: 44 million. In prior elections early voters more or less mirrored the general electorate, or skewed Republican because of military absentee ballots. The Obama campaign combined its data-driven field operation with grassroots enthusiasm to shift markedly who showed up before Election Day. Black churches organized "Souls to the Polls" programs to rally parishioners to vote en masse, especially on the Sunday before the election. In Ohio alone 119,000 churchgoers were bused to polling places to cast their ballots. Suddenly early voting was controversial.

Sometime around New Year's Day in 2011 Florida state officials and political consultants met to map out a new election bill. To write it they recruited the man behind the state's notoriously inexact "felon voter" purge of 2000, now serving as general counsel to the Florida Republican Party. Another attendee, Jim Greer, former chair of the state party, admitted that cries of voter fraud were simply "a marketing ploy" and recounted the advice he was given by consultants: "We've got to cut down on early voting because early voting is not good for us." He testified under oath, "I was upset because the political consultants and staff were talking about voter suppression and keeping Blacks from voting." The party leader's credibility was shaky; he would go to prison for financial misconduct. But other attendees confirmed the discussions.

The new law cut early voting from fourteen days to eight. No more "souls to the polls." "I know that the cutting out of the Sunday before Election Day was one of their targets only because that's a big day when the Black churches organize themselves," a Republican consultant confirmed to the *Palm Beach Post.* As the bill moved through the legislature, debate rubbed raw. State senator Mike Bennett reasoned, "Do you read the stories about the people in Africa? The people in the desert, who literally walk two and three hundred miles so they can have the opportunity to do what we do, and we want to make it more convenient? Why would we make it any easier?"

Florida also lurched backward when it came to restoring voting rights to people with a past criminal conviction. Of all the people in the country who were denied voting rights for this reason, one third lived in Florida. When Jeb Bush was governor he had begun to ease the state's lifetime ban on voting by ex-offenders. His successor, Charlie Crist, also a Republican, made ending the state's policy a campaign plank when he was elected in 2006. The governor could grant blanket pardons to restore voting rights but needed the assent of his elected cabinet. Crist found himself stymied by other Republicans, but by term's end he had restored voting rights to 156,000 people. The far more conservative Rick Scott then became governor and repealed Crist's executive actions during his second month in office. He made the policy more restrictive than it had been under Bush: even nonviolent former felons who had completed their sentences were denied the right to vote, and Scott added long waiting periods and often hearings before rights could be restored. Once again about 1.5 million Floridians paid taxes but could not vote unless the governor and his cabinet personally restored their rights, one at a time.

Across the country lawmakers echoed the idea articulated by the speaker of the Minnesota House of Representatives. Defending a voter ID bill on a talk radio show in 2011, Kurt Zellers declared of voting, "I think it's a privilege, it's not a right."

"Free and Fair"

Democrats and voting rights groups had successfully blocked many of the changes in earlier years, but this blitz caught them flatfooted. The Republicans now moved with strategic ferocity. As soon as they had so much as a pinkie on a lever of power—in states, Congress, or the courts—they used this leverage to change the rules of politics.

By contrast Democrats pursued no broad party strategy to expand democracy. Obama had declined to take public campaign funds for his 2008 race, the first major party nominee to refuse the subsidy since its creation more than three decades earlier. The system had collapsed, he argued with some plausibility, and he vowed to fight for reform to revive it. But when he took office he never proposed changes (the first Democratic president since the 1940s to fail to put forward a campaign finance plan) and downplayed the structural democracy reform measures that might have given his own supporters a greater say in government. His administration refused to designate more state agencies to register voters under the "Motor Voter" law. Democrats in the White House and Congress moved no new voting reform legislation, even when they had a filibuster-proof majority in 2009.

The new state laws were not secret, of course; legislators enacted them in plain view. But the pattern had not been fully noticed. A key moment came in the fall of 2011, one year before the presidential election. Wendy Weiser, an intense attorney who worked for the Brennan Center for Justice, found herself answering increasingly panicked phone calls from civic groups and legislative aides in unexpected states. Weiser and her colleague Lawrence Norden worked through the summer with law students and interns analyzing the new voting statutes and poring over regulations. In October they published *Voting Law Changes in 2012*. Weiser and Norden calculated that the cutbacks already in place could make it significantly harder for 5 million citizens to vote. Enough electoral votes were at risk to decide the presidency. The punchy statistic led the *New York Times* front page.

The widely publicized study helped break open a national debate on the voting wars. Civil rights groups routinely met with Attorney General Eric Holder and pressed him to awaken the Justice Department's Civil Rights Division, which had lately filed few voting rights cases. Now the Department began to move. Investigations by the *New York Times*, *USA Today*, and other newspapers, as well as coverage in increasingly polarized cable television, drove the issue. Fox News long had warned darkly against "voter fraud." Now, with equal fervor, the liberal network MSNBC began to decry and document "voter suppression."

Among the electorate the mood began to shift, most dramatically in Ohio. Elections were especially fraught in the Buckeye State because of its eighteen coveted electoral votes. In 2004, had only sixty thousand votes gone the other way, John Kerry would have been elected president despite losing nationwide by 3 million votes. (Republicans might have demanded a national popular vote, and perhaps Democrats would have found new respect for the wisdom of the framers.) That year many voters in Cleveland, Columbus, and other cities gave up amid polling-place chaos and long lines that stretched into the next morning. Stung, Ohio instituted thirty-five days of early voting. The reforms worked: four years later the election unfolded smoothly. One and a half million Ohioans voted early, and they were older, poorer, less educated, and more likely to be women than those who voted on Election Day. Then, in 2011, the new Republican governor, John Kasich, pressed through a sweeping election bill on a party-line vote that cut back early voting. In response Democrats gathered more than 300,000 signatures on a petition to give voters the chance to negate the law. The Republicans reversed. For the first time in the state's history, legislators quickly undid their own law to avoid a voter repeal—in part, out of fear that a ballot measure would drive turnout. One key restriction remained, however: voting was not permitted during the seventy-two hours before Election Day. This surgically sliced out the "souls to the polls" Sunday heavily used by African American voters. In 2012 the Obama campaign sued, and a federal court reinstated early voting throughout the state.

Still other courts found that provisions of the U.S. Constitution blocked other voting law changes. In Florida the League of Women Voters challenged the latest version of the state's laws designed to crack down on voter registration drives. A federal court ruled that many of the restrictions fell afoul of the First Amendment, which protects voter registration as a form of expression. But the damage had been done: during the time the drives were suspended, registration rates dropped 14 percent statewide.

Nationally it had become clear that these were not, after all, neutral and technical changes to an arcane body of law but a concerted bid to affect the vote. Obama's campaign strategist David Axelrod called them a "calculated strategy" to "hold down voter turnout." Public opinion research commissioned by voting rights advocates showed citizens divided. Many were fearful of fraud and broadly supportive of voter ID. But they were very skeptical of election law changes engineered by partisans to benefit their own incumbency or party, and they embraced core notions of political equality, rooted in the Declaration of Independence and the idea that we are all "created equal."

The U.S. Department of Justice blocked some of the changes, using its power under Section 5 of the Voting Rights Act. And in the spring of 2012, with millions of votes at stake and public attitudes changing, voting rights groups and other nonprofit organizations went to court. Relatively new groups, including the Brennan Center and the Advancement Project, worked closely with the Lawyers Committee for Civil Rights Under Law, which was first convened by President Kennedy in 1962. The American Civil Liberties Union brought suits in Pennsylvania and other states. The League of Women Voters challenged Wisconsin's law. The Open Society Foundations, founded by billionaire George Soros, funded public opinion research to find the best ways to talk about voting.

When the civil rights attorneys went to court, they got a surprisingly warm reception. Despite rising political polarization in legislatures, judges moved with rare unanimity to protect voting rights. In several key states the federal Voting Rights Act was invoked to dam up changes. For example, a panel of three federal judges blocked Texas's voter ID law. Another federal appeals court prompted South Carolina to narrow the scope of its new law: citizens without an ID could still vote if they had a "reasonable impediment" to procuring the paperwork. Fear of fraud was reason enough to uphold the law, the court ruled, though it noted that there was no evidence of voter impersonation, while 130,000 voters lacked the required ID. Judge Brett Kavanaugh, a leading conservative, wrote the opinion.* He explained the postponement: "The Voting Rights Act of 1965 is among the most significant and effective pieces of legislation in American history. Its simple and direct legal prohibition of racial discrimination in voting laws and practices has dramatically improved the Nation, and brought America closer to fulfilling the promise of equality espoused in the Declaration of Independence and the Fourteenth and Fifteenth Amendments to the Constitution."

Some courts relied on state constitutional provisions. Recall that the U.S. Constitution refers to "the right to vote" in various places but never squarely declares that the right exists. By contrast all but one state charter explicitly and affirmatively protects the right to vote. Courts in Wisconsin and Missouri ruled that proposed voter ID laws violated citizens' fundamental rights. A two-week-long trial embarrassed Pennsylvania. First, the state agreed in court papers that there "have been no investigations or prosecutions of in-person voter fraud." Then officials admitted that the number of registered voters who lacked ID was ten times higher than previously estimated, about 758,000 in all. Although the state had promised to make free identification available, witnesses described "long lines, short hours, and misinformed clerks" at the government offices. When, despite the fiasco, the trial court judge upheld the law, the state supreme court quickly reversed him and blocked it. Confusion continued. Just days before the election, some Philadelphia residents told canvassers that they could not vote because they did not have "the papers."

Voter ID laws certainly incited controversy. Did they actually suppress turnout? Answers to that question are surprisingly elusive. Many factors determine turnout. Poor voters in Georgia voted in droves for Obama, but even so, voting laws may have kept turnout lower than it might

---

*Kavanaugh even then was considered a strong possibility for a Supreme Court appointment. (He wrote much of Kenneth Starr's report on the Monica Lewinsky scandal. His defenders insist that he was responsible only for the G-rated sections.)

have been. And only a few states have implemented the tightest rules. Maybe those who lack identification would not have voted anyway. So far, even those who are opposed to the laws have been reluctant to claim an impact on turnout. In 2014 the Government Accountability Office issued perhaps the most significant study of the impact of strict voter ID laws. GAO is the nonpartisan think tank that reports to Congress, and lawmakers from both parties rely on it to assess the effectiveness of government programs. Its findings about depressed turnout were, well, depressing: the new laws do, in fact, dampen voting—but not for everyone. The researchers focused on two states with strict new laws, Kansas and Tennessee. Turnout dropped more than in comparable states, at least 1.9 percent more in Kansas and 2.2 percent more in Tennessee, and the declines "were attributable to changes in those two states' voter ID requirements." Turnout fell most among African Americans, young people, and new voters. The *Washington Post* calculated at least 122,000 fewer voters. (Finally a government program that works as intended!)

In a signal victory for the public interest legal groups, by Election Day 2012 every single one of the harshest laws had been blocked, blunted, postponed, or repealed. Strikingly the rulings came from state and federal judges—from those appointed by Democrats and those appointed by Republicans. Voters overwhelmingly were able to cast their ballots without incident.

"We Have to Fix That"

On Election Day 2012, 98 million Americans went to the polls; 32 million had already voted early. There was little evidence of open disenfranchisement. Tea Party groups that had threatened, implausibly, to mobilize 1 million vigilantes to police "fraud" had little impact.

But the balloting did not unfold perfectly smoothly. In many places voters were met with chaos and long lines. The best estimate suggests that more than 200,000 Floridians gave up in frustration. That the state had cut its early voting timeline nearly in half was one factor; high turnout, 71 percent of registered voters, combined with a long and complex ballot was another. Still evidence suggests that poorer and minority-dominated counties had less equipment, fewer poll workers, and longer lines.

Thanking supporters on Election Night, President Obama delivered a generic homage to the glories of democracy. "I want to thank every American who participated in this election," he said as cheers washed over him. "Whether you voted for the very first time or waited in line for a very long time"—here he was interrupted by a surprising burst of applause. He looked away from the teleprompter and said pointedly, "By the way, we have to fix that."

In January 2013, at his Second Inaugural, he reiterated the point, this time linking current challenges to democracy to the ideals of the country's founding: "Our journey is not complete until no citizen is forced to wait for hours to exercise the right to vote." Two weeks later an elderly voter who had had to wait in line sat in the gallery with First Lady Michelle Obama at the State of the Union address.

Facing a divided Congress, Obama pushed for no new voting legislation. Instead he resorted to a time-honored governmental method for doing nothing: he appointed a presidential commission. At the Brennan Center a young research and program associate thumbtacked on an office corkboard the then-ubiquitous photo of McKayla Maroney, the seventeen-year-old gymnast who scowled after winning a silver medal at the 2012 Olympics. "McKayla is 'Not Impressed' with the voting commission," the caption snarked. In fact Obama's Presidential Commission on Election Administration worked a rare surprise. To chair it he named Benjamin Ginsberg, Mitt Romney's campaign counsel who had led Bush's Florida recount legal team, and Robert Bauer, the former White House counsel who served as chief lawyer for Obama's own campaign. Another member was a Disney executive experienced in moving customers along in theme park waiting lines (or at least keeping them happy while they queued). The panel worked for a year and produced a compelling blueprint. It embraced proposals to modernize voter registration and urged a national standard of no more than thirty minutes spent waiting in line to vote.

In effect the war on voting had been fought to a draw: voting rights activists had kept the worst laws from taking effect, and the impact on turnout was minimal. In 2013, for the first time in years, more bills were introduced in state legislatures to expand voting than to restrict it. Courts had drawn a line, making clear that, given the mismatch between the fundamental right of democratic participation and the rickety machinery of American democracy, they would not allow partisans free rein to manipulate the system.

Then the Supreme Court entered the fray.

13

Five to Four

STARTING IN 2010 the U.S. Supreme Court, led by Chief Justice John Roberts, issued a series of dramatic rulings that struck down long-standing laws of democracy. Its rulings on voting, campaign money, redistricting, and other matters significantly reshaped the terrain on which these issues are fought.

Of course courts have always played a part in the fight over democracy in America—but frequently a bit part. Despite Tocqueville's observation, "There is almost no political question in the United States that does not sooner or later resolve itself into a judicial question," the shape of democracy in America, for most of its history, has not been a judicial question. Courts have found varying ways to avoid "political questions," "political rights," and the "political thicket."

But in the 1950s and 1960s courts became increasingly involved. Judges helped break long-standing and widely recognized barriers to effective representation, through means such as the "one person, one vote" rulings. Judges have been called on to adjudicate election rules, everything from how "provisional ballots" are counted to the appropriate number of days for early voting. And in the 1980s and 1990s they helped greatly expand the number of minorities in office with a second generation of Voting Rights Act cases that undid electoral systems that had diluted minority voting power. In *Thornburgh v. Gingles* in 1986 the Supreme Court unanimously voided North Carolina's use of multimember districts that had made it all but impossible for Black voters to elect their preferred candidates in the face of white bloc voting. The Court went on to strike down at-large elections and other Progressive Era schemes that had made it harder for communities to achieve representation. In their place, the justices ordered the creation of majority-minority districts. Over time, voting rights law would become mired in acronyms and technical formulas, revolving around tests of "bivariate regression analyses" and "vote dilution" and "disparate impact." Over the course of four decades the Court stayed involved, but when it came to the law of democracy it rarely made sudden or transformative moves as it had during the Warren era—and as it would under John Roberts.

The Roberts Court's activist conservatism was hardly news, though it has mostly moved cautiously. The 2008 decision in *District of Columbia v. Heller* announcing an individual right to gun ownership under the Second Amendment made clear that strong gun laws were still "presumptively constitutional." And Justice Roberts voted with the majority to uphold the Affordable Care Act in 2012 under the Constitution's "taxing power." But the Court's aggressive moves to strike down laws that try to expand democratic rights are unprecedented.

Jeffrey Toobin, a *New Yorker* correspondent, made a telling point after one such ruling: "Every Chief Justice takes on a project. Earl Warren wanted to desegregate the South. Warren Burger wanted to limit the rights of criminal suspects. William Rehnquist wanted to revive the powers of the states. It increasingly appears likely that, for John Roberts, the project will be removing the limits that burden wealthy campaign contributors—the 'whole point' of the First Amendment, as he sees it."

Citizens United

American governance has a built-in conflict. We have a political system rooted in the ideal of "one person, one vote," the norm of political equality. And we want the benefits of a market economic system, with its inevitable accumulation of wealth, which can be translated into political power. How to reconcile these? For more than a century, since the birth of the modern economy, Americans have wrestled with this dilemma. At some points money dominated; at others, effective controls were put in place. The challenge grew more acute after 1960, when expensive television advertising drove escalating campaign costs. Through it all the balance was set by the democratically accountable branches of government. Most recently a bipartisan bill sponsored by Arizona Republican John McCain and Wisconsin liberal Democrat Russ Feingold won passage in 2002 after five years of legislative effort. It capped huge contributions that had come to dominate the financing of political parties. President George W. Bush signed the Bipartisan Campaign Reform Act, grumpily.

For most of the twentieth century the courts kept their hands off campaign finance laws. Judges did not even view campaign contribution limits principally through the lens of the First Amendment. That changed in 1976, with *Buckley v. Valeo*, the foundational modern case.

Voting law changes have tended to follow assassinations or wars. Campaign finance laws follow scandal. That was the case after the Equitable Life Assurance Society's Versailles-themed costume ball in 1905. And though it was hardly the main attraction, campaign cash was a constant presence in the welter of scandals that made up Watergate. Campaign finance regulation had been a much-mocked patchwork for years. Lyndon Johnson called it "more loophole than law." Congress at the time took a first stab at reform by imposing contribution limits and requiring disclosure of gifts to federal campaigns. The law would go into effect in April 1972, so Nixon's reelection campaign lurched into a frenzy of illicit fundraising, all aimed at grabbing as much money as possible before midnight on deadline day. Commerce Secretary Maurice Stans found himself gathering large amounts of cash. One suitcase crammed with $200,000 from a fugitive financier was kept secret, Stans testified, because it had been "pledged" before the deadline. Nixon's administration dunned a multinational corporation, International Telephone & Telegraph, for support in exchange for settlement of an antitrust case. Milk producers were hit up to have price controls lifted. New York Yankees owner George Steinbrenner funneled money into thirty-three dummy campaign committees in Ohio. When the burglars were caught in the Democratic National Committee headquarters on June 17, 1972, investigators traced their funding through a labyrinth of bank accounts and committees, some in Mexico. As the mysterious "Deep Throat" told Bob Woodward in the film version of their garage encounter, it paid to "follow the money." (Yet another iconic quote that was never actually said.)

Amid the investigations, indictments, and constitutional crises over the president's secret tapes that would eventually prove his guilt, Congress moved forward to enact a far more ambitious new campaign finance law. The Federal Election Campaign Act revision passed after Watergate imposed contribution and spending limits on federal campaigns. It created a public financing system for presidential campaigns so that general election candidates would stop privately fundraising altogether, turning instead to federal funds. The law also limited expenditures by committees independent of campaigns. James Buckley, a member of the Conservative Party and a former U.S. senator from New York, sued. He was backed by the American Civil Liberties Union, which regarded the law to be a violation of speech rights.

The Supreme Court delivered a monumental and confusing opinion, with multiple parts and no justice's name attached. *Buckley v. Valeo* held, most critically, that money is a form of speech. Justice Potter Stewart said it bluntly during oral argument: "Money is speech and speech is money." The opinion was only slightly more circumspect: "A restriction on the amount of money a person or group can spend on political communication during a campaign necessarily reduces the quantity of expression." Thus curbs on campaign gifts or spending would be allowed only under limited circumstances, and only for the purpose of fighting corruption or its appearance. All other goals—to promote political equality, say, or rein in soaring campaign costs—were deemed insufficient reasons to regulate campaign giving and spending. *Buckley* upheld the law limiting the size of contributions, but it barred restrictions on spending by candidates or by independent groups. The justices tried to grapple with long-standing conflicts between protecting liberty and promoting equality. Instead they drew a line between contributions (which could be limited) and expenditures (which could not). Thus the Court sent the political system wobbling off in a dangerous direction. Candidates could raise unlimited funds, but only in relatively small amounts, all the while worried that an ideological committee or a bored millionaire opponent would suddenly emerge. Of all the justices who ruled in *Buckley*, only one had significant electoral experience. Byron "Whizzer" White, the former NFL player, had run John F. Kennedy's campaign in Colorado. White's foreboding dissent warned that the Court was making a mess. "There are many illegal ways of spending money to influence elections," he wrote. "One would be blind to history to deny that unlimited money tempts people to spend it on whatever money can buy to influence an election." Officeholders would now be forced to spend ever larger amounts of time fundraising. "I regret that the Court has returned them all to the treadmill."

Buckley carved odd contours, but Congress found ways to try to limit the impact of campaign cash. Corruption was interpreted broadly. The public financing system worked well for about two decades, though it eventually succumbed to the fact that it did not allocate enough money to candidates. Over time operatives found loopholes, and funds flowed outside the system, such as large unregulated "soft money" contributions to parties that served as poorly disguised campaign gifts. The Supreme Court upheld most campaign finance laws, but it applied *Buckley*'s already implausible distinctions in ways that chipped away at effective controls. For example, it ruled that a political party could make unlimited expenditures on behalf of *its own candidates* as long as they were supposedly independent.

No grassroots movement rallied to oppose campaign laws. In contrast to the fight over voting laws, no whisper campaign about "fraud" preceded the legal push either. Instead a dedicated band of libertarian and conservative legal activists set out to change the Supreme Court's doctrine. Senator Mitch McConnell of Kentucky was the chief foe of campaign finance regulation. He organized a small, skilled group of deregulatory lawyers; the most aggressive and effective was James Bopp Jr., general counsel of the anti-abortion National Right to Life Committee and vice chair of the Republican National Committee. Bopp launched an armada of lawsuits seeking to allow more money in politics. His work was encouraged by the U.S. Chamber of Commerce, the National Committee on Marriage, which fought attempts to legalize same-sex marriage, and other conservative groups. Bradley Smith, a former chair of the Federal Election Commission, bragged of waging "long term ideological warfare." Beginning in 2006 McConnell's band began to win cases that chipped away at provisions of campaign finance law. In one case early in John Roberts's tenure as chief justice, the Court examined television ads that attacked a candidate just days before an election. They were not campaign commercials at all, Roberts wrote, unless they expressly urged voters to oppose a candidate. When it came to campaign limits, "enough is enough," he thundered.

Then came *Citizens United*. At first it offered few signs of being a constitutional convulsion. There was no trial. The plaintiffs never asked for a sweeping ruling. The case revolved around an arcane application of campaign law. A conservative nonprofit group had produced a documentary film, *Hillary: The Movie*, presented on pay-per-view television. The Federal Election Commission regulated it as an advertisement. Eventually the group appealed to the Supreme Court. Usually justices seek to find narrow grounds for a decision (a doctrine called "constitutional avoidance"). The Court could have ruled that the regulatory agency erred in treating *Hillary: The Movie* as an ad rather than, say, a *movie*, as Citizens United's lawyer Theodore Olson urged. It could have ruled that the film fell under the well-established doctrine that publishers could avail themselves of the "freedom of the press" protected in the First Amendment. Or it could have found that pay-per-view did not fit the definition of "broadcast" under a 2002 federal law.

But at oral argument the government's lawyer made an agonizing mistake. Justice Samuel Alito asked, "The government's position is that the First Amendment allows the banning of a book if it's published by a corporation?" The lawyer squirmed, but eventually answered that the government could ban publication of a book using corporate funds, even a five-hundred-page tome that on the last page urged a vote against a candidate. Sympathetic observers winced: the correct answer was *No, it cannot be banned; it's a book.* The regulation sought to address the impact on elections of hundreds of millions of dollars of barely disguised campaign television ads, not the pervasive risk of books. At the end of the term in June 2009, instead of issuing a ruling the justices announced they were not ready to decide. They asked for a second round of arguments, after making it clear they were poised to take a major step.

The Court finally issued *Citizens United* on January 21, 2010. Justice Anthony Kennedy wrote for a five-vote majority. The opinion upended doctrine dating back a century and campaign finance laws that had been on the books for six decades. Most attention focused on the holding that corporations could not be barred from spending on behalf of candidates. The ban on corporate spending in elections dated back to the 1907 Tillman Act, which prohibited corporate contributions in federal campaigns. (It was assumed to cover independent expenditures too.) In 1947 the Taft-Hartley Act made explicit that corporations and unions could not directly spend their treasury funds on electioneering. Every time it passed a law on the subject Congress had only strengthened this prohibition. The law long treated corporations—with capital amassed for business purposes—differently from natural persons.

Kennedy's passionate opinion was achingly abstract. A First Amendment romantic, he described a country rather different from the one many Americans would recognize. "The censorship we now confront is vast in its reach," he warned. "The Government has muffled the voices that best represent the most significant segments of the economy." Justice John Paul Stevens was withering in his dissent. Congress had grappled for many years with the question of how to ensure that private money did not overwhelm the political system and drown out the voices of the broad mass of citizens. "While American democracy is imperfect, few outside the majority of this Court would have thought its flaws included a dearth of corporate money in politics," he wrote.

The Court's ruling shocked many. It seemed to hold that "corporations are people," as presidential candidate Mitt Romney later memorably said. At first many worried that large, publicly traded firms would pour funds into campaigns. In 2010 Exxon had profits of $45 billion. The day before *Citizens United*, it could not legally spend those profits to support a federal candidate; the day after, it could. In fact, so far, corporations generally have not spent this way. This may be a temporary lull, a matter of social mores rather than law. It may be because corporations get what they want from government by other means, such as lobbying. But it is striking nonetheless.

The greater impact came from a less understood part of the Court's ruling, that independent expenditures could not corrupt *as a matter of constitutional law*. Gone was the standard that had allowed the crafting of rules to protect against the appearance of undue influence by campaign contributors. It was this holding, less celebrated or reviled in 2010, that shook politics. A lower court struck down the long-standing limits on contributions to political action committees, assuming they spent independently from candidates. Now they could raise unlimited sums. In theory those funds could come from corporations and unions.

In practice, rather abruptly, the funds came from the bank accounts of a relative handful of wealthy individuals. Thus Super PACs proliferated. Regulatory agencies froze, unable to keep up with changes in spending.

Six days after the Court announced its ruling in *Citizens United*, Obama delivered his State of the Union address. Most of the justices sat stone-faced in black robes in the front row, as in previous years. Obama looked down at them and declared, "With all due deference to separation of powers, last week the Supreme Court reversed a century of law that I believe will open the floodgates for special interests—including foreign corporations—to spend without limit in our elections." Democrats applauded; Republicans sat quietly. "I don't think American elections should be bankrolled by America's most powerful interests, or worse, by foreign entities." Justice Alito shook his head angrily. Television viewers could read his lips, mouthing, "Not true." Who was right?

Plainly, Obama. The amount of independent spending exploded. In the five years after *Citizens United*, $2 billion was spent on campaigns by supposedly independent committees, vastly more than in previous eras. When Justice Kennedy held that this spending could not corrupt, he rested on two premises: first, that the spending would be disclosed, and second, that it would be genuinely independent. Are those premises valid? One is reminded of Chico Marx in *Duck Soup*: "Who you gonna believe, me or your own eyes?"

Disclosure was spotty. Six hundred million dollars of the spending was "dark money," spent by nonprofit groups that claimed the right not to disclose their donors at all. Laws allow genuine nonprofit issue-advocacy groups such as the Sierra Club and the National Rifle Association to keep donors secret. Now political committees claimed to be charitable organizations. For example, Crossroads GPS, a nonprofit "social welfare" organization supposedly established for charitable purposes by Bush alumnus Karl Rove, spent nearly half of its tax-exempt funds on political campaigns. Of the $180 million it raised for the 2012 election, one donation was for $22.5 million, another for $18 million, and still another for $10 million—all given anonymously. At least fifty people or corporations gave $1 million to Rove's fund.

At the same time, the façade of putative independence quickly dropped. The 2012 presidential campaign was marked by a disturbing new phenomenon: billionaires seeming to sponsor presidential candidates like racehorses. In the most widely publicized example, a political action committee dedicated to the candidacy of former House Speaker Newt Gingrich raised almost its entire budget from casino owner Sheldon Adelson and his family, who donated more than $20 million. This means that one individual effectively funded nearly the entirety of a presidential campaign. By Election Day Adelson and his wife had spent $93 million to support Republican presidential candidates.

Candidates took to attending fundraisers for the "independent" Super PACs that loved them. This was deemed kosher as long as they slipped away before the actual request for funds was made. The co-founder of Rick Perry's 2012 Super PAC, Make Us Great Again, was Perry's former chief of staff and co-owned a private island with a chief strategist for the campaign. The chief financier of the Super PAC backing another Republican, Rick Santorum, traveled with the candidate. Santorum insisted he had "no idea what Foster Friess [was] doing to *my* super PAC." ("My"?) Two years later progressive billionaires joined the fray. Environmentalist Tom Steyer gave $71 million to his own political action committee, Next Generation Climate Action, to back candidates who supported action on global warming. Former New York mayor Michael Bloomberg spent $27 million to back an eclectic array of Democratic and Republican candidates, mostly supporters of stronger gun safety laws. Early omens suggested an even greater role for billionaires in 2016. In one of the first cattle calls for Republican presidential candidates, men who would be president trooped to Las Vegas in what was dubbed "the Sheldon Primary." Governor Chris Christie of New Jersey felt compelled to apologize personally to the pro-Israel Adelson when he accidentally (but accurately) called the

West Bank the "occupied territories." (Christie's eventual campaign slogan: "Telling it like it is.")

Chief Justice Roberts has signaled his Javert-like determination to hunt down traces of the campaign finance laws and their justifications. He made clear that even trace elements of political equality might be enough to render a law unconstitutional. Arizona had enacted a public financing system after a sordid corruption scandal that sent the state's governor to prison. It was challenged in court. At the oral argument before the Supreme Court in 2013, Roberts announced that he had been digging through the state's website: "Well, I checked the Citizens' Clean Elections Commission website this morning, and it says that this act was passed to, quote, 'level the playing field' when it comes to running for office. Why isn't that clear evidence that it's unconstitutional?" In other words, even a constitutionally sound anticorruption law would be fatally tainted by the possibility that it also promoted equality.

The new constitutional landscape—and its implications for the voter—was clearest in a 2014 case, *McCutcheon v. Federal Election Commission.* A coal mining business owner from suburban Birmingham, Alabama, Shaun McCutcheon, was perturbed by his inability to give more than $117,000 to political candidates and a party committee for one election cycle. Joined by the Republican National Committee and Senator McConnell, he sued. The Supreme Court, again by a vote of 5 to 4, for the first time struck down a direct contribution limit in federal law. The rule in question was not hugely important; it was frequently evaded. But Roberts's rationale startled. Describing the gratitude a candidate feels toward those who have financially supported his campaign, the jurist wrote, "Ingratiation and access are not corruption. . . . They embody a central feature of democracy—that constituents support candidates who share their beliefs and interests, and candidates who are elected can be expected to be responsive to those concerns." Call this a Freudian slip opinion. By definition, in a congressional race contributors from all over the country are not constituents.

During the oral argument for the case, Justice Scalia called it "fanciful" to think that a senator would feel more gratitude for a contribution to a party committee than for "a PAC which is spending enormous amounts of money in his district or in his State for his election." This was judicial chutzpah of a high order, since Supreme Court rulings created that precise situation. Justice Elena Kagan interjected, to laughter, "I suppose that if this Court is having second thoughts about its rulings that independent expenditures are not corrupting, we could change that part of the law." Gumption aside, Scalia had a point. Some critics who style themselves "realists" argue that the key goal should be to make it easier for parties to fundraise because they serve broad functions in forging coalitions and engaging the public, in contrast to freelance ideologues who pull their parties to the extreme. These critics blame the 2002 federal Bipartisan Campaign Reform Act. By closing down unlimited contributions to parties, the critics insist, the law forced aspiring kingmakers to set up their own political infrastructure. Allow considerably looser rules for parties, and sensible leaders will reassert control over American politics. These "realists," though, have an unrealistic nostalgia for political parties that have not existed in decades. Often they were mostly shells through which candidates moved funds to purchase thirty-second advertisements on television. In any case, today the once bright (if irrational) line between expenditures and contributions has been smudged or erased. We are, in effect, in a deregulated zone. Candidates can raise unlimited sums through phony independent committees. And loose clusters of outside groups back ideological goals in a way that might once have been the province of parties. Also, some formal party committees raise ample funds and remain a strong leadership tool, such as the Republican and Democratic campaign committees.

No, the biggest problem is not only that funds flow outside the parties—but where the money comes from in the first place.

Over the past decade two great trends contended when it came to the role of money in politics: small donors empowered by the Internet and large donors ushered in by the Supreme Court. Small donors were coming to play an encouraging, ever-larger role. Beginning with the McCain campaign in 2000, then Democrat Howard Dean in 2004, and especially Obama in 2008, individual citizens found ways to participate by clicking over to campaign websites and donating. In 2016, Bernie Sanders ran for president eschewing a Super PAC. He raised an astounding $232 million with an average gift of, as jubilant rallygoers would shout, "twenty-seven dollars." But Sanders so far was an anomoly. Few congressional candidates could match his grassroots pull. In most of the races that would decide power, after *Citizens United*, big money still was winning in a rout. Just fifty individuals and spouses made up more than 33 percent of the funds raised by Super PACs in the 2014 election; donors giving $200 or more made up 85 percent. Probably the most startling evidence of the new role of wealthy individuals is this, according to a calculus by Kenneth Vogel of *Politico*: "In 2014, the top one hundred donors to Super PACs gave more money than the 4.75 million other donors to federal campaigns, *combined*."

That sobering figure suggests that America's electoral system, in one key way at least, has slid back a century.

The Political Thicket Revisited

In a second major area, gerrymandering, the Court helped tilt the terrain of American politics by refusing to act.

Partisan gerrymandering was the very sort of machination James Madison feared when he argued for the Elections Clause, which gave Congress power to overrule state officials. Only during the brief revolutionary moment of *Baker v. Carr* and *Reynolds v. Sims* in the 1960s did the justices shed their normal reluctance to jump in. The Warren Court cast aside worries about finding justiciable standards and declared that population equality among legislative districts was needed to satisfy the Equal Protection Clause of the Fourteenth Amendment. Political equality was considered an acceptable goal and a reflection of the spirit of the Constitution as an evolving democratic document.

Traditional malapportionment, which gave rural voters disproportionate power, was banished; districts had to be equal in size. Under federal law and in accordance with judicial precedent, they had to pass other tests as well: they had to be "compact" and "contiguous," with all the parts of the district being next to each other. Yet party leaders found they could squeeze out seats even within these confines.

Partisan gerrymandering devolved into a never-ending cycle, with lines of propriety blurred. Democrats pressed their advantage first. In 1981 California congressman Phil Burton sat at his favorite table at Frank Fat's Chinese restaurant in Sacramento and drew the state's electoral map to benefit Democrats. He called one district "my contribution to modern art," adding, "It's gorgeous. It curls in and out like a snake." Tools were crude. Burton would assess what kinds of cars residents drove. (Volvos: wealthy Democrats. Buicks: middle-class Republicans. Chevys: middle-class Democrats.) A decade later, as the next redistricting cycle approached, Republican officials allied with the Congressional Black Caucus to take advantage of the Voting Rights Act. The party set up a pop-up group, Fairness for the 90s, that steered conservative funds to provide computer support for African American and Hispanic groups seeking minority representation. The resulting electoral maps pulled Black voters out of swing districts and ensured that more minority lawmakers were elected—and fewer white progressive Democrats. The new political reality in the South was set in cement: more Black lawmakers, returned to office with ever larger supermajorities, and more conservative officeholders overall.

By the redistricting cycles that followed the 2000 and 2010 censuses, political parties had perfected the art of gerrymandering. Lines were etched with computer-aided precision for partisan purposes. In some states both parties worked together to protect incumbents, what law professor Samuel Issacharoff calls a "political cartel." In 2002 eighty-one members of Congress faced no major-party opponent. In 2004, when the incumbent president narrowly beat his challenger, only seven congressional incumbents were defeated, and all but twenty-seven House victors won easily, the vast majority in landslides. In some states parties brazenly pressed their advantage. Michigan shrank by a single House seat in the 2000 census but managed to squeeze six incumbent Democratic lawmakers to compete with one another in three congressional districts. In Florida one congressional district was ninety miles long and no more than three miles wide. "You could say about this district," reported the *Economist*, "that you could kill most of the constituents by driving down the road with the car doors open."

Everything is bigger in Texas, they say, and that is where the lines were rigged most brazenly. Two years after the 2000 census Republicans won control of the legislature. U.S. House Majority Leader Tom DeLay, at the peak of his power in Washington, did not want to wait for the next census. In 2003 he called a special session of the legislature to enact a mid-decade redistricting. DeLay flew home to oversee the session and raised millions of dollars in corporate money to back the plan. Democratic lawmakers lacked the votes to block the move. They bolted. Dozens fled to New Mexico and Oklahoma, hoping to deny the quorum needed to pass the plan. The federal Department of Homeland Security set aside its hunt for terrorists to join the hunt for the "Killer Ds." Airports were alerted. Some of the Democrats were located holed up at the Holiday Inn in Ardmore, Oklahoma. Eventually enough of them trickled back to Austin to constitute a quorum, allowing the plan to pass. Texas's delegation flipped from being 17–15 Democratic to 21–11 Republican after the 2004 election. But DeLay's tactics cost him dearly: he was indicted and convicted for his role in steering allegedly illegal funds to the effort, though an appeals court overturned his conviction. After leaving Congress he was best known for appearing on the television show *Dancing with the Stars.*

The mid-decade Texas redistricting seemed to offer the Supreme Court an ideal chance to limit how far lawmakers could go. Since *Reyn-*

olds v. Sims and *Baker v. Carr* the justices had wrestled with what standards to apply to fair redistricting. In *Reynolds* the Court breezily set out broad standards and assumed that later judges would, well, figure it out. That proved hard. In *Vieth v. Jubelirer* in 2004, Justice Scalia had written that "no judicially discernible and manageable standards for adjudicating political gerrymandering claims have emerged." Perhaps this was true for a typical gerrymander, but surely Texas's nakedly partisan scheme, in the middle of a decade, solely to squeeze political advantage, would trigger constitutional concern. Instead the Supreme Court washed its hands. *League of United Latin American Citizens v. Perry* struck down one district that violated the Voting Rights Act, but it too left for another day the question of whether there was a standard that would make partisan gerrymandering unconstitutional.

Courts were now in full retreat from trying to figure out how to enforce the concept of "one person, one vote." This time it was Republicans who benefited; after the 2010 census sharply gerrymandered districts would lock in Republican dominance in many states. In the 2012 Pennsylvania election Democratic candidates for Congress won more votes than Republicans, but the Republicans won thirteen of eighteen seats. The same tilt happened in other states where Democrats won most of the votes, including Virginia (Republicans held eight of eleven seats) and North Carolina (nine of thirteen). Obama won Ohio that year, as did twelve Republican House members but only four Democrats.

Other factors are at play, of course. A century of migration, housing discrimination, and poverty have packed minority voters into cities, together with younger people and college-educated progressive urbanites. In Pennsylvania in 2012, for example, Obama's statewide win came from an 83 percent blowout in Philadelphia and Pittsburgh. Republicans are winning white rural votes at an equal clip. After what the writer Bill Bishop dubbed the "Big Sort," it is hard to find genuinely "swing" legislative districts: liberals eat Korean tacos with other liberals, while conservatives crowd megachurches in the outer Sunbelt suburbs. It is difficult to imagine a system of legislative line-drawing that would provoke two-party competition in Harlem or Amarillo, Texas. Polarization in Washington may partly reflect a divided country. Still, creative proposals for instant runoff voting or districts represented by multiple members of Congress might better provide a "mirror" of the electorate, though such reforms will run up against the now ingrained assumption that single-member districts are the norm.

"Racial Entitlement"

The terms of the Voting Rights Act were parsed and refined in numerous cases, addressing issues ranging from the permissible use of race in drawing legislative districts to defining the amount of intent needed to prove racial discrimination in voting. The Supreme Court repeatedly upheld the act's most critical provision, Section 5, starting in 1966. Congress reauthorized it in 1970, 1975, and 1982. In 2006 it was again up for renewal.

In 2006, congressional leaders from both parties stood on the Capitol steps and pledged action. John Lewis, now a U.S. representative from Georgia, stood in the well of the House, in front of giant photographs, telling the story once again of his march across the Edmund Pettus Bridge. "Yes, we've made some progress; we have come a distance," he said. "The sad truth is, discrimination still exists. That's why we still need the Voting Rights Act, and we must not go back to the dark past." His fellow Georgian, Republican Phil Gingrey, countered, "A lot has changed in forty-plus years. We should have a law that fits the world in 2006."

Southern conservatives offered an amendment to the act. It targeted the law's most controversial part. Under Section 5 states and some counties with a history of discrimination had to seek permission from the Justice Department or from a federal court before changing voting laws or procedures. For example, when a town wanted to close polling places in Black neighborhoods but keep them open in white areas, it had to seek approval in advance. This was far more effective than the law's Section 2, which allowed a lawsuit to allege racial discrimination after the fact; by the time an expensive case drags through the courts, the officials chosen by a biased system could have been in power for years. Over time Section 5 became a mostly bureaucratic box to check, since localities knew what would be prohibited. Thousands of preclearance applications were sent in before every election. Procedures had been loosened over time, so that counties or states could more easily receive judicial approval to "bail out" of the law. But the formula for where preclearance was required, contained in Section 4, had not been changed since 1975. Congress heard ample testimony—more than ninety witnesses at twenty-one hearings, producing a fifteen-thousand-page legislative record—that discrimination and racially polarized voting remained stronger in the covered jurisdictions, concentrated in the South, than in other parts of the country.

In the face of such testimony, and given the real-world calculus that redrawing the coverage map would have produced a fractious scramble that might have doomed the bill, the amendment to end preclearance was defeated. With strong support from the Bush administration, the Voting Rights Act reauthorization passed Congress—in the Senate by 98 to 0. At the White House signing, applauded by civil rights leaders, President Bush declared, "By reauthorizing this act Congress has reaffirmed its belief that all men are created equal."

A suit challenging the act and Section 5 then came before the Supreme Court in April 2009, brought by a small municipal utility district in Austin, Texas. Conservative justices shelled the attorneys defending the law. They made clear that they viewed the act with disdain and saw Congress's deliberations as cursory at best. Above all, they insisted, times had changed. "Is it your position that today southerners are more likely to discriminate than northerners?" Roberts demanded. He scoffed at the idea that the preclearance requirement had warded off bad voting laws: "You know, I have this whistle to keep away the elephants. . . . Well, there are no elephants, so it must work."

Yet the Court did not strike down the Voting Rights Act or even Section 5. Gone were the talk-radio style queries from the bench. Parts of the opinion read like an NAACP Legal Defense Fund press release. "The historical accomplishments of the Voting Rights Act are undeniable," it intoned. The case avoided a constitutional ruling altogether. Perhaps the canny justices realized it would look dissonant, to put it mildly, if the Court's first major ruling during the first term of the first African American president was to strike down the most famous civil rights statute. But the Court made clear that Section 5 stood on constitutionally shaky ground. Roberts slipped the blade in noiselessly: "In part due to the success of [the Voting Rights Act], we are now a very different Nation. Whether conditions continue to justify such legislation is a difficult constitutional question we do not answer today." The key word in that sentence is *today*. Translation: *Come back to us another time.*

That time came in 2013, in *Shelby County v. Holder*. The Birmingham, Alabama suburbs have been a fertile incubator of constitutional backlash. (Shaun McCutcheon, in whose suit the Supreme Court began to target limits on direct campaign contributions, lives less than an hour away.) Shelby County wanted to change its voting system without seeking permission in advance, so it challenged the constitutionality of the Voting Rights Act.

Plainly some things had changed in the South. Turnout among minority voters had surged. Yet there was new evidence too why such a law was still needed. The 2009 *Northwest Austin* case had been heard before the new wave of voting restrictions, such as voter ID. Far from being obsolete, the act was stretched taut holding back new laws; it had blocked voting law changes in Texas, North Carolina, South Carolina, and other states. On the other hand, strict voting laws were proliferating above the Mason-Dixon line as well, in states such as Ohio, Wisconsin, and Pennsylvania that were not covered by the act's preclearance provisions.

To Chief Justice Roberts, that was then, and this is now. He grilled the federal government's lawyer:

> **Roberts:** Do you know which state has the worst ratio of white voter turnout to African American voter turnout?
>
> **Solicitor General Donald Verrilli:** I do not.
>
> **Roberts:** Massachusetts. Do you know what has the best, where African American turnout actually exceeds white turnout? Mississippi.

Verrilli noted that the Voting Rights Act had been the subject of lengthy, grinding investigation by Congress. Each time it was reauthorized, support grew. Most recently, in 2006 it passed the Senate 98 to 0. Justice Scalia scoffed. The Voting Rights Act, he declared, is a "racial entitlement": "Whenever a society adopts racial entitlements, it is very difficult to get out of them through the normal political processes. I don't think there is anything to be gained by any Senator to vote against continuation of this act." *Racial entitlements*. Attendees gasped.

"Even the name of it is wonderful: *The Voting Rights Act*," Scalia mocked. "Who is going to vote against *that* in the future?"

The Supreme Court issued *Shelby County v. Holder* in the last week of the term, June 25, 2013. Again it was a 5 to 4 ruling. The majority rested its opinion on the view that things had changed in the South. Roberts wrote, "African American voter turnout has come to exceed white voter turnout in five of the six States originally covered by Section Five, with a gap in the sixth State of less than one half of one percent." Given state control over voting, the "extraordinary" circumstances that prompted the Voting Rights Act's preclearance regime simply did not exist. However, the Court did not strike down Section 5; rather, by invalidating the coverage formula it rendered the protection unusable. "Section Five is the automobile. Section Four is the key. They took away the key," explained civil rights lawyer Elaine Jones.

Justice Ruth Bader Ginsburg wrote a stern dissent: "Throwing out preclearance when it has worked and is continuing to work to stop discriminatory changes is like throwing away your umbrella in a rainstorm because you are not getting wet." The Court said that the Voting Rights Act no longer matched "current conditions," but those conditions included the act itself. Ginsburg was now the Court's senior liberal, following the retirement of John Paul Stevens. This passionate demurral caught the public's attention and began to etch her status as a folk hero, the subject of "Notorious R.B.G." T-shirts and Internet memes.

Scalia's gibes reflected more than bullying. The Fifteenth Amendment to the Constitution explicitly had given Congress authority to assure voting rights. The amendment's framers—acting a decade after *Dred Scott*—did not trust judges to assure the system's fairness. The modern Court showed a similar disdain for the legislative branch in *Citizens United*, where it was simply assumed that any campaign finance law passed by legislators must have been designed to squelch speech and entrench incumbents. Together the two cases were seen as marking a new era of judicial activism. In the *Lochner* era a century ago, justices blocked regulation of the marketplace on spurious constitutional grounds. In the era of *Citizens United* and *Shelby County*, an activist court displayed similar aggressiveness in blocking democratic reforms enacted by popularly chosen branches of government.

"We Couldn't Eat the Birth Certificate"

Just hours after the Supreme Court issued *Shelby County* in 2013, Texas implemented its new voter identification law. The statute was nakedly partisan and almost comically precise in its construction. The state's attorney general Greg Abbott rushed to put the rules in place. Abbott was a candidate for governor, who might benefit from the law's tilt.

The U.S. Justice Department promptly sued Texas, as did voting rights groups. The suits relied on constitutional protections for the right to vote, as well as on Section 2 of the Voting Rights Act, which is still on the books. This section prohibits voting practices that discriminate against minorities. But plaintiffs usually cannot obtain relief until after the offending law is already in effect, which shifts the burden of proof of discrimination onto the law's challengers, a much tougher standard. Section 2 had rarely been used to address voting law changes; instead it was wielded to address issues such as at-large elections, north and south. Now it was one of the few vehicles left for redress.

Lawyers and investigators for the Justice Department fanned out across Texas, accumulating evidence and contacting witnesses who might face disenfranchisement. Vishal Agraharkar was an attorney representing the Mexican American Legislative Caucus and the Texas NAACP. A first-generation immigrant whose family hailed from India, Agraharkar spent his high school years in Houston. In September 2013 he drove hours on end through south and west Texas, scouring for possible witnesses. Interstate 35 took him toward the border. One afternoon, after attending a service at the Living Faith Church in Cotulla, he addressed the fifty congregants in halting Spanish, telling them about the case, describing the new law, and encouraging them to come forward for help. He took notes, left business cards, and headed for the door, damp with sweat. A plaque on the wall caught his attention. Yes, Cotulla was the small town where Lyndon Johnson had taught school in 1928, the very place where he had seen "the pain of prejudice." Johnson told Congress in 1965 that that searing experience drove him to fight to create the Voting Rights Act: "I have that chance . . . and I mean to use it." The Welhausen School, where LBJ taught years before, had been converted into the church. Without realizing it, Agraharkar had come to the same town, the same spot, looking for evidence of disenfranchisement and inequality where Johnson had seen it decades before.

The clash over the Texas voting bill produced a compelling nine-day trial. Sammie Louise Bates—the elderly woman who declared she "couldn't eat the birth certificate"—testified by video as the lead witness. In October 2014 the judge in *Veasey v. Perry*, Nelva Gonzales Ramos, issued her decision. It stretched to 143 fact-crammed pages. She found that 608,470 Texas voters lacked an appropriate ID. She reported that the legislature had rammed the proposal through, turning aside any efforts to make the law less burdensome for minority and poor voters. Ramos noted that the state had provided only 279 substitute "free" voter ID cards. And she found only two cases in the previous decade of in-person voter impersonation—the only kind of fraud that a harsh ID rule would block—and one of those involved a fake ID, thus unlikely to have been stopped by the law. The judge ruled that the law amounted to an unconstitutional "poll tax."

A squall of appeals and motions followed. Texas asked the Supreme Court to allow it to implement the law, even though *Veasey v. Perry* found it deliberately discriminatory. The case joined a confusing jumble of lawsuits and arguments in the weeks before the 2014 election, when early voting was already under way in many states. The Supreme Court did not cover itself in glory. Before dawn on a Saturday, in a ruling emailed to reporters, the justices let the Texas law stand for the 2014 election. They also blocked a new voter law in Wisconsin, but allowed restrictions in North Carolina and Ohio to proceed. The common thread was a desire not to change rules too close to an election. Justices Ginsburg, Kagan, and Sonia Sotomayor vigorously dissented. They wrote that the Texas case was distinct, the harm more clearly delineated by a full trial: "The greatest threat to public confidence in elections in this case is the prospect of enforcing a purposefully discriminatory law, one that likely imposes an unconstitutional poll tax and risks denying the right to vote to hundreds of thousands of eligible voters."

Amid the legal flurry Chicago federal appeals judge Richard Posner weighed in. The ACLU and civil rights groups challenged Wisconsin's voter ID law, the one enacted amid the shouting in Madison. A federal trial court blocked the law; a three-judge appeals court reversed that.

Posner's intervention was procedurally idiosyncratic: he tried but failed to have the trial court's ruling heard by a wider group of appeals judges. Posner wrote a forty-three-page dissent. The judge, of course, had written the opinion *upholding* Indiana's voter ID law, the ruling affirmed by the Supreme Court in *Crawford v. Marion County* in 2008. At the time, before Indiana's milder version of voter ID had gone into effect, Posner found inadequate facts to justify overturning the legislation. Like other judges, he treated the law as a low-stakes technicality. In *Reflections on Judging*, a book published in 2012, he hinted at a change of heart, calling the new laws "voter suppression." His dissent made clear that his conversion was complete.

Posner's Wisconsin dissent is a pungent masterpiece. With withering precision he noted that there was little proof of fraud in the state: "Some of the 'evidence' of voter-impersonation fraud is downright goofy, if not paranoid, such as the nonexistent buses that according to the 'True the Vote' movement transport foreigners and reservation Indians to polling places." In Wisconsin (as elsewhere) it costs money to obtain the underlying documents needed to procure the voter ID card. Posner is known for using cost-benefit calculation in legal analysis. Here he found that the burdens of the new law vastly outweighed possible gains: "As there is no evidence that voter-impersonation fraud is a problem, how can the fact that a legislature says it's a problem turn it into one? If the Wisconsin legislature says witches are a problem, shall Wisconsin courts be permitted to conduct witch trials?"

Finally, he went after the blasé opinion written by other judges who would uphold Wisconsin's law. Some scholars have observed that the fight over new voting laws kicked up much dust but ultimately had little impact. There was no evidence of voter fraud, but also no evidence of wide disenfranchisement and impact on voters. Posner found that view implausible. He slammed an article coauthored by Reagan's attorney general Edwin Meese III. "The authors' overall assessment is that 'voter ID laws don't disenfranchise minorities or reduce minority voting, and in many instances enhance it,'" Posner wrote. "In other words, the authors believe that the net effect of these laws is to increase minority voting. Yet if that is true, the opposition to these laws by liberal groups is senseless. If photo ID laws increase minority voting, liberals should rejoice in the laws and conservatives deplore them. Yet it is conservatives who support them and liberals who oppose them." Posner concluded that those who pushed new laws to restrict the vote, and those who fought against them to expand access, probably knew what they were doing.

The Source of All Power

By 2015 American politics appeared pathologically dysfunctional. In the thirty-five years since Reagan's election in 1980, Washington has had a divided government—with parties splitting control—for all but seven years. Partisan Congresses barely even tried to undertake their most basic tasks of passing budgets, appropriating funds, and confirming nominees.

But the Supreme Court rolled ahead, notably functional, if fractious. The country had settled into a routine: every June, when the justices released their opinions, breathless and often confused cable television reporters, standing on the Court's marble front steps, struggled to parse the opinions. June 2015 was only the latest blockbuster season finale. One day the Court swatted aside the latest challenge to the Affordable Care Act. (The law shouldn't be called "Obamacare" but "SCOTUS-care," harrumphed Scalia in dissent. The majority's logic was "pure applesauce.") The next day, with a flourish, the Court ruled that states could not discriminate against same-sex marriages and enshrined marriage equality as the law of the land. Celebratory crowds hugged on First Street in front of the Court. That night the White House was lit in the rainbow colors of gay pride.

But the Court wasn't finished. On June 29, with notably less hoopla, it issued one last major ruling: this one on democracy. *Arizona Legislature v. Arizona Independent Redistricting Commission* signaled strong encouragement by a tenuous majority of the justices for states—for the people—to take up the job of democracy reform.

At issue was partisan gerrymandering, the very topic that had long bedeviled the Court. For two decades justices had denounced the growing trend but found no "judicially discernable and manageable" standards. Meanwhile voters had acted. They used the direct democracy tools established during the Progressive Era. In a 2000 ballot measure Arizona gave the job of redistricting to an independent panel. In 2010, after several attempts, California's Republican governor Arnold Schwarzenegger won a ballot measure to create a nonpartisan panel to draw lines, for state legislators as well as the U.S. Congress. That reform was coupled with another innovation enacted the same year: the top two vote getters in the primaries would proceed to the general election, regardless of which party they came from. Thus, in a heavily Democratic district two candidates will run in the general election, and an appeal to Republicans or independents may be enough to cobble a winning coalition. In Florida liberals won a ballot measure to change the state's constitution to bar districts "drawn with the intent to favor or disfavor a political party or an incumbent."

Arizona's Republican legislators sued; they were unhappy with the lines drawn by the panel and, perhaps, frustrated by their inability to gerrymander like a proper legislative majority. The suit relied on the U.S. Constitution's Elections Clause. Recall that this provision from the founding era gives Congress the power to override manipulative state election laws. The challenge fixated on the wording: "The Times, Places and Manner of holding Elections for Senators and Representatives shall be prescribed in each State by the Legislature thereof." Ah, "the Legislature." That meant, the Arizona Republicans argued, that congressional district lines could be drawn only by the body that met in ill-fitting suits under the state capitol dome—not the people, even when a state constitution gives citizens lawmaking power. This argument had barely been heard in the previous century of popular lawmaking. If the justices struck down Arizona's panel, they would have had to invalidate other states' congressional redistricting reforms and might have had to imperil dozens of other laws enacted by voters.

In a vote of 5 to 4 the justices upheld Arizona's independent commission. This time Justice Kennedy joined the four liberals. The original constitutional provision, they noted, was not understood to focus on the *legislature*. The Supreme Court often now fixates on the definitions of words, taken out of context, with both sides wielding dictionaries. During the eighteenth-century ratification fight, Justice Ginsburg noted, "participants in the debates over the Elections Clause used the word 'legislature' interchangeably with 'state' and 'state government.'" The clause did not seek "to diminish a State's authority to determine its own lawmaking processes." As the majority then showed, over time the states had encompassed "the People" in the lawmaking power—explicitly, in Arizona's constitution. The People are the source of all power and are well within their rights to reserve some portion of it for themselves. In dissent Chief Justice Roberts made a compelling case that *legislature* has a fixed meaning, but to choose that approach would have condemned citizens to powerlessness when it comes to avoiding gerrymandering and political entrenchment—the opposite of the framers' intent.

This ruling was hardly the granite foundation of a new jurisprudence. It was five votes to four, though not the familiar conservative voting bloc. Kennedy, the eternal swing justice, happened to care about gerrymandering. Earlier in his career he was a lobbyist in Sacramento; perhaps he took note of the brief submitted by the conservative lawyer Ted Olson on behalf of three former Republican governors of California in support of the bipartisan commission. It would be rash to discern a general shift in the Roberts Court, especially since the chief justice himself wrote an angry dissent.

One aspect of the ruling could prove noteworthy: its embrace of the Elections Clause and what it means. The majority quoted Madison's warning at the Constitutional Convention—that "it was impossible to foresee all the abuses" that legislators could concoct. While the case did not actually turn on Congress's power to enforce strong election laws, that latent power rang from every page. The same day, the justices declined an appeal from another case, this one addressing voting, which also relied on the Elections Clause. Arizona and Kansas had tried to require voters to produce proof of citizenship, such as a passport or a birth certificate, in order to register. The majority's ruling provided an answer to the question the Court itself had posed in earlier cases. The People—capitalized in the decision wherever possible—are the source of all power in the government. And citizens can—and, by implication, should—take up the task of reform where judges cannot and will not. The remedy could be structural; it could be implemented with the direct vote of the citizens.

14

2016

The 2016 election unfolded with tremendous strains on the health of American democracy. We know it has gone backward before. Is this another period of retreat? Elections can be a time when the fractures become evident. But they also can be a time when public pressure builds for change, often unexpectedly.

Begin with the core act of voting. How bad were things in 2016?

The concerted push to make it harder to vote was felt with full force that year. In fifteen states new restrictive laws were in effect for the first time in a presidential election. Nearly twice as many citizens voted, or tried to, as did two years before. Some may be deterred or dissuaded. At the very least the weeks before Election Day will likely be clogged with last-minute fights, voting machine snafus, and emergency trips to the courtroom—close combat over polling-place hours, early voting, and purges of names from voter lists. It was also the first presidential election since the Supreme Court gutted the Voting Rights Act. Below the gaze of national media, that law had blocked mischief such as a sudden and mysterious shift in polling-place locations.

Sixteen years after Florida 2000, when a Klieg light of national attention briefly illuminated the fractured system, election administration varied widely across the country. We've inherited a patchwork of state control and local autonomy—a system that grows out of the fact that the thirteen independent states had varying voting rules at the time of the Revolution. No national standards govern matters such as how many voting machines there should be. The spanking-new electronic machines purchased with fanfare and controversy after 2000 were up to fifteen years old. They rely on obsolete technology (such as zip drives). The Presidential Commission on Election Administration warned that they may fail en masse at some point in the next decade. Forty-three states have voting machines whose key components are at least ten years old, putting them in the danger zone.

Yet there were positive trends as well. Most voters were able to cast ballots without incident. Nearly one third voted early—a wildly popular innovation. States began to make it easier to register to vote. As of summer 2015, for example, nearly half the states had instituted online registration. Eight instituted "portable" registration, which allows citizens who have moved to cast a valid ballot even if they have not yet changed their registration record. In ten states voters could correct their file or register on the spot on Election Day. The country has moved far from eighteenth-century scenes of mayhem at polling places.

Then there was a newly potent threat to the power of the vote: the power of big political money. From the founders forward, Americans have understood that economic inequality could dilute political equality. Hence the debates over the property requirement to vote. "Not the rich, more than the poor" would be the electors, insisted Madison in Federalist 57, with power held by "the humble sons of obscurity and unpropitious fortune." Concentrated economic power was understood to pose a threat to American democracy at the turn of the twentieth century. Over the past four decades powerful forces have pulled the economy toward a level of inequality of wealth and income unseen since then. The share of national wealth flowing to the top 1 percent soared from 9 percent in 1974 to 24 percent in 2016. The last time the United States had such concentrated wealth was in 1928, at the end of the Roaring Twenties; the last time before that, we had no income tax. As wealth has concentrated, politics has changed.

Some perspective: recall the scandal that led to the first federal campaign finance law, that electric moment when J. P. Morgan's man confessed to the campaign contribution from New York Life. That gift was *$48,702*. How much would that be worth today? In terms of purchasing power, that contribution would have been about $1.3 million in 2012. That year Sheldon Adelson spent at least *$93 million* on behalf of Republican presidential candidates. The sums spent today do not equal those of the Gilded Age. They are far greater.

The garish hoopla of presidential politics can obscure the quiet flow of money. In July 2015 the Federal Election Committee reported that Super PACs for single presidential candidates—raising unlimited funds—brought in four times what their campaigns did. Donald Trump raised relatively little, relying on free television exposure and social media, while Sanders was powered by small donors. Hillary Clinton raised a growing amount from small donors, but spent much of August 2016 dashing between fundraisers, with donors now able to give her campaign and party committees jointly six-figure gifts. Even bigger money continued to flow, though often in obscured ways. At first, libertarian billionaires Charles and David Koch vowed that the groups they back would spend $900 million to elect a president. But they and others recoiled from Donald Trump. Instead funds were steered to bolster Republican control in Congress. Few congressional candidates of either party relied principally on small donors.

Once it was understood that the democratically accountable parts of government could address this challenge. But the Roberts Court has made it far harder for the elected branches to enact laws to address the risks of big money in the political system. Funds now flow outside the parties, but that is not really the problem. Nor, really, is the sheer amount spent on politics. As critics gladly point out, Americans spend more on potato chips in a year than campaigns do on advertising. The greatest risk to voters is the dilution of their voice, the crushing of the opportunity for political participation and meaningful representation.

To this mix add the rigidity introduced by gerrymandering and the general dilemmas of districting. It takes not an electoral wave but a tsunami to change majority control of many legislative bodies. In part this is due to partisan line-drawing, in part to the built-in distortions of winner-take-all elections in a country where partisans and ethnic groups crowd together. Voters had less and less reason to show up.

For these and other reasons voter turnout skidded ever lower. In 2014 little more than one in three eligible voters, 35.9 percent, cast ballots. That was the lowest turnout in seventy-two years. (In 1942 many had a good excuse: they were overseas fighting World War II.) In California, Texas, New York, and eight other states, fewer than 30 percent of eligible voters cast ballots in 2014. Even states with hot Senate races such as Georgia and North Carolina only slightly outpaced the national average. Midterm turnout always lags behind presidential elections, but the 22-point collapse from the 2012 turnout was unprecedented. It was unclear whether it reflects an even more stark splitting of the relevant electorates or a general retreat from political engagement.

Difficult voting rules, new power for big money, widespread gerrymandering, all combined with low turnout and public disinterest: this did not portend great health for American democracy going forward. At the very least these factors make governing hellishly difficult. They have ratcheted up partisanship in Congress and other governing bodies. Debt crises, shutdowns, and stand-offs have become the norm. This is, in part, the product of the sorting of the two major political parties into clear ideological opposites. Voters gain from greater clarity, but they lose from the inability of the system to govern. As political scientists Norman Ornstein and Thomas Mann have diagnosed, our increasingly ideological parties have collided with our Madisonian system of checks, balances, and multiple veto points. Voters have little reason to expect that their stated policy goals, expressed by their votes, will result in the hoped-for outcomes. Others contend that the malaise goes far deeper. It is hardly news that some voices in our democracy seem to be heard more often than others. Recently political scientists have documented the skew. One study goes so far as to show that the views of average voters have *zero* impact on policymakers when the wealthy or organized interest groups hold a different position.

Regardless of the diagnosis, the illness is evident. In basic ways the political system is broken. What can be done about it?

"Make No Little Plans"

Voting rules play only a partial role in this story, as this book suggests. Often other things—from the economy to party mobilization and political leadership—matter more. But one thing we know is that sometimes bold reforms of existing institutions can restore some of the meaning to the right to vote. There are solutions: the next wave of reforms, which, with proper ambition, can significantly improve the state of American democracy. As the great Chicago architect Daniel Burnham said, "Make no little plans; they have no magic to stir men's blood and probably themselves will not be realized."

Despite the energetic effort to restrict voting, since 2012 more states had passed laws to improve voting and expand participation than to restrict it. Among the most promising developments are those in the area of voter registration. A system of universal, automatic voter registration—a truly modern system—would be transformative. How would it work? Government would take responsibility to ensure that every eligible voter is on the rolls. Existing statewide computerized databases would be updated with information from departments of motor vehicles, social welfare agencies, universities and schools, all electronically. Voters would have a chance to correct their records on

Election Day. Those who do not want to be registered could opt out.

All this would mark a paradigm shift in how Americans run elections. After all, more people are hindered from voting due to the ramshackle system than are disenfranchised on purpose by even the worst new laws. Fully implemented, this change would add up to 50 million people to the rolls, permanently. It would cost less. And it would bolster security by reducing the chance for error, duplicate registrations, and records clogged with the dearly departed. It would also bring the United States in line with other major democracies. Great Britain, Canada, Germany, and France boast registration rates above 90 percent. Ours is as much as 30 percentage points lower. That's one kind of American exceptionalism we choose not to boast about.

Intriguingly, amid partisan combat over topics such as voter identification laws, Republicans and Democrats have come to agree on the basic tenets of reform. The Brennan Center for Justice, which I lead, first put out a proposal for universal registration in 2007 and has since worked to advance it. Quietly, even amid partisan shelling on issues like voter ID, modernization has moved forward with minimal controversy in states.

Oregon saw a breakthrough in the spring of 2015. Kate Brown, a backbench legislator serving a term as secretary of state, was unexpectedly catapulted to the governor's chair after a scandal forced the occupant's resignation. Brown pushed through a law she had drafted while representing her crunchy Portland neighborhood. Churches, unions, and voting rights groups organized to back it. Under the new Oregon law, any citizen who has or has updated a driver's license will *automatically* be registered to vote. When the law went into effect in 2016, it added 300,000 people to the rolls on the very first day. This marks a radical shift in voter registration, with government taking on the responsibility for building and maintaining an accurate list. Oregon was able to take this step, in part, because its computerized statewide voter database was in strong shape.

The Oregon model generated enthusiasm. In October 2015 California enacted a law establishing automatic registration at the state's DMVs. Implemented, it could add up to 6 million eligible voters to the rolls. West Virginia and Vermont enacted it, and Connecticut pledged to do so. Illinois and New Jersey's Republican governors vetoed it, though such setbacks were temporary. Governor Tim Pawlenty of Minnesota vetoed a similar bill in 2009, saying, "Registering to vote should be a voluntary, intentional act." But we don't regard paying taxes, signing up for Selective Service, or showing up for jury duty as voluntary. A more telling criticism is the fear that noncitizens who have driver's licenses will be registered, some without even realizing it. Conservatives worry they will vote; immigrant advocates worry they will be deported. States have found different ways to avoid that trap. Above all, everyone is given the ability to opt out and stay off the rolls.

And there are other reforms to revitalize the systems of democracy, each of which has begun to make progress. A surprising coalition of conservative evangelicals and progressives has pressed to reform felony disenfranchisement laws. Senator Rand Paul, the libertarian Republican from Kentucky, has become a national leader in the push. Proposals to restore Justice Department oversight of the Voting Rights Act would extend the reach of Section 5 nationwide, with a new tighter formula for which states must comply and what practices are covered. With the U.S. Supreme Court again blessing citizen initiatives, states will consider redistricting reforms, including using independent commissions. The Presidential Commission on Election Administration has urged uniform national standards for elections, including how many poll workers should help staff polling sites.

Even the Electoral College could yield to state innovation. Five times in the country's history, the winner of the popular vote has lost. (Political scientists, with admirable clarity, call this the "wrong winner" problem.) In a more typical year candidates stump or spend only in a shrinking number of swing states. In 2012 the Romney and Obama campaigns spent $463 million on television ads in ten general election states, and almost nothing anywhere else. Thirty-nine states never got a candidate visit before the general election. There are ways around the Electoral College without enacting a constitutional amendment, just as states introduced citizen voting into Senate elections even before the Seventeenth Amendment. Under the National Popular Vote plan, states pledge to cast their electoral votes for the winner of the overall tally. The pledge goes into effect only when enough states sign up to produce a winner. As of July 2015 eleven jurisdictions producing 165 electoral votes had signed up—nearly two-thirds of the way toward rendering the Electoral College a vestigial organ. Some have urged a different reform of the Electoral College. In Pennsylvania, Wisconsin, Michigan, and Virginia, Republican lawmakers have toyed with the idea of ending the granting of electors to the winner of the popular vote in the state. Instead the electors would go to whoever wins each congressional district. Inevitably, given the concentration of Democratic and minority voters in cities, this would produce a wildly unfair structural bias toward Republican presidential candidates. Add to this the gerrymandering produced by party control of the redistricting process in those states, and it would amount to a breathtakingly misguided attempt to tilt the rules away from a popular vote for president. So far lawmakers have pulled back from actually attempting this move. Under the Constitution states do have the power to allocate their electors, and Maine and Nebraska now award electoral votes by congressional district. But such a move would be subject to the Voting Rights Act, at least in populated diverse states, and would more generally prompt a constitutional controversy unseen in recent years. Far better to focus on Electoral College reforms that benefit neither party but would boost competition and political engagement.

Then there's election integrity. The most significant risk, we learned, came in the form of cybersecurity threats from abroad, as Russia hacked Clinton campaign and Democratic party servers. The attack went further than leaking salacious emails. In his investigative report, Special counsel Robert Mueller III described how Russia broke into registration databases, state boards of elections, the network of at least one Florida county, and software vendors' systems, too. There is no evidence it infiltrated voting machines. An entire office building in St. Petersburg, Russia, crowded with hackers, served as the headquarters for a multimillion-dollar dark money operation aimed at helping Trump win the presidency. They fabricated rumors and bought ads—all anonymously. Russian president Vladimir Putin's trolls simply took advantage of our loophole-plagued campaign finance laws. Thank *Citizens United* and the wild-west deregulation that grew out of it. At an angry congressional hearing, Senator Al Franken rebuked the Facebook general counsel, noting that ads such as the ones purporting to be from a "community of Second Amendment supporters, guns lovers & patriots" were purchased using *rubles*.

And, yes, those who are concerned about protecting the right to vote should recognize the inevitability of voter identification. Many identification regimes protect integrity without disenfranchising voters. Technology offers the possibility for even greater security. Instead of the thumbed-through sheets used today, why not use electronic poll books? Poll workers could look up a voter's record on an electronic tablet. The voter's picture could be included in the signature book. If a citizen lacks ID but is registered, a photo would be taken, which would serve as identification going forward. The details of such a plan would matter greatly. But done right, an upgrade could point to an end to the divisive voter ID battles of recent years. A plausible election-integrity agenda will give legislative allies firm ground on which to stand. They can insist that only eligible citizens vote—but every eligible citizen must be able to vote.

In some ways the most challenging issue is campaign finance—most profound, and hardest to address. The Supreme Court has foreclosed some of the most necessary changes. Even so, many significant reforms still can be enacted under current constitutional rules. The single most important, by far, would be to institute a system of voluntary public financing for campaigns that focus on small donors. Some version of public financing is not a new idea. Public financing for presidential campaigns was in place since the 1976 election, and it worked well for several decades. All major party candidates participated until the 2000s. The system provided matching funds for contributions received in primary elections, and a simple grant of funds to be used in the general election. The system worked, in significant ways. For two decades presidential campaign finance scandal receded, even as congressional races grew more dependent on a chase for funds. Because candidates agreed to a voluntary spending limit, resources were more equal and competition enhanced. In three of the first five times public financing was used in a presidential race, the challenger won: Jimmy Carter in 1976, Ronald Reagan in 1980, Bill Clinton in 1992. (That robust level of competition would be the envy of any congressional district.) But over time the system became outdated. Politicians realized they could still raise large sums for parties even as they purported to refrain from fundraising for themselves (a practice gently named "soft money"). Today the 1970s-vintage system sits quietly, unused. It simply does not provide enough resources, especially at a time of mega-spending by Super PACs. The Supreme Court made it harder in 2011, when it prevented Arizona's public financing system from giving extra support to candidates who faced a free-spending opponent, on the theory that doing so would somehow chill the speech of the wealthy candidate.

But a new model of public financing has emerged that taps the participatory energy of small donors. It would be firmly constitutional. In part this new approach simply recognizes recent decades' hurricane of technological change. Online fundraising reflects genuine citizen participation in ways that could not have been imagined in the time of Theodore Roosevelt or Watergate. An advanced version of small-donor public financing has been used in New York City since 1989. Small contributions receive a taxpayer match, currently at a 6:1 ratio. Candidates meld grassroots organizing and fundraising. Living-room kaffee klatsches suddenly produce as much campaign money as sessions with real estate lobbyists. The system does not negate all campaign finance imbalances: Mayor Michael Bloomberg still spent over $266 million to win his three races against publicly financed opponents. But in typical races that did not involve Gotham's second wealthiest single individual, public financing has opened unprecedented opportunities to run. Varying versions of this approach have been suggested for congressional and presidential races. Small-donor public financing would not pretend to get all private money out of politics (a task that is futile, and not really desirable). But it would boost the voices of voters and incentivize participation—a less puritanical and more democratic set of goals—while reducing opportunities for corruption.

15

The 2020 Election

SOME ERAS are quiet. In others, great forces clash, bringing about breakthroughs in participation—or a lurch backward. That's where we are today: one of the most intense moments in our history in the fight for a meaningful right to vote.

When the presidential election year began, there was every reason to expect record turnout. In the 2014 midterm, participation had plunged to the lowest level in seven decades. But Donald Trump's astounding election to the presidency provoked a massive response. Two years later, midterm turnout soared to the highest level in more than a century. In 2020, experts worried about problems with voting machines, Russian hacking, purges of citizens from the voting rolls, long lines, and so on—and a flood of voters. It promised to be a busy year.

Then came the pandemic.

In January, as word trickled out about COVID-19 spreading around the world, a senior epidemiologist who worked for New York City confided the alarm among public health professionals: it was, she said, like watching a tsunami head for shore, and nobody on land understood what would soon hit them.

By mid-March, the pandemic convulsed the United States. All will remember those surreal, terrifying days. Travel was shut off to China and then Europe, businesses and government offices began to close, supermarket shelves emptied. In New York City, ambulance sirens wailed through the night. Soon it became clear that COVID-19 would upend the election, too. Much of the country shut down on Friday, March 13. That day, Louisiana postponed its presidential primary. Other states began to do the same.

Wisconsin, the only state that did not move the date of its April primary, slid into chaos. Republicans blocked the Democratic governor's last-minute bid to postpone the balloting. Poll workers, many of whom were civic-minded elderly people at extra risk from the virus, vanished. Milwaukee cut its polling places from 182 to five. In the days before the election, nearly a million people requested absentee ballots, with many unsent, others rejected, and confusion in the counting. On primary day, House speaker Robin Vos, who had refused to postpone the primary, told citizens not to worry. "You are incredibly safe to go out," he explained. As he spoke, Vos wore a full-length plastic protective gown, surgical gloves, and a hospital mask. Milwaukee public health authorities had ordered people to stay home, but to cast ballots, thousands had to wait in line. Citizens were forced to choose between their health and their right to vote.

It was plain that Wisconsin's bedlam might repeat around the country in November. With the path of the pandemic unclear, with second and third waves of illness expected later in the year, and no certainty about how to protect oneself, turnout could collapse. The health crisis could become a democracy crisis. Quite literally, there might not have been a free and fair election in 2020.

Voting rights groups had never faced a challenge like this before. Quickly they shifted focus. Even as its offices shut down, with attorneys spiriting away files and boxes of stationery as if fleeing an invading army, the Brennan Center for Justice published a plan for what states would need to do to run safe elections. Initial estimates pegged the cost at $2 billion, though later it was increased to $4 billion. The blueprint set out the elements that would become familiar by year's end.

First, everyone needed access to vote by mail. Already, that was how millions of people cast ballots. The Brennan Center plan did not urge a move to universal vote by mail; few states were ready for that, and many people wanted other options. Rather, the plan urged officials to ask all citizens if they wanted a ballot. In an earlier time, vote by mail seemed less secure than in-person options. But computer barcodes on envelopes and other measures perfected in recent years allayed fraud concerns, ensuring that vote by mail as it was used by millions was secure.

Then early voting would need to be expanded, to ease crowding on Election Day. Many Black citizens, in particular, voted early and were wary of absentee ballots, noting that the postal service poorly served their neighborhoods. There would need to be investments to create safe in-person polling places, including basic items such as gloves, masks, and other PPE supplies at a time when hospitals were still running short. Registration would be rethought; organizers had planned to spend the spring going door-to-door signing up first-timers. Most states let citizens register online, but deadlines would have to be changed.

The Leadership Conference on Civil and Human Rights, the preeminent lobbying coalition in Washington led by former Justice Department official Vanita Gupta, endorsed the plan and began to mobilize support on Capitol Hill. Throughout the year, the Leadership Conference worked with the Brennan Center, Stacey Abrams's group Fair Fight, and a few others as an informal steering committee. Hyperactive organizers and attorneys suddenly found themselves marooned at home, working intensely as children demanded attention and spouses competed for Wi-Fi. Toggling from one Zoom call to the next, whispering on secure Signal chat groups, they organized a mass policy response in those first weeks of COVID's hallucinatory alternate reality.

For a brief moment, even in Washington, D.C., the scale of the disaster dissolved partisan divisions. Economic activity was falling by an annual rate of 32 percent. As the economy shuddered to a halt—not a recession, as many noted, but a medically induced coma—Congress began to pass a series of massive economic stimulus bills. On March 27, with bipartisan support, Congress authorized $400 million for states to run safe elections in November as part of a $2 trillion spending bill. It was not enough, ultimately totaling only 10 percent of the need, but it was a start.

In the end, most states made it easier to vote during the pandemic. Five states already ran elections by mail and did not need to do much. Some asked residents if they wanted to apply to get an absentee ballot. Others had to change the rules so people could vote that way. By the fall, eight in ten voters nationwide could cast ballots by mail if they wanted to. Only Texas, Louisiana, Mississippi, Tennessee, and Indiana required a specific excuse.

Voting Amid Crisis

It turns out there was precedent for all this. The COVID crisis of 2020 was not the first time Americans had to vote amid disruption.

In November 1864, the Civil War still dragged on, with hundreds of thousands dead or wounded. Abraham Lincoln thought he was likely to lose the election to former general George McClellan, who proposed ending the war with slavery intact. Lincoln was so gloomy about his chances that he wrote a memo to his Cabinet, to be unsealed only after Election Day, that assumed he had lost. (He urged his officials "to save the Union between the election and the inauguration, as [his opponent] will have secured his election on such ground that he can not possibly save it afterwards.") Last-minute military victories, especially the Army's capture of Atlanta, swung support toward Lincoln. Challenging circumstances led to innovation. The first widespread use of absentee ballots let Union soldiers vote, providing Lincoln's margin of victory.

Two days after his reelection, Lincoln spoke to a crowd serenading him at the White House. There were "emergencies," he noted. "But the election was a necessity," he declared. "We can not have free government without elections; and if the rebellion could force us to forego, or postpone a national election, it might fairly claim to have already conquered and ruined us."

That determination to keep democracy functioning was also evident when Americans voted during other national emergencies.

In 1918, the influenza pandemic that infected more than one in four Americans intersected with Election Day. A second wave emerged near Boston in September. The political campaign that year was intense: World War I was still underway, some women were voting for the first time, and "dry" candidates were making a hard push for prohibition.

Local and state authorities sought to maintain the integrity of the election while protecting public safety. Health officials in D.C. decided to reopen churches, schools, and theaters shortly before Election Day. In San Francisco, health officials mandated that people wear face masks while in public or in groups of two or more. All poll workers and voters were required to wear masks on Election Day, prompting the *San Francisco Chronicle* to call it "the first masked ballot ever known in the history of America." Still "in most places the election was held with relatively few complications," one study later concluded. The flu changed political practices: mass meetings were replaced by direct mail and newspaper ads. Turnout suffered.

During World War II, as described in chapter 10, many were overseas or away from home. In 1942, with strong support from First Lady Eleanor Roosevelt, Congress passed the Soldier Voting Act, which let service members vote absentee in federal elections and helped states send them ballots. This bill was delayed by Southern opposition because it did not require soldiers, white or Black, to pay the poll tax. In 1944, Congress strengthened the law. Eventually, at least 2.6 million soldiers cast ballots—enough to make a difference in that year's contentious presidential election.

Decades later, fears were rampant about a terrorist attack in 2004, the first presidential election held after 9/11. A train bombing in Madrid that spring was seen as an effort to influence Spain's elections. The House of Representatives made clear that the election would not be delayed. By 419 to 2, it declared that "the actions of terrorists will never cause the date of any Presidential election to be postponed," and that "no single individual or agency should be given the authority to postpone the date of a Presidential election."

COVID, in other words, was not unlike other times the country had to adjust election plans in a crisis. But it was the first time that a major-party candidate for President, let alone the incumbent with access to the bully pulpit, saw the crisis as an opportunity to collapse turnout.

"Rigged"

Trump began to heckle the election in March, spewing an escalating set of charges against vote by mail. He started just after he signed the stimulus into law. The Democrats' spending proposal had "levels of voting that if you ever agreed to it, you'd never have a Republican elected in this country again." As sometimes happened, he had blurted out his motive: "levels of voting," the fear of an expanded electorate. Then—as if remembering his lines—Trump began to insist that the problem was not turnout, but fraud. Dozens of times he tweeted false claims. The election would be, he warned, "the most RIGGED Election in our nations [*sic*] history."

This was not the first time Trump shouted voter fraud without evidence. In 2016, the newly elected president claimed he, not Hillary Clinton, really had won the popular vote if you "deduct" 3 to 5 million illegal voters. (Invisible voters, evidently, since nobody saw them.) He created a commission to prove his nonsensical claim; the panel imploded and shut down without finding misconduct. Trump largely had dropped the issue. But now, as he pounded away at the election, *Politico* reported that bogus charges of fraud had gone from a complaint to the campaign's strategy.

It all came at a time of agonizing social tension. COVID hit Black communities with extra force. Then, on Memorial Day, a Minneapolis police officer murdered a Black man, George Floyd, a death captured on video by a horrified teenager. Within days, racial justice protests exploded nationwide. By one count, 15 to 20 million people marched in the first week in June to decry police brutality and demand justice. In some cities, protests turned violent. Near the White House, federal officers fired tear gas and rubber bullets to clear Lafayette Square—the spot where suffragists a century before, and so many others, had protested—allowing Trump to walk across and brandish a Bible in front of a local church damaged by arson.

Trump's attacks began to worry other Republicans. Vote by mail had never been particularly controversial (as opposed to, say, identification requirements). Florida and Arizona Republicans long built campaigns around absentee balloting by retirees. Before the pandemic, polls showed that people from both parties generally supported it, as well as early voting. After Trump's fusillade, that shifted, with Democrats now far more likely to want to vote remotely and Republicans saying they would not.

Throughout the year, as tens and then hundreds of thousands died in the pandemic, Trump fell behind Democratic nominee Joe Biden in the polls. Panicked, he responded by instinct, stoking visceral fears of urban disorder and shady fraud, aiming to undermine confidence. In July he suggested delaying the election. (Presidents do not have the power to do that. Election Day was set by statute in the 1840s.) By the fall, he would not commit to a "peaceful transfer of power." "We're going to have to see what happens," he told a news conference.

In the first presidential debate, he refused to condemn violent white supremacist groups. "Who would you like me to condemn?" he asked moderator Chris Wallace. "Proud Boys," interjected Biden. They were a far-right group known for brawling in the streets.

"Proud Boys," Trump said, swiveling to the audience and looking to the camera, "stand back—and stand by."

The Mobilization

Trump's tantrums could mesmerize. Far from Washington, though, and far more quietly, an unprecedented civic effort coalesced to ensure a safe election. In other years, campaigns or political parties have become a cause, a mass mobilization event. In 2020, in some respects, it was democracy itself, under assault from the virus and president, that served as an emotional rallying cry.

To start with, Congress never sent states enough money, so private philanthropy stepped in. America's Gilded Age–level of wealth concentration made a difference. Just one mogul, Facebook founder Mark Zuckerberg, with his wife, Priscilla Chan, provided $350 million for states to run elections safely, nearly matching the amount Congress had spent.

Businesses mobilized in other less gaudy ways. Patagonia (the outdoorsy clothing company whose fleece vests were iconic business wear in Silicon Valley), Levi's, PayPal, and a handful of other progressive-minded firms had organized a coalition to ensure employees could get time off to vote. Eventually, Time To Vote included more than one thousand major national retailers and manufacturers including Walmart, McDonald's, and Nike. With other business groups, it focused on recruiting poll workers. All told, businesses recruited at least 350,000 new people to work at the polls.

Athletes rallied, as well. National Basketball Association players were holed up at Disney World, playing an eerie season without fans. They began to speak out. Many wore the Black Lives Matter slogan on their jerseys. In August, as racial justice protests tore through Kenosha, Wisconsin, Milwaukee Bucks players refused to participate in playoff games. The players union brokered a deal: teams would make their arenas available as polling places, and the players would return. In Atlanta, the Hawks' head coach worked at the polls, his face obscured by a mask. Nearly 300,000 people voted at the stadiums. Megastar LeBron James, long politically active in Ohio and now a Los Angeles Laker, formed a new organization, More Than a Vote. It worked with civil rights lawyers to recruit forty thousand poll workers. "We didn't tell you who to go vote for. We didn't pick one side versus the other side," James told a press conference after the election. "We just wanted to educate you, enlighten you, and empower you. And let you know how important your right is."

State and local officials, meanwhile, had to rewrite their plans. Many had been preparing for possible hacking by Russia or other foreign interests. Microsoft engineers and Brennan Center lawyers had partnered to hold "tabletop" exercises with county officers, gaming out what to do if things went wrong. (*Your machines jam. So make sure there are extra ballots.*) Quickly these became planning sessions on how to make polling places safer, how to count absentee ballots quickly, and other urgent 2020 needs.

All this unfolded in a year when more than ever people were at home, online, checking Twitter, watching cable news, obsessively "doomscrolling" through bad news late into the night. Fears about the election rattled public confidence. When the post office announced delays in the mail, at best an ill-considered move in the middle of a pandemic when absentee balloting would be key, cable television obsessively covered what looked like a plot to steal the election but turned out to be cronyism and incompetence.

The news media began to explain that it would take longer than usual to tally the ballots—and that would not be reported as "chaos" or a sign of chicanery, but simply a sign that officials were counting carefully. Television news anchors told viewers to settle in not for Election Night, but Election Week. One poll showed that two thirds of respondents did not expect to know the results immediately, and most understood it could take up to a week.

The weeks before the election saw a pile-up of lawsuits. In states that vote by mail, most people deposit ballots in secure drop boxes, often in government offices or at libraries. The Trump campaign pelted officials with lawsuits trying to stop the use of those boxes. Most courts rejected the campaign's efforts. At the same time, rights groups and Democrats sued to ease access during the pandemic (such as ensuring that ballots postmarked by Election Day could be counted for a few days after). These suits had more success, but when cases reached the U.S. Supreme Court, partisan and divided, it turned back voting rights claims. Often it did this without hearing oral arguments and without explanation (in what lawyers call the "shadow docket"). Once again, courts dashed any hopes that they would lead in expanding the right to vote.

Harris County, Texas, is a microcosm of a changing country. It includes vibrant, diverse Houston, ringed by its growing suburbs. The county government was led by twenty-nine-year-old Lina Hidalgo. She had taken a leave as a law student at New York University to challenge a long-time incumbent and won, finding herself presiding over a $5 billion budget. After a disorganized primary held early in the pandemic, she hired a thirty-four-year-old McKinsey consultant to get ready for November. They "hit the ground running," reported *Texas Monthly*, "embracing an array of innovative ideas, including 24-hour voting, drive-through voting, and ballot drop boxes." They recruited eleven thousand poll workers to staff early voting locations as well as Election Day polling places, and invested in personal protective equipment. Republicans in the state capital noticed. The state of Texas sued Hidalgo to stop her from sending out absentee ballots. Then the governor announced there could only be one drop box per county, meaning that Harris County with 4.7 million people and Loving County, with sixty-seven residents, each would be allowed one. The Brennan Center, representing the Anti-Defamation League and others, sued to challenge that move but lost at the state supreme court. Hidalgo prevailed when the state tried to block drive-through voting.

Similar clashes tumbled out across the country. It all involved tens of thousands of activists and officials, and hundreds of millions of dollars.

Then, in the end, Election Day arrived—and it was remarkably normal. Polling places saw little violence. Long lines, which marred the start of early voting, largely evaporated (though in Georgia and other places, as before, it was Black and Latino citizens who disproportionately had to wait in line). The emergency measures proved popular and effective.

Despite the pandemic, despite voter suppression and lies, the country saw the highest turnout since 1900. Overall participation soared, rising 7 percent from four years before. Nearly half of voters used absentee or mail, twice as many as the last presidential election. One in four voted early in person. In keeping with earlier years, but perhaps surprisingly given Trump's racialized hysteria on the topic, Black people were more likely to vote early in person than by mail, in contrast to other groups.

Notably, the relaxed rules and expanded electorate did not seem to have benefitted one party over the other. Republicans unexpectedly gained eleven seats in the House of Representatives. In the Senate, expected Democratic victories failed to materialize, leaving the party two seats short of a majority with only two runoff elections to come. The GOP gained in state legislative races, as well.

But Joe Biden defeated Donald Trump. It wasn't really close. Biden and his running mate, Kamala Harris, won 51.3 percent of the popular vote to Trump's 46.3 percent, the highest share for a challenger since Franklin Roosevelt ousted Herbert Hoover in 1932. An electoral coalition led by women and voters of color lifted into office the first woman, Black person, or South Asian to serve as vice president—and only the second Catholic president ever. But the quirks of the Electoral College risked turning a decisive popular vote win into defeat for the second time in a row, and the third time in two decades. Key states were achingly close. Biden and Harris eked out a 306–232 Electoral College win with just 44,000 votes in key states.

The election had been extraordinarily well run. The federal Department of Homeland Security declared, "The November 3rd election was the most secure in American history. . . . There is no evidence that any voting system deleted or lost votes, changed votes, or was in any way compromised." (Trump responded to the announcement by firing the key official who protected elections from cyber threats.) Election officials agreed. The Republican secretaries of state contacted by the media all reported they saw no evidence of misconduct. Attorney General William Barr publicly confirmed that there was no widespread fraud. Privately to the president, he called the claims "bullshit."

All this confirmed: voter fraud in the United States is vanishingly rare. As described earlier in this book, you are more likely to be struck by lightning than to impersonate another person at the polls, for example. A comprehensive analysis found only thirty-one credible instances of fraud between 2000 and 2014 out of 1 billion ballots cast. Wild claims amount to a conspiracy theory, nothing more.

Trump joined the list of presidents defeated for reelection. Ten incumbents had lost before him. In the past century they included George H. W. Bush, Jimmy Carter, Gerald Ford, and Herbert Hoover. All conceded and pledged their respect for the public's democratic choice. "The people have spoken and we respect the majesty of the democratic system," Bush had declared. Gerald Ford had wired Jimmy Carter, "I congratulate you on your victory." Respect for voters and acceptance of the result are core tenets of democracies and mark a stable political system. As former White House chief of staff Mick Mulvaney reassured in the *Wall Street Journal*, "if he loses, Trump will concede gracefully." (Even asking the question, Mulvaney wrote, "probably says as much about those asking it as the answer does about President Trump.")

And at that moment, Trump began an assault on America's democratic institutions, a direct attack on the legitimacy of the vote never before seen in the country's history.

The Big Lie

It began on Election Night. It was widely understood that ballots cast in person would likely favor Republicans, but that absentee votes would favor Democrats. Pundits called it the "Red Mirage" or "Blue Shift." This would be especially important in Pennsylvania and Michigan, where the law prevented absentee ballots from being tabulated until after Election Day. (Republican legislators had refused to change the rules.) As results trickled in over the first hours, the presidential race seemed closer than expected. Then Fox News called Arizona for Biden. It looked highly likely he had won, all over but the counting.

Early the next morning, Trump went before supporters in the East Room of the White House. "Frankly, we did win this election," he said to cheers.

"The Big Lie" was a description of a Nazi propaganda technique. As the U.S. government's secret psychological profile of Adolf Hitler explained in 1943, the dictator lived by the belief that "people will believe a big lie sooner than a little one; and if you repeat it frequently enough people will sooner or later believe it." Trump's claim that the election was fraudulent and stolen fit that description perfectly, since the reality was so diametrically opposite.

For four days, in Pennsylvania, Michigan, Georgia, and other key states, election officials and volunteers counted ballots in cavernous convention centers, with observers from both parties standing by and television cameras trained on the scene. Outside, Trump supporters shouted, "stop the steal" and "stop the count." Michigan and Wisconsin had long backed Democrats but swung to Trump in 2016; now they were declared for Biden. The biggest surprise came in Georgia, which had not chosen a Democrat in nearly three decades. Black voters and a suburban shift powered the Biden ticket to a narrow win.

As the counting continued, Trump supporters became more agitated, and more visible. Some election officials, facing screaming crowds and death threats, went into hiding. A cellphone message warned Philadelphia's Republican city commissioner that he and colleagues were "the reason why we have the Second Amendment." Meanwhile Democratic groups, who had been primed to hit the streets, held back, restrained after a series of fretful conference calls organized by the AFL–CIO and other groups.

For four days, officials tallied ballots in Pennsylvania. Finally, late in the morning on Saturday, November 7, the television news networks called the state for Biden and Harris. Now it was Democrats who poured into the streets, banging pots and pans and celebrating in strongholds like Brooklyn and Chicago. For one half of a divided country, it was a moment of exuberance and release.

Just then, Rudolph Giuliani was in the middle of a bizarre press conference. Giuliani's operatic career deserves its own book. Once a crusading anti-corruption prosecutor in New York, then the city's two term mayor, a onetime presidential candidate, he now served as President Trump's lawyer. His erratic efforts in Ukraine to procure political dirt on Biden and his family had led directly to Trump's impeachment. His odd pocket dials to reporters and heavy drinking were tabloid fodder. The big corporate law firms Trump had counted on to run his legal team pulled out. Rudy Giuliani was in charge.

Trump had announced a press conference at the Four Seasons, presumably the swank downtown hotel. Instead, microphones were hurriedly set up in front of Four Seasons Total Landscaping, located in a strip mall in Philadelphia's industrial fringe, near a sex shop and a crematorium. In a scene reminiscent of the television satire *Veep*, campaign aides rushed to insist that was the plan all along. With no evidence, Giuliani and other speakers insisted that there had been massive fraud. "Some of the ballots looked suspicious," Giuliani charged. Philadelphia was run by a "decrepit Democratic machine." Midway through Giuliani's monologue, a British reporter interrupted with news that the television networks had just called the election for Biden. Giuliani scoffed. "Who was it called by?" "All of them." Trump's lawyer raised his hands and looked skyward. "Networks don't get to decide elections. Courts do."

Trump had hoped that judges, many of whom he had appointed, would overturn the election. When Supreme Court justice Ruth Bader

Ginsburg died, he nominated Amy Coney Barrett for the seat. Barrett was confirmed just eight days before Election Day. Trump explained, "I think this will end up in the Supreme Court, and I think it's very important that we have nine Justices."

Trump and his backers filed dozens of lawsuits demanding that the results be overturned, alleging fraud, or claiming illegal practices. Some tried to exclude the votes of Detroit, Philadelphia, Atlanta, and Milwaukee—all cities with heavily Black and Latino electorates. Again and again, the evidence crumbled. In a remarkable string of losses, sixty-three courts ruled on these cases—and all sixty-three ruled against Trump. Republican and Democratic judges joined in. Claims of misconduct in Detroit, the Michigan Supreme Court ruled, are "incorrect and not credible." A conservative Wisconsin Supreme Court justice called the bid to overturn that state's vote "the most dramatic invocation of judicial power I have ever seen. Judicial acquiescence to such entreaties built on so flimsy a foundation would do indelible damage to every future election."

Pennsylvania's twenty electoral votes were crucial to Biden's win. Trump sued to stop the state from certifying the victory despite the 6.8 million votes cast, or at least to discard those of the 1.2 million people who voted by mail in Philadelphia and Pittsburgh. A conservative federal trial judge heard the case. In a five-hour argument, Giuliani admitted the Trump campaign "doesn't plead fraud." A few days later the judge issued a scorching ruling. Trump's lawsuit was marred by "strained legal arguments without merit and speculative accusations . . . unsupported by evidence." He added, "In the United States of America, this cannot justify the disenfranchisement of a single voter, let alone all the voters of its sixth most populated state." Trump's lawyers quickly appealed. A three-judge panel, all Republicans, rejected the claims a week later. "Charges of unfairness are serious. But calling an election unfair does not make it so. Charges require specific allegations and then proof. We have neither here," wrote Judge Stephanos Bibas, a Trump appointee.

The president's lawyers denounced the ruling. "The activist judicial machinery in Pennsylvania continues to cover up the allegations of massive fraud," one tweeted. "On to SCOTUS!" Trump himself tweeted a photo of Amy Coney Barrett doctored to show beams of incandescent light coming from her eyes. The Supreme Court never even heard the case.

Repeatedly the courts repudiated Trump's claims. In that important way, the system worked—the institutions held. But the more Trump brayed about the election being stolen, the more his supporters believed him. Other Republican political leaders shrugged; none would state the obvious fact that Joe Biden had prevailed. "What is the downside for humoring him for this little bit of time? No one seriously thinks the results will change," one Republican leader anonymously told the *Washington Post* in early November. But Trump's incessant false claims of fraud, together with the silence of party leaders, cemented the view among supporters: Biden was not legitimately president. Seventy percent of Republicans believed he had won only through fraud, as of late November. That number has barely budged since.

The Electoral College

Trump's attempt to overturn the election exposed creaky constitutional machinery. As we all now know too well, the popular vote does not choose the president. In 2000 and 2016, the popular vote winner was denied the White House; it almost happened in 2004 as well. (George W. Bush, first elected president despite losing the popular vote, would have been defeated despite winning it.) The process for counting, certifying, and tallying the electoral count was set by the Twelfth Amendment to the Constitution, and by a dismayingly muddled statute passed in 1887, the Electoral Count Act.

Still, the basics were fairly simple. States certified the winners, under their own laws, based on the citizens' vote. Legislators could not simply override that. The U.S. Supreme Court recently had noted that "legislatures no longer play a role" in deciding who gets electors. States had to complete their count by December 8 and cast the electoral votes on December 14.

Trump and his dwindling band of strategists began to spin ever wilder theories of how the results could be reversed. Biden had won Michigan by a comfortable 154,000 votes, fourteen times greater than the margin by which Trump had carried the state four years earlier. The Wayne County canvassing board, a normally sleepy body, certified Biden the winner, reversed itself, then reversed itself again. It turned out the president had called two of its otherwise anonymous members. Trump then summoned the state's two top legislative leaders to an Oval Office meeting. At the airport in Detroit, angry protesters organized by voting rights groups swarmed the lawmakers. When they got to the White House, the officials told the president that constitutionally they could not overturn the public's choice.

On November 19, Giuliani held a press conference at the Republican National Committee. "There was a plan—from a centralized place—to execute these various acts of voter fraud," he declared with no evidence. He explained, "I know crimes, I can smell them." As he ranted, dark trickles began to pour down his face, hair dye mingled with sweat. Giuliani turned the microphone to another lawyer, Sidney Powell. Once she had been a respected prosecutor. Now she descried a conspiracy involving a voting machine manufacturer, a computer server based in Germany, and "Communist money" led by Venezuelan dictator Hugo Chávez, who, sadly, had been dead for seven years. Her delusions proved too odd even for Trump's team, which announced within days that she was "practicing law on her own." (Later, when a voting machine company sued her, Powell's defense was that no "reasonable" person could have believed her claims.)

Nevertheless Powell persisted. On the Fox Business cable channel, she vowed to "release the Kraken," a monster lawsuit that would undo the election. Eventually she met with Trump in the Oval Office, where he mulled whether to appoint her "special counsel" to find election fraud. She was accompanied by retired general Michael Flynn, Trump's first National Security Advisor, convicted of lying to the FBI, who had recently opined that Trump could deploy the military to seize power and "re-run" the election. Trump began to put more and more pressure on the Justice Department to intervene. According to notes from a conversation with the acting Attorney General, the president implored, "just say that the election was corrupt + leave the rest to me and the R[epublican] Congressmen." His demands for action worried military leaders. General Mark Milley, chair of the Joint Chiefs of Staff, reportedly likened Trump's supporters to "brownshirts in the streets," Hitler's paramilitary force before he took power.

The false fraud claims were outlandish, absurd, but lucrative. Trump and the Republican party raised $250 million in November and December with the pretense that the election was still in doubt. (It was a grift. Few of those funds were used to contest the results. The GOP's lead lawyer privately described Trump's lawsuits as "a joke.") Fox News began to lose viewers to One American News Network and Newsmax, more extreme networks. Devotees of the bizarre online conspiracy theory known as Qanon—which believed that the world was run by a satanic cult that imprisoned and ate children—spread more rumors. The Republican Party moved quickly from "what is the downside for humoring him" to adopting his lie. Texas sued Pennsylvania, Georgia, Michigan, and Wisconsin, arguing those states should not have expanded ballot access during the pandemic. It was legally nonsensical. On December 11, the U.S. Supreme Court unanimously tossed the suit out in a one-page order, noting that one state has no standing to sue another to object to how it runs its elections.

Soon the deadline approached for states to certify their results. Some Republican officials, under great pressure, held firm. In Arizona, Republican Governor Doug Ducey was signing the paperwork to award the state's electors to Biden when his cellphone played "Hail to the Chief," apparently his ringtone when Trump would call. Ducey silenced it. On December 14, as set by federal law, the states cast their electoral votes, confirming Biden's win.

Georgia

In 2018, Georgia had been roiled by an epic race for governor. Stacey Abrams, a new, rare political character, was the Democratic nominee. The party leader in the state legislature and a former tax attorney, a young Black woman, she also wrote romance novels under the pen name Selena Montgomery. Over the previous decade, she had led registration drives in the state that brought Black voters to parity with whites. Abrams faced Brian Kemp, a conservative Republican who was Secretary of State and thus supervised the election in which he ran. Kemp's office had purged 1.4 million people from the rolls, while questioning the registrations of 53,000 more—overwhelmingly Black—because of typos. Kemp won by 55,000 votes out of 4 million cast. Abrams decried the vote suppression, acknowledging his win but declaring "this is not a concession speech." She became a national icon, and Democrats chose her to deliver the response to Trump's State of the Union Address. But she refused entreaties to run for the U.S. Senate. Instead, she focused on establishing a new group, Fair Fight, to organize voter protection efforts in the state and around the country. As in other eras, the fight for voting rights now was a core party priority for one of the parties. In this case, the protest leader and the politician were one and the same person.

Under state law, two Senate seats in Georgia would go to a runoff on January 5. The outcome would decide control of the U.S. Senate. Odds heavily favored Republicans, since Democrats typically performed less well in runoffs, which had lower turnout and a shorter window to organize. Neither Democratic candidate had ever held elected office. Raphael Warnock was a pastor at Ebenezer Baptist Church, Dr. Martin Luther

King Jr.'s pulpit in downtown Atlanta. Jon Ossoff, a thirty-two-year-old rail-thin documentary filmmaker, previously had lost a suburban congressional race. Both had amassed huge financial support but were expected to fall short.

But Trump stewed over his loss in Georgia, and the unwillingness of its Republicans to nullify the results and hand him the state's electoral votes. Reality was left far behind. Lin Wood, an attorney who worked with the president's team, urged Republicans to boycott and demanded the arrest of the incumbent Republican senators for insufficient zeal. The two Republican incumbents, in turn, called for the resignation of election officials. National Republican leaders feared Trump would join calls for a boycott.

In Georgia as elsewhere, fraud claims were nonsense. The state organized a recount of its ballots, with election officials from around the country pouring into the state to help. It was the biggest hand recount ever. Biden's lead held. The state's electoral machinery, notably, was entirely in the hands of Republicans. Now Trump bitterly attacked Secretary of State Brad Raffensperger. "Stop the Steal" protesters besieged his house. Gabriel Sterling, who oversaw the recount, strode into a press conference shaking with anger. "Someone's going to get shot," said Sterling. "Someone's gonna get killed." In early January, Trump called Raffensperger and pressured him to cook the results. "What I want to do is this. I just want to find 11,780 votes, which is one more than [the 11,779 vote margin of defeat] we have, because we won the state," Trump told Raffensperger. He said the Georgian's failure to undo the results was "a criminal offense" and threatened prosecution ("that's a big risk to you"). Raffensperger taped the call, and released the recording two days before Georgians would choose their senators.

Democrats who typically sat out runoff elections voted in high numbers, many of them organized by Abrams's voting rights machine, many by nonpartisan groups like the New Georgia Project, many of them just furious at Trump's attempts to overturn the state's election results. By early morning on Wednesday, January 6, both Warnock and Ossoff had won. The state once represented by segregationist leader Richard Russell now would be represented by a Black minister and a Jewish millennial. And the Democrats would take control of the U.S. Senate.

Later that day would come the joint session of Congress to formalize the electoral count and declare Biden the winner.

The Insurrection

For more than a century, the ceremony of counting the electoral votes has been an empty ritual, if at times awkward, even poignant. Richard Nixon as vice president had to declare John F. Kennedy the victor. Al Gore did the same, gaveling down a handful of lawmakers angry about the Florida fiasco. Mike Pence would preside over the formal announcement of Biden's and Harris's victory.

Trump continued to tell his supporters that the election had been stolen, and urged them to take to the streets. On December 13, at a raucous rally in Washington, D.C., the Proud Boys shouted "four more years" and speakers claimed that voting machines had secretly switched results. When it was over demonstrators tore down Black Lives Matter banners and fought with counter-protesters. It was a dry run. Trump and his backers next set their sights on the day of the ceremonial counting of the votes as the true day of reckoning.

"Big protest in D.C. on January 6th," the President of the United States tweeted on December 19. "Be there, will be wild!"

His supporters began setting up Facebook groups, posting photos of weapons, making clear they would fight. Trump began to insist that Vice President Pence "has the power to reject fraudulently chosen electors." Trump pulled Pence into the Oval Office, and introduced a law professor, John Eastman, who mapped out an illegal plan for Pence to simply reject the electoral votes of key states and hand Trump the presidency—a constitutional coup. On January 5, Pence told Trump at lunch that he had no authority to do that and would certify Biden as the winner. It must have been an interesting lunch.

The next morning, tens of thousands of Trump's supporters gathered at the Ellipse south of the White House. The Proud Boys—"Stand back, and stand by"—were in full force. So were the Oath Keepers militiamen, who had been guarding political strategist Roger Stone at his hotel. Rudolph Giuliani implored the crowd, "Let's have trial by combat." Speakers spun wild tales of fraud. The law professor, John Eastman, described voting machines with secret compartments stuffed with hidden Biden ballots. Representative Mo Brooks of Alabama told the crowd to "start taking down names and kicking ass." He noted how "our ancestors" sacrificed their "blood, their sweat, their tears, their fortunes, and sometimes their lives" and asked the audience if they were "willing to do the same."

Then Trump spoke. After months of lying, of telling his followers that the election had been stolen, that democracy itself was at risk, now he told them what to do. "If Mike Pence does the right thing, we win the election." He urged them to march to the Capitol and promised to join them. "After this, we're going to walk down, and I'll be there with you."

"And we fight. We fight like hell. And if you don't fight like hell, you're not going to have a country anymore," he finished.

The whole world knows what happened next. The mob included many white supremacists and even neo-Nazis. Thousands of men wearing red Make America Great Again hats and carrying Trump banners stormed the Capitol, assaulting police officers, smashing glass, and forcing their way into the building. They aimed to stop the counting of the presidential votes. Some carried Confederate flags. Some bellowed, "Hang Mike Pence!"

In the House and Senate chambers, dozens of Republicans were still trying to overturn the election and had just begun to debate. Guards and police rushed in, hustled Pence and House Speaker Nancy Pelosi to safety, and barred the doors, with guns drawn. A Capitol Police officer and four other people died that day. The insurrectionists injured one hundred forty police officers. One adherent of the Qanon conspiracy theory, Ashli Babbitt, was shot by a guard as the mob tried to break into the House chamber. As the rioters sacked the Capitol, Trump tweeted, "Mike Pence didn't have the courage to do what should have been done to protect our Country and our Constitution . . ." Republican leader Kevin McCarthy, in hiding, called the president and begged him to call off the mob. "Well, Kevin," Trump reportedly replied, "I guess these people are more upset about the election then you are." Rioters took over the Senate chamber and ransacked Speaker Pelosi's office. Late in the day, after hours of delay, National Guard troops recaptured the Capitol.

Late that night, the congressional sessions to count the electoral votes resumed. Senator Josh Hawley of Missouri, who had been photographed raising a supportive fist at the insurrectionists earlier in the day, demanded that the election be overturned. Senator Ted Cruz of Texas urged that a commission decide the election as it had in 1877, choosing Rutherford Hayes over Samuel J. Tilden. That was the political equivalent of a Freudian slip, conveying more truth than intended. The corrupt deal ended Reconstruction and led to a century of segregation, disenfranchisement, and brutality. Even after the Capitol had been overrun, 138 House Republicans—two thirds of the caucus—voted to overturn the citizens' choice. McCarthy, who only hours earlier had beseeched Trump to pull back his violent supporters, voted to overturn the result of the 2020 election. Eight senators did so as well. No evidence of fraud or misconduct had been produced or brought to the floor of Congress that day.

A week later, the House of Representatives impeached Donald Trump—for the second time—for his role instigating the insurrection. One week after that, on January 20, 2021, before a Capitol still ringed with troops for protection, Biden and Harris took the oath of office.

Let's pause to recognize the magnitude of the constitutional breach: a defeated president, refusing to respect the results of the election, falsely and repeatedly claiming fraud, tried to overturn it. Eventually he provoked a violent attack on the U.S. Capitol designed to stop the counting of the people's votes for president. Trump's actions during those three months, between the election and the end of his term, were the worst things he did as president—and arguably the worst thing any president has done in years. The sight, on television, of a terrorist mob storming and occupying the seat of government, is agonizing to watch. The whole world saw it.

The day before Biden's swearing in, Mitch McConnell spoke angrily in the Senate. "The mob was fed lies," he declared. "They were provoked by the president and other powerful people, and they tried to use fear and violence to stop a specific proceeding of the first branch of the federal government." But soon party lines hardened again. McConnell came out against conviction, and as he retreated from his strong words, any bipartisan consensus on the insurrection and its causes began to crumble. Seven Republican senators voted to convict Trump in the impeachment trial, but that was short of the two thirds needed. Had he been convicted, under the Constitution the Senate could have barred him from ever seeking the presidency again.

But the Big Lie had taken hold. Belief that the election had been stolen, that Trump really won, that voters of color and political machines and voting machines somehow had rigged the democracy, now was a passionately embraced view held by tens of millions of Republicans. One of the nation's two political parties now organized itself around a delusion. It was transforming into something familiar in Europe but new to the United States: an antidemocratic faction, melding white nationalism, conspiracy thinking, and a hostility to democratic norms.

16

The Clash Over the Vote

On March 26, 2021, Georgia governor Brian Kemp sat at a polished table, brow furrowed, pen in hand. Six middle-aged white men in dark suits flanked him. They posed in front of an oil painting of a slave plantation. Kemp was there to sign the Election Integrity Act, a statute born in controversy, targeting Black, Latino, and Asian voters, which would help set off a high-decibel national debate. As the men stood stiffly, Representative Park Cannon, a Black Democratic legislator, knocked on the door of the governor's office. Two beefy state troopers grabbed her by both arms and arrested her, dragging her through the halls and out of the Capitol.

In a lurid flash the tableau captured a dramatic political story. In the early months of 2021, the Big Lie drove state legislatures across the country to mount an attack on voting rights—the most concerted attempt to roll back voting since the Jim Crow era.

By the Brennan Center's ongoing count, Republican legislators introduced more four hundred bills in forty-eight states to restrict the vote. These were not just thrown in the hopper by backbenchers hoping for a few good hours on Twitter. By October 2021, thirty-three bills in nineteen states had become law. Many of these proposals aimed to undo the practices that had successfully expanded access the previous year—

especially those that let citizens vote by mail or early. Others expanded purges (which removed people from the rolls) or authorized partisans to harass citizens. The push came hardest in states with the fastest-growing minority populations, states that had flipped to the Democrats or were threatening to do so. And the proposed restrictions uncannily hit hardest Black, Latino, and Asian citizens. Many of these measures once would have been stopped or slowed by the Voting Rights Act and its requirement that such changes be "precleared" by the Justice Department or a federal court. Now, thanks to the Supreme Court, legislators could act with impunity.

The fight first came into view in Georgia. Vote by mail had been enacted there by Republicans, but in 2020 it was heavily used by Democrats. The legislature prepared to effectively repeal it for those under sixty-five—meaning that older, whiter, more conservative citizens could still vote absentee. The proposal ended early voting on the Sunday before Election Day, the day Black churches organized "souls to the polls" drives. It repealed automatic voter registration, which Brian Kemp had proudly created as secretary of state just a few years before.

For some Republicans, it went too far. The state's lieutenant governor refused to preside over the legislative debate. Lobbyists for major corporations including Delta Air Lines and Coca Cola—long allies of the Georgia Republican party—urged a retreat. The behind-the-scenes scramble had some impact. As finally passed, the restrictions were less severe—but they were just as targeted. The new law banned mobile voting centers, for example, which only had been used in Atlanta. It made it a crime to give water or snacks to people waiting in line at a polling place, in a state where Black people were far more likely than white people to have to queue for long periods. It cut back on drop boxes and required more proof of identity to vote absentee.

At the last minute, sponsors slipped in perhaps the most dangerous provision. It sought to undermine the independent officials who had stood up to Trump and declared Biden the victor. The law created a new election board responsible to the Republican legislature, taking power away from the secretary of state. The law also effectively let the legislature remove county election officials (raising the risk that state lawmakers could simply take over the machinery in Democratic Atlanta). It was a new ominous twist: aiming not only to limit who could vote but rig who could count the votes. Not just vote suppression, but election subversion.

Georgia's law had a concussive impact. President Biden denounced it as "Jim Crow in the Twenty-First Century." Corporations that had professed fealty to racial equality the year before during Black Lives Matter protests now felt pressure from their own employees to do something. Executives, led by Ken Frazier, the CEO of Merck, and Ken Chenault, former CEO of American Express, signed protests and took out full-page ads. Major League Baseball moved the All-Star game out of Atlanta. The Georgia House, in turn, voted to revoke a jet fuel tax break that benefitted Delta Air Lines in punishment for its criticism of the new law. Senator Mitch McConnell, long the champion of *Citizens United*, now warned corporations to "stay out of politics."

Voting restrictions moved forward in other states. The governors of Iowa and Florida signed new laws. Ugly motives were barely concealed. An Arizona legislator who sponsored that state's proposals made headlines when he said that he did not think everyone should vote. At a hearing on a restrictive bill, Representative John Kavanaugh explained that when it came to voters, "Quantity is important but we have to look at quality as well." Texas bill S.B. No. 7 originally said it aimed to protect the "purity of the ballot box," a phrase from the state's constitution used to justify all-white primaries in the Jim Crow era. The wording was removed only after it was called out during a contentious debate on the bill.

Increasingly it became clear that a key strategic goal was to remold state election machinery to hand control to partisans. New laws and proposals targeted who would count the votes, stripping power from election officials. These schemes aimed to ensure that in 2024, independent officials could not stand up to political bullying as they had in 2020.

In Texas, legislation neared passage in June 2021 that would cut back on early voting, and impose criminal penalties on local officials who widely send out ballot applications. It barred drive-through voting and twenty-four-hour polling places, the innovations implemented by Lina Hidalgo in Harris County in 2020. It prohibited voting on Sunday mornings, the time used by Black churches for "souls to the polls" organizing drives. And it gave partisan judges the power to overturn election results. Following the trend set by Georgia, it imposed vague new criminal penalties on election officials if they modified or suspended rules in an emergency unless it is "expressly authorized" by the state's election code. "Other portions of S.B. No. 7 impose criminal penalties for activities involving counting ballots, dealing with mail-in ballot applications, mailing early voting material, provisional ballots, ballot duplication, and poll watchers," a watchdog group summarized.

With an hour left to go, Democratic lawmakers bolted, leaving the Senate short of a quorum and temporarily killing the bill. The governor called a special session in July to focus on restrictive election laws. When it began, Democrats slipped out of Austin, chartered a plane, and flew out of state. Texas governor Greg Abbott threatened to arrest them. Eventually they would trickle back to Texas, and the legislation eventually passed, but not before the lawmakers made a point on the national stage.

"We are now taking the fight to our nation's Capitol," the Democrats said in a statement. "We are living on borrowed time in Texas." They resurfaced in Washington, D.C., where they joined a movement demanding federal action.

For the People

It had the makings of an epic clash: State legislatures were rushing to restrict the vote. At the same time, Congress had the power to stop that voter suppression in its tracks—legally and constitutionally. The great question was whether it had the political will to do so.

Already, for the first time in decades, Democrats and progressives had begun to put democracy reform at the center of their politics. The new focus took shape after the 2016 election. Trump's victory startled many Americans, shaken by the country's divisions and the rise of angry white nationalism as a mainstream political force. Many saw Trump as part of a global backlash against pluralist, multiracial democracy.

In Grand Rapids the morning after Trump won, a twenty-eight-year-old named Katie Fahey sat in her kitchen and scrolled, wincing, through her social media feed. She tapped out a Facebook post. "I'd like to take on gerrymandering in Michigan," she wrote. "If you're interested in doing this as well please let me know." She added a smiley face emoji. Within weeks thousands of volunteers had signed up, and drafted a ballot measure to set up a nonpartisan commission to conduct redistricting. Relying only on volunteers, Fahey's group gathered signatures in the snow to qualify the proposal for the ballot. It won, as did similar laws in Colorado, Missouri, and Utah. That same day, in Florida, voters ended that state's notorious felony disenfranchisement system, which had barred 1.4 million from voting. A ballot measure to restore the right to vote for people with a past felony conviction needed 60 percent to win. Organizers, many of them formerly incarcerated, enlisted conservatives, religious leaders, and police chiefs. Instead of hiding they went door to door, asking to have their rights restored. Amendment Four passed with a surprising 64 percent. Republican legislators quickly moved to undo the change, and civil rights groups were challenging that in court.

Politicians responded to the surge in public support for reform. Sixteen states plus the District of Columbia had passed or implemented automatic registration, boosting rates across the country. Most were Democratic-leaning states, but not all. Alaska voters enacted it by ballot measure. In Illinois, Republican governor Bruce Rauner signed it into law after legislators passed it unanimously.

In 2017, Democrats took control of the U.S. House of Representatives. Nancy Pelosi returned as Speaker. It was far from obvious that party leaders would embrace reform. (Representative Steny Hoyer, Pelosi's deputy and longtime rival, had told me previously, "If we win, let me tell you what we're going to focus on: not this. People don't care.") Why the shift? A new political action committee, End Citizens United, had mobilized Democratic candidates who announced they would shun corporate funds. The group was explicitly political. Forty new lawmakers were elected with a pledge to make political reform a top priority. Pelosi introduced the For the People Act with the symbolically significant denominator H.R.1

It was novel to find democracy reform at the center of either party's agenda, and some lawmakers were uneasy. A cluster of Democratic House members quietly resisted. On a street near the Capitol one morning, a congressman told me he would oppose the plan, and that few cared. His timing was off. At that very moment, a block away, Representative Alexandria Ocasio-Cortez, the newly elected firebrand from New York City, challenged a panel of witnesses, "Let's play a game." Methodically she drew them out to show how porous campaign finance and ethics laws were. A video of the exchange went viral, quickly amassing 40 million views, making it the most watched political video ever on Twitter, all on the arcane topic of election and lobbying law. The caucus quickly fell in line, and H.R.1 passed the House on March 8, 2019. It was the most sweeping democracy reform plan to pass either chamber of Congress in half a century.

Now it was January 2021, and somewhat to their surprise after the ups and downs of the election season, the Democrats had control of the White House, House, and Senate. (With a fifty-fifty split, the vice president breaks Senate ties to give the party the control.) And with states rushing to pass restrictive laws, federal voting rights legislation suddenly seemed not like a "nice to do" item or a "want to do" but a "must do."

The For the People Act would set national election standards, guaranteeing access to vote by mail and requiring adequate early voting. It would extend automatic voter registration nationwide. It also addressed redistricting: establishing guidelines to block racial and partisan gerrymandering, and setting up independent commissions to draw lines. The bill included significant campaign finance reform. It would require disclosure of "dark money," the funds used in elections that were not disclosed. It also would revive the federal system of public financing of campaigns, with matching funds provided for small individual contributions to congressional or presidential candidates.

The voting and redistricting provisions, in particular, would override the actions of state governments. Congress has the power to do this under the Constitution's Elections Clause. (That's the provision James Madison insisted on, using "words of great latitude" because it was "impossible to foresee the abuses" legislatures might dream up, described in Chapter 2.) The Supreme Court recently reaffirmed that sweeping authority. In a 2019 ruling, an opinion written by Chief Justice Roberts noted, "the Framers gave Congress the power to do something about partisan gerrymandering in the Elections Clause," and even pointed to H.R.1 as a prime example.

A second piece of important legislation moved along a parallel track. It aimed to restore the full strength of the Voting Rights Act after it was gutted by the Supreme Court. It would reestablish "preclearance," which had been the law's most effective element. The legislation was renamed the John Lewis Voting Rights Advancement Act. To overcome the justices' skepticism about whether the Voting Rights Act could be constitutional at all, sponsors painstakingly amassed data and evidence of continued racial discrimination. The measure would not pass the House until August 2021.

Biden had not campaigned on avid support of voting legislation. But like many, he was shaken by the election and Trump's effort to overturn it. He had sponsored earlier laws to reauthorize the Voting Rights Act. His true passion as a young legislator was campaign reform. In the spring of 1993, he paid an off-the-record visit to President Bill Clinton in the Oval Office. Democrats were drafting campaign finance reform, and I attended as Clinton's aide working on the legislation. Go further, Biden urged. Try to enact full public financing of campaigns. It would change Washington. Biden's voluble passion was striking, his idealistic language not often heard in the Oval Office. The bill Democrats proposed that year was far weaker than Biden hoped for, and it failed in any event. At the time Biden had little organizational backing for his stance.

Now an energized grassroots movement pressed for action. For decades, democracy reform failed to reach the top tier of progressive goals partly because of divisions between civil rights groups, led by people of color, and good government groups, principally white and suburban. That was especially true on issues including redistricting reform and campaign finance. Not this time: melding voting rights with anti-corruption proposals turned out to be a force magnifier. Now explicitly political committees, including a group led by former Attorney General Eric Holder that pressed for redistricting reform, and Stacey Abrams's Fair Fight Action, played prominent roles. Progressive grassroots networks including Indivisible and MoveOn joined insurgent groups that arose in the racial justice movement, such as Black Voters Matter. Traditional reform lobbies Public Citizen and Common Cause had their own coalition. Labor unions, once skeptical of reform, mobilized members. It was the broadest push in decades. Fretful commentators who thought a trimmed-down bill might find an easier path to passage misread the political strategy: narrower bills have narrower constituencies of support.

Once again H.R.1 passed the House. Now it was also introduced as the lead bill in the Senate: S.1. Majority Leader Charles Schumer repeatedly declared, "failure is not an option." The legislation was wildly popular. A tape of a private briefing held by the conservative Koch network, leaked to Jane Mayer of the *New Yorker*, suggests its potency. The group's pollster had tested arguments against the measure, and found, disconcertingly, that Republicans as well as independents and Democrats strongly supported the bill. Better not to try to argue against it, he explained, since turning public opinion would be "incredibly difficult."

Better to rely on, instead, "under-the-dome-type strategies" to obstruct the bill. As Senator Ted Cruz of Texas told lobbyists in his own leaked phone call, this was "an all-hands moment."

Indeed, the legislation would soon crash hard into the arcane rules of the U.S. Senate. It takes sixty senators to end a filibuster, and thus allow a vote on legislation. The filibuster is not in the Constitution. In fact, the framers considered and rejected the idea of requiring supermajorities. It was used throughout the twentieth century especially to thwart civil rights legislation. Then, as parties grew more polarized, it became used to block . . . well, almost anything. It is simply assumed that legislation require sixty votes. In 2013, for example, after the massacre of elementary school children at Sandy Hook, legislation to strengthen background checks for gun purchases had 90 percent public support and a majority of the Senate. It died due to a filibuster. Senate officials tallied as many "cloture" motions to end a filibuster in the past decade as in the entire previous half century.

Now, as in earlier eras, the filibuster was being used to block vital voting rights legislation.

In 2020, Representative John Lewis died. Lewis, of course, had led the march on Edmund Pettus Bridge that led to the passage of the Voting Rights Act. Since 1987, he had served in Congress, where he was a revered figure. At Lewis's nationally televised funeral, Barack Obama stood over the late Congressman's casket. The former president demanded action on voting rights, not in 1965, but now: "Let's honor him by revitalizing the law that he was willing to die for." Obama called for passage of the For the People Act. "And if all this takes eliminating the filibuster—another Jim Crow relic—in order to secure the God-given rights of every American, then that's what we should do." Obama's pungent words stung. As president he had done little to advance the issue. Now he had crystalized a new growing consensus among Democrats: the filibuster must go.

Senators had changed the filibuster before. In 1974, they cut the number of votes needed to end a filibuster from sixty-seven to sixty. In the past decade, Republicans and Democrats had ended it for Supreme Court, lower court, and executive branch nominations. Exceptions already were carved out for bills ranging from budget reconciliation to military base closings and trade agreements, all of which required only a majority.

In 2021, two Democratic senators, Joe Manchin of West Virginia and Kyrsten Sinema of Arizona, made clear they did not want to eliminate the filibuster. Manchin's stance perplexed. He was a former secretary of state who had sponsored the predecessor reform bill in years past, but now insisted on Republican support—an impossibility in the polarized Congress. He declared he would not back S.1. Then he proposed the elements of a stripped-down version of the bill that—while less sweeping—still included key voting, redistricting, and campaign finance rules. When Senator Schumer tried to begin debate on June 22, fifty Republicans objected, stopping the bill, at least for now. Later in the summer they blocked votes on redistricting and "dark money" campaign spending. In September, Manchin and other Democrats formally introduced the new version of the legislation, now rechristened the Freedom to Vote Act. Even in its new form, it would be the most significant voting right bill in decades.

Will there be enough political pressure and momentum to force action, including the possibility of a carve-out to the filibuster for election laws? Will the Freedom to Vote Act simply die in the Senate, a victim of the crowded congressional calendar? Will Joe Biden throw the full weight of the White House behind the urgent need for reform?

In early summer, Biden spoke at the National Constitution Center in Philadelphia. He had hastily scheduled the speech after Black leaders challenged him to do more in a White House meeting. The president strode into the atrium of the museum where he had once served as board chair and in simpler times could regularly be found in the lobby, schmoozing and having coffee. Ringed by flags, Biden decried the Big

Lie. He urged action on H.R.1, winning thunderous applause, and the John Lewis Voting Rights Advancement Act. He noted that the Justice Department had doubled the number of lawyers working to protect voting rights. He was particularly incensed by the new provisions finding their way into state laws that gave partisans the power to declare the winner. "To me, this is simple," he said. "This is election subversion—who gets to count whether or not your vote counted at all." Rhetorically Biden raised the stakes sky high. "I've said it before: We are facing the most significant test of our democracy since the Civil War. That's not hyperbole. Since the Civil War. The Confederates back then never breached the Capitol as insurrectionists did on January the sixth." Rhetorically Biden drew a red line. Would such powerful words produce action?

Shortly before Biden walked out to speak, amplifiers blared a soundtrack of classic rock. On came "We Won't Get Fooled Again," the 1971 song by The Who about dashed revolutionary hopes. (*Meet the new boss / Same as the old boss.*) Reformers hoped that was not an omen.

Conclusion

A Democracy Moment

It is now 246 years since the Declaration of Independence launched the nation with a vision of political equality, with government continually bound to earn the "consent of the governed." Americans have since developed a distinct style of social reform, as we hold contemporary institutions up to the light of those ideals. We make progress by looking backward. We do this even though we know well that founding-era Americans did not match their words with deeds—the men, so many of them enslavers, would be surprised and often dismayed by the democracy we've become. As the United States has grown and changed, the vote has become the principal way that consent is sought and offered. The founders would far more easily understand the institutional challenges—including the role of money and manipulative structures of representation—that have grown up to deprive that vote of its power and meaning.

The history in this book has not unfolded in a straight line. Democracy has expanded and contracted. And the story has not featured a simple cast of heroes and villains. Some readers might find it disconcerting that pressure for a meaningful democracy did not always come, in the first instance, from below. Though it often came from activists and organized cadres, at times it came from simple partisan calculation.

The fight to rescue our democracy today will likewise call on different actors. The characters are familiar: politicians, parties, the courts, and the public. All have their role to play.

Political Leaders

Yes, an unexpected place to start. Politicians, of course, are not to be relied on for visionary leadership. Their job is to advance themselves, to get elected, to amass and wield power. But at the best and most critical moments their self-interest aligns with that of the voters and of democracy itself. When prodded, shamed, or enlisted, they have played a central role. Like tuning forks, they are starting to respond to the public. There is the making of a sharp divide.

In our system the two political parties endure, but over time they have shed identities and even swapped roles. In the late nineteenth century, the GOP was the voting rights party, pressing for the Fifteenth Amendment and equal rights. In the twentieth century, both parties had jumbled ideological factions, and northern Republicans worked with liberal Democrats to expand the vote for women and minorities.

Now the story is starker, and far more uncomfortable to tell. Donald Trump touched something visceral and tribal. He leapt to the fore of the Republican field not only due to his celebrity but also because of his outspoken anti-immigrant sentiment. More than five years since then, the party has transformed itself into something not before seen in the United States—a unified white nationalist movement akin to parties in Europe. Yes, there had been American politicians like Trump before, but racist Alabama governor George Wallace finished third when he ran for president in 1968; Trump won. What he has let loose resembles to what we see in Hungary and Poland, in the French party led by Marine Le Pen, in the forces that produced Brexit in Great Britain, and in the Hindu nationalism of Indian prime minister Narendra Modi. In many of those countries, with proportional representation or parliamentary systems, the nationalist faction was small, and mainstream conservatives still could offer ballast or find ways to exclude the authoritarians. In the United States, though, we have a two-party system with winner-take-all elections. When a faction captures one of the parties, it has a much greater chance to gain power.

All that was disturbing enough, but there is a new twist. Now Trump had fixated on a new enemy: not just immigrants, or "Hillary," but our democratic system itself. "Build the Wall" in 2016 has been replaced by "Stop the Steal" in 2021. Fealty to Trump's Big Lie became an organizing principle of the Republican Party. In Georgia, state party committees censured Brad Raffensperger. House Republicans pushed out Liz Cheney, who had backed impeachment, as the party whip. In Arizona, the state senate launched a farcical "audit" of the ballots in Maricopa County, the state's biggest. It was conducted by a company called the Cyber Ninjas (not, implausibly, a parody account), headed by someone who had never run an election audit but had circulated conspiracy theories. Contractors pored over ballots looking for "bamboo fibers" that would prove China had swung the election to Biden. (In the end, the Ninjas found that Biden won by a bigger margin than previously estimated.) Willingness to recognize the result of the 2020 election meant you were a dreaded "RINO," a Republican In Name Only. "Weak," as Trump repeatedly would call those who respected the public's choice. In the past, party operatives tweaked rules because they could, not because there was some groundswell of grassroots demand. Now suppressing the vote is a surefire way to rouse Republican voters.

All this raises sharp questions for Republican politicians and party elites. They know the Big Lie is a lie. They know there was no substantial voter fraud in 2020, but also that shrinking the electorate is one way to stave off demographic change. With cunning and speed they have organized changes in state laws to give Republican politicians control over the counting. Republican candidates for secretary of state, the chief election officer in most states, overwhelmingly deny that Biden won the election. Increasingly conservative activists embrace not just the Big Lie but the January 6th insurrection itself. As former George W. Bush speechwriter David Frum wrote despairingly, "what the United States did not have before 2020 was a large national movement willing to justify mob violence to claim political power. Now it does." Perhaps 2020 was just a dress rehearsal for 2024.

Is there a pro-democracy faction left in the Grand Old Party? Will the party contest every election with bogus claims of "voter fraud"? Much depends on the answers. And much depends, too, on whether a substantial cohort will be repelled by the party of insurrection. Many mocked the "Never Trumpers," conservative Republicans who broke with their party's nominee through organizations such as the Lincoln Project and publications like *The Bulwark*. Their numbers never were huge. But as experts sift data from the 2020 election, it seems clear that suburban voters—many of them conservative on economic issues, in other words, the very swing voters some see as mythical—swung to Biden in large enough numbers to deliver victory. (Black and Latino citizens actually supported Trump at higher rates than four years before, while making up a smaller share of the electorate.)

What about the Democrats?

It has been many years since the Democrats focused on democracy. Obama, for example, never proposed new legislation on voting or campaign finance, the first time a president of his party failed to do so since Grover Cleveland's second term. As Republicans began to rail about fraud and persuaded courts to deconstruct campaign finance law, most Democrats barely responded. Party strategists assured incumbents that the public did not care—it was all process, arcane, *boring*. People, they assured, cared only about "kitchen table" issues, about policies that provided tangible benefits. That was never actually true: as distrust of government rose, some Democratic pollsters noted that many citizens would be more willing to trust government to act in their interest if they first saw corruption addressed.

Still, after the Trump presidency—and especially his calamitous last year in office—that was emphatically no longer the case. The fights for voting rights, and democracy reform more generally, now are central to the Democrats' political identity. Hence the designation of sweeping democracy reform as H.R.1 and S.1., the first bills in each chamber for the session. As the party becomes more comfortable as an explicitly multiracial coalition, the fight against vote suppression has become a defining shared goal. Party establishment figures such as Pelosi and Schumer became hard-to-replace champions.

This is all a bit new. After the civil rights movement of the 1950s and 1960s, we grew accustomed to thinking of progress solely as the province of prophetic voices, of organizers and agitators outside partisan politics. Partly that was just gauzy nostalgia. As this book showed, progress for voting rights always eventually required the hard-eyed calculus of practical politicians, leaders who saw their self-interest advanced by widening democratic participation. These roles could clash: think of suffragist Alice Paul and Woodrow Wilson. At times these conflicts would lead to extraordinary creative progress, as in the dance between Dr. King and LBJ. But they were always distinct roles.

Now there are Democratic Party officeholders whose political platform, coalitions, and strength come from their advocacy on voting rights. Stacey Abrams is a revered figure among advocates, a powerful Black woman who writes articles (for *Foreign Affairs*, no less) in defense of "identity politics," and a political leader who dominates the multiracial Democratic party of Georgia without holding office. In 2022, she is expected to run for governor. Support for H.R.1 became a reliable fundraising pitch and surefire applause line. Movement leaders took powerful positions in the Biden administration. Vanita Gupta, who ran the Leadership Conference, became the Justice Department's number three official. Kristen Clarke, director of the Lawyers Committee for Civil and Human Rights, which organized thousands of attorneys to do voter protection work, became Assistant Attorney General for Civil

Rights, the first Black woman confirmed to the role. The Brennan Center's Myrna Pérez became a top federal judge on the Second Circuit Court of Appeals.

Democrats now must ensure that this focus deepens as a party commitment. Some older party operatives still see voter suppression as something that can be "out-organized," no doubt if those campaigners are handed more money to get-out-the-vote. Putting aside whether that's true—you cannot out-organize a well-executed gerrymander—it reflects a traditionalist mindset, the notion that voting rights is a constituency desk issue to woo Black supporters rather than a central policy goal. The emerging Democratic majority, long anticipated, is taking its time showing up. Black, Latino, and Asian voters, college-educated voters, and women are the core of the party's coalition. But seven in ten voters still are white. White voters without a college degree were 44 percent of the electorate. (Indeed, the Democratic data firm Catalist reported in a review of the 2020 election, Biden did 8 percent worse among Latinos than Clinton had four years before. He won by eking out more votes from Trump's white working-class base and college-educated voters.) A robust democracy agenda, including anti-corruption measures such as campaign finance reform as well as voting rights, appeals notably to that wider, ethnically diverse coalition.

Some might find the spectacle of senior political leaders duking it out on the issues of voting and democracy to be discomfiting: Both major parties have abused the rules; given the chance, for example, both gerrymander with gusto. Isn't progress best made through bipartisan cooperation? At times that is true. Two decades ago, campaign finance reform legislation gained momentum when Republican John McCain joined with Democrat Russell Feingold. Because it is easier to block change than enact it under the American system of multiple veto points, at times reform has come when its partisan impact is unclear or neatly balanced. The many organizations and activists who work on these issues have also struggled to maintain a nonpartisan posture. But policy victories usually are won when one major faction of one party, at least, embraces change as a selling point.

Political Parties

Reformers have long hissed at political parties as the villains of the story. At times there has been a hygienic aspect to reform: an effort to cleanse politics of politics. Yet there is no ambiguity about the fact that engaged political parties can be both the engine of mass public participation and the driver of reforms designed to expand and perfect the ability of that participation to be felt in the halls of power. They can mobilize broad coalitions to win major change. Political realists are right to see stronger parties as a key to making government work better, with less paralysis and fragmentation. But polarized rump parties—a club of donors, lobbyists, operatives, and lawmakers—can pull politics to the extremes and make governing harder, not easier. The key here is to understand the mass nature of truly successful political parties. Some experts, seeing the volume of funds that flow outside the formal structure of political parties to independent spenders and funding coalitions, nostalgically pine for a time, supposedly a decade or two past, when the parties were great and could play their assigned role. Politics would be mended if we could only tweak the campaign finance laws to let parties, as well as PACs, raise unlimited funds from today's new-breed billionaires. Yet that recent halcyon time is an illusion. The parties of the past half century have often been mostly conduits to funnel contributor checks to television station managers. National legislative party leaders supposedly wielded more power then, though in fact throughout nearly the entire twentieth century it was committee chairs who had risen through seniority who governed.

We need to find a way to recapture an earlier notion of what political parties were. No, we can't expect to see torchlight parades down Main Street (or K Street). The component elements of the strong parties of the past have vanished, whether labor unions or urban political machines. (Evangelical churches among conservatives, and Black churches among Democrats, are among the remaining strong community-based grassroots institutions that have played an informal role in party coalitions.) Today's social media points to a new way of energizing and engaging millions of ordinary citizens in political activity. Reformers should swallow hard and consider loosening the laws so parties can more easily raise larger sums. That way they could better compete with outside spenders and play their role as aggregators and organizers for otherwise restless politicians. One legal fix that would make a difference would be to enable campaigns and grassroots groups to share and combine social media networks and email lists. When the Obama campaign concluded in 2012, with an estimated 4.4 million names in its servers, it could legally give that list to the Democratic National Committee—but the party could not hand it to a successor presidential campaign. Martin Van Buren would find that baffling at best.

The Courts

Many readers might be surprised to learn that the judicial branch, and judges, have played only a limited role in the creation of American democracy. Although in the past half century courts have necessarily served as umpires to adjudicate partisan election disputes and to parse the fine points of representation and line drawing, for the most part courts have kept clear from the fray. In recent years a bifurcation has been evident. Many courts (federal and state, Democratic- and Republican-appointed) have stepped forward to protect voting rights, and even to uphold campaign finance laws. But the far more divided, more partisan U.S. Supreme Court has been emphatically more willing to intervene and to rewrite the rules of democracy on behalf of the more powerful. *Citizens United* and *Shelby County*, activist interventions to weaken democratic protections, were followed by *Rucho v. Common Cause* in 2019, where the Court refused to police extreme partisan gerrymandering—and even barred federal courts from hearing such cases.

And now, the Court has a super-majority of dedicated conservatives. Chapter 13 of this book is entitled "Five to Four." Now it would be "Six to Three." Republicans won the popular vote in only one out of the past eight presidential elections, yet six of the nine justices were appointed by that party. Indeed, a majority of the court had been named by presidents who took office despite losing the popular vote, a first in American history. This new super-majority included Neil Gorsuch, nominated after the Republican Senate refused even to hold a hearing on President Obama's nominee to replace Antonin Scalia, Merrick Garland, the first such refusal in a century. It also included Amy Coney Barrett, rushed through in the closing hours of GOP control in 2020, just eight days before Election Day. The new Court in its first year surprised many by treading cautiously on some intense social issues. When it came to democracy, though, the Court continued its trend of being extraordinarily activist—and when it came to major rulings on democracy issues, the Republican-appointed justices usually voted in a way that benefitted the Republican Party.

Shelby County had gutted the most effective part of the Voting Rights Act. Another provision of the law, though, still was in effect. Section Two authorized after-the-fact lawsuits. Only after *Shelby County* did civil right lawyers deploy it to challenge the newfangled voting restrictions, and at first they had some success. In 2016, a three-judge federal appeals court struck down a North Carolina voting law, ruling that its provisions "target African Americans with almost surgical precision." Another federal appeals court blocked and then softened Texas's harsh ID law in a case brought by the Brennan Center and others. ("We couldn't eat the birth certificate.") But the U.S. Supreme Court never had weighed in on how the Voting Rights Act could still be used to fight the new methods of vote suppression.

In July 2021, the Court gave its answer: the Voting Rights Act was still on the books, but barely usable. In *Brnovich v. DNC*, Justice Samuel

Alito wrote an opinion backed by the five other Republican-appointed justices. He fretted that Congress had established "radical" ideas for how to advance racial justice when it amended the law in 1982 to target laws with a discriminatory impact, not just intent. Instead, Alito set out "guideposts" that amounted to an instruction manual for those who want to restrict the franchise. Perhaps most galling, the decision explained that states can pass laws simply to placate the fear of fraud, presumably among white voters, even if the resulting policy hurts actual minority citizens.

Brnovich capped a decade of rulings that retreated from enforcing democratic protections. The justices rebuffed Trump's most lurid conspiracy theories in 2020, but that was cold comfort. Republican lawyers now eye ways to use the Constitution to bar state courts or election officials from making it easier to vote. In a perverse twist, they cite the Elections Clause—the very provision being debated by the framers on the very first page of this book—which was designed to curb the tendency of legislators to suppress the vote and gerrymander. (Madison and colleagues didn't use that word, of course, since it hadn't been coined—and Elbridge Gerry was in the room!) These legal activists now insist, in fact, that the Constitution sought to reserve all authority to those very legislatures, since they are mentioned explicitly in the text. Give points for creativity. As many as four justices seem ready to embrace this approach. While conservatives concoct novel theories, voting rights lawyers now must earn their stripes by finding ways to keep cases out of court.

So when it comes to the Constitution and American democracy, courts speak loudly.

But courts are far from the sole venue for constitutional advocacy. Americans care passionately about the Constitution and its interpretation. In recent years, two movements have shown the centrality of that mission and the chance for success. The National Rifle Association and other gun rights advocates persuaded the Supreme Court to reverse its interpretation of the Second Amendment. In *District of Columbia v. Heller* in 2008, the Court held for the first time that the "right to keep and bear arms" guaranteed a personal right to own a gun. That followed decades of advocacy to shift scholarly, public, and governmental views. Marriage equality supporters won an even more astounding shift in public opinion, then in state laws, and then finally judicial doctrine. Both of these movements understood that constitutional interpretation was not abstract but a fighting faith around which millions would mobilize.

They knew that to win in the court of law, you must first win in the court of public opinion. Far from novel, this strategy has been embraced by those seeking constitutional change from the beginning. Whether they know it or not, activists take their cue from Lincoln. During his debates with Stephen Douglas over the spread of slavery, he explained the centrality of public education. "Public sentiment is everything," he declared. "With public sentiment, nothing can fail; without it, nothing can succeed. Consequently he who molds public sentiment goes deeper than he who enacts statutes or pronounces decisions. He makes statutes and decisions possible or impossible to be executed."

Of course when it comes to voting, constitutional amendments have enshrined the right. The Fourteenth, Fifteenth, Nineteenth, Twenty-fourth, and Twenty-sixth do so explicitly. The Seventeenth gave citizens the right to vote, at last, for all elections for members of both houses of Congress. Many activists lately have mobilized for a constitutional amendment to address campaign finance. Others, chafing at the Supreme Court's refusal to block restrictive election laws, have begun to discuss an amendment that would explicitly protect the right to vote. Nearly all state constitutions have such a provision, so it is unclear what the import of such a change would be, other than to give federal courts a more explicit duty to enforce that right.

Scholars John Kowal and Wilfred Codrington note that many constitutional amendments over the years have strengthened democracy. Amendments come in waves. "In recurring cycles, bursts of energy that add several new amendments in the span of a few years are followed by decades-long dry spells," they write. But they note, "when we consider the twenty-seven amendments to the Constitution as a whole, it is no exaggeration to say that much of what we consider the very heart of our national charter—from its protections for free speech and religion to its guarantees of due process and equal protection of the laws—derive not from the 4,543 words in the framers' beta version of our national charter, but rather from the 3,000 words added in periodic upgrades." Advocates must weigh the opportunity costs—in energy, focus, and funds—of waging that fight over the drive to win shorter-term goals. But they should not find it impermissible to discuss ways to strengthen the Constitution to bolster its core democratic values.

At the very least, it is worth remembering that when it comes to the right to vote and other democracy measures, citizens—not courts—have made the most profound changes in constitutional law.

The People

That brings us to our role—all of us, the people. The fight for the vote has been driven, above all, by the aspirations of those who seek to make their voices heard. It has never been a smooth glide. At every step of the way, entrenched groups, fearing change, have fought back and tried to reduce the opportunity for political participation and power.

Do people care about the rules of democracy? For a long time, conventional thought said no: too abstract. Others have worried that even talking about voter disenfranchisement would dissuade people from participating.

Thus far that has not been the case. People have grown angry that others are trying to curb their rights and are mobilizing to express that anger. They vote to protest the assault on their right to vote. Look no further than North Carolina. Soon after *Shelby County*, the state slammed through the country's most ambitious bill at the time to restrict voting. Soon protesters began to sit in at the state capitol, numbers swelling each week; after a month five thousand deluged the capitol to protest the new laws. A rally in Asheville attracted ten thousand protesters. They called the flashpoint "our Selma." The protests lifted to prominence the leader of the state NAACP, Reverend William Barber III, a mountainous man whose rumbling cadences combined the oratory of an old-school church leader and the snark of a millennial. In 2016, the Moral Mondays movement helped defeat the incumbent governor. (The legislature promptly responded by stripping the new governor of many of his powers.) Barber now leads Repairers of the Breach and launched a Poor People's Movement nationwide. "We declare that voter suppression is sin," he has said.

Until recently, simmering anger did not translate into a full mobilization for action across society. At other times in American history, such as the Progressive Era or the civil rights movement, millions of citizens came together in a profusion of efforts at the local, state, and eventually the national level. They formed organizations, filed lawsuits, wrote books, staged marches, raised funds, even went to jail.

Now once again a growing number of Americans realize that the very tenets of our democracy are at stake. The election of Donald Trump in 2016 caused many people to rethink how strong our system really was. A bookshelf's worth of bestselling titles such as *How Democracies Die*, *On Tyranny*, *The Twilight of Democracy*, and *Trumpocalypse* noted that the constitutional order was upheld by many things beyond elections: checks and balances, independent courts and law enforcement, respect for the rule of law, an apolitical military. All those guardrails faced stress in Trump's term. Free elections alone do not guarantee representation, but they are utterly essential. Now that core element of any constitutional democracy is under relentless assault. For the first time ever, a president aimed to discredit the system itself, a national leader following an authoritarian's playbook. If Republicans succeed in changing the rules for who decides the results of elections, that moves from voter suppression to election subversion. As the conservative scholar Robert Kagan wrote in late 2021, "the constitutional crisis is already here."

Coming years could be ugly. Even if Trump himself does not run again, Trumpism will live on. Demagoguery does not always win the first time. The Roman Republic lasted for four centuries, longer than our own government. It was battered in 133 BC by Tiberius Gracchus, a wealthy, bumptious populist who proposed greater economic and political equality but stirred violence among his supporters and overrode the republic's norms and election rules. For Gracchus, it ended poorly: he was murdered during a riot. But the damage had been done. Ever more brazen attacks on the republic's institutions, often in the name of the people, followed for decades. Julius Caesar was smarter than Gracchus and, when it came his time to seize power, more ruthless. His successor, Augustus, ended the republic.

And yet all these convulsions may be labor pains for a new, more hopeful, more equal and diverse country. Few nations undergo demographic change of such velocity without disruption. The 2020 census not just showed that Latinos now are nearly 19 percent of the population, with Asians doubling their share over two decades to nearly 6 percent, but that the number of people only identifying as white in the United States actually fell, something that had never happened since the first census in 1790. These changes have produced a backlash, of course. But they also point toward a renewed America, a multiracial democracy held together by commitment to common ideals.

One positive sign comes from the rise in participation itself. For years, American voting rates stubbornly remained among the lowest in the democratic world. In 2016, in the first edition of this book, I surmised that our social forces—television saturated, isolated, with millions "bowling alone," even the secret ballot itself—all dampened turnout. (Imagine a rule that said you could root for any sports team of your choice—but only in private, without heading to a bar, watching a game with friends, tailgating at a stadium, or cheering in the stands. Active support for teams would wither.) One great task for this generation, I wrote, was to find a way to make political engagement as celebratory and compelling for those who rarely see thousands of other like-minded people in the flesh at a rally or parade. That was all before the Trump explosions of 2016, the women's march of 2017, the surge of suburban women to the polls in 2018, producing a Democratic sweep, or the Black Lives Matters movement of 2020, and the extraordinary jump in participation in both parties. Once again Americans are holding the equivalent of torchlight parades.

And as in earlier eras, democracy itself has become not just the means for expression but a cherished value and urgent goal. In 2020, the election was saved by businesses and judges and journalists and public health experts, by community activists by the thousands, and by hundreds of thousands of citizens who scrambled and improvised to make sure a fair and safe election took place. Our democracy will only sustain if that mobilization continues. As during the Revolution and other times when the push for representation became a public creed, the ideal of our founding—that government is legitimate only when it rests on the "consent of the governed"—must remain a fighting faith for millions. Two centuries of activists, from Ben Franklin and Frederick Douglass to Alice Paul and John Lewis, found joy and purpose in doing so.

American politics can be dispiriting—it's a messy, jarring, jumbled patchwork of candidates, causes, and elections. But at stake is more than just an effort to craft a workable self-governing republic. Democracy has embedded within it a moral sense—that every individual is of equal worth and has the agency to shape the most important institutions affecting his or her life.

It is possible in reading the push and pull of the stories in this book to lose sight of that moral thread. Lots of people smash and grab for advantage. Republicans today are trying to limit the vote. So what else is new? Democrats rely more on younger, poorer, more diverse voters. They want more opportunities for their supporters to vote. Isn't each party just pressing its own advantage? I think we should resist the temptation to see facile moral equivalence. If the American creed is to mean anything, it is that the basic glue holding the country together is the aspiration set out by Jefferson in that Declaration. The fight for the vote over the years has been more than a clash of classes, parties, factions, races, and interests. It has been a long drive, stumbling, retreating, but ultimately in one direction: toward fulfilling that ideal. So we should all regard it as not just wrong but fundamentally illegitimate, indeed un-American, for anyone to try to make it harder for another American to vote. This fight over first principles should no longer surprise us. In fact, it is typical, and understandable.

It turns out John Adams was right in 1776: "there will be no end of it." Once again the story of American democracy is being written. The fight to vote is at the heart of American history. It is up to all of us to advance that fight and keep it at the center of debate today, where it belongs.

ACKNOWLEDGMENTS

THIS BOOK IS the product of a decade's worth of work with dedicated colleagues in an intense fight over democratic rights.

I begin by thanking Alice Mayhew. Once again I have been extraordinarily fortunate to have her as my editor. She conceived of this volume and understood the importance of the fight for democracy. Her rigor, insistence on quality, savvy editing, and astounding knowledge continue to make working with her a remarkable experience. I am grateful for the skilled and diligent work of her colleague Stuart Roberts. And thank you to the committed team at Simon & Schuster led by Jonathan Karp, including Maureen Cole, Stephen Bedford, Jackie Seow, Ellen Sasahara, Elisa Rivlin, Lisa Healy, and Judith Hoover. Rafe Sagalyn, my agent, once again has been enthusiastic, insightful, and tremendously helpful (among other things, by suggesting the title). My colleague Jeanine Plant-Chirlin partners with them, does world-class work, and understands the power of books to advance ideas.

I am grateful to colleagues who read all or part of the manuscript. They include Samuel Issacharoff, one of the great experts on democracy in American law; Frederick A. O. Schwarz; Jennifer Weiss-Wolf, whose enthusiasm and acumen in reading multiple drafts is greatly appreciated; Wendy Weiser; Vishal Agraharkar; Ted Widmer; Poy Winichakul; Jonathan Alter; Roland Lewis; Jim Lyons; Vivien Watts; Jordan Sayah; Claire Silberman; Michael Li; Myrna Perez; Lawrence Norden; Martin Waldman; and Sandra Waldman. I received valuable insight from experts including Rick Pildes, Larry Kramer, Jeff Shesol, and Robert A. Caro, whose books taught me so much about the true story of American democracy and whose encouragement means so much to me. Thanks to friends including George Stephanopoulos, Fred Kaplan, Jennifer Callahan, Gene Sperling, Steve Bowman, and Cliff Sloan for support and wisdom. Of course, any errors and opinions are mine alone.

Throughout much of the research and writing of the book, I worked with my assistant Amy Lee Goodman, a talented author in her own right. Her skilled research and management of the fact-gathering and -checking was greatly helpful. She worked with Audrey Greene, a keen legal researcher even before law school. Their effort is especially visible in the chapter on women's suffrage (appropriate since they are graduates of Wellesley and Barnard, respectively). In the final stretch Beatriz Aldereguia came to work with me—and has quickly become an invaluable collaborator, research-whiz, taskmaster, and supporter. Her work ethic astounds. I am grateful for assistance from Brennan Center interns and volunteers: indefatigable researchers Molly Seligman and Miriam Bial, Samuel Ison and Alex Lipton. Thanks to Carol Anderson and Chesley Martin for copyediting support.

I wrote this book while having the privilege to lead a remarkable institution, the Brennan Center for Justice at NYU School of Law. The Center bears the name and carries the legacy of the late Supreme Court Justice William J. Brennan, Jr. (This is my second book where his jurisprudence has been central—in the last one, in debates over originalism and the living constitution, and in this one, in the landmark cases such as *Baker v. Carr.*) The Center works to revitalize and reform the systems of democracy and justice, and we are deeply engaged in many of the fights discussed in this book. It is a gift to get to work with a dedicated team, in a good cause, who labor ferociously hard at a high level of skill and intellectual integrity.

I gained much from the expertise of numerous attorneys and policy professionals at the Center. In addition to those who read the manuscript, I want to thank for their help Tomas Lopez, Jonathan Brater, Daniel Weiner, Ian Vandewalker, Carson Whitelemons, Jennifer Clark, Erik Opsal, Alicia Bannon, and the staff of our Democracy Program—in particular its visionary leaders Wendy Weiser, Larry Norden, and Myrna Perez—for their input and support. The Center's executive and management team have been wonderfully supportive: vice presidents Tony

Butler, John Kowal, Jeanine Plant-Chirlin, Vivien Watts, and Jennifer Weiss-Wolf, and program directors including Nicole Austin-Hillery, Inimai Chettiar, Liza Goitein, and Faiza Patel. General counsel Elisa Miller provided valuable legal advice. The entire Brennan Center Board of Directors has been a superb source of strength and encouragement. Particular thanks go to Patricia Bauman and Bob Atkins, our wonderful cochairs (Bob doubles as an energetic voting rights attorney), as well as Board colleagues and advisors including Jim Johnson, Gail Furman, Dan Kolb, Larry Pedowitz, Adam Winkler, Tom Jorde, Wendy Neu, Christine Varney, Jerry Rosenfeld, and Nancy Brennan. New York University School of Law is a remarkable academic institution and a creative and supportive partner for the Center. Special thanks to Dean Trevor Morrison for his leadership and enthusiasm, and his colleagues Burt Neuborne, Helen Hershkoff, and past deans Ricky Revesz and John Sexton, now finishing his tenure as president of NYU.

The Brennan Center has been joined over the years by a wide array of foundation and individual supporters and is grateful for their generosity and steadfast commitment to reforming and revitalizing American democracy. Many thanks to the Center's longstanding, leading supporters of this work: The Bauman Foundation, Patricia Stryker and the Bohemian Foundation, Carnegie Corporation of New York, Lee and Amy Fikes, Ford Foundation, The Joyce Foundation, The JPB Foundation, The Kohlberg Foundation, John D. and Catherine T. MacArthur Foundation, The Mai Family Foundation, Mertz Gilmore Foundation, The John and Wendy Neu Foundation, Open Society Foundations, Rockefeller Brothers Fund, Rockefeller Family Fund, Bernard and Anne Spitzer Charitable Trust, Scott Wallace and the Wallace Global Fund, and Vital Projects Fund, as well as to the Partners of the Democracy Alliance. There are many other supporters, too, whose partnership is invaluable.

Finally, my family has been enthusiastic, tolerant, supportive, bemused and somewhat incredulous that I would take on a project like this so soon after the last book. My wife, Liz Fine, is an endless wonder, a source of strength and love for our family while moving and shaking in the worlds of government and business. Our kids have grown up a bit with each book. Now they are all young adults, far flung (Brooklyn, Georgia, Providence, and beyond), connected by family text chats, and a source of pride, joy, and enthusiastic support: Ben Waldman, Susannah Waldman, and Josh Waldman. Thanks as well to my parents and my brother, Steve, for unending support.

There is great joy in knowing that this work is part of the long stream of American history. One of the most enjoyable aspects of writing this was to discover heroes and heroines in the nooks and crannies of history. Given the NYU Law connection, I have been especially intrigued by—and take inspiration from—our predecessor Inez Milholland, a creative battler for democracy on a white horse. We should all aim so high.

Michael Waldman
New York City
October 2015

For this new edition, I am so grateful to Bob Bender of Simon & Schuster, who encouraged this new edition and edited this "first draft of history." Given the stellar works of history he has edited, it is a particular privilege to work with him. Thanks, as well, to Jonathan Karp, who recognized the intense new interest in the topic in a time of insurrection and drama. Many thanks to my Brennan Center colleagues Alan Beard and Carolyn Schachtel; Emma Diller, and Kayla Forbes for fast and very helpful research; and to Jennifer Weiss-Wolf, Jeanine Chirlin, Sean Morales-Doyle, Edna Negron, and Amanda Powers for edits and facts. Special thanks to Harold Ekeh, whose research and writing on the history of voting during previous crises shows some of the ways we've been here before. Thank you, as ever, to Rafe Sagalyn, who has been a skilled and loyal agent for two decades. And a final thank-you to the late Alice Mayhew, who conceived of this book in its original edition, and whose legacy lives on in this and so much else.

Michael Waldman
New York City
October 2021

NOTE ON SOURCES

THE STORY OF the fight for the vote in many ways encompasses the story of America, so the literature is vast. In this book I have tried to look beyond the formalities of the rules that govern voting and representation in order to see what larger forces were at work. Often those forces were political. So the story of the fight to vote inevitably encompasses some of the great themes and most prominent conflicts in American history.

Here are some works that were particularly useful in understanding history's lessons and applying them to today's challenges. Many others, including journal articles and other scholarly books, are cited in the text.

To begin, there are several broad looks at the history of voting and voting laws, though few of them stretch across the whole country's history. Alexander Keyssar's *The Right to Vote: The Contested History of Democracy in the United States*, revised edition (New York: Basic Books, 2009) is the most comprehensive history, with a particularly strong focus on the nineteenth century. In addition to the basic, deep historical research, Keyssar sees the story as a product of the clash of classes, with suffrage expanded principally owing to military conflict. Other foundational works include Chilton Williamson, *American Suffrage from Property to Democracy* (Princeton: Princeton University Press, 1960), which examines in detail the property requirements of colonial times and their abolition; Marchette Chute, *The First Liberty: A History of the Right to Vote in America, 1619–1850* (New York: Dutton, 1971); and Kirk Harold Porter, *A History of Suffrage in the United States* (Chicago: University of Chicago Press, 1918), an earlier book that betrays the prejudices of its time against voting by African Americans. The other broad synthesis is Sean Wilentz, *The Rise of American Democracy* (New York: Norton, 2005). It extends only up to Lincoln's election to the presidency, but it has the advantage of placing the struggle for democracy in the broadest possible context.

To trace voter turnout and participation rates over time, this book relies on the United States Elections Project, a website maintained by Michael P. McDonald, now at Florida State University: http://www.electproject.org/home. McDonald principally uses Voting Eligible Population data. In other words, at a time when women were not allowed to vote he did not include women. This offers the best apples-to-apples chance to understand the shifting levels of participation. The Elections Project is a remarkably valuable resource.

For lawyers, law students, and those most interested in the development of constitutional doctrine, the landmark casebook is Samuel Issacharoff, Pamela S. Karlan, Richard H. Pildes, and Nathaniel Persily, *The Law of Democracy: Legal Structure of the Political Process*, 5th edition (New York: Thomson Reuters, Foundation Press, 2016).

The *New York Times* has digitized its archived content for subscribers to the newspaper. TimesMachine is a tremendous resource, valuable for researchers and procrastinators alike: http://timesmachine.nytimes.com/browser.

Finally, Supreme Court cases are fully covered at the invaluable website SCOTUSblog. It includes decisions, transcripts, briefs, lower court opinions, and learned commentary.

Part I

For the colonial and Revolutionary period, Gordon S. Wood's works on the shift from traditional thinking to a nascent democratic ethos are foundational: *Creation of the American Republic* (New York: Norton, 1969) and *The Radicalism of the American Revolution* (New York: Random House, 1991). Wood argues that the American Revolution really did have a radical democratizing streak. He builds on the work of Bernard Bailyn in arguing that the ideas of the founding generation mattered: Bernard Bailyn, *The Ideological Origins of the American Revolution*, revised edition (Cambridge, MA: Belknap Press, 1992). For a focus on the way the vote evolved during this time, see two books by Robert J. Dinkin: *Voting in Provincial America: A Study of Elections in the Thirteen Colonies, 1689–1776* (Westport, CT: Greenwood Press, 1977) and *Voting in Revolutionary America: A Study of Elections in the Original Thirteen States, 1776–1789* (New York: Praeger, 1982). For more on the Revolution and its first embrace of democracy, Eric Foner's book on Thomas Paine is a treat: *Tom Paine and Revolutionary America* (New York: Oxford University Press, 1976). J. R. Pole, *Political Representation in England and the Origins of the American Republic*, paperback edition (Berkeley: University of California Press, 1971), is an exhaustive examination of the evolving idea of representation (with a comprehensive look at voting and participation rates). Elisha P. Douglass, *Rebels and Democrats*, paperback reprint edition (Chicago: Ivan R. Dee, 1989), is a vivid, hard-to-find look at the conflict between democrats and conservatives within the revolutionary movement.

So much of the primary source material from the nation's founding is now available online. The University of Chicago Press has made thousands of pages available in Philip B. Kurland and Ralph Lerner, editors, *The Founders' Constitution*, http://press-pubs.uchicago.edu/founders/. The papers of key leaders—George Washington, John Adams, Thomas Jefferson, James Madison, Alexander Hamilton, and Benjamin Franklin—are available at Founders Online, National Archives, http://founders.archives.gov. *The Documentary History of the Ratification of the Constitution* is a twenty-six-volume work that collects all the relevant records from the ratification period, including public records, private letters and diaries, newspapers and pamphlets, and more. It is available online at http://rotunda.upress.virginia.edu/founders/RNCN.html (subscription required).

This volume begins with Jefferson's drafting of the Declaration of Independence. Many have explored its articulation of core American principles, which ripened into a democratic creed. Two books influenced this book beyond others in their focus on the role of the "American creed" as a driver for democratic change. Pauline Maier's *American Scripture: Making the Declaration of Independence* (New York: Knopf, 1997) explores how Jefferson's text reflected the broad sentiments of the revolutionary generation. (I first encountered the book while serving as White House director of speechwriting. I most enjoyed her account of the drafting process and how delegates would lobby Jefferson, Adams, Franklin, and the other committee members to get their favorite hometown King George III atrocity into the document.) The other most powerful impact came from Garry Wills's *Lincoln at Gettysburg: The Words That Remade America* (New York: Simon & Schuster, 1992), which teaches how that creed could be wielded by later generations on behalf of social and democratic reform. A recent book describes the special power of the Preamble for African Americans: Danielle Allen, *Our Declaration: A Reading of the Declaration of Independence in Defense of Equality* (New York: Norton, 2014). This is especially valuable as contemporary Americans rightly question the place of Jefferson, who, after all, wrote the Declaration while being attended by a slave.

The Constitution has, of course, spawned thousands of books. James Madison's notes from the Constitutional Convention are available online and also in book format, *Notes of Debates in the Federal Convention of 1787*, reported by James Madison (Athens: Ohio University Press, 1985). The authoritative book on the ratification of the Constitution is Pauline Maier, *Ratification: The People Debate the Constitution, 1787–1788* (New York: Simon & Schuster, 2010). The Federalist Papers are available in many editions, including Alexander Hamilton, James Madison, and John Jay, *The Federalist Papers*, edited by Lawrence Goldman (New York: Oxford University Press, 2008). Over the years each generation has reassessed the charter and its purposes. Among those focusing on voting, representation, and whether the Constitution was a counterrevolution or a move toward democracy are Akhil Reed Amar, *America's Constitution: A Biography* (New York: Random House, 2005) and *The Bill of Rights: Creation and Reconstruction* (New Haven: Yale University Press, 1998);

Sanford Levinson, *Our Undemocratic Constitution: Where the Constitution Goes Wrong (And How We the People Can Correct It)* (New York: Oxford University Press, 2006); and Robert A. Dahl, *How Democratic Is the American Constitution?*, 2nd edition (New Haven: Yale University Press, 2003). Michael Klarman looks at the anti-democratic purposes of the Constitution in *The Framers' Coup: The Making of the United States Constitution* (New York: Oxford University Press, 2016). Jack Rakove of Stanford shows how hard it is to identify one "original intent" of the disputatious framers in *Original Meanings: Politics and Ideas in the Making of the Constitution* (New York: Knopf, 1996).

James Madison, of course, played a critical role in the drafting of the Constitution and its ratification. A gripping narrative about his political education in his first congressional election is Richard Labunski, *James Madison and the Struggle for the Bill of Rights* (Oxford: Oxford University Press, 2006). The role played by Madison and Jefferson in building the first opposition political party, with huge implications for the role of voting, is described in Richard Hofstadter, *The Idea of a Party System: The Rise of a Legitimate Opposition in the United States* (Berkeley: University of California Press, 1970). The best single-volume modern biography is Ralph Ketcham, *James Madison: A Biography* (Charlottesville: University of Virginia Press, 1990).

Part II

Those writing about the United States in the first half of the nineteenth century necessarily explore the explosion of democracy. A pivotal figure is Andrew Jackson, and later generations tend to look at him based on their contemporary concerns. At first narratives focused on Jackson as a man of the West who set himself against Eastern elites. During the Depression and the New Deal, Arthur M. Schlesinger Jr. reset views of Jackson by presenting him as an agent of class conflict, even a proto–Franklin Roosevelt. See especially *The Age of Jackson* (Boston: Little, Brown, 1945). In addition to Schlesinger, the works of Robert V. Remini illuminate Jacksonian Democracy's fights for a stronger central government and against concentrated economic power: *Andrew Jackson and the Course of American Freedom, 1822–1832* (New York: Harper & Row, 1981); *Andrew Jackson and the Bank War* (New York: Norton, 1967); and *Martin Van Buren and the Making of the Democratic Party* (New York: Columbia University Press, 1959). Later books, echoing the impact of the civil rights movement, look at Jackson through the lens of policies toward Native Americans that come painfully close to genocide. Now, once again, writers have focused on Jackson and his followers as an agent of expanded democracy. See, in addition to Sean Wilentz's *The Rise of American Democracy*, his short biography *Andrew Jackson: The American President Series: The 7th President, 1829–1837* (New York: Times Books, 2005); Ted Widmer's *Martin Van Buren: The American Presidents Series: The 8th President, 1837–1841* (New York: Times Books, 2005); and an earlier book, Harry L. Watson's *Liberty and Power: The Politics of Jacksonian America* (New York: Hill & Wang, 1990). Jackson as a populist precursor of modern politics has even made it onto Broadway, with the musical *Bloody Bloody Andrew Jackson* and its punk-influenced songs, including "Populism, Yea Yea."

Other books about this period examine particular aspects of the rise of democracy and the fight for the vote. Rosemarie Zagarri, *Revolutionary Backlash: Women and Politics in the Early American Republic* (Philadelphia: University of Pennsylvania Press, 2008), illuminates a little-known period when women could vote in New Jersey, and their broader political role. A colorful look at how the act of voting evolved throughout the nineteenth century is Richard Franklin Bensel, *The American Ballot Box in the Mid-Nineteenth Century* (Cambridge, UK: Cambridge University Press, 2004), which makes clear that democracy was a tribal, visceral contact sport for much of the country's history. Grand surveys of the political and social history of the pre–Civil War period are Gordon S. Wood, *Empire of Liberty: A History of the Early Republic, 1789–1815* (Oxford: Oxford University Press, 2009) and Daniel Walker Howe, *What Hath*

God Wrought: The Transformation of America, 1815–1848 (New York: Oxford University Press, 2007).

Abraham Lincoln's evolving political views—and the undergirding concept of political equality—have been the subject of reams of writing. The best recent synthesis is Eric Foner, *The Fiery Trial: Abraham Lincoln and American Slavery* (New York: Norton, 2010). Other useful assessments are Don E. Fehrenbacher, *Prelude to Greatness: Lincoln in the 1850s* (Palo Alto, CA: Stanford University Press, 1962); Harry V. Jaffa, *Crisis of the House Divided* (Seattle: University of Washington Press, 1973); William Lee Miller, *Lincoln's Virtues: An Ethical Biography* (New York: Vintage Books, 2003); Alan Guelzo, *Lincoln and Douglas: The Debates That Defined America* (New York: Simon & Schuster, 2009); and Wills, *Lincoln at Gettysburg*.

The extension of the vote to African Americans after the Civil War—and then its cruel withdrawal—has been the subject of a vast historical literature and a reassessment. The definitive modern look at the period is Eric Foner, *Reconstruction: America's Unfinished Revolution, 1863–1877* (New York: Harper Collins, 1988). The story of the enactment of the Fifteenth Amendment is told in William Gillette, *The Right to Vote: Politics and the Passage of the Fifteenth Amendment* (Baltimore: Johns Hopkins University Press, 1969). A comprehensive look at the restriction of voting by African Americans in the South is J. Morgan Kousser, *The Shaping of Southern Politics: Suffrage Restriction and the Establishment of the One-Party South, 1880–1910* (New Haven: Yale University Press, 1974). The constitutional dimensions of this extension of rights and then its betrayal are explained in Eric Foner, *The Second Founding: How the Civil War and Reconstruction Remade the Constitution* (New York: W. W. Norton, 2019). Frederick Douglass's fight for voting rights is a central thread of the magisterial Pulitzer Prize–winning biography by David W. Blight, *Frederick Douglass: Prophet of Freedom* (New York: Simon & Schuster, 2018).

This modern consensus reflects a reversal of earlier, racially ugly views. At first historians were among those who promulgated the notion that

Reconstruction was a calamitous imposition on the South, with the Klan a justified if somewhat bumptious response. See Claude G. Bowers, *The Tragic Era: The Revolution after Lincoln* (New York: Houghton Mifflin, 1929). The significant change came with the writing of historians influenced by the civil rights movement, especially C. Vann Woodward, *The Strange Career of Jim Crow*, revised edition (New York: Oxford University Press, 2002), and *Origins of the New South: 1877–1913*, revised edition (Baton Rouge: Louisiana State University Press, 1981). Among the many recent additions to Foner's and Woodward's work, see Nicholas Lemann, *Redemption: The Last Battle of the Civil War* (New York: Farrar, Straus & Giroux, 2006); Charles Lane, *The Day Freedom Died: The Colfax Massacre, the Supreme Court, and the Betrayal of Reconstruction* (New York: Henry Holt, 2009); and Garrett Epps, *Democracy Reborn: The Fourteenth Amendment and the Fight for Equal Rights in Post–Civil War America* (New York: Henry Holt, 2006). Today Americans continue to see Reconstruction as a flawed but ultimately noble bid to extend racial equality. Xi Wang, *The Trial of Democracy: Black Suffrage and Northern Republicans, 1860–1910* (Athens: University of Georgia Press, 1997), includes an especially good exploration of the efforts by Northerners to protect voting in the South. A good recent narrative of Reconstruction and its ignominious end is A. J. Langguth, *After Lincoln: How the North Won the Civil War and Lost the Peace* (New York: Simon & Schuster, 2014). A comprehensive survey of the Civil War is James M. McPherson, *Battle Cry of Freedom: The Civil War Era* (New York: Oxford University Press, 1988).

The decline of democracy and the suppression of the vote in the North during this period is less widely understood. In addition to Keyssar and other surveys of voting, books that link the disenfranchisement and new role of money to the decline of popular politics include Mark Lawrence Kornbluh, *Why America Stopped Voting: The Decline of Participatory Democracy and the Emergence of Modern American Politics* (New York: New York University Press, 1999); Michael E. McGerr, *The Decline of Popular Politics: The American North, 1865–1928* (New York: Oxford University Press, 1986); Walter Dean Burnham, *Critical Elections and the Mainsprings of American Politics* (New York: Norton, 1971); and a recent, indignant narrative history: Jack Beatty, *Age of Betrayal: The Triumph of Money in America, 1865–1900* (New York: Knopf, 2007). A useful look at trends in New York City throughout the nineteenth century is Edwin G. Burrows and Mike Wallace, *Gotham: A History of New York City to 1898*, paperback edition (New York: Oxford University Press, 1999). A survey of the general political and economic developments of the time is H. W. Brands, *American Colossus: The Triumph of Capitalism, 1865–1900* (New York: Doubleday, 2010).

Part III

The Progressive Era is once again receiving considerable attention; less so, its attitude toward voting and democracy. Because the era does not fit neatly into modern notions of left and right, the kinetic life of Theodore Roosevelt is a good place to start. See H. W. Brands, *T.R.: The Last Romantic* (New York: Basic Books, 1998); Doris Kearns Goodwin, *The Bully Pulpit: Theodore Roosevelt, William Howard Taft, and the Golden Age of Journalism* (New York: Simon & Schuster, 2013); and Sidney M. Milkis, *Theodore Roosevelt, the Progressive Party, and the Transformation of American Democracy* (Lawrence: University Press of Kansas, 2009). General looks at the era include Richard Hofstadter, *The Age of Reform: From Bryan to F.D.R.*, paperback edition (New York: Vintage, 1960); Robert H. Wiebe, *The Search for Order: 1877–1920* (New York: Hill & Wang, 1967); and Michael McGerr, *A Fierce Discontent: The Rise and Fall of the Progressive Movement in America* (New York: Simon & Schuster, 2003). The story of the Seventeenth Amendment has rarely been told. Wendy J. Schiller and Charles Stewart III, *Electing the Senate: Indirect Democracy before the Seventeenth Amendment* (Princeton: Princeton University Press, 2014), look at aspects of the topic. George Henry Haynes, *The Election of*

Senators (New York: Henry Holt, 1906), gives a sense of why Americans thought it was needed. Recent conservative books that are critical of the amendment include Ralph Rossum, *Federalism, the Supreme Court, and the Seventeenth Amendment: The Irony of Constitutional Democracy* (Lanham, MD: Lexington Books, 2001). A sympathetic assessment of voter registration reforms amid prevalent election fraud, by a Progressive journalist, is Joseph P. Harris, *Registration of Voters in the United States* (Washington, DC: Brookings Institution, 1929).

The definitive history of campaign finance, dating back to this time, has been written by a freelance scholar: Robert E. Mutch, *Buying the Vote: A History of Campaign Finance Reform* (New York: Oxford University Press, 2014), and his earlier *Campaigns, Congress, and Courts: The Making of Federal Campaign Finance Law* (New York: Praeger, 1988). Amazingly, given the endless clamor over campaign money, Mutch's books are among the few that trace the legal and constitutional history.

The fight for voting rights for women has not penetrated modern understanding quite as deeply as the fight for racial equality. Few modern Americans—even those engaged in issues of democracy—have heard of Alice Paul, Lucy Burns, or Inez Milholland. The foundational study is Eleanor Flexner and Ellen Fitzpatrick, *Century of Struggle: The Woman's Rights Movement in the United States*, enlarged edition (Cambridge, MA: Harvard University Press, 1995). Another significant and useful volume is Ellen Carol DuBois, *Woman Suffrage and Women's Rights* (New York: New York University Press, 1998). Useful recent biographies and histories include J. D. Zahniser and Amelia R. Fry, *Alice Paul: Claiming Power* (New York: Oxford University Press, 2014); Mary Walton, *A Woman's Crusade: Alice Paul and Her Battle for the Ballot* (New York: St. Martin's Press, 2010); and Linda J. Lumsden, *Inez: The Life and Times of Inez Milholland* (Bloomington: Indiana University Press, 2004). No major recent biography focuses on Susan B. Anthony. Her life and the lives of other women's suffrage leaders is described in Jean H. Baker, *Sisters: The Lives of America's Suffragists* (New York: Hill & Wang, 2006). A contemporary work of journalism has recently been updated and reissued: Doris Stevens, *Jailed for Freedom: America's Women Win the Vote*, revised edition, edited by Carol O'Hare (Troutdale, OR: New Sage Press, 1995).

The mid-twentieth-century eruption of activism on issues of representation and civil rights has received vast attention, of course: histories, memoirs, political science studies, legal monographs. Good summary histories include Michael Klarman, *From Jim Crow to Civil Rights: The Supreme Court and the Struggle for Racial Equality* (New York: Oxford University Press, 2004); Steven F. Lawson, *Black Ballots: Voting Rights in the South, 1944–1969* (New York: Columbia University Press, 1976); and John Hope Franklin, *From Slavery to Freedom*, eighth edition (New York: Knopf, 2000). The comprehensive look at *Baker v. Carr*, *Reynolds v. Sims*, and the Supreme Court's role is J. Douglas Smith, *On Democracy's Doorstep: The Inside Story of How the Supreme Court Brought "One Person, One Vote" to the United States* (New York: Hill & Wang, 2014). The subsequent impact is traced in Stephen Ansolabehere and James M. Snyder Jr., *The End of Inequality: One Person, One Vote and the Transformation of American Politics* (New York: Norton, 2008); they describe the leftward shift in states, especially around spending, due to the rulings. Lyndon Johnson's career is traced in the epic, mesmerizing four-volume *The Years of Lyndon Johnson* by Robert A. Caro. Each book illuminates a different aspect of the way democracy was conducted in the United States in the mid-twentieth century. *The Path to Power* (New York: Knopf, 1982) describes the vote-buying and fraud in Texas in the 1930s, as well as brilliantly illuminating Johnson's role in the nationalization of campaign finance. *Means of Ascent* (New York: Knopf, 1990) describes the fraud that pervaded the 1948 election for U.S. Senate. *Master of the Senate* (New York: Knopf, 2002) tells the story of the 1957 civil rights law, which began to exert federal power over voting in the South in the wake of the systematic denial of the franchise to Black Americans. And *The Passage of Power* (New York: Knopf, 2014) shows how Johnson began to enact the Second Reconstruction.

A definitive modern look at the Voting Rights Act of 1965 is Gary May, *Bending Toward Justice: The Voting Rights Act and the Transformation of American Democracy* (New York: Basic Books, 2013). The Selma march and its impact is described by David J. Garrow, *Protest at Selma: Martin Luther King, Jr., and the Voting Rights Act of 1965* (New Haven: Yale University Press, 1978); Taylor Branch, *At Canaan's Edge: America in the King Years, 1965–68* (New York: Simon & Schuster, 2006); and David J. Garrow, *Bearing the Cross: Martin Luther King, Jr., and the Southern Christian Leadership Conference* (New York: William Morrow, 1985). Two compelling memoirs of the period around Selma are John Lewis with Michael D'Orso, *Walking with the Wind: A Memoir of the Movement* (New York: Simon & Schuster, 1998) and Richard N. Goodwin, *Remembering America: A Voice from the Sixties* (Boston: Little, Brown, 1988), a memoir written by Johnson's speechwriter. The impact of the law is traced in Bernard Grofman and Chandler Davidson, editors, *Controversies in Minority Voting: The Voting Rights Act in Perspective* (Washington, DC: Brookings Institution, 1992) and Chandler Davidson and Bernard Grofman, editors, *Quiet Revolution in the South: The Impact of the Voting Rights Act, 1965–1990* (Princeton: Princeton University Press, 1994).

Part IV

The past twenty years have seen a burst of new interest in the history of American democracy and the way it is straining at the joints today.

The Florida recount debacle is described in Political Staff of the *Washington Post*, *Deadlock: The Inside Story of America's Closest Election* (New York: Public Affairs Press, 2001); E. J. Dionne Jr. and William Kristol, editors, *Bush v. Gore: The Court Cases and the Commentary* (Washington, DC: Brookings Institution Press, 2001); Martin Merzer and the Staff of the *Miami Herald*, *Democracy Held Hostage* (New York: St. Martin's Press, 2001); Jake Tapper, *Down and Dirty: The Plot to Steal the Presidency* (New York: Warner Books, 2001); and Jeffrey Toobin, *Too Close to Call:*

The Thirty-Six-Day Battle to Decide the 2000 Election (New York: Random House, 2001). Two significant national studies followed. A commission chaired by former presidents Gerald Ford and Jimmy Carter released its findings in 2001: National Commission on Federal Election Reform, *To Assure Pride and Confidence in the Electoral Process* (2001), available at http://web1.millercenter.org/commissions/comm_2001.pdf. A second panel was chaired by Carter and former secretary of state James Baker: *Building Confidence in American Elections: Report of the Commission on Federal Election Reform* (September, 2005), http://www.eac.gov/assets/1/AssetManager/Exhibit%20M.pdf. The U.S. Commission on Civil Rights probed Florida's record in 2000: *Voting Irregularities in Florida During the 2000 Election* (Chapter 5, "The Reality of List Maintenance"), at http://www.usccr.gov/pubs/vote2000/report/ch5.htm.

An explosion of popular and scholarly books looked at the voting system: Lorraine C. Minnite, *The Myth of Voter Fraud* (Ithaca: Cornell University Press, 2010); Lawrence R. Norden, *The Machinery of Democracy: Protecting Elections in an Electronic World* (Chicago: Chicago Review Press, 2007); Spencer Overton, *Stealing Democracy: The New Politics of Voter Suppression* (New York: Norton, 2006); Tracy Campbell, *Deliver the Vote: A History of Election Fraud, an American Political Tradition—1742–2004* (New York: Basic Books, 2006); Andrew Gumbel, *Steal This Vote: Dirty Elections and the Rotten History of Democracy in America* (New York: Nation Books, 2005); Jeff Manza and Christopher Uggen, *Locked Out: Felon Disenfranchisement and American Democracy* (New York: Oxford University Press, 2006); Heather K. Gerken, *The Democracy Index: Why Our Election System Is Failing and How to Fix It* (Princeton: Princeton University Press, 2009). Conservatives who argue that voter fraud is prevalent and are in support of current voter restriction laws include John Fund, *Stealing Elections: How Voter Fraud Threatens Our Democracy* (New York: Encounter Books, 2008), and John Fund and Hans von Spakovsky, *Who's Counting?: How Fraudsters and Bureaucrats Put Your Vote at Risk* (New York: Encounter Books, 2012). Abigail Thernstrom, *Voting Rights—and Wrongs:*

The Elusive Quest for Racially Fair Elections (Washington, DC: AEI Press, 2009), offers a critique of the Voting Rights Act and its recent evolution.

The recent "voting wars" have been covered extensively as well. See Richard L. Hasen, *The Voting Wars: From Florida 2000 to the Next Election Meltdown* (New Haven: Yale University Press, 2012). Hasen is a prolific writer on voting issues and hosts a key blog, Election Law Blog, http://electionlawblog.org/. Ari Berman of *The Nation* was an early chronicler of the push for new voting laws, elaborated in his gripping *Give Us the Ballot: The Modern Struggle for Voting Rights in America* (New York: Farrar, Straus & Giroux, 2015). The 2012 push for restrictive laws—and its centrality as a Republican strategy—is perceptively covered by Jonathan Alter in *The Center Holds: Obama and His Enemies* (New York: Simon & Schuster, 2013). See also Tova Andrea Wang, *The Politics of Voter Suppression: Defending and Expanding Americans' Right to Vote* (Ithaca: Cornell University Press, 2012), and Darryl Pinckney's idiosyncratic *Blackballed: The Black Vote and US Democracy* (New York: New York Review of Books Press, 2014).

In the wake of *Citizens United*, the hotly debated topic of campaign finance has again received a great deal more scrutiny. Recent works include Lawrence Lessig, *Republic, Lost: How Money Corrupts Congress—and a Plan to Stop It* (New York: Twelve, 2011); Zephyr Teachout, *Corruption in America: From Benjamin Franklin's Snuff Box to* Citizens United (Cambridge, MA: Harvard University Press, 2014); Martin Gilens, *Affluence and Influence: Economic Inequality and Political Power in America* (Princeton: Russell Sage, Princeton University Press, 2012); Kenneth P. Vogel, *Big Money: 2.5 Billion Dollars, One Suspicious Vehicle, and a Pimp—On the Trail of the Ultra-Rich Hijacking American Politics* (New York: Public Affairs, 2014).

Books that tie the new world of big money and low voter turnout to the dysfunction of American government include Jacob S. Hacker and Paul Pierson, *Winner-Take-All Politics: How Washington Made the Rich Richer—and Turned Its Back on the Middle Class* (New York: Simon &

Schuster, 2009); Thomas E. Mann and Norman J. Ornstein, *The Broken Branch: How Congress Is Failing America and How to Get It Back on Track* (New York: Oxford University Press, 2006) and *It's Even Worse Than It Looks: How the American Constitutional System Collided with the New Politics of Extremism* (New York: Basic Books, 2012). Books that argue that traditional reforms have made things worse—and that stronger political parties are among the answers—include Bruce E. Cain, *Democracy More or Less: America's Political Reform Quandary* (New York: Cambridge University Press, 2014); Peter J. Wallison and Joel M. Gora, *Better Parties, Better Government: A Realistic Program for Campaign Finance Reform* (Washington, DC: AEI Press, 2009); and Jonathan Rauch, *Political Realism: How Hacks, Machines, Big Money, and Back-Room Deals Can Strengthen American Democracy* (Washington, DC: Brookings Institution Press, 2015). Recent skeptical looks at American democracy include Francis Fukuyama, *Political Order and Political Decay: From the Industrial Revolution to the Globalization of Democracy* (New York: Farrar, Straus & Giroux, 2014), which looks at political paralysis in countries such as the United States; and Fareed Zakaria, *The Future of Freedom: Illiberal Democracy at Home and Abroad* (New York: Norton, 2003).

What about the Constitution and its impact on democracy law and campaign finance? An influential critique of pre–*Citizens United* Supreme Court cases is Bradley Smith, *Unfree Speech: The Folly of Campaign Finance Reform*, paperback edition (Princeton: Princeton University Press, 2003). Smith is a former Federal Election Commission chair who was part of the drive to strike down laws. Now there is an effort under way to rethink the law from the perspective of those who believe the Constitution does not bar regulation of campaign spending. They include Monica Youn, editor, *Money, Politics and the Constitution: Beyond* Citizens United (New York: Century Foundation Press, 2011); *Conference Summary: Money in Politics 2030: Toward a New Jurisprudence*, Brennan Center for Justice, 2015; Richard M. Hasen, *Plutocrats United: Campaign Money, the Supreme Court, and the Distortion of American Politics*

(New Haven: Yale University Press, 2015); Robert Post, *Citizens Divided: Campaign Finance Reform and the Constitution* (Cambridge, MA: Harvard University Press, 2014); Jeffrey D. Clements, *Corporations Are Not People: Why They Have More Rights Than You Do and What You Can Do About It* (San Francisco: Berrett-Koehler, 2012); and Burt Neuborne, *Madison's Music: On Reading the First Amendment* (New York: New Press, 2014). Neuborne provocatively argues that democracy is an unspoken theme throughout the Constitution, just as federalism and separation of powers are. A similar view is expressed by Justice Stephen Breyer in two books, *Active Liberty: Interpreting Our Democratic Constitution* (New York: Vintage, 2006) and *Making Our Democracy Work: A Judge's View* (New York: Vintage, 2010). The Supreme Court's outsized and damaging role in democracy today is covered in Jeffrey Toobin, *The Oath: The Obama White House and the Supreme Court* (New York: Anchor Books, 2012) and decried in Erwin Chemerinsky, *The Case Against the Supreme Court* (New York: Viking, 2014) and Ian Millhiser, *Injustices: The Supreme Court's History of Comforting the Comfortable and Afflicting the Afflicted* (New York: Nation Books, 2015).

During and after the 2016 election, a steady drip of popular and historical books looked at the key trends undermining democratic institutions. Carol Anderson's *One Person No Vote: How Voter Suppression Is Destroying Our Democracy* (New York: Bloomsbury Publishing, 2018) spelled out the racial justice dimensions of recent voting law changes. The evolving role of big money in politics was the subject of Jane Mayer's *Dark Money: The Hidden History of the Billionaires Behind the Rise of the Radical Right* (New York: Anchor Books, 2016). David Daley's *Ratf**d: Why Your Vote Doesn't Count* (New York: W. W. Norton, 2016) focused on Operation Redmap, which masterminded the drive to gerrymander electoral districts after the 2010 election. Richard L. Hasen summed up the woes of election administration in *Election Meltdown: Dirty Tricks, Distrust, and the Threat to American Democracy* (New Haven: Yale University Press, 2020).

Other books focused on solutions, many of which would be familiar to readers of this book. Leah Greenberg and Ezra Levin, the founders of the nationwide progressive grassroots network Indivisible, published *We Are Indivisible: A Blueprint for Democracy After Trump* (New York: Simon & Schuster, 2019). Others include David Daley's *Unrigged: How Americans Are Battling Back to Save Democracy* (New York: W. W. Norton, 2020); Michael Tomasky, *If We Can Keep It: How the Republic Collapsed and How It Might Be Saved* (New York: W. W. Norton, 2019); and former Obama speechwriter David Litt's droll *Democracy in One Book or Less: How It Works, Why It Doesn't, and Why Fixing It Is Easier Than You Think* (New York: Harper Collins, 2020). Two Brennan Center scholars describe how pro-democracy and voting rights amendments became part of the Constitution in John F. Kowal and Wilfred I. Codrington III, *The People's Constitution: 200 Years, 27 Amendments, and the Promise of a More Perfect Union* (New York: The New Press, 2021). Some of the state-based heroes of the emerging democracy movement published books, including Stacey Abrams, *Our Time Is Now: Power, Purpose, and the Fight for a Fair America* (New York: Henry Holt, 2020); and Desmond Meade, *Let My People Vote: My Battle to Restore the Civil Rights of Returning Citizens* (New York: Beacon Press, 2020), by the leader of the drive to eliminate Florida's felony disenfranchisement system. Top quality documentaries also reported on the fights over democracy. They included *All In: The Fight for Democracy,* produced by Abrams, on Amazon; *Slay the Dragon*, about gerrymandering; *Rigged: The Voter Suppression Playbook*; and PBS's *The Vote* about the Nineteenth Amendment.

Trump's election triggered a paroxysm of concern among scholars of democracy and political institutions, many of whom were politically conservative. They worried that Trump was simultaneously revealing the importance of invisible guardrails and norms, and demolishing them. See Steven Levitsky and Daniel Ziblatt, *How Democracies Die* (New York: Crown, 2018) (which President Biden read and frequently cited); a book by Yale scholar of fascism Timothy Snyder, *On Tyranny: Twenty*

Lessons from the Twentieth Century (New York: Crown, 2017); Anne Applebaum, *The Twilight of Democracy: The Seductive Lure of Authoritarianism* (New York: Doubleday, 2020). David Frum was a prominent conservative writer. His *Trumpocracy: The Corruption of the American Republic* (New York: HarperCollins, 2018) was an early warning of the seriousness of Trump's threat to the American republic. Political scientist Yascha Mounck in *The People vs. Democracy: Why Our Freedom Is in Danger and How to Save It* (Cambridge: Harvard University Press, 2019) warns of illiberal democracy, in which authoritarian populists undermine democratic institutions in the name of the people. Journalist John Judis chronicled *The Populist Explosion: How the Great Recession Transformed American and European Politics* (New York: Columbia Global Reports, 2016) and *The Nationalist Revival: Trade, Immigration, and the Revolt Against Globalization* (New York: Columbia Global Reports, 2018).

Russian interference in the 2016 election produced many governmental and journalistic investigations. They include the special counsel's report that detailed Russian efforts to hack election systems, published in multiple editions including *The Mueller Report* (New York: Scribner, 2019). A good summary is David Corn and Michael Isikoff, *Russian Roulette: The Inside Story of Putin's War on America and the Election of Donald Trump* (New York: Twelve, 2018).

Finally, Trump's catastrophic final months in office—including his attempt to overturn the election—produced an instant crop of breathless behind the scenes narratives. They include Carol Leonig and Philip Rucker, *I Alone Can Fix It: Donald Trump's Catastrophic Final Year* (New York: Penguin Press, 2021); Michael Wolff, *Landslide: The Final Days of the Trump Presidency* (New York: Henry Holt, 2021) (which argues, in effect, that Trump's effort to undo the election was less threatening than it appeared, since he was insane); Michael C. Bender, *Frankly, We Did Win This Election: The Inside Story of How Trump Lost* (New York: Twelve, 2021); and Bob Woodward and Robert Costa, *Peril* (New York: Simon & Schuster, 2021). These books all focus on Trump's mind, admittedly an interesting topic, rather than the way his Big Lie affected the workings of the democratic system.

Many of the issues relating to voting and democracy, especially those of the 2020 election and 2021 voting fights, are exhaustively addressed in the work of my colleagues at the Brennan Center for Justice at NYU School of Law. The Center's work is available at www.brennancenter.org, and specific studies and scholarship are cited in the text.

NOTES

Introduction

xiii "It was impossible to foresee": *Notes of Debates in the Federal Convention of 1787*, reported by James Madison (Athens: Ohio University Press, 1985), (August 9, 1787), 423–24. The notes were first published in vols. 2–3 of *The Papers of James Madison* (Washington, 1840).

xiii the U.S. Supreme Court struck down: *Shelby County v. Holder*, 570 U.S. 529 (2013).

xiii voters could present: Senate Bill 14 (SB14). Act of May 16, 2011, 82d Leg., R.S., ch. 123, 2011 Tex. Gen. Laws 619.

xiv "I had to put $42": Plaintiffs' Exhibit 1090 cited in *Veasey v. Perry*, No. 13-CV-00193, 2014 WL 5090258 (S.D. Tex. Oct. 9, 2014).

xvii Voter turnout plunged in 2014: In 2014, 35.9 percent of eligible voters cast ballots for congressional candidates. To find a lower rate we must go back to 1942, when 33.9 percent voted. The source for turnout data used in this book is the invaluable website compiled by Michael McDonald, now at the University of Florida: "National General Election VEP Turnout Rates, 1789–Present," last updated June 2014, U.S. Elections Project, http://www.electproject.org/national-1789-present. McDonald's numbers show voters as a share of the Voting Eligible Population (VEP), that is, those citizens eligible to vote. Other assessments use the Voting Age Population (all adults) or total population.

xvi "There will be no end of it": John Adams to James Sullivan, May 26, 1776, The Founders' Constitution, volume 1, chapter 13, document 10, http://press-pubs.uchicago.edu.

xvii "voter suppression": Richard A. Posner, *Reflections on Judging* (Cambridge, MA: Harvard University Press, 2013), 85.

1: "The Consent of the Governed"

3 The story got better with each retelling: From John Adams to Timothy Pickering, August 6, 1822, Founders Online, National Archives, January 12, 2014, http://founders.archives.gov/documents/Adams/99-02-02-7674. Adams's selectively remembered dialogue was set to jaunty music in the Broadway play *1776* ("But Mr. Adams").

4 Jefferson would serenely deny: Noble E. Cunningham Jr., *In Pursuit of Reason: The Life of Thomas Jefferson*, paperback ed. (New York: Ballantine Books, 1987), 46–47.

4 fourteen-year-old slave boy: Annette Gordon-Reed, *The Hemingses of Monticello: An American Family* (New York: Norton, 2009), 125.

4 Jefferson consulted the "declaration of rights": Pauline Maier, *American Scripture: Making the Declaration of Independence* (New York: Knopf, 1997), 126. See also Joseph J. Ellis, *American Sphinx: The Character of Thomas Jefferson*, paperback ed. (New York: Vintage, 1998), 53–70, for an insightful assessment of the many theories about the sources on which Jefferson drew in writing the Preamble. See also Garry Wills, *Inventing America: Jefferson's Declaration of Independence* (New York: Houghton & Mifflin, 1978); Carl Loftus Becker, *The Declaration of Independence: A Study on the History of Political Ideas* (New York: Harcourt, Brace & Jovanovich, 1922).

4 "all men are by nature": Virginia Declaration of Rights, in Bernard Schwartz, *The Bill of Rights: A Documentary History*, vol. 1 (New York: Chelsea House, McGraw Hill, 1971), 235. The Virginia drafters debated at length, recognizing that "all men are by nature" must logically, if very inconveniently, include slaves. As one delegate objected, that notion could be "the forerunner or pretext of civil convulsion." Kevin R. C. Gutzman, *Virginia's American Revolution: From Dominion to Republic, 1776–1840* (Lanham, MD: Lexington Books, 2007), 27–28. Eventually the phrase "when they enter into society" was inserted, supposedly saving the principled distinction.

4 Historians recently have been scrutinizing: Danielle Allen, *Our Declaration: A Reading of the Declaration of Independence in Defense of Equality* (New York: Norton, 2014), 275. See Jennifer Schuessler, "If Only Thomas Jefferson Could Settle the Issue: A Period Is Questioned in the Declaration of Independence," *New York Times*, July 2, 2014.

5 "intended to be an expression": From Thomas Jefferson to Henry Lee, May 8, 1825, Founders Online, National Archives, http://founders.archives.gov/documents/Jefferson/98-01-02-5212.

5 That creed would rebuke civic inequality: For a quirky but compelling modern exploration of the Declaration's strength as a beacon for civil rights, see Allen, *Our Declaration*. For a survey of the ways that subsequent social movements used the Declaration and the promises of its preamble as a tool to critique existing institutions, see Alexander Tesis, *Liberty and Equality: The Life and Times of the Declaration of Independence* (New York: Oxford University Press, 2012).

5 Abolitionists declaimed the preamble: Pauline Maier describes the "sacralization" of the Declaration in *American Scripture*, 197–201.

5 The first women's rights convention: See Sally McMillan, *Seneca Falls and the Origins of the Women's Rights Movement* (New York: Oxford University Press, 2008).

5 "the sheet anchor": Don E. Fehrenbacher, ed., *Lincoln: Speeches and Writings, 1832–1858* (Des Moines, IA: Library of America, 1989), 328.

5 He paraphrased it at Gettysburg: In the Gettysburg Address, Lincoln dates the birth of the nation to 1776 ("four score and seven years ago") rather than 1787. For a timeless discussion of the relationship between Jefferson's words and Lincoln's speech, see Garry Wills, *Lincoln at Gettysburg: The Words That Remade America* (New York: Simon & Schuster, 1992).

5 "economic royalists": Franklin D. Roosevelt, "Acceptance Speech for the Renomination for the Presidency, Philadelphia, Pa.," June 27, 1936, in Michael Waldman, *My Fellow Americans: The Most Important Speeches of America's Presidents, from George Washington to Barack Obama*, rev. ed. (Naperville, IL: Sourcebooks, 2010), 104–5.

5 "the true meaning of [our] creed": Josh Gottheimer, ed., *Ripples of Hope: Great American Civil Rights Speeches* (New York: Basic Books, 2003), 236.

6 Old Sarum: Stephen Farrell, "Old Sarum," History of Parliament Trust, http://www.historyofparliamentonline.org/volume/1820-1832/constituencies/old-sarum.

6 The satirical painter William Hogarth: *An Election*, Sir John Soane's Museum, London.

6 the social contract: John Locke, *Second Treatise on Government* (Mineola, NY: Dover Thrift Editions, 2002).

6 Conflict first flared over the Stamp Act: For a discussion of how the Stamp

Act began a rapid shift in American minds toward an insistence on meaningful representation, see Bernard Bailyn, *The Ideological Origins of the American Revolution*, rev. ed. (Cambridge, MA: Belknap Press, 1992), 161–74.

7 Religious minorities such as Baptists and Catholics: See Elisha P. Douglass, *Rebels and Democrats* (Chicago: Ivan R. Dee, 1983), for a description of how the calls for a change in the relationship with England prompted similar calls for greater democracy within the colonies.

7 "furnish all the necessaries": Forrest McDonald, *Novus Ordo Seclorum: The Intellectual Origins of the Constitution*, reprint ed. (Lawrence: University Press of Kansas, 1985), 25–26.

7 only men with a stake in society: Chilton Williamson, *American Suffrage from Property to Democracy* (Princeton: Princeton University Press, 1960), 5.

7 Not just African slaves: Gordon S. Wood, *The Radicalism of the American Revolution* (New York: Random House, 1991), 56.

7 "to exclude such persons": William Blackstone, *Commentaries on the Laws of England: A Facsimile of the First Edition of 1765–1769* (Chicago: University of Chicago Press, 1979); The Founders' Constitution, volume 2, article 1, section 2, clause 1, document 3, http://press-pubs.uchicago.edu/founders/documents/a1_2_1s3.html.

8 Seven restricted voting to men: Alexander Keyssar, *The Right to Vote: The Contested History of Democracy in the United States*, rev. ed. (New York: Basic Books, 2009), 5. Historians continue to debate just how restricted the franchise was, given varying patterns of property ownership. Keyssar estimates that roughly six of ten white men could vote (7). Donald Ratcliffe forcefully argues that the conventional view—that few white men could vote—simply is wrong: "The Right to Vote and the Rise of Democracy, 1787–1828," *Journal of the Early Republic* 33, no. 2 (2013): 219–54.

8 "by and large the property clauses": see Willi Paul Adams, *The First American Constitutions: Republican Ideology and the Making of the State Constitutions in the Revolutionary Era* (Chapel Hill: University of North Carolina Press, 2001), 197.

8 80 percent of white men: Sean Wilentz, *The Rise of American Democracy* (New York: Norton, 2005), 6.

8 colonial Massachusetts was a "middle class democracy": Robert E. Brown, *Middle Class Democracy and the Revolution in Massachusetts, 1691–1780* (Ithaca: Cornell University Press, 1955). Brown argues that the British were trying to throttle an existing democratic system, rooted in equality—that the Revolution was designed to protect democracy, not foment it.

8 In a brief ritualized moment: For a description of the rudimentary methods of voting in the colonies, accompanied by occasional fisticuffs, see Robert J. Dinkin, *Voting in Provincial America: A Study of Elections in the Thirteen Colonies, 1689–1776* (Westport, CT: Greenwood Press, 1977), 102–3, 105, 120–43.

8 When young George Washington ran: Daniel Okrent, *Last Call: The Rise and Fall of Prohibition* (New York: Scribner, 2010), 47.

9 "My only fear": From George Washington to James Wood, July 28, 1758, Founders Online, National Archives, http://founders.archives.gov/documents/Washington/02-05-02-0278.

9 "swilling the planters with bumbo": Lisa Bramen, "Swilling the Planters with Bumbo: When Booze Bought Elections," *Smithsonian.com*, October 20, 2010.

9 "personal solicitation": Jack Rakove, *Revolutionaries: A New History of the Invention of America* (Boston: Houghton Mifflin Harcourt, 2011), 347. Madison's

views were recorded by his brother-in-law. See "Defeated for Election to Virginia House of Delegates, [April 24] 1777," Founders Online, National Archives, http://founders.archives.gov/documents/Madison/01-01-02-0062, last update June 29, 2015.

9 Sometimes it was done "by view": Dinkin, *Voting in Provincial America*, 133–34.

9 drive off their opponents' backers: Williamson, *American Suffrage*, 40–43.

9 "Rhode Islandism": Tracy Campbell, *Deliver the Vote: A History of Election Fraud, an American Political Tradition 1742–2004*, paperback ed. (New York: Carroll & Graf, 2005), 7; Dinkin, *Voting in Provincial America*, 117. For a vivid description of the corruption in Rhode Island, see Albert E. McKinley, *The Suffrage Franchise in the Thirteen Colonies in America* (Philadelphia: Publications of the University of Pennsylvania, 1905), 458–64.

9 In a Connecticut gubernatorial election: Ratcliffe, "The Right to Vote and the Rise of Democracy," 239.

9 The "multitude": Williamson, *American Suffrage*, 44.

9 they could engage in "mobbing": For a discussion of "mobbing," now renamed "crowd activity" by historians, giving it a patina of populist legitimacy, see Larry D. Kramer, *The People Themselves: Popular Constitutionalism and Judicial Review* (New York: Oxford University Press, 2004), 27–28.

9 The roughnecks organized by Sam Adams: J. R. Pole, *Political Representation in England and the Origins of the American Republic* (Berkeley: University of California Press, 1966), 67.

9 the ideas held by the colonists began to shift: see generally Wood, *The Radicalism of the American Revolution.*

10 "olive branch petition": Robert Middlekauff, *The Glorious Cause: The American Revolution, 1763–1789* (New York: Oxford University Press, 1982), 313.

10 "openly avow their revolt": King George III, Royal Address to Parliament, October 27, 1775. Available at Library of Congress, American Memory Collection, http://memory.loc.gov/cgi-bin/query/r?ammem/rbpe:@field(DOCID+@lit(rbpe1440150a)). In the 2015 Broadway musical *Hamilton*, the Royal Address is transformed into Britpop in the song, "You'll Be Back." ("When push/comes to shove/I will send a fully armed battalion/to remind you of my love.")

10 The very day the Royal Address: Marchette Chute, *The First Liberty: A History of the Right to Vote in America, 1619–1850* (New York: E. P. Dutton, 1971), 193.

10 "England since the conquest": Thomas Paine, *Common Sense*, in *Paine: Collected Writings*, ed. Eric Foner (Des Moines, IA: Library of America, 2009), 19.

10 "If the right of nominating": Maier, *American Scripture*, 92.

10 "a Form of Government": Ibid.

10 On May 10, 1776: Congress's instruction read, "Resolved, that it be recommended to the respective assemblies and conventions of the United Colonies, where no government sufficient to the exigencies of their affairs have hitherto established, to adopt such government as shall, in the opinion of the representatives of the people, best conduce to the happiness and safety of their constituents in particular and Americans in general." John Adams, "[Fryday May 10. 1776.]," Founders Online, National Archives, http://founders.archives.gov/documents/Adams/01-03-02-0016-0116.

10 "totally suppressed": "V. Preamble to Resolution on Independent Governments, 15 May 1776," Founders Online, National Archives, http://founders.archives.gov/documents/Adams/06-04-02-0001-0006.

10 "an epocha": Adams, "[Fryday May 10. 1776.]," Founders Online, National Archives.
10 "We are in the very midst": From John Adams to William Cushing, June 9, 1776, Founders Online, National Archives, http://founders.archives.gov.
11 revolutionaries quickly fell to writing new constitutions: For a general assessment, see Adams, *The First American Constitutions*. Varying approaches to the property requirement for voting are mapped out in the appendix, "Property Qualifications in First State Constitutions and Election Laws," 293–311.
11 New Hampshire had already created: Chute, *The First Liberty*, 183–86.
11 South Carolina too: Ibid., 188.
11 "The principal difficulty lies": "Thoughts on Government, April 1776," Founders Online, National Archives, http://founders.archives.gov; "I. To William Hooper, 27 March 1776," Founders Online, National Archives, http://founders.archives.gov/documents/Adams/06-04-02-0026-0002.
11 "Where ANNUAL ELECTION ends": Gordon S. Wood, *Creation of the American Republic* (New York: Norton, 1969), 167.
12 "that made the new governments in 1776": Ibid., 163.
12 "It was not recollected": Williamson, *American Suffrage*, 114; Chute, *The First Liberty*, 192. Jefferson later branded this the chief defect of the state's constitution:

> This constitution was formed when we were new and unexperienced in the science of government. It was the first too which was formed in the whole United States. No wonder then that time and trial have discovered very capital defects in it.
>
> 1. The majority of the men in the state, who pay and fight for its support, are unrepresented in the legislature, the roll of freeholders intitled to vote, not including generally the half of those on the roll of the militia, or of the tax-gatherers.

Thomas Jefferson, *Notes on the State of Virginia*, ed. William Peden (Chapel Hill: University of North Carolina Press for the Institute of Early American History and Culture, 1954); The Founders' Constitution, volume 1, chapter 13, document 15, http://press-pubs.uchicago.edu/founders/documents/v1ch13s15.html.
12 Jefferson had scratched out a proposed draft constitution: "III. Third Draft by Jefferson, [before June 1776]," Founders Online, National Archives, http://founders.archives.gov/.
12 "the mass of men": Chute, *The First Liberty*, 223.
12 New York actually curbed voting rights: New York State Constitution, Section VII, http://www.nhinet.org/ccs/docs/ny-1777.htm.
12 the "well regulated militia": For a discussion of the role of colonial and revolutionary militias, see Michael Waldman, *The Second Amendment: A Biography* (New York: Simon & Schuster, 2014), especially 3–16.
12 When the Virginia aristocrat George Washington: James Thomas Flexner, *Washington: The Indispensable Man* (Boston: Little, Brown, 1974), 68.
13 "every taxable bearing arms": Chute, *The First Liberty*, 219.
13 "quiet and peaceable behavior": Vermont Constitution, Chapter II, Section 6 (1777), https://www.sec.state.vt.us/archives-records/state-archives/government-history/vermont-constitutions/1777-constitution.aspx.

13 most visibly the Irish immigrant Matty Lyon: See Geoffrey R. Stone, *Perilous Times: Free Speech in Wartime* (New York: Norton, 2004), 17–20; Aleine Austin, *Matthew Lyon: "New Man" of the Democratic Revolution, 1749–1822* (University Park: Pennsylvania State University Press, 1981), for the story of the "Lyon of Vermont."

13 the British Empire's second busiest port: Robert J. Allison, *The American Revolution: A Concise History* (New York: Oxford University Press, 2011), 2.

13 Old and new worlds clashed: A vivid description of Philadelphia is found in James MacGregor Burns, *The Vineyard of Liberty*, paperback ed. (New York: Vintage Books, 1983), 110–16, "Philadelphia: The Experimenters."

13 Not in Pennsylvania: For discussions of the revolution and counterrevolution in Pennsylvania, see generally Wood, *Creation of the American Republic*, 83–90; Williamson, *American Suffrage*, 93–99, 133–37; Richard Alan Ryerson, *The Revolution Is Now Begun: The Radical Committees of Philadelphia, 1765–1776* (Philadelphia: University of Pennsylvania Press, 1978).

14 "was drawn most heavily": Eric Foner, *Tom Paine and Revolutionary America* (New York: Oxford University Press, 1976), 63–64.

14 "every man who pays his shot": Keyssar, *The Right to Vote*, 12.

14 on a rainy day in May: For a discussion of the drafting of the Pennsylvania constitution of 1776, see Douglass, *Rebels and Democrats*, 256–86.

14 Sam Adams, fresh from instigating rebellion: Garry Wills, *Inventing America: Jefferson's Declaration of Independence* (New York: First Mariner Books, 2002), 19–34.

14 the world's most democratic such document: John Keane, *Tom Paine: A Political Life* (London: Bloomsbury, 1995), 152.

14 "Every freeman of the full age": "Constitution of Pennsylvania—September 28, 1776," in *The Federal and State Constitutions Colonial Charters, and Other Organic Laws of the States, Territories, and Colonies Now or Heretofore Forming the United States of America*, compiled and edited under the Act of Congress of June 30, 1906 by Francis Newton Thorpe (Washington, DC: Government Printing Office, 1909), Avalon Project, Yale Law School, http://avalon.law.yale.edu/18th_century/pa08.asp.

15 For a time the drafters even toyed with: Douglass, *Rebels and Democrats*, 266.

15 By 1787 nearly 88 percent: Robert J. Dinkin, *Voting in Revolutionary America: A Study of Elections in the Original Thirteen States, 1776–1789* (New York: Praeger, 1982), 36.

15 Benjamin Franklin was now eighty-one: Joseph C. Morton, *Shapers of the Great Debate at the Constitutional Convention of 1787: A Biographical Dictionary* (Westport, CT: Greenwood, 2006), 101.

15 Today a man owns a jackass: Benjamin Franklin, *The Casket, or Flowers of Literature, Wit and Sentiment* (1828), quoted in Keyssar, *The Right to Vote*, 3.

15 hired Thomas Paine as clerk: Keane, *Tom Paine*, 192–94.

15 "qualified voters": Paine, *Common Sense*, 33.

15 Paine was out of town: Keane, *Tom Paine*, 136–37.

15 "makes scarce any, or no difference": Quoted in Foner, *Tom Paine and Revolutionary America*, 143.

16 "[The] right of voting for representatives": Thomas Paine, *Dissertation on First Principles of Government* (1795), The Founders' Constitution, volume 1, chapter 13, document 40, http://press-pubs.uchicago.edu/founders/documents/v1ch13s40.html. He also borrowed, without attribution, Franklin's metaphor of the mule.

William M. Van der Weyde, ed., *The Life and Works of Thomas Paine*, Patriots' ed., 10 vols. (New Rochelle, NY: Thomas Paine National Historical Association, 1925).

16 They tried repeatedly to repeal the constitution: Robert L. Brunhouse, *The Counter-Revolution in Pennsylvania 1776–1790* (New York: Octagon Books, 1971), 221.

16 "They call it a democracy": Benjamin Rush to Charles Lee, October 24, 1779, in *The Lee Papers, 1754–1811*, vol. 6 (New York: New York Historical Society, 1874), 380–81.

16 "the rich a predominancy in government": Chute, *The First Liberty*, 202.

16 "Disastrous Meteor": Joseph J. Ellis, *Passionate Sage: The Character and Legacy of John Adams*, reprint ed. (New York: Norton, 2001), 63.

17 "The History of our Revolution": From John Adams to Benjamin Rush, April 4, 1790, Founders Online, National Archives, http://founders.archives.gov.

17 "He means well for his Country": Extract of a Letter from Benjamin Franklin to Robert R. Livingston, July 22, 1783, Founders Online, National Archives, http://founders.archives.gov.

17 Ironically all men could vote: Williamson, *American Suffrage*, 101.

17 "Depend upon it, sir": John Adams to James Sullivan, May 26, 1776, The Founders' Constitution, volume 1, chapter 13, document 10, http://press-pubs.uchicago.edu.

17 "many persons" would be disenfranchised: Adams, *The First American Constitutions*, 199.

17 "meant their own rights only": Williamson, *American Suffrage*, 102.

18 It won ratification on a second round: Ibid.

18 Women began to object: Rosemary Zagarri, *Revolutionary Backlash: Women and Politics in the Early American Republic* (Philadelphia: University of Pennsylvania Press, 2008), 29.

18 "I long to hear you have declared an independency": Abigail Adams to John Adams, March 31, 1776, Founders Online, National Archives, http://founders .archives.gov.

18 "As to your extraordinary code of laws": John Adams to Abigail Adams, April 14, 1776, Founders Online, National Archives, http://founders.archives.gov.

2: "Who Are to Be the Electors?"

20 "the excess of democracy": Gerry and other New Englanders were scarred—and scared—by Shays Rebellion, which had ended only months before. Madison, *Notes of Debates* (May 31, 1787), 39–40.

20 an approach influenced by the radical Pennsylvania constitution: Akhil Reed Amar, *America's Constitution: A Biography* (New York: Random House, 2005), 84.

20 "the small ones will find": Madison, *Notes of Debates* (June 30, 1787), 230.

20 "The Senate was formed": Hendrik Hertzberg, *Politics: Observations and Arguments, 1966–2004* (New York: Penguin, 2004), 526.

20 "As States are a collection of individual men": Madison, *Notes of Debates* (June 29, 1787), 215.

20 "[It] does not call for much discussion": James Madison, Federalist 62, in Alexander Hamilton, James Madison, and John Jay, *The Federalist Papers*, ed. Lawrence Goldman (New York: Oxford University Press, 2008), 304.

21 the level of inequality in representation: Robert A. Dahl, *How Democratic Is the American Constitution?*, 2nd ed. (New Haven: Yale University Press, 2003), 49.

21 the delegates in Philadelphia never even considered: See Sanford Levinson, *Our Undemocratic Constitution: Where the Constitution Goes Wrong (And How We the People Can Correct It)* (New York: Oxford University Press, 2006), 51. Levinson writes, "The very notion of popular elections for the Senate was unavailable to them" (61).

21 "The qualifications of the electors": Draft U.S. Constitution, Article I, Section 4, Clause 1, in Madison, *Notes of Debates* (August 6, 1787), 386.

21 a "nefarious institution": Madison, *Notes of Debates* (August 8, 1787), 411.

21 "That instrument was written": Richard Brookhiser, *Gentleman Revolutionary: Gouverneur Morris, the Rake Who Wrote the Constitution*, paperback ed. (New York: Free Press, 2004), xiv.

21 "The mob begin to think and reason": Ibid., 20.

22 Nine out of ten white men: Madison, *Notes of Debates* (August 7, 1787), 402–3.

22 "It was difficult to form": Ibid., 401.

22 "restriction of the right": Ibid., 402.

23 "The right of suffrage": Ibid., 403.

23 He thought a property requirement was a good idea: His views had evolved (or regressed) on this matter. Two years before, Madison's friend Caleb Wallace had asked for advice on how the nascent state of Kentucky might structure its government. In his reply the Virginian offered an early sketch, which he would then apply to the national government. Intriguingly, in the same letter Madison enumerates the ways a state legislature could prohibit its legislators from trampling on fundamental rights—a list that would take familiar form as the Bill of Rights. The right to vote was one of them: "The Constitution may expressly restrain them from medling with religion—from abolishing Juries—from taking away the Habeas corpus—from forcing a citizen to give evidence against himself—from controuling the press—from enacting retrospective laws at least in criminal cases, from abridging the right of suffrage, from taking private property for public use without paying its full Value, from licensing the importation of Slaves, from infringing the confederation, &c &c." From James Madison to Caleb Wallace, August 23, 1785, Founders Online, National Archives, http://founders.archives.gov.

23 "the power will slide into the hands": Madison, *Notes of Debates* (June 26, 1787), 194.

23 "In future times": Madison, *Notes of Debates* (August 7, 1787), 403–4.

23 He did so rarely that summer: David O. Stewart, *The Summer of 1787: The Men Who Invented the Constitution* (New York: Simon & Schuster, 2007), 237–38.

23 "the difference in the way the common people": Madison, *Notes of Debates* (August 7, 1787), 404.

23 "Hereditary Professor[s] of Mathematicks": From Benjamin Franklin to William Franklin: Journal of Negotiations in London, March 22, 1775, Founders Online, National Archives, http://founders.archives.gov.

24 "Property was certainly the principal object": Madison, *Notes of Debates* (July 5, 1787), 245.

24 "Doctr. FRANKLIN expressed his dislike": Madison, *Notes of Debates* (August 10, 1787), 426–27.

24 "of all the objections [to] the federal Constitution": Federalist 57, in Hamilton et al., *The Federalist Papers*, 282.

25 as slightly cleaned up: The provision went through a series of revisions, but none

altered its basic meaning. The drafting history is traced in Jack Rakove, Richard R. Beeman, Alexander Keyssar, Peter S. Onuf, and Rosemarie Zagarri, "Brief in Support of Appellees in *Arizona State Legislature v. Arizona Independent Redistricting Commission*," 18–20, http://www.brennancenter.org/sites/default/files/legal-work/AZ%20Amicus%20of%20Rakove.pdf.

25 "The Times, Places and Manner": U.S. Constitution, Article 1, Section 4, Clause 1. The U.S. Supreme Court has interpreted this clause on only a few occasions; most deal with Congress's power under the clause. *Ex parte Siebold*, 100 U.S. 271 (1879) concerned election judges in Maryland who had been convicted of stuffing the ballot box. They challenged their conviction, arguing that the federal government could not prosecute them for violating state law. The Court ruled that the federal government has sweeping power to regulate state elections—without having to be entirely responsible for them. *Smiley v. Holm*, 285 U.S. 355 (1932) set out the history of the clause; it made clear that Congress has a very broad power to regulate elections and prevent abuses. In *U.S. v. Classic*, 313 U.S. 299 (1941) the Court ruled the Elections Clause applied to primaries and, in *Roudebush v. Hartke*, 405 U.S. 15 (1972), to recounts. Most significant, in *Arizona v. Inter-Tribal Council of Arizona*, 133 S. Ct. 2247 (2013), the modern Supreme Court—in an opinion written by Justice Antonin Scalia, no less—struck down Arizona's requirement that voters show proof of citizenship because Congress, with broad power, preempted it. A few Court cases dealt with what the clause meant for state legislatures. In *Ohio ex rel. Davis v. Hildebrandt*, 241 U.S. 565 (1916), a state constitutional provision allowed voters to overturn the redistricting map drawn by the state legislature. The Court ruled that the provision did not intend to prevent states from deciding where the legislative power rested—and that could include the people themselves. In 2015 the Court heard *Arizona State Legislature v. Arizona Independent Redistricting Commission*, which turned on the meaning of *legislature* (rather than Congress's role). It is discussed in chapter 13 of this book.

26 Two delegates from South Carolina: Jack Rakove, *Original Meanings: Politics and Ideas in the Making of the Constitution* (New York: Knopf, 1996), 223–24.

26 "will sometimes fail or refuse": Madison, *Notes of Debates* (August 9, 1787), 423–24.

27 A roaring debate erupted: The authoritative study of the ratification debate is Pauline Maier, *Ratification: The People Debate the Constitution, 1787–1788* (New York: Simon & Schuster, 2010), 58.

27 Twelve of the thirteen states: Rakove, *Original Meanings*, 102–8.

27 In these elections all free men could vote: See Amar, *America's Constitution*, 17, 503n1.

27 One state, Rhode Island: Maier, *Ratification*, 223–24, 458–59.

28 Summoning the revolutionary spirit of 1776: For overviews of the Anti-Federalists and their objections, see Herbert J. Storing, *What the Anti-Federalists Were For: The Political Thought of the Opponents of the Constitution* (Chicago: University of Chicago Press, 1981); Saul Cornell, *The Other Founders: Anti-Federalism and the Dissenting Tradition in America, 1788–1828* (Chapel Hill: University of North Carolina Press, 1999).

28 "of great importance": Jackson Turner Main, *The Antifederalists: Critics of the Constitution, 1781–1788* (Chapel Hill: University of North Carolina Press, 1961), 149–51.

28 "By altering the time": Quoted in ibid., 150.

28 "the democratic branch": John P. Kaminski, Gaspare J. Saladino, Richard Leffler, Charles H. Schoenleber, and Margaret A. Hogan, eds., *The Documentary History of the Ratification of the Constitution*, vol. 6, digital ed. (Charlottesville: University of Virginia Press, 2009), 1217.

28 "make an unequal and partial division": Jonathan Elliot, ed. *The Debates in the Several State Conventions on the Adoption of the Federal Constitution as Recommended by the General Convention at Philadelphia in 1787*, vol. 2, 2nd ed. (Philadelphia: J. B. Lippincott Company, 1901), 27.

28 James Wilson warned: Wilson spoke at the Pennsylvania ratification convention on November 22, 1787. Elliot, ed., *The Debates in the Several State Conventions*, 441.

28 Six states urged an amendment: Rakove et al., "Brief in Support of Appellees in *Arizona State Legislature v. Arizona Independent Redistricting Commission*," 21. Two states also proposed amendments giving Congress that power if states prevented "free and equal" representation.

28 Hamilton felt it necessary to publish: Federalist 59–61, in Hamilton et al., *Federalist Papers*, 291–303.

29 no proposed amendments expressed outrage: Some amendments did call for a statement that voters have a "common interest in and attachment to the community." Ralph Ketcham, ed., *The Anti-Federalist Papers and the Constitutional Convention Debates*, paperback ed. (New York: Signet Classics, 1986), 223 (Virginia's recommended amendments), 230 (those urged by Rhode Island).

29 Appropriations of funds for an army: Akhil Reed Amar observes this was an attempt to check the possible power of a standing army commanded by the executive: "The particular two-year cutoff meshed perfectly with the gears of the Constitution's electoral clock, which would bring the entire House membership before the American electorate every two years." Akhil Reed Amar, *The Bill of Rights: Creation and Reconstruction* (New Haven: Yale University Press, 1998), 51.

29 slaves were counted as three-fifths of a person: U.S. Constitution, Article 1, Section 2, Clause 3.

30 "With respect to democratic politics": Samuel Issacharoff, Pamela S. Karlan, and Richard H. Pildes, *The Law of Democracy: Legal Structure of the Political Process*, 4th ed. (New York: Thomson Reuters, Foundation Press, 2007), 9–10.

30 "How is it that we hear": Samuel Johnson, "Taxation No Tyranny; an Answer to the Resolutions and Address of the American Congress" (1775), in *The Works of Samuel Johnson*, Yale digital ed., http://www.yalejohnson.com/frontend/sda_viewer?n=108205.

31 President Franklin Roosevelt considered backing: "Fireside Chat," March 9, 1937, American Presidency Project, http://www.presidency.ucsb.edu/ws/?pid=15381.

3: Young America

35 "Rip Van Winkle": Washington Irving, "Rip Van Winkle and the Legend of Sleepy Hollow" (Cambridge, MA: Harvard Classics Shelf of Fiction, 1917), http://www.bartleby.com/310/2/1.html.

35 Benjamin Latrobe: Williamson, *American Suffrage*, 209.

36 "democratic rupture": Wilentz, *Rise of American Democracy*, xix.

36 In 1788, as "Publius": Federalist 10, in Hamilton et al., *The Federalist Papers*, 48–55.

36 "Parties ranked high": *Jones v. California Democratic Party* (Stevens, J., dissenting), 530 U.S. 567 (2000).

36 Former Virginia governor Patrick Henry: See generally Harlow Giles Unger, *Lion of Liberty: Patrick Henry and the Call to a New Nation* (New York: Da Capo Press, 2010), 231–32; Henry Mayer, *Son of Thunder: Patrick Henry and the American Republic* (New York: Grove Press, 2001).

36 "The Edicts": From George Washington to James Madison, November 17, 1788, Founders Online, National Archives, http://founders.archives.gov.

37 "rivulets of blood": Henry Lee reported this bit of rhetorical excitement to Madison. To James Madison from Henry Lee, November 19, 1788, Founders Online, National Archives, http://founders.archives.gov. See also Irving Brant, *James Madison: Father of the Constitution* (New York: Bobbs Merrill, 1950), 237; Ralph Ketcham, *James Madison: A Biography* (New York: Macmillan, 1971), 275.

37 He found himself forced to compete frenetically: For vivid descriptions of this pivotal election, see Richard Labunski, *James Madison and the Struggle for the Bill of Rights* (Oxford: Oxford University Press, 2006); Chris DeRose, *Founding Rivals: Madison vs. Monroe, the Bill of Rights, and the Election That Saved a Nation* (Washington, DC: Regnery, 2011), 246. For a discussion of the Virginia Baptists and Madison's last-minute flip-flop to win their votes, see Steven Waldman, *Founding Faith: Providence, Politics and the Birth of Religious Freedom in America* (New York: Random House, 2008), 100–106.

37 In the end he won by 336 votes: DeRose, *Founding Rivals*, 246.

37 They divided over state debt: For a riveting account of the early fights and the compromises that saved the young country, see Joseph Ellis, *Founding Brothers: The Revolutionary Generation* (New York: Knopf, 2000), 48–80.

38 With Madison he traveled to New York: Federalists warned that they were really on a political organizing trip, though many modern historians doubt this. Madison himself wrote to Jefferson as they planned the jaunt, "Health recreation and curiosity being my objects, I can never be out of my way." But they did return to Philadelphia with a party in the making. Given the opprobrium still aimed at parties, an indirect approach seems at least plausible. For a discussion of the trip and the controversy that still surrounds it, see "Editorial Note: The Northern Journey of Jefferson and Madison," Founders Online, National Archives, http://founders.archives.gov.

38 Madison publicly changed his mind: James Madison, "A Candid State of Parties," *National Gazette*, September 22, 1792, Founders Online, National Archives, http://founders.archives.gov. For a discussion of Madison's emergence as the organizer of the Republican Party, the first national party, see Ketcham, *James Madison*, 304–36.

38 "Parties are unavoidable": James Madison, "On Parties," *National Gazette*, ca. January 23, 1792, Founders Online, National Archives, http://founders.archives.gov.

38 The task of winning power: Richard Hofstadter, assessing Madison's approach in "A Candid State of Parties," observes wryly, "Gone, now that Madison is a party leader, are the old references to the turbulence and violence of faction. Gone too, now that Madison is the leader of a party which he is convinced can soon well command the loyalty of an overwhelming majority, are his speculations about the best way to check the most dangerous of all factions, the majority faction." Richard Hofstadter, *The Idea of a Party System: The Rise of a Legitimate Opposition in the United States* (Berkeley: University of California Press, 1970), 84.

38 "Citizen Genêt": Gordon S. Wood, *Empire of Liberty: A History of the Early Republic, 1789–1815* (Oxford: Oxford University Press, 2009), 185–89.

39 Matty Lyon, the Vermont militiaman: See Robert D. Rachlin, "The Sedition Act of 1789 and the East-West Political Divide in Vermont," *Vermont History* 78, no. 2 (2010): 123–50; Stone, *Perilous Times*, 17–18.

39 "well fed, well dressed": Wood, *Radicalism of the American Revolution*, 275.

39 whether he claimed to love pork rinds: Patrician George H. W. Bush claimed to love the crunchy snack as well as the game of horseshoes. See Herbert S. Parmet, *George Bush: The Life of a Lone Star Yankee* (New York: Scribner, 1997), 88.

39 "they had not snored": Wood, *Radicalism of the American Revolution*, 275.

40 candidates "stood for office": The shift is effectively described by Melvin I. Urofsky, *Money and Speech: Campaign Finance Reform and the Courts* (Lawrence: University Press of Kansas, 2005), 4–7.

40 a request by settlers for wider suffrage: The Northwest Ordinance reads, "[No] person [shall] be eligible or qualified to act as a representative unless he shall have been a citizen of one of the United States three years, and be a resident in the district, or unless he shall have resided in the district three years; and, in either case, shall likewise hold in his own right, in fee simple, two hundred acres of land within the same; Provided, also, That a freehold in fifty acres of land in the district, having been a citizen of one of the states, and being resident in the district, or the like freehold and two years residence in the district, shall be necessary to qualify a man as an elector of a representative." Northwest Ordinance, July 13, 1787, Avalon Project, Yale Law School, http://avalon.law.yale.edu/18th_century/nworder.asp.

40 "In 1796, seven out of sixteen states": Jill Lepore, "Party Time," *New Yorker*, September 17, 2007; Edward J. Larson, *A Magnificent Catastrophe: The Tumultuous Election of 1800, America's First Presidential Campaign* (New York: Free Press, 2007), 200–204.

41 a smaller share of Americans: McDonald, "National General Election VEP Turnout Rates, 1789–present."

41 "the Revolution of 1800": Thomas Jefferson to Spencer Roane, September 6, 1819, The Founders' Constitution, volume 3, article 1, section 8, clause 18, document 16, http://press-pubs.uchicago.edu/founders/documents/a1_8_18s16.html.

41 Nearly 4 million people: Department of Commerce, U.S. Bureau of the Census, "Population of States and Counties of the United States, 1790–1990," compiled and edited by Richard Forstall (Washington, DC: Government Printing Office, March 1996), 4, http://www.census.gov/population/www/censusdata/PopulationofStatesandCountiesoftheUnitedStates1790-1990.pdf.

41 As the French writer Alexis de Tocqueville noted: Hugh Brogan, *Alexis de Tocqueville: Prophet of Democracy in an Age of Revolution* (London: Profile Books, 2010), 183.

41 Between 1812 and 1821: Richard Hofstadter, *The American Political Tradition and the Men Who Made It*, rev. ed. (New York: Knopf, 1973), 49.

41 Veterans of the War of 1812: A point made by Judith Shklar, "American Citizenship: The Quest for Inclusion," Tanner Lectures on Human Values, University of Utah, May 1 and 2, 1989, 401, http://tannerlectures.utah.edu/_documents/a-to-z/s/shklar90.pdf.

42 In 1821 Massachusetts held a constitutional convention: The Massachusetts, Virginia, and New York conventions are described in Merrill D. Peterson, ed., *Democracy, Liberty, and Property: The State Constitutional Conventions of the 1820s*, reprint ed. (Indianapolis: Liberty Fund, 2010).

42 a "perfect and complete" example: Ibid., 69.
42 Once again Massachusetts rejected: Williamson, *American Suffrage*, 191.
42 That would not change for three more decades: Arthur M. Schlesinger Jr., *The Age of Jackson* (Boston: Little, Brown, 1945), 343; Alan Tarr, *Understanding State Constitutions* (Princeton: Princeton University Press, 1998), 127.
42 Madison and Monroe, both retired: Williamson, *American Suffrage*, 233.
42 Asthmatic and fading, Madison: Ketcham, *James Madison*, 637.
42 His powdered hair: A vivid description of Madison at the convention is in David O. Stewart, *Madison's Gift: Five Partnerships That Built America* (New York: Simon & Schuster, 2015), 298–99.
42 Apparently, due to illness: David E. Johnson, *John Randolph of Roanoke* (Baton Rouge: Louisiana State University Press, 2012), 29.
42 He named his plantation Bizarre: Daniel Walker Howe, *What Hath God Wrought: The Transformation of America, 1815–1848* (New York: Oxford University Press, 2007), 82.
43 "I am an aristocrat": Johnson, *John Randolph of Roanoke*, 6.
43 "Are we men?": *Proceedings and Debates of the Virginia State Convention of 1829–1830: To which are Subjoined, the New Constitution of Virginia, and the Votes of the People* (Richmond, VA: Samuel Sheperd, 1890), 316.
43 Pointing at Madison, who averted his gaze: Johnson, *John Randolph of Roanoke*, 219–20.
43 His arguments would be echoed: One of the founders of modern conservatism wrote an admiring biography: Russell Kirk, *Randolph of Roanoke: A Study in Conservative Thought* (Chicago: University of Chicago Press, 1951).
43 the fight over suffrage was noisiest in New York: Williamson, *American Suffrage*, 197.
43 The unlikely instigator: The best recent biography of Van Buren is Ted Widmer, *Martin Van Buren: The American President Series: The 8th President, 1837–1841* (New York: Times Books, 2005).
43 "As I invariably slept": "The Little Magician" himself recounted the story (claiming that it was funny, but false). Martin Van Buren, *The Autobiography of Martin Van Buren* (Washington, DC: Government Printing Office, 1920), 199.
43 "this class of men": Nathaniel H. Carter, William L. Stone, and Marcus T. C. Gould, *Proceedings of the New York Constitutional Convention 1821, Assembled for the Purpose of Amending the Constitution of the State of New York* (Albany: E. and E. Hosford, 1821), 257; Peterson, *Democracy, Liberty, and Property*, 185.
43 "The tendency of universal suffrage": Carter et al., *Proceedings of the New York Constitutional Convention 1821*, 221. See also Kenneth Vines and Henry Glick, "The Impact of Universal Suffrage: A Comparison of Popular and Property Voting," *American Political Science Review* 61, no. 4 (1967): 1079.
44 New Jersey, the one state: Zagarri, *Revolutionary Backlash*, 31–32.
44 before the War of 1812: See Jamin B. Raskin, "Legal Aliens, Local Citizens: The Historical Constitutional and Theoretical Meanings of Alien Suffrage," *University of Pennsylvania Law Review* 141 (1993): 1391.
44 In the South rising support for slavery: See Carl T. Bogus, "The Hidden History of the Second Amendment," *University of California at Davis Law Review* 31 (1998): 309.
44 "to patrol for the public safety": Williamson, *American Suffrage*, 227, 232.

45 "corrupt bargain": The appointment of Clay and Jackson's sulfurous reaction to it are described in Robert V. Remini, *Andrew Jackson and the Course of American Freedom, 1822–1832* (New York: Harper & Row, 1981), 98.
45 By 1828 all states but two: In South Carolina and Delaware the legislature still chose presidential electors. Harry L. Watson, *Liberty and Power: The Politics of Jacksonian America* (New York: Hill & Wang, 1990), 94.
45 turnout among white men was 27 percent: McDonald, "National General Election VEP Turnout Rates, 1789–Present."
46 cheap postage rates and the free "franking privilege": Richard R. John, "Affairs of Office: The Executive Departments, the Election of 1828, and the Making of the Democratic Party," in *The Democratic Experiment: New Directions in American Political History*, ed. Meg Jacobs, William J. Novak, and Julian E. Zelizer (Princeton: Princeton University Press, 2003), 58.
46 Van Buren took his organizing skills nationwide: See Robert V. Remini, *Martin Van Buren and the Making of the Democratic Party* (New York: Columbia University Press, 1959).
46 "The driving energy of Jacksonian democracy": Schlesinger, *The Age of Jackson*, 67.
46 "The Monster": Robert V. Remini, *Andrew Jackson and the Bank War* (New York: Norton, 1967), 15.
47 "I can remove all the constitutional scruples": Quoted in Hofstadter, *The American Political Tradition*, 59.
47 "The Bank, Mr. Van Buren": Quoted in Remini, *Andrew Jackson and the Course of American Freedom*, 366.
47 "It is to be regretted": Jackson's veto message is included in Waldman, *My Fellow Americans*, 25–29.
47 Biddle spent lavishly: Remini, *Andrew Jackson and the Bank War*, 99.
47 "If the Bank, a mere monied corporation": Ibid.
48 "In Jackson's view of America": Sean Wilentz, *Andrew Jackson* (New York: Times Books, 2005), 83.
48 This scene echoed Election Day: Howe, *What Hath God Wrought*, 490.
48 Now parties printed ballots: Keyssar, *The Right to Vote*, 40.
49 In one article attacking Van Buren: John G. Gasaway, "Tippecanoe and the Party Press Too: Mass Communication, Politics, Culture, and the Fabled Presidential Election of 1840," PhD dissertation, University of Illinois at Urbana, 1999, 228.
49 there were Barnburners: Jed Handelsman Shugerman, *The People's Courts: Pursuing Judicial Independence in America* (Cambridge, MA: Harvard University Press, 2012), 90.
49 Loco Focos: The glorious profusion of factions is documented in Wilentz, *Rise of American Democracy*; the origin of the Loco Focos is described on 421–23.
49 The democratic impulse was so strong: Shugerman, *The People's Courts*, 77.
49 "a new word entered the American vocabulary": *Booze*, of course. Widmer, *Van Buren*, 138.
50 "the log cabin and the palace": Wilentz, *Rise of American Democracy*, 504.
50 "With them we'll beat little Van": Howard Da Silva, *Tippecanoe and Tyler Too, Politics and Poker: Songs to Get Elected By*, Monitor Records, Smithsonian Folkways, 2004.
50 Turnout soared to 80 percent: McDonald, "National General Election VEP Turnout Rates, 1789–Present."

4: "Sheet Anchor"

51 America's democratic ferment: Robert H. Wiebe argues that Europeans were so fascinated by the tumultuous egalitarianism of American society that they actually paid little attention to its politics. See Robert H. Wiebe, *Self-Rule: A Cultural History of American Democracy* (Chicago: University of Chicago Press, 1995), 41–60.

51 Reform Act of 1832: For a discussion of the Reform Act and its significance, see John A. Phillips and Charles Wetherell, "The Great Reform Act and the Political Modernization of Britain," *American Historical Review* 100, no. 2 (1995): 411–36.

51 English reform proponents: Williamson, *American Suffrage*, 296–97.

52 "Americans use associations": Alexis de Tocqueville, *Democracy in America*, ed. and trans. Harvey C. Mansfield and Delba Winthrop (Chicago: University of Chicago Press, 2000), 489.

52 records from disputed elections: Richard Franklin Bensel, *The American Ballot Box in the Mid-Nineteenth Century* (Cambridge, UK: Cambridge University Press, 2004).

52 When Abraham Lincoln voted: Ibid., 287n3.

53 provoked a miniature civil war: See Erik J. Chaput, *The People's Martyr: Thomas Wilson Dorr and His 1842 Rhode Island Rebellion* (Lawrence: University Press of Kansas, 2013); Howe, *What Hath God Wrought*, 599–602. Original documents and contemporary news coverage are gathered at the fascinating website The Dorr Rebellion, http://library.providence.edu/dps/projects/dorr/index.php.

53 The soldiers hid, feasting and drinking: Williamson, *American Suffrage*, 259.

53 "Governor" Dorr dashed off to Washington: See Arthur May Mowry, "Tammany Hall and the Dorr Rebellion," *American Historical Review* 3, no. 2 (1898): 292–301.

54 a significant U.S. Supreme Court decision: *Luther v. Borden*, 48 U.S. 1, 12 L. Ed. 581 (1849).

54 The small convention held there: The description of Seneca Falls is drawn from the classic history Eleanor Flexner and Ellen Fitzpatrick, *Century of Struggle: The Woman's Rights Movement in the United States*, enlarged ed. (Cambridge, MA: Harvard University Press, 1995), 66–72.

55 "We hold these truths to be self-evident": *Proceedings of the Woman's Rights Conventions, Held at Seneca Falls & Rochester, N.Y., July & August, 1848* (New York: Arno Press, New York Times, 1969), 5.

55 "Marx of the Master Class": Hofstadter, *The American Political Tradition*, 67–91.

56 "Our union—it must be preserved": John Meacham, *American Lion: Andrew Jackson in the White House* (New York: Random House, 2008), 136.

56 Contemporaries joked: Wilentz, *Rise of American Democracy*, 319.

56 "Taking the proposition literally": Hofstadter, *The American Political Tradition*, 74.

56 "political and social equality": Ibid., 79.

56 Abraham Lincoln did not start his political career: See Eric Foner, *The Fiery Trial* (New York: Norton, 2010), 3–62.

56 "that the elective franchise should be kept pure": Paul Simon, *Lincoln's Preparation for Greatness: The Illinois Legislative Years* (Champaign: University of Illinois Press, 1989), 130. Simon first published the book in 1965, long before he became a bow-tied U.S. senator.

56 he even attacked Van Buren: Michael Burlingame, *Abraham Lincoln: A Life*, vol. 1, paperback reprint ed. (Baltimore: Johns Hopkins University Press, 2013), 108.

57 "What I do say is": Fehrenbacher, *Lincoln: Speeches and Writings, 1832–1858*, 328.

57 "I am not, nor have ever been": Fourth Lincoln-Douglas Debate, Charleston, Illinois, September 18, 158, in ibid., 636.

58 twenty-two states and territories: For a pioneering rediscovery of voting by noncitizens over the years, see Raskin, "Legal Aliens, Local Citizens," 1391. See also Kirk Harold Porter, *A History of Suffrage in the United States* (Chicago: University of Chicago Press, 1918), 115–34.

58 Order of the Star Spangled Banner: Howe, *What Hath God Wrought*, 826–27.

58 The "American Party": Ibid.

58 "As a nation, we begin": Letter to Joshua F. Speed, August 24, 1855, in Fehrenbacher, *Lincoln: Speeches and Writings, 1832–1858*, 363.

59 Lincoln secretly invested in: Harold Holzer, *Lincoln and the Power of the Press: The War for Public Opinion* (New York: Simon & Schuster, 2014), 188–94.

59 "That is the electric cord": "Speech at Chicago, Illinois, July 10, 1858," in Don E. Fehrenbacher, *Lincoln: Speeches and Writings, 1859–1865* (Des Moines: Library of America, 1989), 456.

59 "All honor to Jefferson": Letter to Henry L. Pierce and Others, April 6, 1859, in ibid., 19.

59 "What, to the American slave": James Daley, ed., *Great Speeches by Frederick Douglass* (Mineola, NY: Dover Thrift Editions, 2013), 26.

5: "The Bullet and the Ballot"

61 "I have had but one idea": Frederick Douglass, "What the Black Man Wants," in Daley, *Great Speeches by Frederick Douglass*, 51. The speech was delivered to the Thirty-second Annual Meeting of the Massachusetts Anti-Slavery Society in Boston on January 26, 1865. Many books erroneously date it to April, a more portentous month. See Frederick Douglass, "What the Black Man Wants," in William D. Kelley, Wendell Phillips, and Frederick Douglass, *The Equality of All Men before the Law Claimed and Defended in Speeches by Hon. William D. Kelley, Wendell Phillips, and Frederick Douglass* (Boston: Rand and Avery, 1865), ser. 3, 37, cited in Xi Wang, *The Trial of Democracy: Black Suffrage and Northern Republicans, 1860–1910* (Athens: University of Georgia Press, 1997), 310n18.

62 "It is not your intention": "Speech of Frederick Douglass," *Boston Post*, April 5, 1865.

62 "the greatest question": David Herbert Donald, *Lincoln* (New York: Simon & Schuster, 1995), 467.

62 "frees the slave and ignores": Foner, *Fiery Trial*, 291.

62 Congress took steps: Quintard Taylor, *In Search of the Racial Frontier: African Americans in the American West, 1528–1990* (New York: Norton, 1998), 121.

62 Lincoln's brilliant Second Inaugural Address: See Garry Wills, "Lincoln's Greatest Speech," *Atlantic*, September 1999; Ronald C. White, Jr., *Lincoln's Greatest Speech: The Second Inaugural* (New York: Simon & Schuster, 2001).

62 "sacred effort": Allen Thorndike Rice, *Reminiscences of Abraham Lincoln by Distinguished Men of His Time* (New York: Classic Reprint, 2012), 262–63.

62 "Guns are firing": Gideon Welles, *The Civil War Diary of Gideon Welles, Lincoln's*

Secretary of the Navy: The Original Manuscript Edition (Champaign: University of Illinois Press, 2014), 621.

63 "It is also unsatisfactory to some": Speech on Reconstruction, April 11, 1865, in Fehrenbacher, *Lincoln: Speeches and Writings, 1859–1865*, 699.

63 "That means nigger citizenship": Donald, *Lincoln*, 588.

63 Lincoln gave them reason to think: Foner, *Fiery Trial*, 332.

64 "When the fight is over": John Jay, *The Political Situation in the United States: A Letter to the Union League* (London: Rivingtons, 1866), 51; Keyssar, *The Right to Vote*, 69.

64 "a great oversight": William Nelson, *The Fourteenth Amendment: From Political Principle to Judicial Doctrine* (Cambridge, MA: Harvard University Press, 1988), 46.

64 a white political militia known as "The Thugs": A. J. Langguth, *After Lincoln: How the North Won the Civil War and Lost the Peace* (New York: Simon & Schuster, 2014), 147.

64 Section 2 had a more immediate impact: It reads, "Representatives shall be apportioned among the several states according to their respective numbers, counting the whole number of persons in each state, excluding Indians not taxed. But when the right to vote at any election for the choice of electors for President and Vice President of the United States, Representatives in Congress, the executive and judicial officers of a state, or the members of the legislature thereof, is denied to any of the male inhabitants of such state, being twenty-one years of age, and citizens of the United States, or in any way abridged, except for participation in rebellion, or other crime, the basis of representation therein shall be reduced in the proportion which the number of such male citizens shall bear to the whole number of male citizens twenty-one years of age in such state." U.S. Constitution, Amendment XIV, Section 2.

65 Such promiscuous presidential speechmaking: See Jeffrey Tulis, *The Rhetorical Presidency* (Princeton: Princeton University Press, 1987), 87–94.

65 "intemperate, inflammatory and scandalous": "Proceedings of the Senate Sitting for the Trial of Andrew Johnson, President of the United States, on Articles of Impeachment Exhibited by the House of Representatives," Article X, http://law2.umkc.edu/faculty/projects/ftrials/impeach/articles.html.

65 In 1865 five jurisdictions had ballot initiatives: William Gillette, *The Right to Vote: Politics and the Passage of the Fifteenth Amendment* (Baltimore: Johns Hopkins University Press, 1969), 25.

65 "Your noble and humane predecessor": Philip S. Foner, ed., *Frederick Douglass on Slavery and the Civil War: Selections from His Writings* (Mineola, NY: Dover Thrift Editions, 2003), 26.

65 "Those damned sons of bitches": James Oakes, *The Radical and the Republican: Frederick Douglass, Abraham Lincoln and the Triumph of Antislavery Politics* (New York: Norton, 2007), 255.

65 The First Reconstruction Act: See Eric Foner, *Reconstruction: America's Unfinished Revolution, 1863–1877* (New York: Harper Collins, 1988), 271–80.

66 "the people of the South": Langguth, *After Lincoln*, 171.

66 Many nations ended slavery: Foner, *Reconstruction*, 279.

66 the Union general Ulysses S. Grant: H. W. Brands, *The Man Who Saved the Union: Ulysses S. Grant in War and Peace*, paperback ed. (New York: Anchor, 2013), 417.

66 Southern Blacks cast 450,000 votes: Gillette, *The Right to Vote*, 41.

66 "We must establish the doctrine": Hans Louis Trefousse, *Thaddeus Stevens: Nineteenth Century Egalitarian* (Chapel Hill: University of North Carolina Press, 1997), 218.

67 "race, color, nativity": *Congressional Globe*, volume 61, part 2, February 9, 1869.

67 "it will be taken as a solemn national declaration": *Nation*, February 11, 1869.

67 "For the first time in our lives": Wendell Phillips in the *National Anti-Slavery Standard*, February 30, 1869, quoted in James McPherson, *The Struggle for Equality* (Princeton: Princeton University Press, 1964), 426.

67 "It was one of the ironies": McPherson, *The Struggle for Equality*, 426–27.

68 It was just a decade after the notorious *Dred Scott* decision: *Dred Scott v. Sanford*, 60 U.S. 393 (1857). Lincoln, among others, argued that the Court had illicitly conspired to expand slavery. See Harold Holzer, *Lincoln at Cooper Union: The Speech That Made Abraham Lincoln President* (New York: Simon & Schuster, 2004), 136–37. Opposition to the *Dred Scott* case was an early, unifying party plank for the Republicans (211).

68 Both parties knew an enfranchised Northern Black vote: According to William Gillette, "The enfranchisement [of] between 130,000 and 171,000 Negro voters in the border states, the Northeast, the Middle West, and the Far West could change the political complexion of state and national politics. This Negro vote would be Republican, and it might cost the Democrats Maryland, Delaware and New Jersey, while assuring the Republicans control of Connecticut, Indiana, Ohio, and Pennsylvania." Gillette, *The Right to Vote*, 80.

68 the "lower orders": Lori D. Ginzberg, *Elizabeth Cady Stanton: An American Life* (New York: Hill and Wang, 2009), 128.

68 "Think of Patrick and Sambo": Ellen Carol DuBois and Richard Candida Smith, eds., *Elizabeth Cady Stanton, Feminist as Thinker: Reader in Documents and Essays* (New York: New York University Press, 2007), 128.

69 "I must say I do not see how": Philip S. Foner, ed., *Frederick Douglass on Women's Rights*, paperback ed. (New York: Da Capo Press, 1992), 87.

69 "the bullet and the ballot go together": Edwin G. Burrows and Mike Wallace, *Gotham: A History of New York City to 1898*, paperback ed. (New York: Oxford University Press, 1999), 982–83.

69 "Politics got in our midst": A stirring description of the rise of Black political activism in the South is in Foner, *Reconstruction*, 282–83.

69 "Every tenth negro": Ibid., 291.

69 "It is the hardest thing in the world": Richard Bailey, *Neither Carpetbaggers nor Scalawags: Black Officeholders During the Reconstruction of Alabama, 1867–1878* (Montgomery, AL: New South Books, 2010), 239.

70 between 264 and 324 Black men: J. Morgan Kousser, "The Voting Rights Act and the Two Reconstructions," in *Controversies in Minority Voting: The Voting Rights Act in Perspective*, ed. Bernard Grofman and Chandler Davidson (Washington, DC: Brookings Institution, 1992), 139–40.

70 Eighteen Black men: Foner, *Reconstruction*, 353.

70 P. B. S. Pinchback: See Nicholas Lemann's description—"an outsized figure: newspaper publisher, gambler, orator, speculator, dandy, mountebank—served for a few months as the state's Governor and claimed seats in both houses of Congress following disputed elections but could not persuade the members of either to seat him." Nicholas Lemann, *Redemption: The Last Battle of the Civil War* (New York: Farrar, Straus & Giroux, 2006), 197.

70 Claude Bowers, a Columbia University professor: See Claude G. Bowers, *The Tragic Era: The Revolution after Lincoln* (New York: Houghton Mifflin, 1929).
70 "wave of counterrevolutionary terror": Foner, *Reconstruction*, 425–44.
70 Thousands were killed: Kousser, "The Voting Rights Act and the Two Reconstructions," 141–42.
70 the 1870 massacre in Eutaw, Alabama: Melinda Meek Hennessey, "Political Terrorism in the Black Belt: The Eutaw Riot," *Alabama Review: A Quarterly Journal of Alabama History* 33, no. 1 (1980): 43–47.
71 In 1873 alone they brought: Keyssar, *The Right to Vote*, 107; Wang, *The Trial of Democracy*, 120–21.
71 In one Louisiana parish: Langguth, *After Lincoln*, 348.
72 "a political bargain": Ibid., 352.

6: The Gilded Age

73 "What is the chief end of man?": Mark Twain, "The Revised Catechism," *New York Tribune*, September 27, 1871, analyzed in Arthur L. Vogelback, "Mark Twain and the Tammany Ring," *PMLA* 70, no. 1 (1955): 69–77.
74 Meet the iconic Boss Tweed: Kenneth D. Ackerman, *Boss Tweed: The Rise and Fall of the Corrupt Pol Who Conceived the Soul of Modern New York* (New York: Carroll & Graf, 2005), 17.
74 recent accounts have suggested: Ibid., 340.
75 Tweed never actually said: Ibid., 139.
75 Voting Democratic, they feared African American competition: James M. McPherson, *Battle Cry of Freedom: The Civil War Era* (New York: Oxford University Press, 1988), 609–11.
75 In all, 25 million immigrants: U.S. Bureau of the Census, Historical Statistics of the United States. Colonial Times to 1970, Part 1, Bicentennial Edition (Washington, DC. U.S. Government Printing Office, 1975), 105, https://ia700407.us.archive.org/4/items/HistoricalStatisticsOfTheUnitedStatesColonialTimesTo1970/us_historical_statistics_colonial_times_to_1970.pdf.
75 When the radical reformer Henry George: George Seldes, *Witness to a Century* (New York: Ballantine Books, 1987), 20.
75 "all of the signers of the Declaration of Independence": Joseph P. Harris, *Registration of Voters in the United States* (Washington, DC: Brookings Institution, 1929), 6.
75 "In a contested election case in Colorado": Ibid., 12–13.
76 Backlash ensued: The revolt by intellectuals against democracy and voting is described in Michael E. McGerr, *The Decline of Popular Politics: The American North, 1865–1928* (New York: Oxford University Press, 1986), 46–48.
76 "A New England village of the olden time": Francis Parkman, "The Failure of Universal Suffrage," *North American Review* 127, no. 263 (1878): 7, 10, 4.
77 the "best men": McGerr, *The Decline of Popular Politics*, 42–43.
77 "universal suffrage can only mean": Charles Francis Adams Jr., "The Protection of the Ballot in National Elections," *Journal of Social Science* 1 (New York: Leypoldt and Holt, June 1869), 109.
77 E. L. Godkin: Burrows and Wallace, *Gotham*, 980.
77 "our times and lands searchingly in the face": Walt Whitman, *Democratic Vistas* (New York: Liberal Arts Press, 1949), 2.

77 "Redemption of the North": Keyssar, *The Right to Vote*, 117–71.

77 reformers tried to reimpose a form of property requirement: The fight over the effort to impose economic strictures on voting in New York City is chronicled in Burrows and Wallace, *Gotham*, 1032–33.

77 "would no longer find themselves in contest": Ibid., 1033.

77 "ignorant voters": Ibid.

78 "uncivilized classes in Brooklyn": Ibid.

78 a "menace to the rights of people": McGerr, *The Decline of Popular Politics*, 50.

78 pauper exclusions barred thousands: Keyssar, *The Right to Vote*, 135.

78 The Supreme Court had blessed this approach: In *Minor v. Happersett*, an 1874 case dealing with women's rights, the Court noted that noncitizens could vote in Alabama, Arkansas, Florida, Georgia, Indiana, Kansas, Minnesota, and Texas—so it was acceptable to deny women, who were undoubtedly citizens, the privilege of suffrage.

78 The law kindled draft riots: See Barnet Schechter, *The Devil's Own Work: The New York City Draft Riots and the Fight to Reconstruct America* (New York: Walker Books, 2005).

78 "Under our complex system": *In re Wehlitz*, 16 Wis. 468 (1863).

79 California's 1879 constitution declared: California Constitution, Article II ("Right of Suffrage"), http://archives.cdn.sos.ca.gov/collections/1879/archive/1879-constitution.pdf.

79 Some states required voters: Ron Hayduck, *Democracy for All: Restoring Immigrant Voting Rights in the United States* (London: Routledge, 2006), 37.

79 "sad feature" of the law: Ibid.

79 Other states imposed literacy tests: Keyssar, *The Right to Vote*, 145.

80 In Chicago the new system: Ibid., 154–55.

80 In New York City in 1908: Ibid., 157.

80 "Our registration and ballot laws": Ray Stannard Baker, "Negro Suffrage in a Democracy," *Atlantic Monthly*, November 1910.

81 the "Australian ballot": The introduction of the Australian ballot is described in Joseph Pratt Harris, *Election Administration* (Washington, DC: Brookings Institution, 1934), 152–65.

81 One Tammany Hall leader perfumed the party tickets: Jack Beatty, *The Age of Betrayal: The Role of Money in America, 1865–1900* (New York: Knopf, 2007), 207. The innovative politician was "Big Tim" Sullivan, who later authored the first major urban gun control law.

82 The number of third parties: See Mark Kornbluh, *Why America Stopped Voting: The Decline of Participatory Democracy and the Emergence of Modern American Politics* (New York: New York University Press, 1999), 124–5.

82 Newspapers previously had been overtly partisan: See McGerr, *The Decline of Popular Politics*, 107–37.

82 "without fear or favor": "Business Notice," *New York Times*, August 19, 1896.

82 three years after the U.S. Army left: Kousser, "The Voting Rights Act and the Two Reconstructions," 141.

82 In one Tennessee district: The story of disenfranchisement in Tennessee is told in J. Morgan Kousser, *The Shaping of Southern Politics: Suffrage Restriction and the Establishment of the One-Party South* (New Haven: Yale University Press, 1974), 104–23.

82 In Louisiana the governor swore to follow: Ibid., 46.

83 its 1888 platform declared "unswerving devotion": The party platform read, "We reaffirm our unswerving devotion to the National Constitution and the indissoluble Union of the States; to the autonomy reserved to the States under the Constitution; to the personal rights and liberties of citizens in all the States and Territories of the Union, and especially to the supreme and sovereign right of every lawful citizen, rich or poor, native or foreign born, white or Black, to cast one free ballot in public elections, and to have that ballot duly counted. We hold the free and honest popular ballot and the just and equal representation of all the people to be the foundation of our Republican government and demand effective legislation to secure the integrity and purity of elections, which are the fountains of all public authority. We charge that the present Administration and the Democratic majority in Congress owe their existence to the suppression of the ballot by a criminal nullification of the Constitution and laws of the United States." "Republican Party Platform of 1888," June 19, 1888, American Presidency Project, http://www.presidency.ucsb.edu/ws/?pid=29627. Four years later, in a section titled "Southern Outrages," the party platform declared, "We denounce the continued inhuman outrages perpetrated upon American citizens for political reasons in certain Southern States of the Union." "Republican Party Platform of 1892," June 7, 1892, American Presidency Project, http://www.presidency.ucsb.edu/ws/?pid=29628.

83 Twenty times in the last two decades of the nineteenth century: Kousser, *The Shaping of Southern Politics*, 263.

83 Opponents dubbed the mild measure the "Lodge Force Bill": See Wang, *The Trial of Democracy*, 232–52. The Lodge bill had several key provisions. It authorized a chief election supervisor for each judicial circuit, who could appoint election supervisors when asked by citizens. It expanded the role of existing federal supervisors, giving them power to supervise voter rolls and challenge qualifications. And it established the U.S. Board of Canvassers to supervise the counting of votes. In effect the federal government would now determine who had won elections, including state races (236–37).

83 Southern white leaders also feared the rising Populist movement: See Lawrence Goodwyn, *Democratic Promise: The Populist Moment in American Life* (New York: Oxford University Press, 1976).

83 In the South the Farmers Alliance: For a pioneering discussion of the cross-racial coalition as part of the Populist Era, see C. Vann Woodward, *The Strange Career of Jim Crow*, rev. ed. (New York: Oxford University Press, 2002) and *Origins of the New South: 1877–1913*, rev. ed. (Baton Rouge: Louisiana State University Press, 1981), 235–63. Dr. Martin Luther King Jr. cited Woodward's work in his great speech before the Alabama statehouse in 1965. See also Frederick D. Ogden, *The Poll Tax in the South* (Birmingham: University of Alabama Press, 1958), 10–20.

84 Mississippi moved first: The Mississippi Plan is described in Kousser, *The Shaping of Southern Politics*, 139–45, 154–55.

84 In 1890 Black voters still outnumbered: Morton Stavis, "A Century of Struggle for Black Enfranchisement in Mississippi: From the Civil War to the Congressional Challenge of 1965—and Beyond," *Mississippi Law Journal*, no. 57 (1987): 603; Richard H. Pildes, "Democracy, Anti-Democracy and the Canon," *Constitutional Commentary* 17 (2000): 603.

84 "disenfranchised not only the ignorant and vicious Black": Kousser, *Shaping of Southern Politics*, 144.

84 Over the next eighteen years: Mississippi (1890), South Carolina (1895), Louisiana

(1898), North Carolina (1900), Alabama (1901), Virginia (1902), Texas (1902), and Georgia (1908) all enshrined white supremacy and Black disenfranchisement in their constitutions, mostly by convention. Pildes, "Democracy, Anti-Democracy and the Canon," 301n29.

84 Virginia's convention met: Susan Breitzer, "Virginia Constitutional Convention (1901–1902)," *Encyclopedia Virginia*, Virginia Foundation for the Humanities, January 16, 2015, http://www.encyclopediavirginia.org/Constitutional_Convention_Virginia_1901-1902.

85 To raucous cheers Glass declared: Delegates "wildly cheered" Glass's line, according to the New Deal–era Federal Writers Project's guide, *Virginia: A Guide to the Old Dominion*: "With the turn of the century came the virtual elimination of the Negro from Virginia politics. . . . The *Lynchburg News* found in 1905 of the 147,000 Negro voters qualified under the former constitution, only 21,000 were registered and of these less than half had paid their poll taxes and qualified." Federal Writers Project, *Virginia: A Guide to the Old Dominion* (Richmond: Governor of Virginia, 1941).

85 "This plan will eliminate the darkey": *Report of the proceedings and debates of the Constitutional Convention, state of Virginia: held in the city of Richmond June 12, 1901, to June 26, 1902, Vol. II* (Richmond: Heritage Press, 1906) 3076.

85 It took effect without public ratification: The Constitution was upheld as the legitimate governing document by the state supreme court in *Taylor v. Commonwealth*, June 18, 1903, Virginia Law Register 9, no. 5 (1903): 381–83.

85 In desperation Black activists turned to the courts: A good summary of cases from this period is found in Michael Klarman, *From Jim Crow to Civil Rights: The Supreme Court and the Struggle for Racial Equality* (New York: Oxford University Press, 2004), 28–39.

85 it neutralized the Fourteenth Amendment's protection: *The Slaughter-House Cases*, 83 U.S. 36 (1876).

85 the notorious 1872 Colfax massacre: *United States v. Cruikshank*, 92 U.S. 542 (1876). For a harrowing description of the massacre and the case, see Charles Lane, *The Day Freedom Died: The Colfax Massacre, the Supreme Court, and the Betrayal of Reconstruction* (New York: Henry Holt, 2008).

86 "Thus the first of the modern reactionary constitutions": Porter, *A History of Suffrage in the United States*, 223. The Mississippi constitution was upheld in *Sproule v. Fredericks*, 69 Miss. 898 (1892). Its literacy test was upheld in *Williams v. Mississippi*, 170 U.S. 213 (1898).

86 Previously the Court had upheld Mississippi's literacy tests: The 9–0 ruling in *Williams* is shocking to read. The justices quote the Mississippi Supreme Court's opinion: "By reason of its previous condition of servitude and dependencies, this race had acquired or accentuated certain peculiarities of habit, of temperament, and of character which clearly distinguished it as a race from the whites; a patient, docile people, but careless, landless, migratory within narrow limits, without forethought, and its criminal members given to furtive offenses, rather than the robust crimes of the whites. Restrained by the federal Constitution from discriminating against the negro race, the convention discriminates against its characteristics, and the offenses to which its criminal members are prone." "But," the U.S. Supreme Court held, "nothing tangible can be deduced from this."

86 *Giles v. Harris*: 189 U.S. 475 (1903).

86 the canon of major constitutional cases: These are *Dred Scott v. Sanford*, 60 U.S. 393 (1857); *Plessy v. Ferguson*, 163 U.S. 537 (1896).

86 "the decisive turning point": Pildes, "Democracy, Anti-Democracy and the Canon," 295, 309. Pildes notes that the case received little attention in constitutional law casebooks, despite its significance.

86 Alabama had one of the most democratically robust systems: Chandler Davidson and Bernard Grofman, eds., *Quiet Revolution in the South: The Impact of the Voting Rights Act, 1965–1990* (Princeton: Princeton University Press, 1994), 44.

86 "We women are in the same boat": R. Volney Riser, *Defying Disenfranchisement: Black Voting Rights Activism in the Jim Crow South* (Baton Rouge: Louisiana State University Press, 2010), 207.

87 a "declaration in the air": *Giles v. Harris*, 488. The plaintiff brought a suit in "equity," meaning he asked the courts to order that an action be taken. Giles could still have sued for damages, the Court ruled, which kept the door open for suits several decades later to challenge the white primaries in southern states.

87 This judicial period is known as the "*Lochner* era": *Lochner v. New York*, 198 U.S. 45 (1905). Some modern conservatives believe the case is unfairly derided. See David E. Bernstein, *Rehabilitating Lochner: Defending Individual Rights from Progressive Reform* (Chicago: University of Chicago Press, 2011). Not all: Chief Justice John Roberts, in his dissent from the decision establishing marriage equality, *Obergefell v. Hodges*, harshly refers to *Lochner* sixteen times. Like *Lochner*, he asserted, the majority in *Obergefell* turn "personal preferences into constitutional mandates." *Obergefell v. Hodges*, 576 U.S. 644 (2015) (Roberts, C.J., dissenting).

87 "If my fellow citizens": Oliver Wendell Holmes to Harold J. Laski, March 4, 1920, in *Holmes-Laski Letters*, vol. 1, ed. Mark de Wolfe Howe, abridged by Alger Hiss (New York: Atheneum, 1963), 194.

88 "By the decision of the Supreme Court": From Charles Waddell Chesnutt, May 2, 1903, in *The Booker T. Washington Papers*, vol. 7, ed. Louis R. Harlan and Raymond W. Smock (Champaign: University of Illinois Press, 1977), 136.

88 Even in Alabama: In fact an opponent of the constitution was elected governor in the same election.

88 "In Mississippi after 1890": Keyssar, *The Right to Vote*, 114.

88 In 1965, on the eve of the Voting Rights Act: Richard H. Pildes, "The Politics of Race," *Harvard Law Review* 108 (1995): 1360.

88 Tom Watson of Georgia: The classic biography is C. Van Woodward, *Tom Watson: Agrarian Rebel*, paperback reissue ed. (1938; New York: Oxford University Press, 1978).

88 "Now the People's Party says to these two men": Ibid., 220.

89 "the unreconstructed rebel": Jeff Shesol, *Supreme Power: Franklin Roosevelt vs. the Supreme Court* (New York: Norton, 2010), 312.

89 never left his hotel suite: Robert A. Caro, *The Years of Lyndon Johnson: Master of the Senate* (New York: Knopf, 2002), 83.

89 racist southerners still controlled: Caro, *Master of the Senate*, xiv.

90 a troubled man named Charles Guiteau: The story of Charles Guiteau and his deluded preparation for the assassination of President Garfield is told in Candice Millard, *Destiny of the Republic: A Tale of Madness, Medicine and the Murder of a President* (New York: Random House, 2011), 137–39.

90 an earnest former general: Garfield's 1881 inaugural address also eloquently

denounced disenfranchisement of African Americans: "Under our institutions there [is] no middle ground for the negro race between slavery and equal citizenship. There can be no permanent disenfranchised peasantry in the United States. Freedom can never yield its fullness of blessings so long as the law or its administration places the smallest obstacle in the pathway of any virtuous citizen." *Inaugural Addresses of the Presidents of the United States* (Washington, DC: U.S. Government Printing Office, 1989), Bartleby.com, 2001, www.bartleby.com/124/.

90 he backed civil service reform: The Pendleton Civil Service Reform Act, Chapter 27, 22 Statute 403. The story of its passage is told in Ari Hoogenboom, *Outlawing the Spoils* (Urbana: University of Illinois Press, 1961). Hoogenboom argues that the reform was a classic case of "the outs versus the ins." Matthew Josephson takes a more jaundiced view, claiming the act was pushed by businessmen in reaction to the rough-edged party operatives. See Matthew Josephson, *The Politicos, 1865–1896* (New York: Harcourt, Brace, 1938).

91 America's "clientelist" period: See Francis Fukuyama, *Political Order and Political Decay: From the Industrial Revolution to the Globalization of Democracy* (New York: Farrar, Straus & Giroux, 2014), 135–49.

91 Federal patronage began to shrink: Fukuyama points out that patronage did not disappear overnight at the federal level: "In 1882, only 11 percent of the civil service was classified [subject to merit, not patronage, selection]; the number grew to 46 percent by 1900. (This figure was to reach 80 percent under Franklin D. Roosevelt and 85 percent in the immediate post–World War II period, declining thereafter.)" Fukuyama, *Political Order and Political Decay*, 153.

91 "American colossus": See generally H. W. Brands, *American Colossus: The Triumph of Capitalism, 1865–1900* (New York: Doubleday, 2010).

91 crude oil production: "U.S. Field Production of Crude Oil," U.S. Energy Information Administration, http://www.eia.gov/dnav/pet/hist/LeafHandler.ashx?n=PET&s=MCRFPUS1&f=A.

91 Railroad revenues more than tripled: Richard Franklin Bensel, *The Political Economy of American Industrialization, 1877–1900* (Cambridge, UK: Cambridge University Press, 2000), 296.

91 By World War I the wealthiest 1 percent: Paul Krugman, "Why We're in a New Gilded Age," *New York Review of Books*, May 8, 2014.

91 "What do I care about the law?": Brands, *American Colossus*, 8.

92 "The Royal Feast": *New York World*, October 30, 1884, reprinted, among other places, on the website HarpWeek, http://elections.harpweek.com/1884/cartoon-1884-large.asp?UniqueID=30&Year=.

92 "rum, Romanism and rebellion": Brands, *American Colossus*, 405.

92 "If Blaine had eaten": Robert E. Mutch, *Buying the Vote: A History of Campaign Finance Reform* (New York: Oxford University Press, 2014), 14.

92 "an alarming merger": Ibid., 16.

92 "the corrupt use of large sums of money": E. L. Godkin, "The First American Corrupt Practices Act," *Nation*, April 17, 1890, 308, quoted in ibid., 17.

92 "You shall not press down": Michael Kazin, *A Godly Hero: The Life of William Jennings Bryan* (New York: Knopf, 2006), 61.

93 250 speeches to 5 million people: Ibid., 66.

93 Mark Hanna organized: There have been few recent studies of this foundational figure in American politics. The best book is the biography by Herbert Croly, the founder of the *New Republic* magazine and a leading progressive thinker: *Marcus*

Alonzo Hanna: His Life and Work (New York: Macmillan, 1912), available online at Internet Archive, https://archive.org/details/marcusalonzohan03crolgoog. The other leading work is Thomas Beer, *Hanna* (New York: Doubleday, 1929). A look at Hanna in the context of recent politics is William T. Horner, *Ohio's Kingmaker: Mark Hanna, Man and Myth* (Columbus: Ohio State University Press, 2010). It bears a blurb from Karl Rove, who told reporters Hanna was a role model.

93 His possibly apocryphal quip: This quote is ubiquitous. Rather remarkably it is very hard to find an original source. Sadly, Hanna may never have said it. (Surely he thought it.)

93 "Mr. Hanna always did his best": Croly, *Marcus Alonzo Hanna*, 220.

93 The campaign printed 120 million pieces: Kazin, *A Godly Hero*, 66–67.

93 "He has advertised McKinley": Brands, *American Colossus*, 542.

93 Now firmly the party of business: A point made by Klarman, *From Jim Crow to Civil Rights*, 31.

94 "the System of 1896": Walter Dean Burnham, "The Changing Shape of the American Political Universe," *American Political Science Review* 59 (March 1965): 7–28.

94 It had peaked in 1896: See McDonald, "National General Election VEP Turnout Rates, 1789–Present."

7: The Age of Reform

97 "invisible empire": Doris Kearns Goodwin, *The Bully Pulpit: Theodore Roosevelt, William Howard Taft, and the Golden Age of Journalism* (New York: Simon & Schuster, 2013), 246.

98 "fierce discontent": The line comes from TR's famous "man with the muckrake" speech. See Theodore Roosevelt, "The Man with the Muck Rake," in Waldman, *My Fellow Americans*, 65–67. The best survey histories of the Progressive Era are Richard Hofstadter, *The Age of Reform: From Bryan to F.D.R* (New York: Knopf, 1955); Robert H. Wiebe, *The Search for Order: 1877–1920* (New York: Hill & Wang, 1967); Michael McGerr, *A Fierce Discontent: The Rise and Fall of the Progressive Movement in America* (New York: Simon & Schuster, 2003).

98 "The President is at liberty": Woodrow Wilson, *Constitutional Government* (New York: Columbia University Press, 1908), 70.

98 Glenn Beck and other modern television hosts: For an explanation of Glenn Beck's obsession with Wilson and the Progressives, see David Greenberg, "Hating Woodrow Wilson," *Slate*, October 22, 2010. Hating Wilson, one journalist reported, had become "a secret handshake" among Beck supporters. Mark Liebovich, "Being Glenn Beck," *New York Times Magazine*, September 29, 2010.

98 "We can have democracy": This quote was reported after Brandeis's death. Evidently a former congressman, Edward Keating, a friend and confidant of the justice, related it pseudonymously as "Raymond Longergan" in the magazine *Labor*. The article was reprinted in Irving Dillard, ed., *Mr. Justice Brandeis, Great American* (St. Louis: Modern View Press, 1941), 42, http://babel.hathitrust.org/cgi/pt?id=mdp.39015009170443;view=1up;seq=56. The quote appears nowhere else in Brandeis's papers. As with so many of the most quotable quotes, it is not entirely clear whether it is apocryphal. The editor of his papers, sifting through Keating's writings, concludes, "While there is no positive proof Brandeis ever said these exact words, he expressed a similar sentiment numerous times. If it is not a

Brandeis quote, it is at least a Brandeisian one." Peter Scott Campbell, "Democracy v. Concentrated Wealth: In Search of a Louis D. Brandeis Quote," Green Bag, 16: 2d 251, http://www.greenbag.org/v16n3/v16n3_articles_campbell.pdf.

99 On February 1, 1905: For a description of the party and the painful morning after for Mr. Hyde and the Equitable, see Patricia Beard, *After the Ball: Gilded Age Secrets, Boardroom Betrayals, and the Party That Ignited the Great Wall Street Scandal of 1905* (New York: Harper Collins, 2003), 171–78.

100 "Why Mr. President": Ron Chernow, *Titan: The Life of John D. Rockefeller, Sr.* (New York: Random House, 1999), 591.

100 "We bought the son of a bitch": Ibid.

100 the "bearded iceberg": Shesol, *Supreme Power*, 27.

100 The star witness was George Perkins: Mutch, *Buying the Vote*, 37–38.

101 "Life Insurance Campaign Gifts": *New York Times*, September 16, 1905. These and the archival *New York Times* stories in the notes that follow are retrieved from the invaluable site Times Machine, which makes a full century of news coverage available.

101 other companies contributed too: "Campaign Offerings from Other Companies; New York Life Not the Only Insurance Contributor; One Helped Both Parties," *New York Times*, September 17, 1905.

101 "a key moment in the development of progressivism": Robert Harrison, *Congress, Progressive Reform, and the New American State* (New York: Cambridge University Press, 2004), 45; Mutch, *Buying the Vote*, 45–61.

101 Up in Boston: See Melvin I. Urofsky, *Brandeis: A Life* (New York: Pantheon Books, 2009), 155–80.

101 Prosecutors arrested Perkins: Prosecutors charged him with grand larceny from the insurance company for having paid the campaign contribution. "Perkins Is Arrested and Denies Wrongdoing," *New York Times*, March 29, 1906.

102 "Sooner or later": Edmund Morris, *Theodore Rex* (New York: Random House, 2001), 360. In an article after Roosevelt left office, a journalist reported that Roosevelt said this in Des Moines, Iowa, in 1903. Lindsay Denison, "Seven Years of Roosevelt," *The Circle*, March 1909, 134.

102 William Chandler: Mutch, *Buying the Vote*, 45–47.

102 Progressive state governments began to enact reform: Ibid., 46; Anthony Corrado, *The New Campaign Finance Sourcebook* (Washington, DC: Brookings Institution, 2005), 10.

102 "the advocate of both mob violence": Stephen Kantrowitz, *Ben Tillman and the Reconstruction of White Southern Supremacy* (Chapel Hill: University of North Carolina Press, 2000), 157.

102 Tillman Act: The story of the passage of the Tillman Act is told by Mutch, *Buying the Vote*, 45–61. See also Robert E. Mutch, *Campaigns, Congress, and Courts: The Making of Federal Campaign Finance Law* (New York: Praeger, 1988), 1–7.

103 "Go back and read": Adam Liptak, "A Justice Responds to Criticism from Obama," *New York Times*, February 4, 2010, http://www.nytimes.com/2010/02/04/us/politics/04scotus.html?_r=0.

103 "a very radical measure": "Theodore Roosevelt, Seventh Annual Message, December 7, 1907," Miller Center Presidential Speech Archive, http://millercenter.org/president/speeches/speech-3779.

104 "To destroy this invisible government": Platform of the Progressive Party, August 7, 1912, *American Experience*, PBS, http://www.pbs.org/wgbh/americanexperience/features/primary-resources/tr-progressive/.

104 "We stand at Armageddon": H. W. Brands, *T.R.: The Last Romantic* (New York: Basic Books, 1998), 719.

104 The 1912 campaign was one of history's most remarkable: See James Chace, *1912: Wilson, Roosevelt, Taft and Debs—The Election That Changed the Country* (New York: Simon & Schuster, 2004).

104 "the central doctrine": Sidney Milkis, *Theodore Roosevelt, the Progressive Party, and the Transformation of American Democracy* (Lawrence: University Press of Kansas, 2009), 224.

104 "I like the Fourth of July": Ibid., 229.

105 President William Howard Taft clung to the most traditional concepts: Ibid., 89.

105 In 1898 South Dakota became the first state: John J. Dinan, *The American State Constitutional Tradition* (Lawrence: University Press of Kansas, 2006), 85.

105 "TR's crusade made universal use": Milkis, *Theodore Roosevelt, the Progressive Party, and the Transformation of American Democracy*, 2–3.

106 "unnecessary to dilate upon": Federalist 62, in Hamilton et al., *The Federalist Papers*, 304.

106 In the 1890s alone: George Henry Haynes, *The Election of Senators* (New York: Henry Holt, 1906), 59–63; Wendy J. Schiller and Charles Stewart III, *Electing the Senate: Indirect Democracy before the Seventeenth Amendment* (Princeton: Princeton University Press, 2014), 8.

106 In Colorado in 1903: George H. Haynes, "Election of Senators by State Legislatures," in *The Senate of the Untied States*, vol. 1 (Boston: Houghton Mifflin, 1938), 90–91.

106 "charges of corruption": Haynes, *The Election of Senators*, 51.

106 U.S. senators who doubled as industry representatives: See a classic account by William Allen White, *Masks in a Pageant* (New York: Macmillan, 1928), 79: "A United States senator in 1889, with few exceptions, represented something more than a state, more even than a region. He represented principalities and powers in business. One senator, for instance, represented the Union Pacific Railway System, another the New York Central, still another the insurance interests of New York and New Jersey."

106 "In one of the North Pacific States": Haynes, *The Election of Senators*, 177.

106 a "state for sale": Lincoln Steffens, "Rhode Island: A State for Sale," *McClure's Magazine*, February 1905, http://www.unz.org/Pub/McClures-1905feb-00337.

107 "That his reputation": David Herbert Donald, *Lincoln* (New York: Simon & Schuster, 1995), 266.

107 "An honest politician": Doris Kearns Goodwin, *Team of Rivals: The Political Genius of Abraham Lincoln* (New York: Simon & Schuster, 2005), 217.

107 "has done everything with the Pennsylvania legislature": Henry Demarest Lloyd, "The Story of a Great Monopoly," *Atlantic Monthly*, March 1881.

107 "a dozen raw oysters": Robert Bowden, *Boies Penrose: Symbol of an Era* (New York: Greenberg, 1937), 191.

107 To mark that festive moment: Schiller and Stewart, *Electing the Senate*, 61; Walter Davenport, *Power and Glory: The Life of Boies Penrose* (New York: G. P. Putnam's Sons, 1931), 76–78.

107 "squeeze bills": Paul B. Beers, *Pennsylvania Politics Today and Yesterday: The Tolerable Accommodation* (University Park: Pennsylvania State University Press, 1980), 53.

107 "I believe in the division of labor": James E. Watson, *What I Saw: Memoirs of a United States Senator from Indiana* (Indianapolis: Bobbs-Merrill, 1936), 294.

107 "There isn't going to be any election": Davenport, *Power and Glory*, 158. Reviewing

the book, *Time* raved in *Time*-ese that it was the story of a "bold, bad man." "Boiese Would Be Boise," *Time*, November 23, 1931.

108 "Politics does not determine prosperity": David Graham Phillips, "The Treason of the Senate," *Cosmopolitan* 40, no. 5 (1906): 488.

108 "The men with the muck rakes": See Waldman, *My Fellow Americans*, 63–67.

108 The Omaha convention: The party convention resolutions read, in part, "RESOLVED, That we favor a constitutional provision limiting the office of President and Vice-President to one term, and providing for the election of Senators of the United States by a direct vote of the people." George Brown Tindall, ed., *A Populist Reader: Selections from the Works of American Populist Leaders* (New York: Harper & Row, 1966), 95. The platform is also available at "The Omaha Platform: Launching the Populist Party," History Matters, George Mason University, http://historymatters.gmu.edu/d/5361/.

108 Already creative ferment: For a discussion of the role played by state efforts to give voters de facto voice in choosing senators, see Kris W. Kobach, "Rethinking Article V: Term Limits and the Seventeenth and Nineteenth Amendments," *Yale Law Journal* 103, no. 7 (1994): 1971–2007. Two decades later Kobach would play a leading role in pushing for laws to reduce voting rights as the controversial secretary of state of Kansas.

109 legislative candidates would run newspaper ads: Wendy J. Schiller, "Climbing and Clawing Their Way to the U.S. Senate: Political Ambition and Career Building 1880–1913," paper presented at the annual meeting of the Western Political Science Association, March 11, 2004, 5, http://www.politics.as.nyu.edu/docs/IO/4744/ws1201.pdf.

109 "on the first ballot": Robert Rienow and Leona Train Rienow, *Of Snuff, Sin and the Senate* (Chicago: Follett, 1965), 290.

109 The "Oregon Plan" spread: See Schiller and Stewart, *Electing the Senate*, 111–16. Historians debate how widespread the primary system was and how much influence it had over the choices made by legislators. Schiller and Stewart estimate that about one third of elections relied on direct primaries.

109 By 1911 about half of new senators: Haynes, "Election of Senators by State Legislatures," 104.

109 Illinois voters backed direct election: Rienow and Rienow, *Of Snuff, Sin and the Senate*, 291.

109 twenty-five states joined the call: Russell L. Caplan, *Constitutional Brinksmanship: Amending the Constitution by National Convention* (New York: Oxford University Press, 1988), 61–65; Thomas H. Neale, *The Article V Convention for Proposing Constitutional Amendments: Historical Perspectives for Congress*, CRS Report No. 42592 (Washington, D.C.: Congressional Research Service, 2012), 8–9, https://www.fas.org/sgp/crs/misc/R42592.pdf.

109 "the great corporations which control": Walter Clark wrote in the *Yale Law Journal* for December 1906; see Caplan, *Constitutional Brinksmanship*, 64.

110 "The legislature is the arena": Senator William Borah, speaking on Election of Senators by Direct Vote, on January 19, 1911, 61st Congress, 2nd session, *Congressional Record*, 1106.

110 "I have sinned": Senator Robert LaFollette, speaking on S. Rept. 35, on May 22, 1911, 62nd Congress, 1st session, *Congressional Record*, 1435.

110 Boies Penrose himself proposed: Anthony Madonna, Mark E. Owens, and Joel Sievert, "Building a Record: Amending Activity, Position Taking, and the

Seventeenth Amendment," paper presented at the Midwest Political Science Association, September 20, 2013.

110 Southern Democrats once had supported: John Buenker, "The Urban Political Machine and the Seventeenth Amendment," *Journal of American History* 56, no. 2 (1969): 305–22.

110 As ratified, the Seventeenth Amendment: U.S. Constitution, Amendment XVII, Section 1.

111 Then, a century later: Most scholarship about the Seventeenth Amendment has focused on its impact on federalism. See Vikram David Amar, "Indirect Effects of Direct Election: A Structural Examination of the Seventeenth Amendment," *Vanderbilt Law Review* 49 (1996): 1347.

111 Popular legislating swept through the West: See Nathaniel Persily, "The Peculiar Geography of Direct Democracy: Why the Initiative, Referendum and Recall Developed in the American West," *Michigan Law & Policy Review* 2 (1997): 11.

111 By 1920 in roughly half the states: Dinan, *The American State Constitutional Tradition*, 85–86. A current list of state constitutional provisions providing for referendum or initiative is on 94n151.

112 Proposition 13 launched the national "tax revolt": See Robert Kuttner, *Revolt of the Haves: Tax Rebellions and Hard Times* (New York: Simon & Schuster, 1980).

112 "poorly designed policies": Richard J. Ellis, *Democratic Delusions: The Initiative Process in America* (Lawrence: University Press of Kansas, 2002), 2.

112 Voters themselves voted to establish primary elections: A complete list of provisions enacted by ballot measure is available at the National Conference of State Legislatures' Ballot Measures Database, www.ncsl.org. See also "Brief of Brennan Center for Justice at NYU School of Law in Support of Appellees," *Arizona State Legislature v. Arizona Redistricting Commission et al.*, 20–21.

112 "From the ruins of the political machines": Hofstadter, *The American Political Tradition*, 419.

112 Compared to later reform movements: Hofstadter saw the Progressives as falling victim to moral absolutism. In the managerial 1950s, disillusioned by the failures of Marxism and unnerved by McCarthyism, Hofstadter wrote that William Jennings Bryan and his Progressive successors appeared "very strongly to foreshadow the cranky pseudo-conservatism of our time." Hofstadter, *The Age of Reform*, 19.

113 as a countervailing power to the heft of business: For the pioneering and still classic twentieth-century articulation of this view, see John Kenneth Galbraith, *American Capitalism: The Concept of Countervailing Power* (New York: Houghton Mifflin, 1952).

113 Reformers won changes in many state laws: John Judis, *The Paradox of American Democracy: Elites, Special Interests and the Betrayal of Public Trust* (New York: Pantheon Books, 2000), 5–9; Richard Pildes, "Romanticizing Democracy: Political Fragmentation, and the Decline of American Government," *Yale Law Review* 124 (2014): 804.

113 But the very mechanism by which reformers pursued change: Ruy A. Teixeira, *The Disappearing American Voter* (Washington, DC: Brookings Institution, 2011), 20.

113 Often moralistic professionals: See Wiebe, *The Search for Order*, 165.

113 "I ain't up on sillygisms": William Riordon, *Plunkitt of Tammany Hall: A Series*

of Very Plain Talks on Very Practical Politics (New York: Signet Reprint Editions, 1995), 8. Justice Antonin Scalia quoted the Tammany sachem in his dissent from a decision that held it violated a low-level government employee's First Amendment right when she was dismissed due to party affiliation. *Rutan v. Republican Party of Illinois*, 497 U.S. 62 (1990) (Scalia, J., dissenting).

8: Silent Sentinels

115 where she had plunged into the frenzied suffragist movement: For an accounting of Alice Paul's education as an activist in London, see an excellent biography, J. D. Zahniser and Amelia R. Fry, *Alice Paul: Claiming Power* (New York: Oxford University Press, 2014), 65–104.

115 Once, dressed as a maid: Robert S. Gallagher, "I Was Arrested, Of Course . . . ," *American Heritage*, February 1974. In this interview Alice Paul debunks the idea that she also hid on the roof as well as the balcony at the Guild Hall—a story that was too good to check.

116 "to avail ourselves of the strong arm": Ellen DuBois, *Woman Suffrage and Women's Rights* (New York: New York University Press, 1998), 90.

116 For the centennial of the Declaration of Independence: Flexner and Fitzpatrick, *Century of Struggle*, 163–64; The Declaration of Rights of the Women of the United States by the National Woman Suffrage Association, July 4, 1876; David M. Dismore, "The Suffragists; Protest on Independence Day, 1876: You Are There," *Ms. Magazine*, July 4, 2012.

116 "My natural rights": Ann D. Gordon, "The Trial of Susan B. Anthony," Federal Judicial Center, Federal Judicial History Office, Washington, DC, 2005, 46, http://www.fjc.gov/history/docs/susanbanthony.pdf.

116 the justices ruled that the Fourteenth Amendment: *Minor v. Happersett*, 88 U.S. 162 (1874).

117 "the living Constitution": See Adam Winkler, "A Revolution Too Soon: Woman Suffragists and the 'Living Constitution,'" *New York University Law Review* 76 (November 2001): 1457.

117 The Court nearly nullified: *United States v. Cruikshank*, 92 U.S. 542 (1875).

117 Judges would cite *Minor* up until the 1960s: See, for example, *Stone v. Smith*, 159 Mass. 413 (Mass. 1893) (upholding a literacy test as a constitutional qualification for the right to vote); *Lackey v. United States*, 107 F.114, 116, 120 (6th Cir. 1901) (holding that Congress's power to enforce the Fifteenth Amendment prohibition against racial discrimination in the exercise of the franchise extends only to state actors and not private citizens), *cert denied*, 21 S.Ct. 925 (1901); *Breedlove v. Suttles*, 302 U.S. 277, 283 (1937) (upholding payment of a poll tax as a prerequisite to voting); *Pirtle v. Brown*, 118 F. 218, 221 (6th Cir. 1941) (upholding the use of a poll tax as an appropriate state condition on the exercise of the franchise); *W.M.C.A., Inc. v. Smith*, 202 F.Supp. 741, 751 (S.D.N.Y. 1962) (upholding a legislative apportionment plan that diluted the power of urban voters).

117 As western states entered the union: For a timeline of states giving women the vote, see Marjorie Spruil Wheeler, *One Woman, One Vote: Rediscovering the Women's Suffrage Movement* (Portland, OR: New Sage Press, 1995), 375–77.

118 "The right of citizens": U.S. Constitution, Amendment XIX.

118 "'Small but vociferous'": "Wilson Evades Vast Crowd: Goes by Side Streets to Hotel While Suffrage Parade Is On," *New York Times*, March 4, 1913.

119 a pageant rich with symbolism: See Sarah J. Moore, "Making a Spectacle of Suffrage: The National Woman Suffrage Pageant, 1913," *Journal of American Culture* 20, no. 1 (1979): 89.

119 "As far as I can see": Michelle Bernard, "Despite the Risk, African American Women Marched for Suffrage, Too," *Washington Post*, March 3, 2013, http://www.washingtonpost.com/blogs/she-the-people/wp/2013/03/03/despite-the-tremendous-risk-african-american-women-marched-for-suffrage-too/.

119 Ida B. Wells ignored the choreography: Zahniser and Fry, *Alice Paul*, 149.

119 They heckled, spat, threw objects: The melee is described in the *Baltimore Sun*, March 4, 1903, quoted in Flexner and Fitzpatrick, *Century of Struggle*, 256. See also "5,000 Women March, Beset by Crowds; Demonstration at Capital Badly Hampered and Congress Is Asked to Investigate," *New York Times*, March 4, 1913.

119 Milholland steered her steed: Mary Walton, *A Woman's Crusade: Alice Paul and the Battle for the Ballot* (New York: St. Martin's Press, 2010), 175.

120 Paul's committee presented Congress with a petition: Flexner and Fitzpatrick, *Century of Struggle*, 257.

120 Using the flashiest new technology: Ibid., 261.

120 Gradually women in seventeen states: See Keyssar, *The Right to Vote*, A. 17–20, for a full accounting of the state legal and referenda victories.

120 "tied to a conviction": A Scott Berg, *Wilson* (New York: G. P. Putnam's Sons, 2013), 487.

121 Wilson spoke at the group's convention: Woodrow Wilson, "Address at the Suffrage Convention, Atlantic City, New Jersey," September 8, 1916, American Presidency Project, http://www.presidency.ucsb.edu/ws/?pid=65395.

121 her resemblance to a Gibson Girl: Linda J. Lumsden, *Inez: The Life and Times of Inez Milholland* (Bloomington: Indiana University Press, 2004), 40.

121 Alice Paul arranged for a memorial service: Zahniser and Fry, *Alice Paul*, 252; "Tribute at Capitol for Mrs. Bossevain; Statuary Hall Crowded at Memorial Service Held for Young Suffrage Leader," *New York Times*, December 26, 2016.

122 "The world must be made safe": Woodrow Wilson, *War Messages*, 65th Cong., 1st Sess., Senate Doc. No. 5, Serial No. 7264, Washington, DC, 1917, 3–8, passim.

122 In previous military conflicts: For the argument that military conflict has been a principal driver of the expansion of suffrage, see Pamela S. Karlan, "Ballots and Bullets: The Exceptional History of the Right to Vote," *University of Cincinnati Law Review* 71 (Summer 2003): 1345–72.

122 On January 9, 1917: Katherine H. Adams and Michael L. Keene, *Alice Paul and the American Suffrage Campaign* (Urbana: University of Illinois Press, 2008).

122 In October 1917 Paul herself: Doris Stevens, *Jailed for Freedom: America's Women Win the Vote*, rev. ed., ed. Carol O'Hare (Troutdale, OR: New Sage Press, 1995), 111.

122 "As members of the disenfranchised class": Lucy Burns, "A Suffrage Trial in Washington," *Liberator*, no. 8 (October 1918): 20, https://www.marxists.org/history/usa/culture/pubs/liberator/1918/08/v1n08-oct-1918-liberator.pdf.

122 "We are being imprisoned": Stevens, *Jailed for Freedom*, 113.

123 "The President has succumbed": Zahniser and Fry, *Alice Paul*, 301.

123 "This is a people's war": Woodrow Wilson, *Address of the President of the United States Delivered in the Senate of the United States, September 30, 1918* (Washington, D.C.: Government Printing Office, 1918); "Wilson Makes Suffrage Appeal, but Senate Waits," *New York Times*, October 1, 1918.

124 "Dear son": The story of the Tennessee vote is told in Carol Lynn Yellin and

Janann Sherman, *The Perfect 36: Tennessee Delivers Women's Suffrage* (Oak Ridge, TN: Iris Press, 1998), 117. See also Jennie Cohen, "The Mother Who Saved Suffrage," History in the Headlines, The History Channel, August 16, 2010, http://www.history.com/news/the-mother-who-saved-suffrage-passing-the-19th-amendment.

9: "One Person, One Vote"

126 "Clear it with Sidney": For the role of labor and its mobilization, see generally Steven Fraser, *Labor Will Rule: Sidney Hillman and the Rise of American Labor* (New York: Free Press, 1991). Did FDR actually say "Clear it with Sidney"? The *New York Times* reported he did: Arthur Krock, "Hillman as a Liability; Hannegan's Denial He Was 'to Clear with Sidney' Is Linked with Byrnes," *New York Times*, September 13, 1944. Others say he did not. It became a significant issue in the 1944 election, with anti-immigrant and anti-Semitic overtones. See Richard Norton Smith, *Thomas E. Dewey and His Times* (New York: Simon & Schuster, 1982), 409–10.

126 Caro vividly describes: Robert A. Caro, *The Years of Lyndon Johnson: The Path to Power* (New York: Knopf, 1982), 721, 739.

127 The election turned on the results of Precinct 13: See Robert A. Caro, *The Years of Lyndon Johnson: Means of Ascent* (New York: Knopf, 1990), 328.

127 "When I die": Lyndon Johnson's aide Jack Valenti made the same request before his death, except he wanted to stay active in Texas. See William Safire, "Cemetery Vote," in *Safire's New Political Dictionary*, revised ed. (New York: Oxford University Press, 2008), 107.

127 "With a little bit of luck": Benjamin C. Bradlee, *Conversations with Kennedy* (New York: Norton, 1975), 25.

127 It's a potent historical myth: David Greenberg, "Was Nixon Robbed? The Legend of the Stolen 1960 Presidential Election," *Slate*, October 14, 2000.

127 "They said terrible things about you": John F. Kennedy, "Remarks in Chicago to Democratic Precinct Workers," October 19, 1962, American Presidency Project, http://www.presidency.ucsb.edu/ws/?pid=8983; Hugh Sidey, *President Kennedy* (New York: Athenaeum, 1964), 337.

128 In Georgia in 1942: Walter Dean Burnham, "Democracy in Peril: America's Turnout Problem and the Path to Plutocracy," Roosevelt Institute, Working Paper No. 5, December 2010, 3, http://www.nextnewdeal.net/wp-content/uploads/2010/12/burnham-white-paper-pdf.pdf.

128 "The past is never dead": William Faulkner, *Requiem for a Nun* (New York: Library of America, 1994), 73.

128 To steer legislation through Congress: See Ira Katznelson, *When Affirmative Action Was White: An Untold History of Racial Inequality in Twentieth-Century America* (New York: Norton, 2005).

129 seats be apportioned by population: U.S. Constitution, Article I, Section 2, Paragraph 3. The original Constitution infamously counted only three-fifths of slaves, but since 1868 congressional seats have been apportioned among states by population: Fourteenth Amendment, Section 2.

129 they moved not to the frontier to farm: See generally Robert G. Dixon Jr., *Democratic Representation: Reapportionment in Law and Politics* (New York: Oxford University Press, 1968), 58–90.

129 The 1920 census: The failure to reapportion in the 1920s is told in Charles W. Eagles, *Democracy Delayed: Congressional Reapportionment and Urban-Rural Conflict in the 1920s* (Athens: University of Georgia Press, 2010), 32–84.

130 "in nineteen states": J. Douglas Smith, *On Democracy's Doorstep: The Inside Story of How the Supreme Court Brought "One Person, One Vote" to the United States* (New York: Hill and Wang, 2014), 18.

130 beginning in the 1890s: Dixon, *Democratic Representation*, 82–84.

130 In the most extreme example: Smith, *On Democracy's Doorstep*, 16.

130 "Opting for what became known": Ibid.

131 in 1956, faced with Supreme Court rulings: See J. Douglas Smith, *Managing White Supremacy: Race, Politics, and Citizenship in Jim Crow Virginia* (Chapel Hill: University of North Carolina Press, 2002), 295.

132 The new approach was articulated: *United States v. Carolene Products Co.*, 304 U.S. 144 (1938), fn. 4.

133 Justice Louis D. Brandeis even paid him secretly: See Bruce Allen Murphy, *The Brandeis/Frankfurter Connection: The Secret Political Activities of Two Supreme Court Justices* (New York: Oxford University Press, 1982).

133 In 1946 he wrote for a six-vote majority: *Colegrove v. Green*, 328 U.S. 549 (1946).

133 The state's smallest congressional district: The smallest had a population of 112,116, and the largest a population of 914,000. *Colegrove*, 567 (Black, J., dissenting).

134 "We were shocked": Bernard Taper, *Gomillion versus Lightfoot: The Tuskegee Gerrymander Case* (New York: McGraw Hill, 1962), 34. Taper's long-forgotten book, based on a *New Yorker* article, is a psychologically astute chronicle of an important case.

134 Frankfurter wrote the opinion: *Gomillion v. Lightfoot*, 364 U.S. 339 (1960).

134 what law professors call the "reapportionment revolution": *Baker v. Carr*, 369 U.S. 186 (1962). The phrase comes from Issacharoff et al., *The Law of Democracy*. For the history of the case, see Gene S. Graham, *One Man, One Vote: Baker v. Carr and the American Levellers* (Boston: Little, Brown, 1972). For a description of the political background and community role, see Stephen Ansolebehere and Samuel Issacharoff, "The Story of *Baker v. Carr*," in *Constitutional Law Stories*, 2nd ed., ed. Michael Dorf (New York: Foundation Press, 2009), 271–94.

134 "Well, are you going to win?": Graham, *One Man, One Vote*, 216–17.

134 Frankfurter harangued his colleagues: Seth Stern and Stephen Wermiel, *Justice Brennan: Liberal Champion* (New York: Houghton Mifflin, 2010), 185, report a one-hour diatribe. Others write that Frankfurter orated for four and a half hours. See Noah Feldman, *Scorpions: The Battles and Triumphs of FDR's Great Supreme Court Justices* (New York: Twelve, 2010), 418. Perhaps it felt like four hours.

135 When new clerks arrived: Stern and Wermiel, *Justice Brennan*, 196.

135 Within one year of the decision: "Districting Case Stirs Revolution; Year Later, 19 Legislatures Are Reapportioned," *New York Times*, April 1, 1963.

135 "the most important case": Earl Warren, *The Memoirs of Earl Warren* (New York: Doubleday, 1977), 306.

135 Prime Minister William Gladstone's proposal: See "The Liberal Programme," *New York Times*, September 23, 1892. The House of Lords repeatedly defeated the bill. Plural voting did not end until 1950.

136 The phrase had rarely been used: A search of the *New York Times* archives, for example, shows it was used almost exclusively in the international context, first

to describe English electoral reform, and then as Africans demanded political equality in the 1950s.

136 Remarkably it made its way to the Supreme Court: The etymology of "one person, one vote" was traced by Smith, *On Democracy's Doorstep*, 98–99.

136 "The Africans require": Nelson Mandela interview with Brian Wildlake, "The New Republic," ITN Television, May 1961, quoted in Alexis C. Madrigal, "Nelson Mandela's First TV Interview, May 1961," *TheAtlantic.com*, December 6, 2013, http://www.theatlantic.com/international/archive/2013/12/nelson-mandelas-first-tv-interview-may-1961/282120/; Smith, *On Democracy's Doorstep*, 99–100.

136 According to newspaper reports: "1,000 Africans Greet McLeod," *New York Times*, March 28, 1961: "About 1,000 Africans greeted Ian McLeod, English Colonial Secretary, with a boisterous demonstration when he arrived [in northern Rhodesia]. . . . The crowd surged toward the Colonial Secretary shouting 'Freedom' and 'One Man, One Vote.'" The phrase was in growing use as African colonies sought independence. See, for example, "Ghana Gets Plan to Be a Republic," *New York Times*, March 8, 1960 ("In a broadcast speech [Prime Minister Kwame Nkrumah] said the keynote of the new constitution was 'one man, one vote and the unity of Africa, namely the political union of African countries'"); "Kaunda Bars Violence," *New York Times*, March 13, 1959 ("He urges his followers to reject violence as a means to his goal of 'one-man-one-vote democracy'").

136 As the day's orations rumbled: See Taylor Branch, *Parting the Waters: America in the King Years 1954–63* (New York: Simon & Schuster, 1988), 879–80. The text of Lewis's draft speech is available in Gottheimer, *Ripples of Hope*, 238–40.

137 "One man, one vote is the African cry": The text as delivered is available at the University of Maryland Voices of Democracy U.S. Oratory Project, http://voicesofdemocracy.umd.edu/lewis-speech-at-the-march-on-washington-speech-text/.

137 "I don't know why people are so mad at me": Evan Thomas, *Robert Kennedy: His Life* (New York: Simon & Schuster, 2000), 110–11.

137 "In this case that is what the ideal is": Transcript of arguments, *Gray v. Sanders*, January 17, 1963, Oyez Project at IIT Chicago-Kent College of Law, accessed March 28, 2015.

137 "The conception of political equality": *Gray v. Sanders*, 372 U.S. 368 (1963).

137 it struck down Georgia's congressional map: *Wesberry v. Sanders*, 376 U.S. 1 (1964).

137 the justices specified for the first time: *Reynolds v. Sims*, 377 U.S. 533 (1964).

137 That case arose as a sideshow: The fascinating (if sometimes confusing) machinations among the lawyers, civic groups, and business interests in Alabama that produced *Reynolds v. Sims* are detailed in Smith, *On Democracy's Doorstep*, 116–38, especially 122–23.

138 His attention focused on the assassination: Melissa Cully Anderson and Bruce E. Cain, "Venturing onto the Path of Equal Representation: The Warren Court and Redistricting," in *Earl Warren and the Warren Court: The Legacy in American and Foreign Law*, ed. Harry N. Schieber (New York: Lexington Books, 2006), 45.

138 "Legislators represent people": *Reynolds v. Sims*, 562, 565.

139 By 1968 ninety-three of ninety-nine: Smith, *On Democracy's Doorstep*, 281.

139 Everett Dirksen: See ibid., 263–80.

139 "The six million citizens": Quoted in Morris K. Udall, "Reapportionment II—

Where Do We Go from Here?," Congressman's Report, December 11, 1964, http://www.library.arizona.edu/exhibits/udall/congrept/88th/641211.html.

139 Under its terms: See Peter Wolf, "An Antiapportionment Amendment: Can It Be Legally Ratified," *American Bar Association Journal*, April 1966, 326–31.

139 Each time it fell short: "State Apportionment Plan Loses in Senate," *CQ Almanac 1965*, 21st ed. (Washington, DC: Congressional Quarterly, 1966), 520–32; "Senate Lets Reapportionment Ruling Stand," *CQ Almanac 1966*, 22nd ed. (Washington, DC: Congressional Quarterly, 1967), 505–11.

140 State legislatures quietly began: John R. Vile, *Encyclopedia of Constitutional Amendments, Proposed Amendments, and Amending Issues, 1789–2002* (Santa Barbara, CA: ABC-CLIO, 2002), 429; Fred P. Graham, "Efforts to Amend the Constitution on Districts Gain; One-Man, One-Vote Ruling Spurs First Bid for Charter Convention Since 1787," *New York Times*, March 18, 1967.

10: Walls of Jericho

142 in 1915 the U.S. Supreme Court: *Guinn v. U.S.*, 238 U.S. 347 (1915).

142 Methods turned more devious: For a good review of the issue of white primaries and the successful legal drive to prohibit them, see Darlene Clark Hine, *Black Victory: The Rise and Fall of the White Primary*, 2nd ed. (Columbia: University of Missouri Press, 2003); Michael J. Klarman, "The White Primary Rulings: A Case Study in the Consequences of Supreme Court Decisionmaking," *Florida State University Law Review* 29 (2001): 55.

142 By 1940 only 151,000 African Americans: David J. Garrow, *Protest at Selma: Martin Luther King, Jr., and the Voting Rights Act of 1965* (New Haven: Yale University Press, 1978), 6.

142 Starting in 1927: *Nixon v. Herndon*, 273 U.S. 536 (1927) (invalidated exclusion of African Americans by statute); *Nixon v. Condon*, 386 U.S. 73 (1932) (the same result by party Executive Committee, authorized by statute); *Grovey v. Townsend*, 321 U.S. 649 (1935) (allowing the white primary if done by party convention) (this case would be overruled by *Smith v. Allwright*).

143 "In the glove compartment": Juan Williams, *Thurgood Marshall: American Revolutionary* (New York: Times Books, 1998), 110.

143 The elegant jazz bandleader Duke Ellington: Ibid.

143 "The United States is a constitutional democracy": *Smith v. Allwright*, 321 U.S. 649 (1944).

143 the "real reason": Arthur Krock, "In the Nation: Self-Reexamination Continues in the Supreme Court," *New York Times*, April 4, 1944.

143 "Even at the end of his life": Williams, *Thurgood Marshall*, 112.

143 In the eight years after the decision: See Garrow, *Protest at Selma*, 7. The numbers were still small: in 1940, 151,000 Black southerners were registered; in 1947, 595,000; by 1952, 1,008,614.

143 the Second Reconstruction: See Hine, *Black Victory*, 248.

144 Progress was visible: These states still prevented their Black citizens from voting in large numbers. It would require one more Supreme Court case to fully declare the white primary unconstitutional. See *Terry v. Adams*, 345 U.S. 461 (1953) (a local club, the Jaybird Democrats, could not exclude Black voters, even if it was not a regulated statewide primary).

144 In one hundred counties in seven states: U.S. Commission on Civil Rights, *Report on Voting* (1961), http://www.crmvet.org/docs/ccr_61_voting.pdf, 44, 138.

144 increasingly arcane questions: The literacy test is reprinted in Bernard Lafayette Jr. and Kathryn Lee Johnson, *In Peace and Freedom: My Journey in Selma* (Lexington: University Press of Kentucky, 2013). A wonderful resource, the website of the Civil Rights Movement Veterans, contains samples of the literacy tests. Many were first gathered by activists for use in lawsuits and law enforcement proceedings.

145 "Write every other word": Rebecca Onion, "Take the Impossible 'Literacy Test' Louisiana Gave Black Voter in the 1960s," *Slate*, June 28, 2013, http://www.slate.com/blogs/the_vault/2013/06/28/voting_rights_and_the_supreme_court_the_impossible_literacy_test_louisiana.html.

145 Other registrars asked Black applicants: See Abigail Thernstrom, *Whose Votes Count? Affirmative Action and Minority Voting Rights* (Cambridge, MA: Harvard University Press, 1989), 15.

145 "Ma'am, would you do one thing": Ibid., 54.

145 the 1957 Civil Rights Act: Public Law 85–315. It also provided for jury trials for violation of civil rights laws. This was the most controversial provision, since southern jurors, invariably white, rarely would convict for violations of civil rights.

145 Another civil rights law: Civil Rights Act of 1960, Public Law 86–449.

145 "We are confronted": John F. Kennedy, "Radio and Television Report to the American People on Civil Rights," June 11, 1963, The American Presidency Project, http://www.presidency.ucsb.edu/ws/?pid=9271.

146 A relentless drive by churches: Two books published on the anniversary of the act look at its enactment. Clay Risen, *The Bill of the Century: The Epic Battle for the Civil Rights Act* (New York: Bloomsbury, 2014) focuses on the civil rights movement and its allies as they lobbied for the law. Todd S. Purdum, *An Idea Whose Time Has Come: Two Presidents, Two Parties, and the Battle for the Civil Rights Act of 1964* (New York: Henry Holt, 2014) focuses more on political leaders, including Johnson's legendary lobbying of Congress. Robert A. Caro describes Johnson's elaborate legislative strategies, including enactment of a seemingly unrelated tax bill and encouragement of a "discharge commission" to bypass the House Rules Committee, controlled by a segregationist chairman. See Robert A. Caro, *The Years of Lyndon Johnson: The Passage of Power* (New York: Knopf, 2014).

146 "Kennedy had charmed King": Taylor Branch, *At Canaan's Edge: America in the King Years, 1965–68* (New York: Simon & Schuster, 2006), 14.

146 "Martin, you're right about that": David J. Garrow, *Bearing the Cross: Martin Luther King, Jr., and the Southern Christian Leadership Conference* (New York: William Morrow, 1985), 368.

146 "We've got to get them passed": Johnson conversation with Martin Luther King Jr., January 15, 1965, in Michael Beschloss, *Reaching for Glory: Lyndon Johnson's Secret White House Tapes, 1964–1965* (New York: Simon & Schuster, 2001), 195–63.

147 "Get me some things you'd be proud of": Lyndon Johnson conversation with Nicholas Katzenbach, December 14, 1964. Quoted in Nick Kotz, *Judgment Days: Lyndon Baines Johnson, Martin Luther King, Jr. and the Laws That Changed America* (New York: Houghton Mifflin, 2005), 245.

147 The Justice Department filed its first voting rights suit: "Central Points," *Time*, March 19, 1965.

148 "Our cry to the state of Alabama": Gary May, *Bending Toward Justice: The Voting*

Rights Act and the Transformation of American Democracy (New York: Basic Books, 2013), 54. King's refrain repeated his call from his May 1957 address at the Prayer Pilgrimage for Freedom, a march on Washington that took place on the Mall.

148 The liberal attorney general pressed instead for an amendment: The Justice Department crafted language, sent to the president in January 1965, that read:

> SECTION 1. The right of citizens of the United States to vote shall not be denied or abridged by the United States or by any State for any cause except (1) inability to meet residence requirements not exceeding sixty days or minimum age requirements, imposed by State law; (2) conviction of a felony for which no pardon or amnesty has been granted; (3) mental incompetency adjudicated by a court of record; or (4) confinement pursuant to the judgment or warrant of a court of record at the time of registration or election.
>
> SECTION 2. The Congress shall have power to enforce this Article by appropriate legislation.

Bruce Ackerman and Jennifer Nou, "Canonizing the Civil Rights Revolution: The People and the Poll Tax," *Northwestern University Law Review* 103, no. 1 (2009): 91–92.

149 A basic agreement was reached on March 1: May, *Bending toward Justice*, 95.

149 To pass such a measure: For a discussion of the interplay between Johnson and congressional Republicans and Democrats, see Julian E. Zelizer, *The Fierce Urgency of Now: Lyndon Johnson, Congress, and the Battle for the Great Society* (New York: Penguin Press, 206–12).

149 "the froth on a warm pail of milk": Purdum, *An Idea Whose Time Has Come*, 211.

149 "He kept his vocal cords lubricated": Ibid.

149 kept their own counsel: Garrow, *Protest at Selma*, 69; Charles Mohr, "Johnson, Dr. King Confer on Rights," *New York Times*, March 6, 1965.

150 Lewis recounts that the march: John Lewis with Michael D'Orso, *Walking with the Wind: A Memoir of the Movement* (New York: Simon & Schuster, 1998), 325.

150 "Mr. Major, I would like to have a word": Roy Reed, "Alabama Police Use Gas and Clubs to Rout Negroes," *New York Times*, March 8, 1965.

150 The troopers rushed forward: Ibid.

151 "I don't see how President Johnson": Lewis with D'Orso, *Walking with the Wind*, 330.

152 "integrating, carpetbagging": Stephan Lesher, *George Wallace: American Populist* (New York: Perseus Books, 1994), 140. A "carpetbagger" was a northerner who traveled to the South during Reconstruction. A "scalawag" was a local white sympathetic to Blacks.

152 "Rarely in history": "The Central Points," *Time*, March 19, 1965, http://www.time.com/time/magazine/article/0,9171,833543,00.html.

152 Students held a sit-in at the base of the Liberty Bell: "Sympathy Demonstrations over Selma Spread across Nation," *New York Times*, March 13, 1965.

152 "heavy load of tension": Lady Bird Johnson, tape-recorded diary, March 13, 1965, in Beschloss, *Reaching for Glory*, 227.

153 "No other son-of-a-bitch": Dan T. Carter, *The Politics of Rage: George Wallace, the Origins of the New Conservatism, and the Transformation of American Politics*, 2nd ed. (Baton Rouge: Louisiana State University Press, 2000), 96.

153 "The six foot four Johnson": Richard N. Goodwin, *Remembering America: A Voice from the Sixties* (Boston: Little, Brown, 1988), 323.
153 With that, Johnson pulled a rattled Wallace: Kotz, *Judgment Days*, 306.
154 "Hell, if I'd stayed in there much longer": Robert Dallek, *Flawed Giant: Lyndon Johnson and His Times, 1961–1973* (New York: Oxford University Press, 1998), 217.
154 "The hell you did": Goodwin, *Remembering America*, 325–27.
154 Johnson phoned Goodwin only once: Ibid., 329.
154 "At times history and fate": Lyndon B. Johnson: "Special Message to the Congress: The American Promise," March 15, 1965, The American Presidency Project, http://www.presidency.ucsb.edu/ws/?pid=26805.
157 "The threat of the free exercise": "Our God Is Marching On," speech at Montgomery, March 25, 1965, in *A Testament of Hope: The Essential Writings of Martin Luther King, Jr.*, ed. James M. Washington (New York, Harper & Row, 1986), 227–30. Sadly the transcript of this pivotal speech is garbled. According to Branch, *At Canaan's Edge*, 169, it simply excludes King's discursive passage on Reconstruction. More amusingly, news transcripts the next day mangled the most famous line, rendering it "The moral arm of the universe is long, but it bends toward justice." (Images of the arm, perhaps holding a beer, are hard to shake.) The version in *A Testament of Hope* includes "arm," not "arc," as does John Lewis's book. A film of the speech, however, shows clearly that King said "arc." The line is a paraphrase from Theodore Parker. Viewers of the film *Selma* might note that none of this appears in the movie's portrayal of the great rally. The King family carefully guards use of his speeches and licensed the speeches for a different movie that has not yet been made. The speech delivered in the film is a scriptwriter's concoction of what a King speech might sound like—borrowing from an early speech during the Montgomery bus boycott.
157 "the Old Negro spiritual": Ibid.
158 "How then shall there be": Remarks of Senator Everett Dirksen, *Congressional Record*, April 22, 1965, 8292–94.
158 The sweeping legislation: Voting Rights Act of 1965, 42 U.S.C. §§ 1973 to 1973aa-6, Avalon Project, Yale Law School, http://avalon.law.yale.edu/20th_century/voting_rights_1965.asp.
158 Section 2 declared:: The Supreme Court found a private right of action in Section 5 of the Voting Rights Act in *Allen v. State Bd. of Elections*, 393 U.S. 544 (1969), and implicitly extended this holding to Section 2 in subsequent cases, most notably *Mobile v. Bolden*, 446 U.S. 55 (1982) and *Thornburg v. Gingles*, 478 U.S. 30 (1986).
158 The legislation did not, however, prohibit poll taxes: See May, *Bending toward Justice*, 158–59, 165–67.
159 "Now John": Lewis, *Walking with the Wind*, 346.
159 In Mississippi, African American registration leaped: Richard M. Valelly, *The Two Reconstructions: The Struggle for Black Enfranchisement* (Chicago: University of Chicago Press, 2004), 207.
160 "When he signed the act he was euphoric": Bill Moyers, *Moyers on America: A Journalist and His Times*, paperback ed. (New York: Anchor Books, 2005), 197.
160 In Mississippi in 2004: CNN exit poll, November 2004, http://www.cnn.com/ELECTION/2004/pages/results/states/MS/P/00/epolls.0.html.
161 By 1904 every ex-Confederate state: For a thorough analysis of the poll tax and its impact, see Ogden, *The Poll Tax in the South*. For a survey of the origins of the poll tax, see Kousser, *The Shaping of Southern Politics*, 63–72.

161 In 1900, when three-quarters of the population: Kousser, *The Shaping of Southern Politics*, 64.
161 "the forgotten man": Franklin D. Roosevelt, "Radio Address from Albany, New York: 'The Forgotten Man' Speech," April 7, 1932, The American Presidency Project, http://www.presidency.ucsb.edu/ws/?pid=88408.
161 Three southern states eliminated: Ogden, *The Poll Tax in the South*, 178–85.
161 "an entering wedge for Negro suffrage": T. Harry Williams, *Huey Long* (New York: Knopf, 1969), 738.
161 "contributed to my very large majority": Steven F. Lawson, *Black Ballots: Voting Rights in the South, 1944–69* (New York: Columbia University Press, 1976), 63.
162 neither lion nor fox: See the classic study of FDR's leadership style, James MacGregor Burns, *Roosevelt: The Lion and the Fox*, paperback reprint ed. (New York: Harcourt, 1984). Burns recounts one meeting between FDR and student leaders. One challenged him about the lack of democracy in the South. Roosevelt parried feebly, "What are we going to do about it? . . . You can't solve that in a year or two." To another student he said of Abraham Lincoln, "He was a sad man, because he couldn't get it all at once" (423). In fact Roosevelt barely used his wiles to advance racial justice in the South.
162 FDR privately wrote: Lawson, *Black Ballots*, 57.
162 a "remnant of the period": Franklin Delano Roosevelt, press conference no. 484, Hyde Park, New York, September 9, 1938, http://www.fdrlibrary.marist.edu/_resources/images/pc/pc0069.pdf.
162 it was "inevitably contrary": Susan Dunn, *Roosevelt's Purge: How FDR Fought to Change the Democratic Party* (Cambridge, MA: Belknap Press, 2012), 237.
162 "At no time and in no manner": Ibid.
162 In 1940 voter turnout: Ira Katznelson, *Fear Itself: The New Deal and the Origins of Our Time* (New York: Norton, 2012), 142.
162 "Polltaxia": The phrase appears to have been coined by the crusading journalist Stetson Kennedy in his 1944 book, *Southern Exposure: Making the South Safe for Democracy*, reprint ed. (Tuscaloosa: University of Alabama Press, 2011).
162 Soldier Voting Act: Absentee Voting in Time of War, Pub. L. No. 78–277, 5 8 Stat. 136 (1944) (repealed in full 1955). For a discussion of its significance, see Karlan, "Ballots and Bullets."
162 NAACP joined with a new coalition: Lawson, *Black Ballots*, 58–59.
162 In fact a constitutional amendment: Ackerman and Nou, "Canonizing the Civil Rights Revolution," 69–70.
163 "It is a travesty": "NAACP against Tax Amendment," *Pittsburgh Courier*, March 31, 1962, quoted in ibid., 70.
163 the Supreme Court struck down the remaining state laws: *Harper v. Virginia Bd. of Elections*, 383 U.S. 663 (1966).
163 The justices never mentioned: Ackerman and Nou, "Canonizing the Civil Rights Revolution," 67.
164 The United States first imposed: Lynne Olson, *Those Angry Days: Roosevelt, Lindbergh and America's Fight over World War II* (New York: Random House, 2013), 217–18.
164 The first proposal was introduced: Wendell W. Cultice, *Youth's Battle for the Ballot: A History of Voting Age in America* (New York: Praeger, 1992), 21–22.
165 Journalists noted that for all the enthusiasm: Jules Witcover, *85 Days: The Last Campaign of Robert F. Kennedy*, revised paperback ed. (New York: William Morrow, 1998), 106.

165 Politicians began to urge: See Jenny Diamond Cheng, "Uncovering the Twenty-Sixth Amendment," PhD dissertation, University of Michigan, 2008, http://search.proquest.com/docview/304573437.
165 "whether the violence, animal energy": *Voting at 18*, 90th Cong., 2d sess., *Congressional Record* 114 (June 27, 1968): 19135.
165 "In these troubled times": Rep. Howard Tenzer, "L.B.J.: A President Who Understands Young People," 90th Cong., 2d sess., *Congressional Record* 114 (June 27, 1968): 19079.
165 the radicals "probably feel": Sen. Marlow Cook, *Senate Judiciary Committee, Subcommittee on Constitutional Amendments, Hearing before the Subcommittee on Constitutional Amendments of the Committee of the Judiciary United States Senate Ninety-First Congress Second Session on S.J. Res. 7, S.J. Res. 19, S.J. Res. 32, S.J. Res. 34, S.J. Res. 38., S.J. Res. 73, S.J. Res. 87, S.J. Res. 102, S.J. Res. 105, S.J. Res. 141, S.J. Res. 147*, 91st Cong., 2nd Session, February 16, 1970, 42.
165 A national commission: National Commission on the Causes and Prevention of Violence, *To Establish Justice, to Insure Domestic Tranquility: Final Report of the National Commission on the Causes and Prevention of Violence* (Washington, D.C.: Government Printing Office, 1969), xix, 224.
165 the day after President Nixon gave his speech: Rick Perlstein, *Nixonland: The Rise of a President and the Fracturing of America* (New York: Scribner, 2010), 435.
165 One adopted the groovy name: Cultice, *Youth Battles for the Ballot*, 98.
166 "overcome the image": United Press International, "Young Lobby Group Chided on Militancy," February 5, 1969.
166 On April 28, 1970, the president opposed: Marjorie Hunter, "Democrats Press 18 Year Old Vote," *New York Times.*
166 Nixon surprised the nation: Richard Nixon, "Address to the Nation on the Situation in Southeast Asia," April 30, 1970, American Presidency Project, http://www.presidency.ucsb.edu.
166 At Kent State University: John Kifner, "4 Kent State Students Killed by Troops," *New York Times*, May 4, 1970.
166 Within days undergrads went on strike: See Todd Gitlin, *The Sixties: Years of Hope, Days of Rage* (New York: Bantam Books, 1987), 410.
166 "Youth in its protest must be heard": Max Frankel, "Hickel, in Note to Nixon, Charges Administration Is Failing Youth; Protests Close over 80 Colleges," *New York Times*, May 7, 1970.
166 an agitated televised press conference: The episode of the visit to the Lincoln Memorial is described in Richard Reeves, *President Nixon: Alone in the White House* (New York: Simon & Schuster, 2000), 218–22.
167 "weirdest day so far": The diary entry was for May 9, 1970. H. R. Haldeman, *The Haldeman Diaries* (New York: G. P. Putnam's Sons, 1994), 163.
167 "There will either be an 18-year-old vote": Associated Press, "Mansfield Sees Filibuster If 18 Year Old Vote Fails," May 10, 1970.
167 "Give someone direct orders": Reeves, *President Nixon*, 225.
167 the Supreme Court confirmed: *Oregon v. Mitchell*, 400 U.S. 112 (1970).
168 "As of now": Quoted in Perlstein, *Nixonland*, 528.
168 "Surely the 25 million baby boomers": Hunter S. Thompson, "The Campaign Trail: The Million Pound Shithammer," February 3, 1972, in *Fear and Loathing at Rolling Stone: The Essential Writing of Hunter S. Thompson* (New York: Simon & Schuster, 2011), 130.

168 "The people most terrified": Perlstein, *Nixonland*, 509.

168 That imaginary winning liberal coalition: See John Aloysius Farrell, "The Youth Vote," *Denver Post*, August 23, 2008, http://www.denverpost.com/thedemocrats/ci_10168450f.

168 the Democratic Party rewrote its rules: See Byron E. Shafer, *Quiet Revolution: The Struggle for the Democratic Party and the Shaping of Post-Reform Politics* (New York: Russell Sage, 1983); Bruce Miroff, *The Liberals' Moment: The McGovern Insurgency and the Identity Crisis of the Democratic Party* (Lawrence: University Press of Kansas, 2007).

169 The use of primaries and direct votes are now seen: The Parti Socialiste in France now chooses its presidential nominee through a primary. In Canada party members have an opportunity to vote directly. The British conservatives have begun to experiment with direct primaries to choose nominees for parliamentary seats. In 2015 the British Labour Party radically expanded the ranks of those who could vote for party leader, in effect creating a primary. Over 422,000 voted, triple the number the prior time the party elected a leader. They chose Jeremy Corbyn, a hard-left candidate supported by only a handful of members of Parliament. See Alberto Nardelli, "Corbyn Has a Huge Mandate but Labour Simply Has to Win Votes from Tories," *Guardian* (London), Datablog, September 12, 2015, http://www.theguardian.com/politics/datablog/2015/sep/12/jeremy-corbyn-mandate-labour-win-votes-tories.

169 they had actually fallen from 1972 to 1992: J. Mijin Cha, *Registering Millions: The Success and Potential of the National Voter Registration Act at 20* (New York: Demos, 2013), 4.

169 National Voter Registration Act: P.L. 103–31, 107 Stat.77, 42 U.S.C. §1973gg et seq. For a summary and history of the act, see Royce Crocker, *The National Voter Registration Act of 1993: History, Implementation, and Effects*, CRS No. R40609 (Washington, DC: Congressional Research Service, 2013).

170 registration rates increased: "Between 1992 and 2012, voter registration increased nationally by over seven percentage points." Crocker, *The National Voter Registration Act of 1993*, 23.

11: Lost Decade

173 "perhaps the strangest phone call": Political Staff of the *Washington Post*, *Deadlock: The Inside Story of America's Closest Election* (New York: Public Affairs Press, 2001), 48.

173 "Circumstances have changed dramatically": Ibid. The Associated Press reported the conversation slightly differently. According to the AP, Gore said, "You don't have to get snippy about this." Later, according to the AP, he lectured Bush, "Let me explain something. Your YOUNGER brother is not the ultimate authority on this." Sandra Sobieraj, Associated Press, "Gore Phones Bush: No Need to Get 'Snippy,'" November 9, 2000.

175 "Stop the fraud": Jake Tapper, *Down and Dirty: The Plot to Steal the Presidency* (Boston: Little, Brown, 2001), 261.

175 "the Brooks Brothers Riot": Several of the "rioters" would go on to significant public office. They included Matt Schlapp, later White House political director, and Garry Malphrus, who became the deputy director of the Domestic Policy Council at the White House. See Al Kamen, "Miami 'Riot' Squad: Where Are They Now?," *Washington Post*, January 24, 2005.

175 the U.S. Supreme Court halted it: *Bush v. Gore*, 538 U.S. 98 (2000).

175 It was implausible enough: How implausible? University of Chicago professor Geoffrey Stone calculates, "In the decade leading up to *Bush v. Gore*, Justices Rehnquist, Scalia and Thomas cast approximately 65 votes in non-unanimous Supreme Court decisions interpreting the Equal Protection Clause. Nineteen of those votes were cast in cases involving affirmative action. . . . Of the 46 votes that these Justices cast in cases that did not involve affirmative action, Justices Rehnquist, Scalia and Thomas collectively cast only two votes to uphold a claimed violation of the Equal Protection Clause. Thus, these three Justices found a violation of Equal Protection in only 4 percent of these cases. For the sake of comparison, over this same period, and in these very same cases, the colleagues of Justices Rehnquist, Scalia and Thomas collectively voted 74 percent of the time to uphold the Equal Protection Clause claim. 74 percent versus 4 percent." Geoffrey R. Stone, "Equal Protection? The Supreme Court's Decision in *Bush v. Gore*," Federal Bar Association, May 23, 2001.

175 Even more jarring: "Our consideration is limited to the present circumstances, for the problem of equal protection in election processes generally presents many complexities." *Bush v. Gore*, 109. Ruth Bader Ginsburg, on reading the draft majority opinion, wrote a draft dissent stating that if there were any Equal Protection violation, it was by state government officials against Black voters. Scalia erupted, charging that Ginsburg was using "Al Sharpton tactics." She dropped the language. Jeffrey Toobin, *Too Close to Call: The Thirty-Six-Day Battle to Decide the 2000 Election* (New York: Random House, 2002), 266–67.

175 Some were reminded of the tape recorder: See, for example, Adam Liptak, "Bush v. Gore Set to Outlast Its Beneficiary," *New York Times*, December 22, 2008.

175 Gore won a half million more popular votes: Did the Court really hand the election to Bush? Gore had publicly urged, "Count every vote," but in court had asked for counts only in four Democratic counties. A consortium of newspapers examined the "undervotes" and concluded that although Bush would have won if the recount had proceeded as requested by Gore, a statewide hand recount might have awarded the presidency to the Democrat. Ford Fessenden and John M. Broder, "Study of Disputed Florida Ballots Finds Justices Did Not Cast the Deciding Vote," *New York Times*, November 12, 2001. However, the *Orlando Sentinel* showed that had the recounts proceeded even in the four counties, they would likely have counted *overvotes* as well—such as when a voter wrote the candidate's name on the ballot as well as making a mark. Had that happened, Gore could have won the recount. See Mickey Kaus, "Everything *The New York Times* Thinks About the Florida Recount Is Wrong," *Slate*, November 13, 2001.

175 "Get over it!": Joan Biskupic, *American Original: The Life and Constitution of Supreme Court Justice Antonin Scalia* (New York: Farrar, Straus & Giroux, 2009), 248.

176 Florida's secretary of state hired a private company: Many details of the purge are revealed in Greg Palast, "Florida's 'Disappeared Voters': Disenfranchised by the GOP," *Nation*, January 18, 2001, http://www.thenation.com/article/floridas-disappeared-voters-disfranchised-gop/. See also U.S. Commission on Civil Rights, *Voting Irregularities in Florida During 2000 Election* (Chapter 5, "The Reality of List Maintenance"), http://www.usccr.gov/pubs/vote2000/report/ch5.htm.

176 "Middle initials didn't need to be the same": David Margolick, Evgenia Peretz, and Michael Schnayerson, "The Path to Florida," *Vanity Fair*, October 2004, http://www.vanityfair.com/news/2004/10/florida-election-2000.

176 "at least 1,100 eligible voters": Scott Hiaasen, Gary Kane, and Eliot Jaspin, "Felon Purge Sacrificed Innocent Voters," *Palm Beach Post*, May 27, 2001.

176 One county checked: Greg Palast, "Ex Con Game: How Florida's 'Felon' Voter-Purge Was Itself Felonious," *Harper's*, March 2002, 48–49, http://www.gregpalast.com/wp-content/uploads/HarpersMagazine-2002-03-0079106-1.pdf.

176 Florida was one of nine states: The other eight were Iowa, Kentucky, Maryland, Nebraska, New Mexico, Tennessee, Virginia, and Wyoming.

176 The Fourteenth Amendment authorizes it: The amendment reduces the number of members of Congress for any state that denies the right to vote "to any of the male inhabitants of such state, being twenty-one years of age, and citizens of the United States, or in any way abridged, except for participation in rebellion, or other crime."

176 the Jim Crow constitutions crafted provisions: For example, in Florida and other southern states, African American men who did not have a job could be convicted of vagrancy, imprisoned, then "leased out" to mines, factories, or farms—a convict leasing system that replicated slavery and disenfranchised the "felons" for good measure. See Douglas A. Blackmon, *Slavery by Another Name: The Re-Enslavement of Black Americans from the Civil War to World War II* (New York: Anchor Books, 2008).

176 possession of one ounce of marijuana: Jeff Manza and Christopher Uggen, *Locked Out: Felon Disenfranchisement and American Democracy* (New York: Oxford University Press, 2006), 8.

177 more than quadrupled: Numbers calculated using Bureau of Justice Statistics, "Corrections Statistical Analysis Tool (CSAT)—Prisoners under the Jurisdiction of State and Federal Correctional Authorities," December 31, 1978–2013, http://www.bjs.gov/index.cfm?ty=nps.

177 By the time of the contest between Bush and Gore: The Citizen Voting Age Population (CVAP) in Florida was 11,081,542; therefore 827,000 is 7.46 percent of the Florida CVAP. See U.S. Census Bureau, "2000 PHC-T-31, Voting-Age Population and Voting-Age Citizens," http://www.census.gov/population/www/cen2000/briefs/phc-t31/tables/tab01-01.pdf.

177 Nationwide, as of 2010: Christopher Uggen, Sarah Shannon, and Jeff Manza, *State-Level Estimates of Felon Disenfranchisement in the United States, 2010* (Washington, DC: Sentencing Project, 2010), 1.

177 designed a "butterfly ballot": Ironically this was done in a democratizing move: increased ballot access for third parties and fringe candidates meant more names on the page.

177 "Israeli occupied territory": Anti-Defamation League of B'nai B'rith, "Pat Buchanan in His Own Words," September 1999, http://archive.adl.org/special_reports/buchanan_own_words/print.html.

177 Even Buchanan's campaign: Jake Tapper, "Buchanan Camp: Bush Claims Are 'Nonsense,'" Salon.com, November 10, 2000.

178 "If I perish, I perish": Political Staff of the *Washington Post*, *Deadlock*, 96; Diane Rado, "Harris Finds Strength in Bible's Esther," *St. Petersburg Times*, November 18, 2000. When the HBO movie *Recount* aired, she objected to her portrayal, including its mirthful rendering of her identification with the beautiful Jewish queen who exposed the hateful Haman and his plot against the Hebrews.

178 In thirty states: Jocelyn F. Benson, *State Secretaries of State: Guardians of the Democratic Process* (Burlington, VT: Ashgate, 2010).

178 Troubling racial patterns: "Rights Commission's Report on Florida Election,"

Washington Post, June 5, 2001. One reason: newly registered Black voters, many casting ballots for the first time, were more likely than white voters to "overvote." See Dan Keating and Jon Mintz, "Florida Black Ballots Affected Most in 2000," *Washington Post*, November 13, 2001.

178 He calculates that if ballots: Allan Lichtman, "The Greatest Unknown Scandal of Our Time," *Huffington Post*, June 24, 2008.

179 The fix called for voting machines: This perhaps apocryphal story is related by Samuel Issacharoff, "Ballot Bedlam," *Duke Law Journal* 64 (2015): 1363, 1377.

179 "between four and six million presidential votes": CalTech/MIT Voting Project, *Voting: What Is, What Could Be*, 2001, 8–9, https://people.csail.mit.edu/rivest/pubs/VTP01.pdf.

179 Help America Vote Act: Public Law 107–252.

179 Many states charged forward: Myrna Pérez, *Voter Purges*, Brennan Center for Justice, September 30, 2008, 1–3, https://www.brennancenter.org/publication/voter-purges.

179 "disenfranchisement by typo": The Brennan Center for Justice led the fight to stop these "no match, no vote" laws. In *Washington Association of Churches v. Reed*, 492 F. Supp.2d 1264 (W.D. Wash. 2006), a federal court struck down Washington State's plan. For an exploration of the problem that prompted the court's ruling, see Justin Levitt, Wendy R. Weiser, and Ana Munoz, *Making the List: Database Matching and Verification Procedures for Voter Registration*, Brennan Center for Justice, March 24, 2006, http://www.brennancenter.org/sites/default/files/publications/Making%20the%20List.pdf.

180 one of every eight names: See Pew Center on the States, *Inaccurate, Costly, and Inefficient: Evidence That America's Voter Registration System Needs an Upgrade*, February 2012, http://www.pewtrusts.org/~/media/legacy/uploadedfiles/pcs_assets/2012/PewUpgradingVoterRegistrationpdf.pdf.

180 sixty million paper registration forms: U.S. Election Assistance Commission, *The Impact of the National Voter Registration Act of 1993 on the Administration of Elections for Federal Office 2007–2008: A Report to the 111th Congress* (2009), 6, http://www.eac.gov/assets/1/AssetManager/The%20Impact%20of%20the%20National%20Voter%20Registration%20Act%20on%20Federal%20Elections%202007-2008.pdf.

180 51 million eligible voters: Pew Center on the States, *Inaccurate, Costly, and Inefficient*, 1; see also U.S. Census Bureau, Current Population Survey, Voting and Registration Supplement (2012), http://thedataweb.rm.census.gov/TheDataWeb_HotReport2/voting/voting.hrml.

180 nearly one in four: Pew Center on the States, *Inaccurate, Costly, and Inefficient*, 2.

180 Twenty-six million voting-age Americans: David Ihrke, *Reason for Moving: 2012 to 2013*, https://www.census.gov/prod/2014pubs/p20-574.pdf.

180 A study by a Harvard political scientist: Thomas Patterson, *The Vanishing Voter: Public Involvement in an Age of Uncertainty* (New York: Vintage, 2003), 178.

180 "The registration laws in force": National Commission on Election Reform, Task Force on the Federal Election System, "Voter Registration," in *To Assure Pride and Confidence in the Electoral Process*, August 2001, 3, http://election2000.stanford.edu/task.force.report.8.2001.pdf.

180 the United States is one of the few democracies: See Jennifer S. Rosenberg with Margaret Chen, *Expanding Democracy: Voter Registration Around the World*, Brennan Center for Justice, June 10, 2009, 2.

180 In 2008, hindered by errors: Heather K. Gerken, "Make It Easy: The Case for Automatic Registration," *Democracy Journal*, Spring 2013, 18.

180 The saga of the Association of Community Organizations for Reform Now: For a measured discussion of the controversy around ACORN, see "The Acorn Story," *New York Times*, editorial, October 16, 2008.

181 three temporary ACORN canvassers: Keith Ervin, "Three Plead Guilty in Fake Voter Scheme," *Seattle Times*, October 30, 2007.

181 The names of professional football players: "Jive Turkey Rides Again," *National Review*, October 10, 2008.

181 In a presidential debate in 2008: FactCheck.org, "The Truth About McCain's ACORN Accusations," *Newsweek*, October 17, 2008; Justin Rood, "McCain Acorn Fears Overblown," ABC News, October 16, 2008.

181 "gift from heaven": Richard L. Hasen, *The Voting Wars: From Florida 2000 to the Next Election Meltdown* (New Haven: Yale University Press, 2012), 70.

181 ACORN quickly collapsed: The reasons for the collapse were essentially unrelated to controversies over voting. Chief among them was the revelation that the brother of the organization's founder had embezzled $1 million and its board of directors were never notified. Campbell Robertson, "Amount Embezzled from ACORN Is Disputed," *New York Times*, October 5, 2009.

181 error rates are high: Fritz J. Scheuren and Wendy Alvey, *Elections and Exit Polling* (Hoboken, NJ: John Wiley & Sons, 2008), 21.

181 The computerized systems prompted intense skepticism: See, for example, Robert F. Kennedy Jr., "Was the 2004 Election Stolen?," *Rolling Stone*, June 15, 2006.

182 "to helping Ohio deliver": Bob Fitrakis and Harvey Wasserman, "Diebold's Political Machine," *Mother Jones*, March 5, 2004.

182 "Ooh, one of those electronic voting dealies": "Electronic Voting," *The Simpsons*, November 4, 2008, https://www.youtube.com/watch?v=IoWJkrlptNs.

182 A task force of top computer scientists: The panel's report is summarized in Lawrence D. Norden with Eric Lazarus, *The Machinery of Democracy: Protecting Elections in an Electronic World* (Chicago: Chicago Academy Press, 2007); Kim Zetter, "Report: Magnet and PDA Sufficient to Change Votes on Voting Machine," *Wired*, December 17, 2007, http://www.wired.com/2007/12/report-magnet-a.

182 the voting machine scare receded: Not without a paradox. Cheap machines and printers routinely jam, helping lead to longer lines.

183 180,000 precincts and 114,000 separate polling places: U.S. Election Assistance Commission, "The 2014 Election Administration and Voting Survey Comprehensive Report," Report to the 114th Congress, July 1 2015, http://www.eac.gov/assets/1/Page/2014_EAC_EAVS_Comprehensive_Report_508_Compliant.pdf.

183 $10,000 fine and three years in prison: *Frank v. Walker*, 17 F. Supp.3d 837, 850 (E.D. Wis., 2014).

184 "Voter fraud, in particular": Justin Levitt, *The Truth About Voter Fraud*, Brennan Center for Justice, November 9, 2007), https://www.brennancenter.org/sites/default/files/legacy/The%20Truth%20About%20Voter%20Fraud.pdf.

184 It is also like a bank robbery: The days of Bonnie and Clyde are long gone. "Some crimes have all but died out. Last year there were just 69 armed robberies of banks, building societies and post offices in England and Wales, compared with 500 a year in the 1990s. . . . The biggest factor may be simply that security measures have improved. Car immobilisers have killed joyriding; bulletproof screens, security guards and marked money have all but done for bank robbery." "The Curious Case of the Fall in Crime,"

Economist, July 20, 2013, http://www.economist.com/news/briefing/21582041-rich-world-seeing-less-and-less-crime-even-face-high-unemployment-and-economic.

184 Russell Kirk invoked: Russell Kirk, *John Randolph of Roanoke: A Study in American Politics*, reprint ed. (Indianapolis: Liberty Fund, 1997), 53. When originally published in 1951, the book was titled *John Randolph of Roanoke: A Study in Conservative Thought*.

184 Carter proposed a nationwide system: Jimmy Carter, "Election Reform Message to the Congress," March 22, 1977, American Presidency Project, http://www.presidency.ucsb.edu/ws/?pid=7218. The story of Carter's proposal and the New Right's opposition to it is told by Rick Perlstein, *Reaganland: America's Right Turn 1976–1980* (New York: Simon & Schuster, 2020), 93–5.

184 The party chair called it "a Republican concept": Warren Weaver Jr., "Carter Proposes End of Electoral College in Presidential Votes," *New York Times*, March 23, 1977. "The national chairman, Bill Brock, said that the proposal 'has merit' and embodied 'a Republican concept,' expanding citizens' opportunity to vote. He said that further safeguards were needed, however."

185 "Fraud and Carter's voter registration scheme": Rick Perlstein, "The Prophetic President," *Washington Spectator*, August 27, 2015, http://washingtonspectator.org/the-prophetic-president.

185 That November, Ohio voters: "Congress and Government 1977: Overview," *CQ Almanac 1977*, 33rd ed. (Washington, DC: Congressional Quarterly, 1978), 747–48, http://library.cqpress.com/cqalmanac/cqal77-1201416.

185 "I know you can't endorse me": The meeting is described in Stephen F. Hayward, *The Age of Reagan: The Fall of the Old Liberal Order, 1964–1980* (New York: Crown Books, 2009), 680; and in Allan J. Lichtman, *White Conservative Nation: The Rise of the American Conservative Movement* (New York: Atlantic Monthly Press, 2008), 344.

185 "It is interesting": William Martin, *With God on Our Side: The Rise of the Religious Right in America* (New York: Broadway Books, 1996), 215.

185 "How many of our Christians": "Paul Weyrich: 'I Don't Want Everybody to Vote' (Goo Goo)," 1980, https://www.youtube.com/watch?v=8GBAsFwPglw.

186 In 2009 ALEC drafted model voter identification bills: ALEC's Public Safety and Elections Task Force approved a model voter ID bill in 2009. Ethan Magoc, "Flurry of Voter ID Laws Tied to Conservative Group ALEC," NBC News, August 21, 2012, http://investigations.nbcnews.com/_news/2012/08/21/13392560-flurry-of-voter-id-laws-tied-to-conservative-group-alec.

186 "a major criminal enterprise": Carolyn Tuft, "Bond Wants Federal Investigation of Problems at City Polls; He Accuses Democrats of 'Criminal Enterprise' in Keeping Polls Open Late; Democrats Criticize Election Board," *St. Louis Post-Dispatch*, November 10, 2000.

186 St. Louis election officials alleged: Jo Mannies and Jennifer LaFleur, "City Mislabeled Dozens as Voting from Vacant Lots; Property Records Appear to Be in Error, Survey Finds; Just 14 Ballots Are Suspect," *St. Louis Post-Dispatch*, November 5, 2001, http://www.brennancenter.org/sites/default/files/legacy/d/download_file_39006.pdf. See also Levitt, *The Truth about Voter Fraud*, 11; Lorraine Minnite and David Callahan, *Securing the Vote: An Analysis of Election Fraud* (New York: Demos, 2003), 49 n. 88.

186 In all, in 2000 and 2002: Levitt, *The Truth About Voter Fraud*, 13.

186 "federal prosecutors indicted far more people": Lorraine C. Minnite, *The Myth of Voter Fraud* (Ithaca: Cornell University Press, 2010), 47.

186 national study by the Walter Cronkite School: Natasha Kahn and Corbin Carson, "Comprehensive Database of U.S. Voter Fraud Uncovers No Evidence That Photo ID Is Needed," News21, August 12, 2012, http://votingrights.news21.com/article/election-fraud/index.html.

187 "There is widespread": John Serebrov and Tova Wang, "Voting Fraud and Voter Intimidation: Report to the U.S. Election Assistance Commission on Preliminary Research and Recommendations," http://graphics8.nytimes.com/packages/pdf/national/20070411voters_draft_report.pdf. The panel suppressed the finding, and then rewrote it to say, "There is a great deal of debate on the pervasiveness of fraud in elections." U.S. Election Assistance Commission, *Election Crimes: An Initial Review and Recommendations for Further Study*, December 2006, http://www.eac.gov/assets/1/workflow_staging/Page/57.PDF. See Ian Urbina, "U.S. Panel Is Said to Alter Finding on Voter Fraud," *New York Times*, April 11, 2007. One of the coauthors described the process in Tova Wang, "A Rigged Report on U.S. Voting?," *Washington Post*, August 30, 2007, http://www.washingtonpost.com/wp-dyn/content/article/2007/08/29/AR2007082901928.html.

187 "it is more likely that an individual will be struck by lightning": Levitt, *The Truth About Voter Fraud*, 4.

187 He formally made combating voter fraud: See U.S. Department of Justice, "Prepared Remarks of Attorney General John Ashcroft, Voting Integrity Symposium, October 8, 2002," http://www.justice.gov/archive/ag/speeches/2002/100802ballotintegrity.htm. For a description of the push to find voter fraud at the Justice Department, see Jeffrey Toobin, "Poll Position: Is the Justice Department Poised to Stop Voter Fraud—or to Keep Voters from Voting?," *New Yorker*, September 20, 2004.

187 "all components of the Department": U.S. Department of Justice, "Department of Justice to Hold Ballot Access and Voting Integrity Symposium: Conference to Focus on Election Fraud, Voting Rights," August 2, 2005, http://www.justice.gov/archive/ag/speeches/2002/100802ballotintegrity.htm.

187 only twenty-four people: See Art Levine, "The Republican War on Voting," *American Prospect*, March 19, 2008.

187 "Many of those charged": Eric Lipton and Ian Urbina, "In Five-Year Effort, Scant Evidence of Voter Fraud," *New York Times*, April 12, 2007, http://www.nytimes.com/2007/04/12/washington/12fraud.html?pagewanted=all&_r=0.

187 An energetic band of partisan activists: Hasen, *Voting Wars*, 42–73.

188 "I too get to work with mold spores": U.S. Department of Justice, Office of Inspector General/Office of Professional Responsibility, *An Investigation of Allegations of Politicized Hiring and Other Improper Personnel Actions in the Civil Rights Division*, July 2, 2008, 20–21, http://www.justice.gov/sites/default/files/opr/legacy/2009/01/13/oig-opr-iaph-crd.pdf.

188 The inspector general concluded that he lied: "We believe that Schlozman made false statements to the Senate Judiciary Committee, both in his sworn testimony and in his written responses to the supplemental questions for the record." Ibid., 53–55.

188 His lawyer denied the charge: David Morgan, "IG: Justice Official Hired Partisans, Lied," CBS News, January 13, 2009, http://www.cbsnews.com/news/ig-justice-official-hired-partisans-lied/. Schlozman's lawyer, William Jordan, said his client had passed a lie-detector test. "The report released today is inaccurate, incomplete, biased, unsupported by the law, and contrary to the facts," he charged, and accused the investigators themselves of "extraordinary bias and lack of ethical and legal standards."

188 its "headquarters" appeared to be a post office box: Brad Friedman, "Mystery Solved! Location of 'American Center for Voting Rights' Found! Exclusive Photographs!," BradBlog, March 25, 2005, http://www.bradblog.com/?p=1283; Richard L. Hasen, "The Fraudulent Fraud Squad: The Incredible, Disappearing American Center for Voting Rights," *Slate*, May 18, 2007.

188 Hearne's group vanished: Hasen, "Fraudulent Fraud Squad."

188 Hearne even declined to mention it: Mark F. (Thor) Hearne II, Arent Fox, http://www.arentfox.com/people/mark-f-thor-hearne-ii#.VTSFL2bIyCR, accessed June 30, 2015.

188 Hans von Spakovsky: The best profile of von Spakovsky and his outsized impact is Jane Mayer, "The Voter-Fraud Myth: The Man Who Has Stoked Fear About Impostors at the Polls," *New Yorker*, October 29, 2012, http://www.newyorker.com/magazine/2012/10/29/the-voter-fraud-myth.

188 It turned out that he: Dan Eggen, "Official's Article on Voting Law Spurs Outcry," *Washington Post*, April 13, 2006; Publius, "Securing the Integrity of American Elections: The Need for Change," *Texas Review of Law and Policy* 9 (2005): 277.

188 President George W. Bush installed him: Dahlia Lithwick, "Do Not Vote for This Guy," *Slate*, September 25, 2007, http://www.slate.com/articles/news_and_politics/jurisprudence/2007/09/do_not_vote_for_this_guy.html. Since then the U.S. Supreme Court has sharply curtailed the president's power to make such appointments. See *NLRB v. Noel Canning*, 134 S.Ct 2550 (2014). A filibuster blocked von Spakovsky's nomination once it became clear he had worked hard to restrict voting rights, as seen by his Democratic opponents.

188 "One doesn't have to look far": Hans A. von Spakovsky, "Smoke of Registration Fraud Leads to Election Fires," Fox News, October 31, 2008. The article summarizes his report, "Stolen Identities, Stolen Votes: A Case Study in Voter Impersonation," Heritage Foundation, March 10, 2008, www.heritage.org.

189 John Fund: See John Fund, *Stealing Elections: How Voter Fraud Threatens Our Democracy* (New York: Encounter Books, 2008).

189 eight of the nineteen hijackers: Ibid.; Minnite, *The Myth of Voter Fraud*, 5–11.

189 Busy Kobach helped draft the 2010 Arizona law: Alan Greenblatt, "Kris Kobach Tackles Illegal Immigration," *Governing*, March 2012.

189 Former House majority leader Dick Armey: Hasen, *Voting Wars*, 44; Rachel Slajda, "Dick Armey: Many Dems Are Voting Early to Commit Voter Fraud," TPM Muckraker, October 21, 2010, http://talkingpointsmemo.com.

190 Describing poor voters: Dick Morris and Eileen McGann, *Power Grab: Obama's Dangerous Plan for a One Party Nation*, Kindle ed. (West Palm Beach, FL: Humanix Books, 2014), location 883.

190 A University of Delaware study: Seventy-three percent of those surveyed supported strict voter ID when accompanied by the photo of a Black man voting, compared with 67 percent support from those shown a photo of a white person or no photo at all. This is considered statistically significant. David C. Wilson, Paul R. Brewer, and Phoebe Theodora Rosenbluth, "Racial Imagery and Support for Voter ID Laws," *Race and Social Problems* 6 (December 2014): 4. See also Christopher Ingraham, "Whites Are More Supportive of Voter ID Laws When Shown Photos of Black People Voting," *Washington Post*, Wonkblog, October 14, 2014.

190 Royal Masset, political director: Kristen Mack, "In Trying to Win, Has Dewhurst Lost a Friend?," *Houston Chronicle*, May 17, 2007.

190 "We did hear complaints": George W. Bush, "Remarks on the Department of

Justice and an Exchange with Reporters, March 20, 2007," in *Public Papers of the President of the United States: George W. Bush, 2007, Book 1 January 1–June 30, 2007* (Washington, DC: Government Printing Office, 2011), 335.

190 At one point Rove: David Johnson and Eric Lipton, "Rove Discussed Firing U.S. Attorneys Earlier Than He Indicated, Emails Show," *New York Times*, March 16, 2007, http://www.nytimes.com/2007/03/16/world/americas/16iht-rove.4930290.html?_r=1.

191 By December 2006 nine U.S. attorneys: For a full recounting of the scandal, see U.S. Department of Justice, Office of the Inspector General and Office of Professional Responsibility, *An Investigation into the Removal of Nine U.S. Attorneys in 2006*, Washington, DC, October 2008, https://oig.justice.gov/special/s0809a/final.pdf.

191 Joshua Micah Marshall: See Paul McLeary, "How TalkingPointsMemo Beat the Big Boys on the U.S. Attorney Scandal," *Columbia Journalism Review*, March 15, 2007.

191 "broad partisan conspiracies": Jay Carney, "Running Massacre," Swampland blog, *Time*.com, January 17, 2007.

191 "The voter fraud wars continue": U.S. Department of Justice, Office of the Inspector General and Office of Professional Responsibility, *An Investigation into the Removal of Nine U.S. Attorneys in 2006*, 170.

191 "What the critics": David C. Iglesias, "Why I Was Fired," *New York Times*, March 21, 2007.

192 "[Pete] Domenici says": U.S. Department of Justice, Office of the Inspector General and Office of Professional Responsibility, *An Investigation into the Removal of Nine U.S. Attorneys in 2006*, 151.

192 "There was an illegitimate basis": Tom Hamburger, "Fired U.S. Attorney Tells of a Lunch with Politics on the Menu," *Los Angeles Times*, May 19, 2007.

192 "First would come the spurious allegations": David Iglesias, *In Justice: Inside the Scandal That Rocked the Bush Administration* (Hoboken, NJ: John Wiley & Sons, 2008), 75. Iglesias had a commendable subsequent career: he was recalled to navy duty and successfully prosecuted war crimes at Guantánamo.

192 "There was no evidence": David Bowermaster, "McKay 'Stunned' by Report on Bush," *Seattle Times*, March 13, 2007.

192 Using a provision in the Patriot Act: Eric Lipton, "Missouri Prosecutor Says He Was Pushed to Resign," *New York Times*, May 10, 2007, http://www.nytimes.com/2007/05/10/washington/10attorney.html.

192 The hasty charges: Charlie Savage, "Missouri Attorney a Focus in Firings," *Boston Globe*, May 7, 2007, http://www.boston.com/news/nation/washington/articles/2007/05/06/missouri_attorney_a_focus_in_firings/; Hasen, *Voting Wars*, 58–59.

193 investigations by Senator Charles Schumer: Tim Shipman, "Mafia Prosecutor Now Has Bush in His Sights," *Telegraph (UK)*, June 3, 2007. Bharara became the high-profile U.S. attorney for the Southern District of New York.

193 firing a prosecutor for failing to find voter fraud: See Michael Waldman and Justin Levitt, "The Myth of Voter Fraud," *Washington Post*, March 29, 2007.

193 At one session the attorney general answered: Dana Milbank, "Maybe Gonzales Won't Recall His Painful Day on the Hill," *Washington Post*, April 20, 2007.

193 "Voter fraud drives honest citizens": *Purcell v. Gonzalez*, 549 U.S. 1, 4 (2006). The Court would rely on *Purcell* in 2014, when it declined to uphold injunctions against several voting law changes in the days before the midterm election.

193 "*Feel* disenfranchised?": Alex Keyssar, "'Disenfranchised?' When Words Lose Their

Meaning," *Huffington Post*, October 22, 2006. Scholars from MIT and Columbia tested the Court's premise. In a public opinion poll, they asked voters how they felt about fraud, whether the risk of others voting improperly affected their own ardor to vote. They found that fears of fraud by others "have no relationship to an individual's likelihood of turning out to vote." See Stephen Ansolabehere and Nathaniel Persily, "Voter Fraud in the Eye of the Beholder: The Role of Public Opinion in the Challenge to Voter Identification Requirements," *Harvard Law Review* 121 (2008): 1737.

193 The appeals court opinion upholding Indiana's law: *Crawford v. Marion County*, 472 F. 3d 949 (CA7 2007).

194 the most frequently cited legal scholar: Fred R. Shapiro, "The Most-Cited Legal Scholars," *Journal of Legal Studies* 29, no. S1 (January 2000).

194 preeminent public intellectuals: See Richard A. Posner, *Public Intellectuals: A Study of Decline* (Cambridge, MA: Harvard University Press, 2002). Posner's list of leading public intellectuals is on page 209. He made number 70.

194 "A great many people who are eligible to vote": *Crawford v. Marion County Election Board*, 953–54 (citing *Clingman v. Beaver*, 544 U.S. 581 (2005)).

194 the type of fraud the statute protected against: *Crawford v. Marion County Election Board*, 553 U.S. 181 (2008). Stevens's opinion was joined by Roberts and Kennedy. Scalia, Clarence Thomas, and Samuel Alito wrote their own opinion agreeing with Stevens on the result.

195 In 1968 Richard M. Nixon's aide: See Kevin Phillips, *The Emerging Republican Majority* (New York: Arlington House, 1969).

195 In 2002 John Judis and Ruy Teixiera: John B. Judis and Ruy Teixeira, *The Emerging Democratic Majority* (New York: Simon & Schuster, 2002).

195 By 2008, 5 million more voters: "Non-Hispanic Whites (66 percent) and Blacks (65 percent) had the highest levels of voter turnout in the 2008 election. Voting rates for Asians and Hispanics were not statistically different from one another at about 49 percent." Thom File and Sarah Crissey, "Voting and Registration in the Election of 2008," *Current Population Reports*, U.S. Census Bureau (2012), 2.

195 In the dozen years after 2000: Thom File, "The Diversifying Electorate: Voting Rates by Race and Hispanic Origin in 2012 (and Other Recent Elections)," U.S. Census Bureau, *Current Population Reports*, 2013, 5.

195 To assemble two electoral vote majorities: See an analysis by Bill Clinton's 1992 pollster, Stanley Greenberg, *Middle Class Dreams: The Politics and Power of the New American Majority* (New Haven: Yale University Press, 1996).

196 first Democrat to win a majority of the popular vote: "Inside Obama's Sweeping Victory," Pew Research Center, November 5, 2008, http://www.pewresearch.org/2008/11/05/inside-obamas-sweeping-victory/.

196 Demographic panic: A point made by Frank Wilkinson, "Why Voter Suppression Is Mostly a Republican Tactic," Bloomberg, November 5, 2012, http://www.bloombergview.com/articles/2012-11-05/why-voter-suppression-is-mostly-a-republican-tactic.

196 in three decades whites would no longer be the majority: William H. Frey, "New Projections Point to a Majority Minority Nation in 2044," Brookings Institution, December 12, 2014.

196 a party that seeks to restrict turnout: Jonathan Chait, "2012 or Never," *New York Magazine*, February 26, 2012.

196 the proposal was only three pages long: Andrew Ross Sorkin, *Too Big to Fail:*

The Inside Story of How Wall Street and Washington Fought to Save the Financial System—and Themselves (New York: Viking, 2009), 465–66.

196 One poll showed that *most* Republican voters: "ACORN," Public Policy Polling, November 19, 2009, http://publicpolicypolling.blogspot.com/2009/11/acorn.html.

196 "registering the poor to vote": Matthew Vadum, "Registering the Poor to Vote Is Un-American," *American Thinker*, September 1, 2011.

196 "There was a time in American history": Peter Beinart, "Should the Poor Be Allowed to Vote?," *Atlantic*, October 22, 2014.

197 "I've had some radical ideas": Daniel Strauss, "GOPer Suggested Voting Should Be Limited to Property Owners (Video)," TalkingPointsMemo, May 20, 2014, http://talkingpointsmemo.com/livewire/ted-yoho-voting-property-owners.

197 "And that makes a lot of sense": Zaid Jilani, "Tea Party Nation President Says It 'Makes a Lot of Sense' to Restrict Voting Only to Property Owners," ThinkProgress, November 30, 2010, http://thinkprogress.org/politics/2010/11/30/132532/tea-party-voting-property/.

197 some political leaders began to assail the Seventeenth Amendment: See Alex Seitz-Wald, "Repeal the 17th Amendment!," Salon.com. August 16, 2012, http://www.salon.com/2012/08/16/repeal_the_17th_amendment/. An impassioned conservative case is Todd Zywicki, "Repeal the Seventeenth Amendment," *National Review*, November 15, 2010, http://www.nationalreview.com/article/252825/repeal-seventeenth-amendment-todd-zywicki. His earlier work includes "Beyond the Shell and Husk of History: The History of the 17th Amendment and Its Implications for Current Reform Proposals," *Cleveland State Law Review* 45 (1997): 165, http://engagedscholarship.csuohio.edu/clevestlrev/vol45/iss2/3.

197 Progressives "favoring centralization": Rick Perry, *Fed Up! Our Fight to Save America from Washington* (Boston: Little, Brown, 2010), 43.

197 Mike Lee of Utah: He spoke as a candidate for the Senate on CNN. Charles Riley, "Repeal 17th Amendment?," CNN.com, July 10, 2010, http://politicalticker.blogs.cnn.com/2010/07/10/repeal-17th-amendment/.

197 Scalia declared the original Constitution "providential": Associated Press, "Scalia, Breyer Spar Over Supreme Court Issues," November 12, 2010.

198 "Prior to the 17th Amendment": Amanda Terkel, "Ted Cruz to ALEC: 'Stand Your Ground' Against Dick Durbin," *Huffington Post*, December 5, 2013, http://www.huffingtonpost.com/2013/12/05/ted-cruz-alec_n_4392721.html?utm_hp_ref=tw.

198 The emerging Democratic majority in presidential contests: Drew Desilver, "Voter Turnout Always Drops Off for Midterm Elections, but Why?," Pew Research Center, July 24, 2014, http://www.pewresearch.org/fact-tank/2014/07/24/voter-turnout-always-drops-off-for-midterm-elections-but-why/.

198 unified control of legislatures in twenty-five states: National Conference of State Legislatures, "2010 Post-Election Party Control of State Legislatures," www.ncsl.org; National Conference of State Legislatures, "2011 State and Legislative Partisan Composition," http://www.ncsl.org/documents/statevote/2010_Legis_and_State_post.pdf.

12: Marching Backward

199 In a raucous session in the legislative chamber: The enactment of the bill is described in Mary Spicuzza, "Legislature Passes Voter ID Bill; Walker to Sign It Wednesday," *Wisconsin State Journal*, May 19, 2011.

200 "common sense reform": James Kelleher, Reuters, "Wisconsin Governor Signs Controversial Voter ID Law," May 25, 2011.

200 Similar scenes: Wendy R. Weiser and Lawrence Norden, *Voting Law Changes in 2012*, Brennan Center for Justice, 2011, 4–6.

200 nineteen states passed twenty-five laws: Wendy Weiser and Diana Kasdan, *Voting Law Changes: Election Update*, Brennan Center for Justice, October 28, 2012, http://www.brennancenter.org/sites/default/files/legacy/publications/Voting_Law_Changes_Election_Update.pdf.

200 The laws took many shapes: The full array of legal changes is set out in Weiser and Norden, *Voting Law Changes in 2012*, 2–4, 19–20, 24.

200 "Texas, you know, is a big handgun state": Representative Patricia Harless, quoted in Frederica Schouten, "More States Require ID to Vote," *USA Today*, June 20, 2011, http://usatoday30.usatoday.com/news/nation/2011-06-19-states-require-voter-ID_n.htm.

201 called it "remarkable": National Conference of State Legislatures, "2011 State and Legislative Partisan Composition."

201 A Republican Party strategy was evident: For excellent descriptions of the Republican push for voting laws in 2011, see Jonathan Alter, *The Center Holds: Obama and His Enemies* (New York: Simon & Schuster, 2013), 71–82.

201 Of the eleven states: Wendy R. Weiser, "Voter Suppression: How Bad? (Pretty Bad)," *American Prospect*, Fall 2014, http://prospect.org/article/22-states-wave-new-voting-restrictions-threatens-shift-outcomes-tight-races.

201 "Voting as a liberal": Peter Wallsten, "In States, Parties Clash Over Voting Laws That Would Affect College Students, Others," *Washington Post*, March 8, 2011. The legislator's candid remarks were posted on YouTube, available as "Bill O'Brien Speaking @ Rochester 9/12 Project Part 2."

201 "Voter ID, which is gonna allow": Kelley Cernetich, "Turzai: Voter ID Law Means Romney Can Win PA," *PoliticsPA*, June 25, 2012. Turzai's effusiveness received wide coverage after it was repeated on the local political blog. See, for example, McKenzie Weinger, "Mike Turzai: Voter ID Helps GOP Win State," *Politico*, June 25, 2012.

201 The public broadly supported: In June 2011 the Rasmussen Reports (a conservative-leaning polling firm) showed 75 percent of likely voters agreeing with this question: "Should voters be required to show photo identification such as a driver's license before being allowed to vote?" Some of the support is overstated. For example, a 2014 Rasmussen poll was headlined, "Despite Justice Department Challenges, Most Still Favor Voter ID Laws" (August 20, 2014, http://www.rasmussenreports.com/public_content/politics/general_politics/august_2014/despite_justice_department_challenges_most_still_favor_voter_id_laws). But the question, with which 74 percent of likely U.S. voters surveyed agreed, did not ask about "voter ID laws." It asked, "Should all voters be required to prove their identity before being allowed to vote?" Since that question encompasses a wider range of proof than the narrow state ID laws (e.g., utility bills, student cards, signature matches), many already in the law without controversy, it is hard to draw the conclusion the headline writer did.

201 Under the Help America Vote Act: 42 U.S. Code §15483(b).

201 Michigan required voters: See, for example, Mich. Comp. Laws 168.523(2).

202 In 2011 Rhode Island required voters: R.I. Gen. Laws § 17-19-24.2, 17-19-24.3. See Simon van Zuylen Wood, "Why Did Liberal African-Americans in Rhode Island Help Pass a Voter ID Law?," *New Republic*, February 7, 2012.

202 About 11 percent: That statistic is derived from multiple sources. The most widely cited study is Brennan Center for Justice, "Citizens Without Proof: A Survey of Americans' Possession of Documentary Proof of Citizenship and Photo Identification," November 2006, http://www.brennancenter.org/sites/default/files/legacy/d/download_file_39242.pdf. The study is critiqued in Hans A. von Spakovsky and Alex Ingram, "Without Proof: The Unpersuasive Case Against Voter Identification," Heritage Foundation, August 2011. The Brennan Center responded in Wendy R. Weiser, Keesha Gaskins, and Sundeep Iyer, "'Citizens Without Proof' Stands Strong," Brennan Center for Justice, August 2011. Other studies found a similar rate of eligible voters who lacked a driver's license or other ID. Most relevant, the Carter-Ford Commission on Electoral Reform in 2001 found that between 6 and 11 percent of voting-age citizens lack a driver's license or alternate state-issued photo ID. See, for example, Commission on Federal Election Reform, "Building Confidence in U.S. Elections," September 2005, 73n22, http://www.eac.gov/assets/1/AssetManager/Exhibit%20M.PDF; Carter-Ford Commission on Election Reform, "To Assure Pride and Confidence in the Electoral Process: Task Force Reports to Accompany the Report of the National Commission on Election Reform, No. VI: Verification of Identity," August 2001, http://election2000.stanford.edu/task.force.report.8.2001.pdf.

202 Black voters were nearly three times as likely: American National Election Studies, "Time Series Study," 2012, extrapolated by Vanessa M. Perez, "Americans with Photo ID: A Breakdown of Demographic Characteristics," Project Vote, February 2015, http://www.projectvote.org/wp-content/uploads/2015/06/AMERICANS-WITH-PHOTO-ID-Research-Memo-February-2015.pdf.

202 Birth certificates can cost: Keesha Gaskins and Sundeep Iyer, *The Challenge of Obtaining Voter Identification*, Brennan Center for Justice, July 18, 2012, 14–15.

202 In the most extreme example, it costs $345: Department of Homeland Security, U.S. Citizenship and Immigration Services, "N-565, Application for Replacement Naturalization/Citizenship Documents," http://www.uscis.gov/n-565.

202 By contrast, the poll tax: According to the government's calculator, $1.50 in 1966 is worth $11.03 in 2015 dollars. http://data.bls.gov/cgi-bin/cpicalc.pl.

202 it comes from a federal statute: 3 U.S.C. §1 (2014).

202 "pipelaying": Jack Maskell, *Postponement and Rescheduling of Elections to Federal Office*, CRS No. RL32623 (Washington, DC: Congressional Research Service, 2014), 3.

202 Hence the first Tuesday: See Kevin J. Coleman, Joseph E. Cantor, and Thomas H. Neale, *Presidential Elections in the United States: A Primer*, CRS No. RL30527 (Washington, DC: Congressional Research Service, 2000), 38.

203 In 2006 about one in five voters: "Early Voting Increased in 2008," Pew Research Center, October 26, 2012, http://www.pewresearch.org/daily-number/early-voting-increased-in-2008/.

203 "Souls to the Polls": Michael C. Herron and Daniel A. Smith, "Souls to the Polls: Early Voting in Florida in the Shadow of House Bill 1355," *Election Law Journal* 11, no. 3 (2012), http://blogs.reed.edu/earlyvoting/?attachment_id=1252.

203 119,000 churchgoers were bused: Alter, *The Center Holds*, 78.

203 To write it they recruited: Dara Kam and John Lantigua, "Architect of Felon Voter Purge Behind Florida's New Limits," *Palm Beach Post*, October 28, 2012. In a lawsuit deposition Emmett "Bucky" Mitchell IV confirmed that he wrote the first draft of the law. Mitchell's role in the 2000 felon voting purge was documented by

the U.S. Civil Rights Commission, *Voting Irregularities in Florida During the 2000 Presidential Election*, chapter 5: "The Reality of List Maintenance," http://www.usccr.gov/pubs/vote2000/report/ch5.htm.

203 "marketing ploy": Dara Kam and John Lantigua, "Former Florida GOP Leaders Say Voter Suppression Was Reason They Pushed New Law," *Palm Beach Post*, November 25, 2012.

203 "I was upset": Lucy Morgan, "Jim Greer Denounces Florida Republican Party Officials as Liars, 'Right-Wing Crazies' in Deposition," *Tampa Bay Times*, July 25, 2012.

203 he would go to prison for financial misconduct: See Peter Golenbock, *The Chairman: The Rise and Betrayal of Jim Greer* (Montgomery, AL: NewSouth Books, 2014), 392. In a jailhouse interview Greer told Golenbock, "We can suppress votes if we want. We can eliminate early voting, and why do we do that? Because it's been shown that Republicans vote on Election Day."

203 "I know that the cutting out": Kam and Lantigua, "Former Florida GOP Leaders Say Voter Suppression Was Reason They Pushed New Election Law."

203 "Do you read the stories": Aaron Sharockman, "Think We Have It Tough? In Africa, People Walk up to 300 Miles to Vote, GOP Senator Says," Politifact Florida, May 6, 2011, http://www.politifact.com/florida/statements/2011/may/06/mike-bennett/think-we-have-it-tough-africa-people-walk-300-mile/.

204 by term's end he had restored: Amy Sherman, "Rick Scott Says Charlie Crist Favors Violent Felons Immediately Getting Their Right to Vote Restored," Politifact Florida, October 27, 2014, http://www.politifact.com/florida/statements/2014/oct/27/rick-scott/rick-scott-says-charlie-crist-favors-violent-felon/.

204 repealed Crist's executive actions: See Erika Wood, "Turning Back the Clock in Florida," blog post, Brennan Center for Justice, 2011.

204 "I think it's a privilege": Eric Roper, "Zellers: Voting Is 'Privilege, Not Right,'" *Minneapolis Star Tribune*, April 26, 2011. When the *Star Tribune* pointed out that the Fourteenth, Fifteenth, Nineteenth, Twenty-fourth, and Twenty-sixth Amendments all referenced a right to vote, Zellers issued a correction: "I fully understand it's a right we all have. I probably should have said it a little bit better at that late hour at night."

204 Obama had declined to take public campaign funds: Adam Nagourney and Jeff Zeleny, "Obama Forgoes Public Funds in First for Major Candidate," *New York Times*, June 20, 2008; Shailagh Murray and Perry Bacon Jr., "Obama to Reject Public Funds for Election," *Washington Post*, June 20, 2008.

205 Weiser and Norden calculated: Weiser and Norden, *Voting Law Changes in 2012*.

205 The punchy statistic: Michael Cooper, "New State Rules Raising Hurdles at Voting Booth," *New York Times*, October 2, 2011.

206 In 2004, had only sixty thousand: Ohio Secretary of State, Election Results, President and Vice President, 2004, http://www.sos.state.oh.us/sos/elections/Research/electResultsMain/2004ElectionsResults/04-1102PresVicePres.aspx. Bush received 2,859,768 votes; Kerry received 2,741,167—a difference of 118,601.

206 One and a half million Ohioans voted early: George Mason University professor Michael McDonald compiled the most reliable records on early voting: "2008 November General Election Early Voting," November 4, 2008, U.S. Election Project, http://www.electproject.org/2008_early_vote. See the federal court's ruling in *Obama for America v. Husted*, 697 F.3d 423, 426 (6th Cir. 2012).

206 a sweeping election bill: H.B. 194 and its provisions are described in Lynda J. Jacobsen,

"Am. Sub. H.B. 194, Final Analysis," Ohio Legislative Service Commission, August 2012, http://www.lsc.ohio.gov/analyses129/11-hb194-129.pdf.

206 Democrats gathered more than 300,000 signatures: Devin Dwyer, "Obama Supporters Score Early Victory in Ohio," ABC News, September 30, 2011, http://abcnews.go.com/blogs/politics/2011/09/obama-supporters-score-early-victory-in-ohio.

206 For the first time in the state's history: Joe Guillen, "Ohio House Votes to Repeal Controversial Election Law," Cleveland *Plain Dealer*, May 8, 2012.

206 a federal court reinstated early voting: *Obama for America v. Husted*, 888 F.Supp.2d 897 (S.D. Ohio 2012), *aff'd* 697 F. 3d 423 (6th Cir. 2012).

206 In Florida the League of Women Voters: *See League of Women Voters of Florida v. Browning*, 863 F.Supp.2d 1155, 1157–58 (N.D. Fla. 2012).

207 a "calculated strategy": Fredreka Schouten, "More States Require ID to Vote," *USA Today*, June 20, 2011.

207 Public opinion research: Voting rights groups summarized the research in *Talking about Voting 2012*, Brennan Center for Justice and Advancement Project, 2012, and *How to Talk About Voting 2014: A Toolkit for Advocates*, Brennan Center for Justice and Advancement Project, 2014.

207 A panel of three federal judges: *Texas v. Holder*, 888 F.Supp.2d 113, 144 (D.D.C. 2012).

208 "The Voting Rights Act of 1965 is among the most significant": *South Carolina v. United States*, 898 F.Supp.2d 30, 36–37, 52 (D.D.C. 2012); David Ingram, "South Carolina Voter ID Law Blocked Until 2013," Reuters, October 10, 2012.

208 all but one state charter: For a comprehensive look at state voting rights' constitutional provisions, see Joshua A. Douglas, "The Right to Vote Under State Constitutions," *Vanderbilt Law Review* 67, no. 1 (2014): 89. Forty-nine states have explicit protections for the right to vote; Arizona's constitution protects it implicitly.

208 Courts in Wisconsin and Missouri: In 2006 the Missouri Supreme Court struck down a voter identification law as unconstitutional under the state constitution. *Weinschenk v. State*, 203 S.W.3d 201, 213 (Mo. 2006). Five years later, Governor Jay Nixon vetoed a measure to place a referendum on the ballot in 2012 that would amend the constitution to allow for voter ID. In Wisconsin two trial courts struck down the state's new law, though the state supreme court overturned the rulings. See *League of Women Voters of Wisc. Educ. Network, Inc. v. Walker*, No. 11 CV 4669, 2012 WL 763586 (Wis. Cir. Ct. Mar. 12), *rev'd*, 357 Wis.2d 360 (Wisc. 2014); *Milwaukee Branch of the NAACP v. Walker*, No. 11 CV 5492, 2012 WL 739553 (Wis. Cir. Ct. Mar. 6, 2012), *rev'd*, 357 Wis.2d 469 (Wisc. 2014).

208 "have been no investigations": Jamelle Bouie, "Pennsylvania Admits It: No Voter Fraud Problem," *Washington Post*, July 24, 2012.

208 "long lines, short hours": Amy Worden, "Witnesses: PennDot Can't Handle Voter ID Demands," *Philadelphia Inquirer*, August 2, 2012.

208 the state supreme court quickly reversed him: *Applewhite v. Commonwealth*, No. 330 M.D. 2012 (Pennsylvania Commonwealth Court, Aug. 15, 2012), *vacated*, 617 Pa. 563 (Pa. 2012). In 2014 the Pennsylvania Supreme Court issued a permanent injunction against the law after a two-week trial, in a fifty-page decision: http://www.pacourts.us/assets/files/setting-647/file-3490.pdf?cb=a5ec29.

208 some Philadelphia residents: Author interviews of canvassers for Obama for America, November 3, 2012.

208 Answers to that question: See, for example, Robert S. Erikson and Lorraine C. Minnite, "Modeling Problems in the Voter Identification–Voter Turnout Debate," *Election Law Journal* 8, no. 2 (2009): 85 ("The moral is simple. We should be wary of claims—from all sides of the controversy—regarding turnout effects from voter ID laws. . . . The effects may be there. By all tests there is nothing to suggest otherwise. But the data are not up to the task of making a compelling statistical argument"); Timony Vercellotti and David Anderson, "Voter-Identification Requirements and the Learning Curve," *PS: Political Science and Politics* 42, no. 1 (2009): 117 ("As others have found, the identification requirements did not have a general effect on turnout when taking into account the entire sample of voters").

208 Many factors determine turnout: For a survey of the various studies that paint a muddled picture of whether there is an impact on turnout, see CalTech/MIT Voting Technology Project, "Voting: What Has Changed, What Hasn't, and What Needs to Change," November 2012, http://vote.caltech.edu/sites/default/files/Voting%20Technology%20Report_1_14_2013.pdf.

209 perhaps the most significant study: *Elections: Issues Related to State Voter Identification Laws*, GAO-14-634, Washington, DC, 2014, http://www.gao.gov/assets/670/665966.pdf.

209 The *Washington Post* calculated: Philip Bump, "Voter ID Laws in Kansas and Tennessee Dropped Turnout by Over 100,000 Votes," *Washington Post*, October 9, 2014.

209 by Election Day 2012: United States Election Project, "2012 November General Election Turnout Rates," September 3, 2014, http://www.electproject.org/2012g; United States Election Project, "2012 November General Election Early Voting," November 6, 2012, http://www.electproject.org/2012_early_vote.

209 Tea Party groups that had threatened: The most prominent, a Texas-based organization called True the Vote, proved to have "more bark than bite." See Abby Rapoport, "What's the Truth about True the Vote," *American Prospect*, October 10, 2012, http://prospect.org/article/whats-truth-about-true-vote.

209 The best estimate suggests: See Scott Powers and David Damron, "Analysis: 201,000 in Florida Didn't Vote Because of Long Lines," *Orlando Sentinel*, January 29, 2013; Christopher Famighetti, Amanda Melillo, and Myrna Pérez, *Election Day Long Lines: Resource Allocation*, Brennan Center for Justice, September 15, 2014, https://www.brennancenter.org/sites/default/files/publications/ElectionDayLongLines-ResourceAllocation.pdf.

210 "I want to thank every American": White House, Office of the Press Secretary, "Remarks by the President on Election Night," November 7, 2012.

210 "Our journey is not complete": White House, Office of the Press Secretary, "Inaugural Address by President Barack Obama," January 21, 2013.

210 an elderly voter who had had to wait: White House, Office of the Press Secretary, "Remarks by the President in the State of the Union Address," February 12, 2013; Emily Heil, "State of the Union Guest Desiline Victor, 102, Will Be the Face of Voting Delays at Address," *Washington Post*, February 11, 2013.

211 a compelling blueprint: *The American Voting Experience: Report and Recommendations of the Presidential Commission on Election Administration*, January 2014, www.supportthevoter.gov/.

13: Five to Four

213 "There is almost no political question": Alexis de Tocqueville, *Democracy in America*, abridged ed., trans. Stephen T. Grant (Indianapolis: Hackett, 2000), 123.

214 the Supreme Court unanimously voided: *Thornburgh v. Gingles*, 478 U.S. 30 (1986). For an analysis of the judiciary's recognition of the increasing importance of racially polarized voting, see Samuel Issacharoff, "Polarized Voting and the Political Process: The Transformation of Voting Rights Jurisprudence," *Michigan Law Review* 90 (1992): 1833.

214 The 2008 decision in *District of Columbia v. Heller*: Justice Scalia wrote that the Court's decision did not affect "presumptively lawful" regulations: "Nothing in our opinion should be taken to cast doubt on longstanding prohibitions on the possession of firearms by felons and the mentally ill, or laws forbidding the carrying of firearms in sensitive places such as schools and government buildings, or laws imposing conditions and qualifications on the commercial sale of arms." *District of Columbia v. Heller*, 554 U.S. 570 (2008).

214 But the Court's aggressive moves: See, for example, *National Federation of Independent Business v. Sebelius*, 567 U.S. 519 (2012), in which the Court came within one vote of striking down the Affordable Care Act, the central domestic policy accomplishment of the Democratic Party in the past generation.

214 "Every Chief Justice": Jeffrey Toobin, "The John Roberts Project," *New Yorker*, April 2, 2014.

215 Most recently a bipartisan bill: Bipartisan Campaign Reform Act of 2002, Public Law, 107-155.

215 Judges did not even view campaign contribution limits: See Mutch, *Campaigns, Congress, and Courts*, 53–80.

215 campaign cash was a constant presence: For a general narrative of the campaign finance scandal that overlapped with Watergate, see J. Anthony Lukas, *Nightmare: The Underside of the Nixon Years* (New York: Viking, 1976), 108–45.

215 "more loophole than law": Lyndon B. Johnson, "Statement by the President upon Signing the Foreign Investors Tax Act and the Presidential Election Fund Act," November 13, 1966, The American Presidency Project, http://www.presidency.ucsb.edu/ws/?pid=28030.

216 New York Yankees owner: Stanley I. Kutler, *The Wars of Watergate: The Last Crisis of Richard Nixon* (New York: Knopf, 1990), 435. Steinbrenner was suspended from baseball for two years. According to Kutler, a player guilty of manslaughter was not similarly suspended; his crime occurred during the off-season.

216 "Money is speech": *Buckley v. Valeo*, transcript of argument, November 10, 1975, 24.

216 "A restriction on the amount of money": *Buckley v. Valeo*, 424 U.S. 1, 16–19, 24–59 (1976). For a full critique of Buckley, see E. Joshua Rosenkranz, *Buckley Stops Here: Loosening the Judicial Stranglehold on Campaign Finance* (New York: Century Foundation Press, 1998); E. Joshua Rosenkranz, ed., *If Buckley Fell: A First Amendment Blueprint for Regulating Money in Politics* (New York: Century Foundation, 1999).

217 "There are many illegal ways": *Buckley v. Valeo*, 424 U.S. at 265 (White, J., concurring in part, dissenting in part).

217 The Supreme Court upheld most: See, for example, *Austin v. Michigan Chamber of Commerce*, 494 U.S. 652 (1990) (upholding ban on using corporate treasury funds

for independent expenditures on political campaigns); *Nixon v. Shrink Missouri Government PAC*, 528 U.S. 377 (2000) (*Buckley* applied to state laws); *McConnell v. Federal Election Commission*, 540 U.S. 93 (2003) (upholding the McCain-Feingold law, the Bipartisan Campaign Reform Act).

217 it applied *Buckley*'s already implausible distinctions: In a confusing pair of cases, known as *Colorado I* and *II*, the Court upheld limits on spending by parties on behalf of their candidates. In the first case, it allowed the spending because it was supposedly done without coordination with the candidates. This was intrinsically a baffling notion: How could party committees, which exist to back office seekers, spend independently of their own candidates? In the second case, the Court upheld the constitutionality of limits on coordinated spending. *Colorado Republican Federal Campaign Comm. v. Federal Election Comm'n*, 518 U.S. 604 (1996) (*Colorado I*); *Federal Election Commission v. Colorado Republican Federal Campaign Commission*, 533 U.S. 431 (2001) (*Colorado II*).

218 Senator Mitch McConnell of Kentucky: Eric Lichtblau, "Long Battle by Foes of Campaign Finance Rules Shifts Landscape," *New York Times*, October 15, 2010.

218 "long term ideological warfare": Ibid.

218 McConnell's band began to win cases: Initial Supreme Court wins include *Federal Election Commission v. Wisconsin Right to Life, Inc.*, 551 U.S. 449 (2007) (allowing corporations to spend to run ads up to Election Day, so long as the ads do not explicitly call for the defeat or election of a candidate); *Davis v. Federal Election Commission*, 554 U.S. 724 (2008), which struck down a provision giving candidates the ability to raise larger sums if they are faced with a free-spending opponent (the "millionaires amendment"). For a discussion of how *Citizens United* extended the logic of *Wisconsin Right to Life*, see Heather K. Gerken, "The Borden Lecture: The Real Problem with *Citizens United*: Campaign Finance, Dark Money, and Shadow Parties," *Marquette Law Review* 97 (2014): 903. An earlier case, *Randall v. Sorrell*, 548 U.S. 230 (2006), invalidated Vermont's campaign finance law, which had imposed mandatory spending limits. That decision was no surprise, since in effect it merely reiterated *Buckley*.

218 "Enough is enough": *Wisconsin Right to Life*, 551 U.S. 449.

219 the government's lawyer made an agonizing mistake: Transcript of argument, *Citizens United v. Federal Election Commission*, March 24, 2009, 27–30.

219 They asked for a second round: According to Jeffrey Toobin, Chief Justice Roberts originally wrote an opinion ruling against the government on narrow grounds. Four other justices wrote a concurrence saying they wanted to strike down campaign finance laws. Roberts switched to join them. The Court would have issued its revolutionary ruling without even a hearing on the arguments. Justice David Souter was so outraged, Toobin reports, that he planned to reveal the backstage machinations in his draft dissent. In a bargain Souter withdrew his dissent (he was retiring), and the Court requested a second hearing on the case. Jeffrey Toobin, *The Oath: The Obama White House and the Supreme Court* (New York: Anchor Books, 2012), 158–69.

219 The opinion upended doctrine: Some defenders of *Citizens United* deny that it upended a century of law. They assert that the decision merely struck down the Supreme Court's *Austin* case, which was seen as an outlier, at odds with *Buckley*'s protection of independent spending. The Tillman Act, they argue, deals with direct contributions from corporations, which can still be banned, not independent spending. See, for example, Ilya Shapiro, "To Fix Our Campaign Finance

System, Liberalize Political Speech," testimony before the Subcommittee on the Constitution, Civil Rights and Human Rights, Committee on the Judiciary, U.S. Senate, July 24, 2010, www.cato.org. But the concept of direct or independent spending was not in use at the turn of the twentieth century. At that time the language was assumed to encompass both. It was clarified and reinforced later, in the 1947 Taft-Hartley Act, not overturned by that second law.

219 The ban on corporate spending: "a money contribution in connection with any election to any political office." Tillman Act, Pub. L. No. 59–36, 34 Stat. 864, 865 (1907) (codified as amended at 2 U.S.C. § 441b(a) (2006)). One Supreme Court case, *First National Bank of Boston v. Bellotti*, 435 U.S. 765 (1978), struck down an outright ban on corporate contributions to state ballot initiative campaigns. That was a narrow ruling, though, that was never extended to candidate races or federal elections. In *Austin* and *McConnell*, the Supreme Court reaffirmed the differential treatment of contributions and spending between corporations and natural persons.

220 Every time it has passed a law on the subject: Congress extended the ban to labor unions in the Taft-Hartley Act and reiterated that it included independent expenditures as well as direct spending. 18 U.S.C. § 610. The Supreme Court recognized this in *U.S. v. International Union United Automobile, Aircraft and Agricultural Implement Workers of America (UAW-CIO)*, 352 U.S. 567 (1957).

220 "The censorship we now confront": *Citizens United v. Federal Election Commission*, 558 U.S. 310, 354 (2010).

220 "While American democracy is imperfect": *Citizens United v. Federal Election Commission*, 557 U.S. at 479 (Stevens, J., dissenting).

220 "corporations are people": Philip Rucker, "Mitt Romney Says 'Corporations Are People,'" *Washington Post*, August 11, 2011.

220 In 2010 Exxon had profits: See Michael Waldman, "Bigger Than *Bush v. Gore*," *New York Times*, January 21, 2010.

220 A lower court struck down: *SpeechNow.org v. Federal Election Commission*, 599 F.3d 686, 689 (D.C. Cir. 2010) (en banc).

220 "With all due deference": White House, Office of the Press Secretary, "Remarks by the President on the State of the Union," January 27, 2010.

221 "Not true": "Alito Mouths 'Not True' as Obama Criticizes Sup Ct for Opening Floodgates to Special Interests," https://www.youtube.com/watch?v=4pB5uR3zgsA.

221 The amount of independent spending exploded: Daniel I. Weiner, *Citizens United Five Years Later*, Brennan Center for Justice, January 2015.

221 In the five years after *Citizens United:* Center for Responsive Politics, "Outside Spending by Disclosure, Excluding Party Committees," https://www.opensecrets.org/outsidespending/disclosure.php.

221 "Who you gonna believe": The line is usually misattributed to Groucho Marx. In the scene Chico is disguised as Groucho, so confusion is understandable.

221 Crossroads GPS: Kim Barker, "New Tax Return Shows Karl Rove's Group Spent Even More on Politics Than It Said," ProPublica, November 25, 2013, http://www.propublica.org/article/new-tax-return-shows-karl-roves-group-spent-more-on-politics-than-it-said.

221 Of the $180 million it raised: Kim Barker, "Crossroads' Tax Returns Shows Big Donors, But Doesn't Name Them," ProPublica, November 18, 2013, http://www.propublica.org/article/crossroads-tax-return-shows-big-donors-but-doesnt-name-them. The group's tax form is available from the Internal Revenue Service.

222 billionaires seeming to sponsor: For a full discussion, see "Brief of *Amici Curiae* the Brennan Center for Justice and Constitutional Law Professors in Support of Respondents," *American Tradition Partnership, Inc. v. Bullock,* March 18, 2012.

222 In the most widely publicized example: Aaron Blake, "Adelsons Give Gingrich Super PAC Another $5 Million," *Washington Post*, April 23, 2012.

222 By Election Day Adelson and his wife: Theodoric Meyer, "How Much Did Sheldon Adelson Really Spend on Campaign 2012?," Pro Publica, December 20, 2012, http://www.propublica.org/article/how-much-did-sheldon-adelson-really-spend-on-campaign-2012.

222 Candidates took to attending fundraisers: Andy Kroll, "The Candidates and the Totally Unrelated Super PACs Who Love Them," *Mother Jones*, January 20, 2012, http://www.motherjones.com/mojo/2012/01/stephen-colbert-citizens-united-super-pac.

222 "no idea": Jackie Koszczuk, "Super PAC? What Super PAC?," *National Journal*, February 9, 2012, http://decoded.nationaljournal.com/2012/02/campaign-2012-weve-memorized-t.php.

222 Environmentalist Tom Steyer: Zach C. Cohen, "Meet the Nine Biggest Super PAC Bankrollers," *National Journal*, December 22, 2014.

222 Former New York mayor Michael Bloomberg: Kenneth R. Vogel, "Big Money Breaks Out," *Politico*, December 29, 2014.

222 "occupied territories": Kenneth R. Vogel, "Chris Christie Apologizes for 'Occupied Territories' Remark," *Politico*, March 29, 2014.

223 "Telling it like it is": www.chrischristie.com, accessed July 11, 2015.

223 "Well, I checked": Transcript of argument, *Arizona Free Enterprise Club's Freedom PAC v. Bennett*, March 28, 2011, http://www.supremecourt.gov/oral_arguments/argument_transcripts/10-238.pdf.

223 A coal mining business owner: Ben Jacobs, "Meet Shaun McCutcheon, the Republican Activist Trying to Make History at the Supreme Court," *Daily Beast*, October 8, 2013.

223 "Ingratiation and access": *McCutcheon v. Federal Election Commission*, 572 U.S. 185 (2014).

224 "fanciful" to think: Transcript of arguments, *McCutcheon v. Federal Election Commission*, October 8, 2013, 51–53.

224 who style themselves "realists": See, for example, Jonathan Rauch, *Political Realism: How Hacks, Machines, Big Money, and Back-Room Deals Can Strengthen American Democracy* (Washington, DC: Brookings Institution Press, 2015).

225 Just fifty individuals and spouses: Center for Responsive Politics, "2014 Outside Spending, by Super PAC," https://www.opensecrets.org/outsidespending/summ.php?chrt=V&type=S, accessed November 17, 2014; Center for Responsive Politics, "Top Individual Contributors to Super PACs," https://www.opensecrets.org/overview/topindivs.php?view=sp&type=src, accessed November 17, 2014; Karen Shanton and Adam Lioz, "The Dominance of Big Money in the 2014 Congressional Elections," Demos, November 20, 2014, http://www.demos.org/publication/dominance-big-money-2014-congressional-elections.

225 "In 2014, the top one hundred donors": Vogel, "Big Money Breaks Out."

226 "my contribution to modern art": John Jacobs, *A Rage for Justice: The Passion and Politics of Phillip Burton* (Berkeley: University of California Press, 1997), 435.

226 Burton would assess what kinds of cars: Juliet Eilperin, *Fight Club Politics: How*

Partisanship Is Ruining the House of Representatives (Lanham, MD: Rowan & Littlefield, 2007), 92.

226 Republican officials allied with the Congressional Black Caucus: The GOP partnership with Black politicians is described in Ari Berman, *Give Us the Ballot: The Modern Struggle for Voting Rights in America* (New York: Farrar, Straus & Giroux, 2015), 183–94. See also Richard L. Berke, "G.O.P. Tries a Gambit with Voting Rights," *New York Times*, April 14, 1991; Thomas B. Edsall, "GOP Goal: Gain Ground by Fostering 'Majority Minority' Districts," *Washington Post*, July 7, 1990.

226 Fairness for the 90s: Thomas Byrne Edsall and Mary D. Edsall, *Chain Reaction: The Impact of Race, Rights, and Taxes on American Politics* (New York: Norton, 1992), 270.

226 By the redistricting cycles that followed: I describe this period in Michael Waldman, *A Return to Common Sense: Seven Bold Ideas to Revitalize Democracy* (Naperville, IL: Sourcebooks, 2007), 89–94.

226 "political cartel": Samuel Issacharoff, "Gerrymandering and Political Cartels," *Harvard Law Review* 116 (2002): 593.

226 In 2002 eighty-one members of Congress: Jeffrey Toobin, "The Great Election Grab," *New Yorker*, December 8, 2003.

226 In 2004, when the incumbent president: Thomas E. Mann, "Redistricting Reform," *National Voter*, June 2005, 4.

227 "You could say about this district": "How to Rig an Election," *Economist*, April 24, 2002.

227 DeLay flew home to oversee: R. Jeffrey Smith, "DeLay's Corporate Fundraising Investigated," *Washington Post*, July 12, 2004.

227 holed up at the Holiday Inn: See Jeffrey Toobin, "Drawing the Line: Will Tom DeLay's Redistricting in Texas Cost Him His Seat?," *New Yorker*, March 6, 2006.

227 he was indicted and convicted: Associated Press, "Texas Appeals Court Upholds Reversal of Tom DeLay's Money-Laundering Convictions," *Dallas Morning News*, October 1, 2014, http://www.dallasnews.com/news/state/headlines/20141001-texas-appeals-court-upholds-delay-reversal.ece.

227 Since *Reynolds v. Sims* and *Baker v. Carr*: Principal cases included *Gaffney v. Cummings*, 412 U.S. 735 (1973); *Davis v. Bandemer*, 478 U.S. 109 (1986); *Vieth v. Jubelirer*, 541 U.S. 267 (2004).

227 "no judicially discernible and manageable standards": *Vieth v. Jubelirer*, 281.

228 Instead the Supreme Court washed its hands: *League of United Latin American Citizens v. Perry*, 548 U.S. 399 (2006).

228 The same tilt happened: "2012 Pennsylvania House Results," "2012 Ohio House Results," "2012 Virginia House Results," and "2012 North Carolina House Results," *Politico*, November 19, 2012.

228 the "Big Sort": See Bill Bishop, *The Big Sort: Why the Clustering of Like-Minded America Is Tearing Us Apart* (New York: Houghton Mifflin, 2008).

229 The Supreme Court repeatedly upheld: *South Carolina v. Katzenbach*, 383 U.S. 301 (1966); *Georgia v. Katzenbach*, 383 U.S. 301, 308 (1966); *City of Rome v. United States*, 446 U.S. 156, 177–78, 183 (1980); *Lopez v. Monterey County*, 525 U.S. 266, 282–85 (1999).

229 Congress reauthorized it: See Fannie Lou Hamer, Rosa Parks, and Coretta Scott King Voting Rights Act Reauthorization and Amendments Act of 2006, 120 Stat. 577; Voting Rights Act Amendments of 1982, 96 Stat. 131; Voting Rights Act Amendments of 1975, 89 Stat. 400; Voting Rights Act Amendments of 1970, 84 Stat. 314.

229 John Lewis, now a U.S. representative: Raymond Hernandez, "After Challenges, House Approves Renewal of Voting Act," *New York Times*, July 14, 2006.

230 Congress heard ample testimony: Spencer Overton, "*Shelby County v. Holder*: Voting Discrimination Remains Concentrated in Covered States," SCOTUSblog, February 14, 2013. The testimony is summarized in the *Brief of Professors Richard Engstrom, Theodore S. Arrington, and David T. Canon as amici curae in support of respondents, Shelby County v. Holder, on writ of certiorari to the United States Court of Appeals*.

230 "By reauthorizing this act": George W. Bush, "Remarks on Signing the Fannie Lou Hamer, Rosa Parks, and Coretta Scott King Voting Rights Act Reauthorization and Amendments Act of 2006, July 27, 2006," *Public Papers of the Presidents: George W. Bush, 2006, Book 2, July 1–December 31, 2006* (Washington, DC: Government Printing Office, 2010), 1448. The president signed Public Law No. 109–246, 120 Stat. 577.

230 "Is it your position": Transcript of argument, *Northwest Austin Municipal Utility District No. 1 v. Holder*, April 29, 2009, 48.

231 "The historical accomplishments": *Northwest Austin Municipal Utility District No. One v. Holder*, 557 U.S. 193, 201, 211 (2009).

232 Do you know which state: Transcript of *Shelby County v. Holder*, February 27, 2013, http://www.supremecourt.gov/oral_arguments/argument_transcripts/12-96.pdf; *Shelby County v. Holder*, 133 S.Ct. 2612, 2619 (2013). Roberts cited Department of Commerce, Census Bureau, "Reported Voting and Registration, by Sex, Race and Hispanic Origin, for States," November 2012, table 4b.

232 "African American voter turnout": *Shelby County v. Holder*. Roberts cited the Department of Commerce, Census Bureau, Reported Voting and Registration, by Sex, Race and Hispanic Origin, for States (Nov. 2012) (Table 4b). The Court also engaged in some creative originalism, citing "the fundamental principle of equal sovereignty" among states. This new-old doctrine held, it seemed, that the federal government had to have an unusually high bar to treat states differently. Previously the Court had ruled that notion "applies only to the terms upon which states are admitted to the Union, and not to the remedies for local evils which have subsequently appeared." *Shelby County*, 570 U.S. 529 (2013) (Ginsburg, J., dissenting) (citing *South Carolina v. Katzenbach*, 383 U.S. 301, 328–29 (1966)). Judge Richard Posner wrote, "[Equal sovereignty] is a principle of constitutional law of which I had never heard—for the excellent reason that . . . there is no such principle." Richard A. Posner, "The Voting Rights Act Ruling Is about the Conservative Imagination," The Breakfast Table, *Slate*, June 25, 2013, http://www.slate.com/articles/ news_and_politics/the_breakfast_table/features/2013/supreme_court_2013/the_supreme_court_and_the_voting_rights_act_striking_down_the_law_is_all.html.

232 "Section Five is the automobile": James Harper, "Panel Urges NAACP to Keep Up Fight for Voting Rights Act," *Houston Forward Times*, July 24, 2013.

233 "Throwing out preclearance": *Shelby County*, 133 S.Ct. at 2650 (Ginsburg, J., dissenting).

233 The U.S. Justice Department promptly sued Texas: The Brennan Center, together with the Lawyers Committee for Civil Rights and the Dechert law firm, represents the Texas NAACP and the state Mexican American Legislative Caucus in these cases. See *Texas NAACP v. Steen* (consolidated with *Veasey v. Perry*), August 5, 2015, http://www.brennancenter.org/legal-work/naacp-v-steen.

234 Vishal Agraharkar: Personal interview. The attorney worked for the Brennan Center for Justice at the time.

235 143 fact-crammed pages: *Veasey v. Perry*.

235 The case joined a confusing jumble: Wisconsin: *Frank v. Walker*, On Application to Vacate Stay, 574 U.S. 929 (2014), October 9, 2014; North Carolina: *North Carolina v. League of Women Voters of North Carolina*, On Application to Recall and Stay, 574 U.S. 927 (2014), October 8, 2014; Ohio: *Husted v. Ohio State Conference of NAACP*, Order in Pending Case, 573 U.S. 988 (2014), September 29, 2014.

235 Before dawn on a Saturday: *Veasey v. Perry*, 135 S.Ct. 9 (Oct. 18, 2014).

235 "The greatest threat to public confidence": *Veasey v. Perry*, 135 S.Ct. 12 (Ginsburg, J., dissent from denial of application to vacate stay).

236 "voter suppression": Posner, *Reflections on Judging*, 85.

236 "Some of the 'evidence'": *Frank v. Walker*, 773 F.3d 783 (7th Cir. 2014) (Posner, J., dissent from denial of rehearing en banc).

237 In the thirty-five years since Reagan's election: Democrats controlled the House throughout Reagan's two terms. From 1987 on, they also held the Senate. Clinton and the Democrats had unified control for two years; in the 1994 election Republicans won both chambers. In 2001 George W. Bush was president, and the GOP held both House and Senate. Later that year Senator James Jeffords of Vermont switched parties, and Democrats fleetingly controlled the upper chamber. Republicans had unified control from 2003 to 2007, the longest modern period of unified government. (The Iraq war was one result.) In 2007 Democrats again took control of both chambers, again facing off against a Republican president. Obama and his party had unified control for two years. In 2010 the GOP won the House, and in 2014, the Senate.

237 latest challenge to the Affordable Care Act: *King v. Burwell*, 576 U.S. 473 (2015).

237 The next day, with a flourish: *Obergefell v. Hodges*, 576 U.S. 644 (2015).

237 one last major ruling: *Arizona Legislature v. Arizona Independent Redistricting Commission*, 576 U.S. 787 (2015).

238 "judicially discernible": *Vieth v. Jubelirer*, 281.

238 In 2010: California Constitution, art. XXI, §§ 1, 2; Prop. 11, adopted November 2008 and Prop. 11, adopted November 2010.

238 That reform was coupled: Proposition 14, Top Two Primary Act, adopted June 2010; codified as California Constitution, art. II, §§ 5 and 6.

238 In Florida liberals won: Fla. Const. art. III, § 20(a-b), § 21(a-b).

239 "participants in the debates": *Arizona Legislature*, 24, 35.

240 the justices declined an appeal: *Kobach v. United States Election Assistance Commission*, 6 F. Supp. 3d 1252 (2015) (7th Circuit) (cert. denied).

14: 2016

242 The Presidential Commission on Election Administration: *The American Voting Experience*, 62.

242 Forty-three states: See Lawrence Norden and Christopher Famighetti, *America's Voting Machines at Risk*, Brennan Center for Justice, September 15, 2015, 4–5, https://www.brennancenter.org/sites/default/files/publications/Americas_Voting_Machines_At_Risk.pdf.

242 nearly half the states: National Conference of State Legislatures, Online Voter

Registration, September 3, 2015, http://www.ncsl.org/research/elections-and-campaigns/electronic-or-online-voter-registration.aspx#table. Moving to an online system cuts costs dramatically. See Matt Baretto et al., *Online Voter Registration (OLVR) Systems in Arizona and Washington: Evaluating Usage, Public Confidence and Implementation Premises,* University of Washington/University of California, 2010, http://www.pewtrusts.org/~/media/legacy/uploadedfiles/pcs_assets/2010/onlinevoterregpdf.pdf.

242 Eight instituted "portable" registration: See the resource page on portable registration, http://www.brennancenter.org/analysis/vrm-states-portability.

242 "Not the rich": Federalist 57, in Hamilton et al., *The Federalist Papers,* 282.

242 The share of national wealth: See Jacob S. Hacker and Paul Pierson, *Winner Take All Politics: How Washington Made the Rich Richer—and Turned Its Back on the Middle Class* (New York: Simon & Schuster, 2009), 13–14.

243 How much would that be worth today: The government's inflation calculator starts in 1913; $48,000 in 1913 would be worth a bit over $1.1 million in 2012. http://data.bls.gov/cgi-bin/cpicalc.pl. The website Measuring Worth calculates the amount as $1.29 million. More expansively, as a share of national wealth, it would have been worth $3,050,000. See Measuring Worth, http://www.measuringworth.com.

243 That year Sheldon Adelson spent: Chris Cillizza, "Sheldon Adelson Spent $93 Million on the 2012 Election: Here's How," *Washington Post,* March 25, 2014, http://www.washingtonpost.com/blogs/the-fix/wp/2014/03/25/sheldon-adelson-spent-93-million-on-the-2012-election-heres-how/. See also Matea Gold, "Koch-Backed Political Network, Built to Shield Donors, Raised $400 Million in 2012 Elections," *Washington Post,* January 5, 2014.

243 Charles and David Koch: Nicholas Confessore, "'16 Koch Budget Is $889 Million," *New York Times,* January 27, 2015; Matea Gold, "Koch-Backed Network Aims to Spend Nearly $1 Billion in Runup to 2016," *Washington Post,* January 26, 2015.

244 Americans spend more on potato chips: George F. Will, "The Democratic Version of Big Brother," *Washington Post,* October 17, 2010.

244 In 2014 little more than one in three: Michael P. McDonald, "2014 November General Election Turnout Rates," United States Election Project, accessed July 2015, http://www.electproject.org/2014g. See Jose A. DelReal, "Voter Turnout in 2014 Was the Lowest Since WWII," *Washington Post,* November 10, 2014.

244 In California, Texas, New York: McDonald, "2014 November General Election Turnout Rates." The states were Alabama, California, Indiana, Nevada, New Jersey, New York, Oklahoma, Tennessee, Texas, and Utah.

244 Georgia and North Carolina: See "The Worst Voter Turnout in 72 Years," *New York Times,* November 11, 2014, for a thorough analysis of regional and other patterns.

244 As political scientists: See Norman Ornstein and Thomas E. Mann, *The Broken Branch: How Congress Is Failing America, and How to Get It Back on Track* (New York: Oxford University Press, 2006) and *It's Even Worse Than It Looks: How the American Constitutional System Collided with the New Politics of Extremism* (New York: Basic Books, 2012).

245 Recently political scientists have documented the skew: Studies documenting the broad impact of economic inequality and campaign money on policymaking are summarized by two leading proponents of that view, Martin Gilens and Benjamin I. Page, "Testing Theories of American Politics: Elites, Interest Groups,

and Average Citizens," *Perspectives on Politics (American Political Science Association)* 12, no. 3 (2014): 565, http://journals.cambridge.org/download.php?file=%2FPPS%2FPPS12_03%2FS1537592714001595a.pdf&code=97d111b3c1871ff390aecae20ceafeb1. Full-length works include Larry M. Bartels, *Unequal Democracy: The Political Economy of the New Gilded Age* (New York: Russell Sage Foundation and Princeton University Press, 2008); Martin Gilens, *Affluence and Influence: Economic Inequality and Political Power in America* (Princeton: Russell Sage, Princeton University Press, 2012); and Hacker and Pierson, *Winner Take All Politics*.

245 "Make no little plans": Charles Moore, *Daniel Burnham: Architect and Planner of Cities* (Boston: Houghton Mifflin, 1928), 147.

246 Great Britain, Canada, Germany: Rosenberg and Chen, *Expanding Democracy*.

246 The Brennan Center: See Wendy Weiser, Michael Waldman, and Renée Paradis, *Universal Voter Registration: Draft Proposal*, Brennan Center for Justice, 2007; see also Waldman, *A Return to Common Sense*, 11–16. The proposal was updated as Wendy Weiser, Michael Waldman, and Renée Paradis, *Voter Registration Modernization: Policy Summary*, Brennan Center for Justice, 2009. See also Heather K. Gerken, "Make It Easy: The Case for Automatic Registration," *Democracy* 28 (Spring 2013): 17–21.

246 Under the new Oregon law: Oregon's new automatic registration system, enacted as H.B. 2177, 78th Leg. Assemb., Reg. Sess. (Or. 2015) (enacted), is codified at Oregon Revised Statutes sec. 247.017 (2015).

247 "Registering to vote should be": Paul Walsh, "Pawlenty Vetoes Motor Voter Registration Bill," Minneapolis *Star Tribune*, May 22, 2009, http://www.startribune.com/pawlenty-vetoes-motor-voter-registration-bill/45841627/.

247 Senator Rand Paul: Benjamin Goad, "Paul Drafts Bill to Restore Voting Rights for Ex-Cons," *The Hill*, February 11, 2014.

247 Proposals to restore: Sponsors would apply the VRA's Section 5 nationwide, with a set of criteria for which states had repeatedly violated voting rights in the past. See, e.g., Voting Rights Advancement Act of 2015, S. 1659, 114th Cong., 1st sess.; Voting Rights Amendment Act of 2014, H.R. 3899, 113th Cong., 2nd sess.

247 Five times in the country's history: Five men became president despite losing the popular vote: John Quincy Adams (1824), Rutherford B. Hayes (1876), Benjamin Harrison (1888), George W. Bush (2000), and Donald Trump (2016).

248 In 2012 the Romney and Obama campaigns spent $463 million: Fair Vote, "Presidential Tracker," http://www.fairvote.org/research-and-analysis/presidential-elections/presidential-tracker/, accessed July 10, 2015. A similar analysis for 2008 is Fair Vote, "Presidential Elections Inequality: The Electoral College in the 21st Century," http://archive.fairvote.org/?page=1729.

248 National Popular Vote: The interstate compact is explained in Hendrik Hertzberg, "National Popular Vote: New York State Climbs Aboard," *New Yorker* (Daily Comment), April 16, 2014, http://www.newyorker.com/news/daily-comment/national-popular-vote-new-york-state-climbs-aboard.

248 Republican lawmakers have toyed with the idea: Dave Wiegel, "Electoral College Rigging Bill Makes Comeback in Michigan," *Bloomberg News*, March 10, 2015, http://www.bloomberg.com/politics/articles/2015-03-10/electoral-college-rigging-bill-makes-comeback-in-michigan.

248 election integrity: See Myrna Pérez, *Election Integrity: A Pro-Voter Agenda*, Brennan Center for Justice, December 2015.

249 Special Counsel Robert Mueller: U.S. Department of Justice, *Report On The Investigation Into Russian Interference In The 2016 Presidential Election, Vol. II of II*, Special Counsel Robert E. Mueller III, Submitted Pursuant to 28 C.F.R. § 600.8(c), 2019, 14-33, https://www.justice.gov/archives/sco/file/1373816/download. See also *Russian Active Measures Campaigns and Interference in the 2016 U.S. Election, Volume 1: Russian Efforts against Election Infrastructure With Additional Views*, Select Committee on Intelligence, U.S. Senate, 116th Congress, 1st Session, Senate Report 116-XX (2019), https://www.intelligence.senate.gov/sites/default/files/documents/Report_Volume1.pdf.

249 There is no evidence: Lawrence Norden and Ian Vanderwalker, *Securing Elections From Foreign Interference*, Brennan Center for Justice (2017), https://www.brennancenter.org/sites/default/files/publications/Securing_Elections_From_Foreign_Interference_1.pdf.

249 An entire office building: Neil MacFarquhar, "Inside the Russian Troll Factory: Zombies and a Breakneck Pace," *New York Times*, February 18, 2018; "The Mueller Report Exposed Weaknesses in U.S. Democratic Institutions that H.R. 1 Would Address," Brennan Center for Justice, July 10, 2019, https://www.brennancenter.org/our-work/research-reports/mueller-report-exposed-weaknesses-us-democratic-institutions-hr-1-would.

249 "community of Second Amendment": Colin Lecher, "Here Are the Russia-Linked Facebook Ads Released by Congress," The Verge, November 1, 2017, https://www.theverge.com/2017/11/1/16593346/house-russia-facebook-ads; U.S. House of Representatives, Permanent Select Committee on Intelligence, HPSCI Minority Open Hearing Exhibits (accessed August 31, 2021), https://intelligence.house.gov/hpsci-11-1/hpsci-minority-open-hearing-exhibits.htm.

249 purchased using rubles: Harper Neidig, "Franken blasts Facebook for accepting rubles for U.S. election ads," *The Hill*, October 31, 2017.

249 single most important: For a general discussion, see Michael Miller, *Subsidizing Democracy: How Public Funding Changes Elections and How It Can Work in the Future* (Ithaca: Cornell University Press, 2013).

250 The Supreme Court made it harder in 2011: *Arizona Free Enterprise Club's Freedom Club PAC et al. v. Bennett*, 131 S. Ct. 2806 (2011).

250 An advanced version: Michael J. Malbin, Peter W. Brusoe, and Brendan Glavin, "Small Donors, Big Democracy: New York City's Matching Funds as a Model for the Nation and States," *Election Law Journal* 11, no. 1 (2012): 3.

250 Mayor Michael Bloomberg still spent over $266 million: In 2001, to win election the first time, Bloomberg spent $73.9 million. In 2005 he spent $84.6 million. In 2009 he spent $108.4 million. See New York City Campaign Finance Board, Campaign Finance Summary, 2009 Citywide Elections, http://www.nyccfb.info/VSApps/WebForm_Finance_Summary.aspx?as_election_cycle=2009. See also Frank Lombardi, "Bloomberg's Campaign Tab: $108,371,685.01. Getting Re-elected to a Third Term as NYC Mayor? Priceless," *New York Daily News*, January 15, 2010, http://www.nydailynews.com/news/bloomberg-campaign-tab-108-371-685-01-relected-term-nyc-mayor-priceless-article-1.460319.

15: The 2020 Election

253 the 2014 midterm: United States Election Project. See also, Editorial, "The Worst Voter Turnout in 72 Years," *New York Times*, November 11, 2014.

253 midterm turnout soared: Emily Stewart, "2018's record-setting voter turnout, in one chart," Vox, November 19, 2018, https://www.vox.com/policy-and-politics/2018/11/19/18103110/2018-midterm-elections-turnout.

253 problems with voting machines: On long lines and their racial dimension, see Hannah Klain, Kevin Morris, Max Feldman, and Rebecca Ayala, *Waiting to Vote* Brennan Center for Justice, June 2020, https://www.brennancenter.org/our-work/research-reports/waiting-vote. On voter purges, see Jonathan Brater, Kevin Morris, Myrna Pérez, and Christopher Deluzio, *Purges: A Growing Threat to the Right to Vote*, Brennan Center for Justice, July 20, 2018, https://www.brennancenter.org/our-work/research-reports/purges-growing-threat-right-vote, and Kevin Morris, "Voter Purges Remain High," Brennan Center for Justice, August 21, 2019, https://www.brennancenter.org/our-work/analysis-opinion/voter-purge-rates-remain-high-analysis-finds. On threats of Russian hacking, see Lawrence Norden and Andrea Córdova McCadney, *Voting Machines at Risk: Where We Stand Today*, Brennan Center for Justice, March 6, 2019, https://www.brennancenter.org/our-work/research-reports/voting-machines-risk-where-we-stand-today, and Christopher R. Deluzio, Liz Howard, Paul Rosenzweig, David Salvo, and Rachael Dean Wilson, *Defending Elections Federal Funding Needs for State Election Security*, Brennan Center for Justice, Pitt Cyber, Alliance for Securing Democracy, and R Street Institute, July 18, 2019, https://www.brennancenter.org/sites/default/files/2019-08/Report_Defending_Elections.pdf.

253 In January: Dr. Annie Fine, personal conversation, January 28, 2020.

254 Nearly a million people: Alison Dirr and Mary Spicuzza, "What we know so far about why Milwaukee only had 5 voting sites for Tuesday's election while Madison had 66," *Milwaukee Journal-Sentinel*, April 9, 2020; Nick Corasaniti and Stephanie Saul, "Inside Wisconsin's Election Mess: Thousands of Missing or Nullified Ballots," *New York Times*, April 9, 2020; Kevin Morris, *Did Consolidating Polling Places in Milwaukee Depress Turnout?*, Brennan Center for Justice, June 24, 2020, https://www.brennancenter.org/our-work/research-reports/did-consolidating-polling-places-milwaukee-depress-turnout.

254 "You are incredibly safe": Kate Sullivan, "Republican Wisconsin assembly speaker wears protective gear while telling voters they are 'incredibly safe to go out,'" CNN, April 7, 2020, https://www.cnn.com/2020/04/07/politics/wisconsin-robin-vos-protective-gear/index.html.

254 Brennan Center for Justice published a plan: Wendy Weiser and Max Feldman, *How to Protect the 2020 Vote from the Coronavirus*, Brennan Center for Justice, March 16, 2020, https://www.brennancenter.org/our-work/policy-solutions/how-protect-2020-vote-coronavirus; Michael Waldman and Wendy Weiser, "What effect will coronavirus have on Tuesday's primaries," *Los Angeles Times*, March 14, 2020.

254 $4 billion: Lawrence Norden, Edgardo Cortés, Elizabeth Howard, Derek Tisler, Gowri Ramachandran, *Estimated Costs of Covid-19 Election Resiliency Measures*, Brennan Center for Justice, April 18, 2020, https://www.brennancenter.org/our-work/research-reports/estimated-costs-covid-19-election-resiliency-measures.

255 computer barcodes: Lisa Danetz, "Mail ballot security features," Brennan Center for Justice, October 16, 2020, https://www.brennancenter.org/our-work/research-reports/mail-ballot-security-features-primer. Security steps include sealed envelopes, a second "security" envelope, and secure drop-boxes. See also Wendy Weiser, "The False Narrative of Vote by Mail Fraud," Brennan Center

for Justice, April 10, 2020, https://www.brennancenter.org/our-work/analysis-opinion/false-narrative-vote-mail-fraud. The first edition of this book expressed worry that absentee balloting could be a source of fraud. However, its widespread use without significant problems—coupled with the new steps taken—allays that earlier concern.

256 $2 trillion spending bill: *Coronavirus Aid, Relief, and Economic Security Act (CARES) Act*, Public Law 116-136, 2020.

256 It was not enough: U.S. Election Assistance Commission, *CARES Grant Funding Chart*, July 22, 2020, https://www.eac.gov/sites/default/files/paymentgrants/cares/FundingChart_CARES.pdf.

256 most states made it easier: Wendy Weiser, Eliza Sweren-Becker, Dominique Erney, and Anne Glatz, *Mail Voting: What Has Changed in 2020,* Brennan Center for Justice, September 17, 2020, https://www.brennancenter.org/our-work/research-reports/mail-voting-what-has-changed-2020.

256 only Texas, Louisiana: Kate Rabinowitz and Brittany Renee Mayes, "At least 84% of American voters can cast ballots by mail in the fall," *Washington Post*, September 24, 2020.

256 "to save the union": "Memorandum on Probable Failure of Reelection, Executive Mansion, Washington, D.C., August 23, 1864," in Fehrenbacher, *Lincoln: Speeches and Writings, 1859–1865*, 624.

256 "But the election": "Response to Serenade, November 10, 1864," ibid., 641.

257 In 1918: For a summary of how the Spanish Flu affected the midterm election, see Bo Erikson, "Voting during a pandemic? Here's what happened in 1918," CBS News, April 7, 2020, https://www.cbsnews.com/news/spanish-flu-pandemic-1918-voting/.

257 Health officials in D.C.: "Washington, D.C.," American Influenza Epidemic of 1918–1919: A Digital Encyclopedia, http://www.influenzaarchive.org., accessed July 5, 2021.

257 In San Francisco: "San Francisco," American Influenza Epidemic of 1918–1919: A Digital Encyclopedia, http://www.influenzaarchive.org, accessed July 5, 2021.

257 "in most places": Jason Marisam, "Judging the 1918 Election," *Election Law Journal: Rules, Politics, and Policy,* June 2010, 141–152, http://doi.org/10.1089/elj.2009.0052.

257 The flu changed political practices: Writing about 1918, one prescient columnist predicted early in the 2020 pandemic, "It was a preview of the campaign that may be in our future, where coronavirus task force briefings replace MAGA rallies and Joe Biden addresses a virtual Democratic National Convention from his rec room." Matthew Continetti, "The Second Masked Ballot," *Washington Free Beacon*, April 10, 2020, https://freebeacon.com/columns/the-second-masked-ballot/.

257 Eventually, at least 2.6 million: Soldier's Vote Act (Armed Forces Absentee Voting Act), ch. 561, 56 Stat. 753 § 2 (1942) (repealed 1955); R. Michael Alvarez, Thad E. Hall, and Brian F. Roberts, Military Voting and the Law: Procedural and Technological Solutions to the Ballot Transit Problem, 34 *Fordham Urban Law Journal* 935 (2007), https://ir.lawnet.fordham.edu/ulj/vol34/iss3/3.

258 "the actions of terrorists": U.S. Congress, House, "Expressing the sense of the House of Representatives that the actions of terrorists will never cause the date of any Presidential election to be postponed and that no single individual or agency

should be given the authority to postpone the date of a Presidential election," H. Res. 728, 108th Congress, 2nd Session, July 22, 2004, https://www.congress.gov/bill/108th-congress/house-resolution/728.

258 "levels of voting": Aaron Blake, "Trump just comes out and says it: The GOP is hurt when it's easier to vote," *Washington Post*, March 30, 2020.

258 Dozens of times: Twitter suspended Trump's account after the January 6, 2021, insurrection. His Tweets were archived and are available on TheTrumpArchive.com, as of August 2021.

258 In 2016, the newly elected president claimed: Cleve R. Wootson, Jr., "Donald Trump: 'I won the popular vote if you deduct the millions of people who voted illegally,'" *Washington Post*, November 27, 2016.

258 He created a commission: Ed Pilkington, "Trump scraps his widely denounced commission on voter fraud," *The Guardian*, January 4, 2018.

258 *Politico* reported: David Siders, "'Rigged election' goes from Trump complaint to campaign strategy," *Politico*, July 31, 2020.

259 15 to 20 million people: Larry Buchanan, Quoctrung Bui and Jugal K. Patel, "Black Lives Matter May Be the Largest Movement in U.S. History," *New York Times*, July 3, 2020.

259 Lafayette Square: An inspector general report confirmed the use of CS (tear gas) and stinger ball grenades (rubber pellets), but found that the attack on protestors was not just to enable the photo opportunity for President Trump. U.S. Department of the Interior, Office of the Inspector General, *Review of U.S. Park Police Actions at Lafayette Park*, Case No. 20-0563, June, 2021, https://www.doioig.gov/sites/doioig.gov/files/SpecialReview_USPPActionsAtLafayettePark_Public.pdf.

259 Before the pandemic: From late 2018 to April 2021, there was a nineteen-point drop in Republican support for allowing voters to vote early or absentee without having to document a reason. Pew Research Center, April, 2021, "Republicans and Democrats Move Further Apart in Views of Voting Access," https://www.pewresearch.org/politics/2021/04/22/republicans-and-democrats-move-further-apart-in-views-of-voting-access/.

259 After Trump's fusillade, that shifted: Amy Gardner and Josh Dawsey, "Trump's attacks on mail voting are turning Republicans off absentee ballots," *Washington Post*, July 7, 2020.

259 delaying the election: Zeke Miller and Colleen Long, "Trump floats idea of election delay, a virtual impossibility," Associated Press, July 30, 2020.

259 "We're going to have to see": Aamer Madhani and Kevin Freking, "Trump won't commit to peaceful transfer of power if he loses," Associated Press, September 23, 2020.

259 "stand back—and stand by": The Commission on Presidential Debates, "September 29, 2020 Debate Transcript," https://www.debates.org/voter-education/debate-transcripts/september-29-2020-debate-transcript/.

260 Mark Zuckerberg: The funds were provided to the Center on Tech and Civic Life, a well-regarded Chicago nonprofit. See Michael Scherer, "Mark Zuckerberg and Priscilla Chan donate $100 million more to election administrators, despite conservative pushback," *Washington Post*, October 10, 2020.

260 the players union: Samatha Raphelson, "NBA Agrees To Use Arenas As Polling Places In Deal To Resume Playoffs," NPR, August 28, 2020, https://www.npr

.org/sections/live-updates-protests-for-racial-justice/2020/08/28/907101601/nba-agrees-to-use-arenas-as-polling-places-in-deal-to-resume-playoffs.

260 Hawks' head coach: Ramona Shelburne and Malika Andrews, "What the work behind political change looks like for LeBron James and star athletes," ESPN.com, Oct 30, 2020, https://www.espn.com/nba/story/_/id/30213500/what-work-political-change-looks-lebron-james-star-athletes.

260 Nearly 300,000 people: Josh Peter, Tom Schad, and Jeff Zillgitt, "How sports arenas ran up score on 2020 election, hosting hundreds of thousands of voters," *USA Today*, November 13, 2020.

261 "We didn't tell you who to go vote for": Mark Medina, "LeBron James on 'More Than a Vote': 'We just wanted to educate you, enlighten you and empower you'," *USA Today*, December 8, 2020.

261 news media began to explain: Alex Weprin, "'This Is Going to Be Wild': TV News Outlets Prepare for 'Unpredictable' Election Night Scenarios," *Hollywood Reporter*, November 1, 2020.

261 two thirds of respondents: Zach Montellaro, "Poll: Two-thirds of voters don't expect to know Biden-Trump winner on election night," *Politico*, September 28, 2020.

262 when cases reached the U.S. Supreme Court: See Wendy Weiser and Daniel Weiner, "The Supreme Court's 'Breathtakingly Radical' New Approach to Election Law," *Politico*, November 22, 2020.

262 "shadow docket": See Edward Foley, "Symposium: The particular perils of emergency election cases," SCOTUSblog (Oct. 23, 2020), https://www.scotusblog.com/2020/10/symposium-the-particular-perils-of-emergency-election-cases/.

262 Harris County: Michael Hardy, "The Best Things in Texas, 2021: Lina Hidalgo and Chris Hollins," *Texas Monthly*, January, 2021, https://www.texasmonthly.com/news-politics/the-best-things-in-texas-2021-lina-hidalgo-chris-hollins/.

262 Anti-Defamation League: *Abbott v. Anti-Defamation League Austin, Sw., & Texoma Regions*, 610 S.W.3d 911 (Tex. 2020). The Brennan Center filed the suit along with the law firm Dechert on behalf of the Anti-Defamation League Austin, Southwest, and Texoma Regions ("ADL"), Common Cause Texas, and an individual Texas voter. A description of the case is here: https://www.brennancenter.org/our-work/court-cases/anti-defamation-league-austin-southwest-and-texoma-regions-vs-abbott.

263 highest turnout since 1900: United States Elections Project. According to Michael McDonald's analysis, in 2020, 66.8 percent of the voting-eligible population voted. In 1900,73.7 percent of VEP participated. (In 1904, turnout was 65.5 percent of VEP.)

263 Overall participation soared: 46 percent voted by mail, 26 percent early, and 26 percent on Election Day. The statistics on the 2020 election are drawn from Pew Research Center, "Behind Biden's 2020 Victory," June 30, 2021, https://www.pewresearch.org/politics/2021/06/30/behind-bidens-2020-victory/.

263 "most secure in American history": Cybersecurity and Infrastructure Security Agency, Department of Homeland Security, Joint Statement From Elections Infrastructure Government Coordinating Council & the Election Infrastructure Sector Coordinating Executive Committees, November 12, 2020, https://www.cisa.gov/news/2020/11/12/joint-statement-elections-infrastructure-government-coordinating-council-election.

263 Trump responded to the announcement: David E. Sanger and Nicole Perlroth, "Trump Fires a Cybersecurity Official Who Called the Election 'the Most Secure in American History,'" *New York Times*, updated December 8, 2020.

264 The Republican secretaries of state: Nick Corasaniti, Reid J. Epstein and Jim Rutenberg, "The Times Called Officials in Every State: No Evidence of Voter Fraud," *New York Times*, November 10, 2020.

264 Attorney General William Barr: Michael Balsamo, "Disputing Trump, Barr Says No Widespread Election Fraud," Associated Press, December 1, 2020.

264 he called the claims "bullshit": Jonathan Swan, "Trump Turns on Barr," Axios, January 18, 2021, https://www.axios.com/trump-barr-relationshipoff-the-rails-b33b3788-e7e9-47fa-84c5-3a0016559eb5.html.

264 vanishingly rare: Brennan Center for Justice, *The Myth of Voter Fraud* (March 20, 2021), https://www.brennancenter.org/issues/ensure-everyamerican-can-vote/vote-suppression/myth-voter-fraud; *Debunking the Voter Fraud Myth*, Brennan Center for Justice (January 31, 2017), https://www.brennancenter.org/our-work/research-reports/debunking-voter-fraud-myth; Levitt, *The Truth About Voter Fraud.*

264 only thirty-one credible instances: Justin Levitt, "A comprehensive investigation of voter impersonation finds 31 credible incidents out of one billion ballots cast," *Washington Post*, August 6, 2014.

264 "the people have spoken": "Transcript of the President's Speech, Conceding His Defeat by Clinton," *New York Times*, November 4, 1992, https://www.nytimes.com/1992/11/04/us/1992-elections-disappointment-transcript-president-s-speech-conceding-his-defeat.html.

264 "if he loses": Mick Mulvaney, "If He Loses, Trump Will Concede Gracefully," *Wall Street Journal*, November 7, 2020.

264 It was widely understood: See, for example, Philip Bump, "Here's why you should be very cautious about proclaiming a winner on Election Day," *Washington Post*, September 2, 2020.

265 "people will believe": Walter C. Langer, *The Mind of Adolf Hitler* (New York: New American Library, 1972), 76.

265 Republican city commissioner: *Election Officials Under Attack*, Brennan Center for Justice and Bipartisan Policy Center, June 2021, 8, https://www.brennancenter.org/sites/default/files/2021-06/BCJ-129%20ElectionOfficials_v7.pdf; Max Marin, "How 'GOP Rebel' Al Schmidt Became the Voice of the 2020 Philly Election—and Trump's Nemesis," Billy Penn, December 1, 2020, https://billypenn.com/2020/12/01/al-schmidt-death-threats-trump-philadelphia-election-zero-fraud-republican-commissioner.

265 Democratic groups: See Molly Ball, "The Secret History of the Shadow Campaign That Saved the 2020 Election," *Time*, February 4, 2021.

266 His odd pocket dials: See Olivia Nuzzi, "A Conversation With Rudy Giuliani Over Bloody Marys at the Mark Hotel," *New York*, December 19, 2019; "A Reporter's Guide to Texting With Rudy Giuliani," *New York*, November 25, 2019; Michael Wolff, *Landslide: The Final Days of the Trump Presidency* (New York: Henry Holt, 2021), 96. Many of Trump's advisors, the book reports, believed that Giuliani was "always buzzed."

266 Four Seasons: Trump's tweet read, "Lawyers News Conference Four Seasons, Philadelphia. 11:00 a.m." The fiasco is described with relish in Annie Carni

and Nic Corasinti, "Which Four Seasons? Oh, not that one," *New York Times*, November 7, 2020.

266 "ballots looked suspicious": Mary Claire Dale, "Trump's legal team cried fraud, but courts found none," Associated Press, November 27, 2020.

266 "Networks don't get to decide": Rudolph Giuliani Press Conference, Four Seasons Total Landscaping, Philadelphia, PA, November 17, 2021, https://www.youtube.com/watch?v=7QTRO9MG6z8.

267 "I think this will end up": David Jackson and Joey Garrison, "Trump says he wants to fill Supreme Court seat quickly in case justices need to settle election dispute," *USA Today*, September 23, 2020.

267 cities with heavily Black and Latino electorates: Kristine Phillips, "'Damaging to our democracy': Trump election lawsuits targeted areas with large Black, Latino populations," *USA Today*, December 1, 2020.

267 all sixty-three ruled: Jacob Kovacs-Goodman, *Post-Election Litigation Analysis and Summaries* Stanford-MIT Healthy Elections Project, March 10, 2021, https://healthyelections.org/sites/default/files/2021-04/Post-Election_Litigation_Analysis.pdf.

267 Michigan Supreme Court: *Constantino v. City of Detroit*, 950 N.W.2d 707 (Mich. 2020).

267 "most dramatic invocation": *Wisconsin Voters Alliance v. Wisconsin Elections Commission*, 2020AP1920-OA, December 4, 2020; Bill Glauber, "After siding with liberals in election cases, conservative Wisconsin Supreme Court Justice Hagedorn finds himself in 'Twilight Zone,'" *Milwaukee Journal Sentinel*, December 18, 2020.

267 "doesn't plead fraud": *Donald J. Trump for President Inc. v. Boockvar*, Motion to Dismiss Hearing Transcript, 118:19–20, 137:18.

267 "strained legal arguments": *Donald J. Trump for President Inc. v. Boockvar*, 4-20-cv-02078-MWB (M.D. PA, November 21, 2020).

267 "Charges of unfairness": *Donald J. Trump for President, Inc. v. Secretary Commonwealth of Pennsylvania*, No. 20-3371; No. 20-3384 (3rd Cir.).

268 "The activist judicial machinery": Jenna Ellis, Twitter post, November 27, 2020, 12:46PM, https://twitter.com/JennaEllisEsq/status/1332380180065738754.

268 Supreme Court never heard: The case was never appealed. On December 8, 2020, the Court refused to hear a different Trump campaign case from Pennsylvania. Adam Liptak, "Supreme Court Rejects Republican Challenge to Pennsylvania Vote," *New York Times*, December 10, 2020.

268 "What is the downside": Amy Gardner, Ashley Parker, Josh Dawsey, and Emma Brown, "Top Republicans back Trump's efforts to challenge election results," *Washington Post*, November 9, 2020.

268 Seventy percent of Republicans: Monmouth University Poll, "National: More Americans Happy About Trump Loss Than Biden Win," November 18, 2020, https://www.monmouth.edu/polling-institute/documents/monmouthpoll_us_111820.pdf/.

268 the Electoral Count Act: 3 U.S.C. §§3-21. See 24 Stat. 373, ch. 90, 49th Cong., February 3, 1887; 62 Stat. 671, P.L. 771, June 25, 1948, enacting Title 3, United States Code, into positive law. See Elizabeth Rybicki and L. Paige Whittaker, *Counting Electoral Votes: An Overview of Procedures at the Joint Session, Including Objections by Members of Congress*, Congressional Research Service, updated December 8, 2020, https://crsreports.congress.gov/product/pdf/RL/RL32717/13.

269 "legislatures no longer play a role": *Chiafalo v. Washington*, 140 S. Ct. 2316 (2020).

269 the president had called: Clara Hendrickson, "Donald Trump called Monica Palmer after Wayne County Board of Canvassers meeting," *Detroit Free Press*, November 19, 2020.

269 At the airport in Detroit: Robin Murdoch and Jack Nissen, "Michigan Senate Leader Shirkey swarmed by activists at airport before flying to meet with Trump," Fox2 Detroit, https://www.fox2detroit.com/news/shirkey-swarmed-by-activists-at-airport-before-flying-to-meet-with-trump.

269 "There was a plan": Jane C. Timm, "Rudy Giuliani baselessly alleges 'centralized' voter fraud at free-wheeling news conference," NBC News, November 19, 2020, https://www.nbcnews.com/politics/donald-trump/rudy-giuliani-baselessly-alleges-centralized-voter-fraud-free-wjheeling-news-n1248273.

269 As he ranted: Martin Pengelly, "Sweaty Rudy Giuliani suffers hair malfunction in latest bizarre press conference," *The Guardian*, November 19, 2020.

269 "practicing law on her own": Eric Tucker, "Trump campaign legal team distances itself from Powell," Associated Press, November 22, 2020.

269 "reasonable" person: Defendants' Motion to Dismiss, *U.S. Dominion Inc. v. Sidney Powell*, Civil Action No. 1:21-cv-00040-CJN (U.S.D.C.D.C., March 21, 2021); Jacqueline Thomsen, "Facing Defamation, Sidney Powell Says 'No Reasonable Person' Thought Her Election Fraud Claims Were Fact," *National Law Journal*, March 22, 2021.

269 Powell persisted: Asawin Suebsaeng, "Trump's Bonkers Oval Office Meeting With Sidney Powell Was Even Too Much for Rudy," The Daily Beast, December 19, 2020, https://www.thedailybeast.com/trumps-bonkers-oval-office-meeting-with-sidney-powell-was-even-too-much-for-rudy; Maggie Haberman and Zolan Kanno-Youngs, "Trump Weighed Naming Election Conspiracy Theorist as Special Counsel," *New York Times*, December 19, 2020.

270 "just say that the election was corrupt": U.S. House of Representatives, Committee on Oversight and Reform, "Committee Obtains Key Evidence of President Trump's Attempts to Overturn the 2020 Election," July 30, 2021. The second-in-command at the department called White House demands that it intervene "pure insanity": Matt Zapotosky, Rosalind S. Helderman, Amy Gardner and Karoun Demirjian, "'Pure insanity': How Trump and his allies pressured the Justice Department to help overturn the election," *Washington Post*, June 16, 2021.

270 "brownshirts in the streets": Carol Leonig and Philip Rucker, *I Alone Can Fix It: Donald Trump's Catastrophic Final Year* (New York: Penguin Press, 2021), 383.

270 $250 million: Shane Goldmacher and Rachel Shorey, "Trump Raised $255.4 Million in 8 Weeks as He Sought to Overturn Election Result," *New York Times*, January 31, 2021.

270 "a joke": Josh Dawsey, "The Republican Party's top lawyer called election fraud arguments by Trump's lawyers a 'joke' that could mislead millions," *Washington Post*, July 12, 2021.

270 Supreme Court unanimously tossed: *Texas v. Pennsylvania*, et al., 592 U.S. ___ (2020). In an unsigned order, the justices said Texas did not have standing to bring the case. Justices Alito and Thomas would have heard the case, but would not grant any other relief. https://www.supremecourt.gov/orders/courtorders/121120zr_p860.pdf.

270 "Hail to the Chief": Ryan Randazzo, "Ducey: Trump did call during vote

certification but he didn't ask to overturn Arizona's results," *Arizona Republic*, December 2, 2020.

271 wrote romance novels: See Selena Montgomery, *Hidden Sins* (New York: HarperTorch, 2006).

271 Kemp's office had purged: Vann R. Newkirk III, "The Georgia Governor's Race Has Brought Voter Suppression Into Full View," *Atlantic*, November 6, 2018.

272 Lin Wood: Ryan Mills and Tobias Hoonhout, "The Conspiracy-Theorist Lawyer Who Would Hand Joe Biden Control of the Senate," *National Review*, November 25, 2020, https://www.nationalreview.com/news/the-conspiracy-theorist-lawyer-who-would-hand-joe-biden-control-of-the-senate/.

272 "Someone's going to get shot": David Wickert and James Salzer, "'This has to stop': Georgia official calls out Trump, U.S. senators over threats to election workers," *Atlanta Journal-Constitution*, December 1, 2020.

272 "What I want to do is this": "Read the full transcript and listen to Trump's audio call with Georgia secretary of state," CNN.com, January 4, 2021, https://edition.cnn.com/2021/01/03/politics/trump-brad-raffensperger-phone-call-transcript/index.html

273 Richard Nixon as vice president: Gillian Brockell, "'Grace and humor': The vice presidents who certified their own election losses," *Washington Post*, January 20, 2021.

273 raucous rally: Ashraf Khalil and Michael Balsamo, "Proud Boy, antifa clashes at D.C. Trump rally ends with stabbings, arrests," Associated Press, December 13, 2020.

273 mapped out an illegal plan: Bob Woodward and Robert Costa, *Peril* (New York: Simon and Schuster, 2021), 225-6. Eastman's plan for a coup was published in full in "Trump lawyer's memo on six-step plan for Pence to overturn the election," CNN.com, September 21, 2021, https://edition.cnn.com/2021/09/21/politics/read-eastman-memo/index.html.

273 Pence told Trump: Maggie Haberman and Annie Karni, "Pence Said to Have Told Trump He Lacks Power to Change Election Result," *New York Times*, January 5, 2021.

274 Oath Keepers: Matthew Mosk, Olivia Rubin, Ali Dukakis, and Fergal Gallagher, "Video surfaces showing Trump ally Roger Stone flanked by Oath Keepers on morning of Jan. 6," ABCnews.com, https://abcnews.go.com/US/video-surfaces-showing-trump-ally-roger-stone-flanked/story?id=75706765.

274 "trial by combat": U.S. Congress, House of Representatives, *Materials in Support of H. Res. 24, Impeaching Donald John Trump, President of the United States, for High Crimes and Misdemeanors, Report by the Majority Staff of the House Committee on the Judiciary*, 117th Cong., 1st Sess., January, 2021, 9, https://judiciary.house.gov/uploadedfiles/house_judiciary_committee_report_-_materials_in_support_of_h._res._24.pdf?utm_campaign=4640-519; Aaron Blake, "'Let's have trial by combat': How Trump and allies egged on the violent scenes Wednesday," *Washington Post*, January 7, 2021.

274 machines with secret compartments: Leonig and Rucker, *I Alone Can Fix It*, 458.

274 "kicking ass": Ryan Bort, "Rep. Mo Brooks on Incendiary Jan. 6th Speech: Trump Made Me Do It," *Rolling Stone*, July 6, 2021, https://www.rollingstone.com/politics/politics-news/mo-brooks-insurrection-speech-lawsuit-1193229/.

274 "fight like hell": U.S. Congress, House of Representatives, *Materials in Support*

of H. Res. 24, 10-11; Brian Naylor, "Read Trump's Jan. 6 Speech, A Key Part Of Impeachment Trial," NPR, https://www.npr.org/2021/02/10/966396848/read-trumps-jan-6-speech-a-key-part-of-impeachment-trial.

274 injured one hundred forty policy officers: Tom Jackman, "Police union says 140 officers injured in Capitol riot," *Washington Post*, January 27, 2021.

275 "Well, Kevin": The exchange was reported by Rep. Jaime Herrera Beutler (R-WA). See press release, "Herrera Beutler Again Confirms Conversation with McCarthy Regarding January 6 U.S. Capitol Attack," Office of Rep. Jaime Herrera Beutler, February 12, 2021, https://jhb.house.gov/news/documentsingle.aspx?DocumentID=402083.

276 "The mob was fed lies": Senator Mitch McConnell, 117th Cong., 1st sess., Congressional Record 167 No. 10 (January 19, 2021): S49.

16: The Clash Over the Vote

277 oil painting: A *Philadelphia Inquirer* columnist identified the painting. Will Bunch, "Georgia governor signed a voter suppression law under a painting of a slave plantation," *Philadelphia Inquirer*, March 25, 2021.

277 Park Cannon: Mark Niesse, Maya T. Prabhu, Greg Bluestein "Georgia representative arrested after governor signs elections bill," *The Atlanta Journal-Constitution,* March 25, 2021.

277 thirty-three bills in nineteen states: *Voting Laws Roundup: October 2021 (updated)*, Brennan Center for Justice, https://www.brennancenter.org/our-work/research-reports/voting-laws-roundup-october-2021.

278 Many of these measures once would have been stopped: See *Voting in America: A National Perspective on the Right to Vote, Methods of Election, Jurisdictional Boundaries, and Redistricting*, 117th Congress, U.S. House of Representatives, Committee on House Administration, Subcommittee on Elections, June 24, 2021 (testimony of Michael Waldman), https://docs.house.gov/meetings/HA/HA08/20210624/112806/HHRG-117-HA08-Wstate-WaldmanM-20210624.pdf.

278 lieutenant governor refused: Greg Bluestein, "Georgia's No. 2 Republican boycotts debate over election restrictions," *Atlanta Journal-Constitution*, March 8, 2021.

278 As finally passed, the restrictions: Nick Corasaniti and Reid J. Epstein, "What Georgia's New Voting Law Really Does," *New York Times*, April 2, 2021.

279 "Jim Crow in the Twenty-First Century": President Joseph Biden, "Statement by President Biden on the Attack on the Right to Vote in Georgia," The White House, March 26, 2021.

279 jet fuel tax break: Robert Hart, "Georgia House Passes Bill Stripping Delta Of A Multimillion Tax Break After It Slammed The State's New Voting Restrictions," *Forbes*, April 1, 2021.

279 "stay out of politics": Teo Armus, "McConnell says companies should stay out of politics—unless they're donating money," *Washington Post*, April 7, 2021.

279 "Quantity is important": Eric Bradner and Dianne Gallagher, "Arizona Republican lawmakers join GOP efforts to target voting, with nearly two dozen restrictive voting measures," CNN, March 11, 2021, https://www.cnn.com/2021/03/11/politics/arizona-republicans-voter-suppression-bills/index.html.

279 "purity of the ballot box": S.B. 7, 87th Leg., Reg. Sess. (Tex. 2021); TEX. CONST.,

art. 6, § 4. See Kayla Harris, "'Purity of the ballot box,' an echo of Jim Crow, stricken from Texas voting bill," *Houston Chronicle,* May 8, 2021.

279 remold state election machinery: See *Democracy Crisis in the Making: How State Legislatures are Politicizing, Criminalizing, and Interfering with Elections*, States United Democracy Center, Protect Democracy, and Law Forward, June, 2021, https://protectdemocracy.org/resource-library/document/democracy-crisis-in-the-making-how-state-legislatures-are-politicizing-criminalizing-and-interfering-with-elections/. See also Richard L. Hasen, *Identifying and Minimizing the Risk of Election Subversion and Stolen Elections in the Contemporary United States* (September 18, 2021), Harvard Law Review Forum, forthcoming 2022, UC Irvine School of Law Research Paper No. 2021-50, Available at SSRN: https://ssrn.com/abstract=3926381 or http://dx.doi.org/10.2139/ssrn.3926381

280 "Other portions": "Memorandum: Democracy Crisis Law Update," States United Democracy Center, Protect Democracy, and Law Forward, June 10, 2021, https://statesuniteddemocracy.org/wp-content/uploads/2021/06/Democracy-Crisis-Part-II_June-10_Final_v7.pdf. This is an update of *A Democracy Crisis in the Making*, April 22, 2021, https://statesuniteddemocracy.org/wp-content/uploads/2021/04/FINAL-Democracy-Crisis-Report-April-21.pdf.

280 Democratic lawmakers bolted: Andrea Zelinski, "Inside the Texas Democratic Walkout That Derailed Senate Bill 7," *Texas Monthly*, June 1, 2021.

281 "I'd like to take on": Tina Rosenberg, "Putting the voters in charge of fair voting," *New York Times*, January 23, 2018. See also, "I'd Like to Take On Gerrymandering in Michigan," *Democracy and Justice: Collected Writings 2019*, Brennan Center for Justice, 2020, 38, https://www.brennancenter.org/sites/default/files/2020-04/2020Annual_Democracy%26Justice_Collected%20Writings.pdf. Brennan Center attorney Michael Li worked with Michigan activists to hone the language of the ballot proposal, and Fahey received the 2019 Brennan Legacy Award.

281 similar laws in Colorado: Annie Lo, *Citizen and Legislative Efforts to Reform Redistricting in 2018*, Brennan Center for Justice, November 7, 2018, https://www.brennancenter.org/our-work/analysis-opinion/citizen-and-legislative-efforts-reform-redistricting-2018.

281 in Florida: The movement is described in Emily Bazelon, "Will Florida's Ex-Felons Finally Regain the Right to Vote?," *New York Times Magazine*, September 30, 2018. See also Desmond Meade, *Let My People Vote: My Battle to Restore the Civil Rights of Returning Citizens* (New York: Beacon Press, 2020).

281 civil rights groups were challenging: Amendment 4 passed in November 2018. Fla. Const. art. VI, § 4. The legislature enacted a law, supposedly to implement the amendment, that said its provisions meant that formerly incarcerated people must have paid all fees, fines, and court costs to regain their right to vote. Fla. Stat. § 98.0751(2)(a). Civil rights groups sued, calling the new law discriminatory, and pointing out that there was no system to tell citizens what they owed, and that the legislature's rollback would mean that only a few hundred thousand of the 1.4 million eligible people would actually be able to vote. The Brennan Center, ACLU, and NAACP Legal Defense and Education Fund won at trial. The judge found the scheme discriminatory—indeed, a form of poll tax—and said that the plaintiffs who could not pay their fines could still register to vote. *Jones v. DeSantis*, 462 F. Supp. 3d 1196 (N.D. Fla. 2020). But in September 2020, a three-judge panel of the Eleventh Circuit Court of Appeals reversed the ruling and upheld the restrictions. *Jones v. Governor of Fla.*, 975 F.3d 1016 (11th Cir. 2020). For a full

explanation of the case and its course, see "Litigation to Protect Amendment 4 in Florida," last updated September 2020, Brennan Center for Justice, https://www.brennancenter.org/our-work/court-cases/litigation-protect-amendment-4-florida.

281 Sixteen states: Nathaniel Rakich, "What happened when 2.2 million people were automatically registered to vote," 538.com, October 10, 2019, https://fivethirtyeight.com/features/what-happened-when-2-2-million-people-were-automatically-registered-to-vote/. See also Kevin Morris and Peter Dunphy, *AVR Impact on State Voter Registration*, Brennan Center for Justice, April 11, 2019, https://www.brennancenter.org/sites/default/files/2019-08/Report_AVR_Impact_State_Voter_Registration.pdf.

281 In Illinois: Kim Geiger, "Rauner signs immigration, automatic voter registration bills into law," *Chicago Tribune,* August 28, 2017. Rauner previously had vetoed an earlier version.

282 End *Citizens United*: Brigit Bowman and Simone Pathé, "How the 'No Corporate PAC' Pledge Caught Fire," *Roll Call*, November 8, 2018; Joshua Jamerson, "107 House Democratic Candidates to Congress: We Want Campaign-Finance Reform," *Wall Street Journal*, October 8, 201.

282 most watched political video: Sam Wolfson, "Why Ocasio-Cortez's lesson in dark money is the most-watched political video," *The Guardian*, February 14, 2019.

282 For the People Act: "Annotated Guide to the For The People Act," Brennan Center for Justice, March 18, 2021, https://www.brennancenter.org/our-work/policy-solutions/annotated-guide-people-act-2021; see also "Testimony on S.1" before the Committee on Rules and Administration, U.S. Senate, 117th Congress, First Session, 103-62 (2021) (Michael Waldman, President, Brennan Center for Justice), https://www.rules.senate.gov/imo/media/doc/Testimony_Waldman.pdf.

283 Constitution's Elections Clause: See Eliza Sweren-Becker and Michael Waldman, "The Meaning, History, and Importance of the Elections Clause," *Washington Law Review*, Vol. 96, No 3, 2021. See also Jack Rakove, "The framers would have been fine with sweeping national election reforms," *Washington Post*, June 15, 2021;

283 *The Elections Clause: Constitutional Interpretation and Congressional Exercise,* 117th Congress, U.S. House of Representatives, Committee on House Administration, July 12, 2021 (testimony of Franita Tolson and Jack Rakove), https://cha.house.gov/committee-activity/hearings/elections-clause-constitutional-interpretation-and-congressional.

283 "the Framers gave Congress the power": *Rucho v. Common Cause*, 139 S. Ct. 2484 (2019).

283 In the spring of 1993: As Special Assistant to the President for Policy Coordination, the author attended the meeting with President Clinton and Senator Biden and at least one other senator (he cosponsored public financing with John Kerry of Massachusetts).

284 Fretful commentators: I discuss this in Michael Waldman, "Why Democrats shouldn't break up their voting rights bill," *Washington Post*, April 2, 2021. See one of many arguing a different view, Edward B. Foley, "Voting rights are in trouble. H.R 1 isn't going to pass—but this could," *Washington Post*, March 8, 2021.

284 "failure is not an option": Yet *another* iconic quote that was never said in real life. It was coined by the screenwriters for the film *Apollo 13*, just like Deep Throat's "follow the money." In this case, the real-life flight director, Gene Kranz, did go on to title his memoir, *Failure Is Not an Option* (New York: Simon & Schuster, 2009).

285 "under-the-dome-type strategies": Jane Mayer, "Inside the Koch-Backed Effort to

Block the Largest Election-Reform Bill in Half a Century," *New Yorker*, March 29, 2021.

285 "all-hands moment": Nicholas Riccardi and Michael Biesecker, "'An all-hands moment': GOP rallies behind voting limits," Associated Press, March 19, 2021.

285 filibuster not in the Constitution: See Caroline Fredrickson, *The Case Against the Filibuster*, Brennan Center for Justice, October 30, 2020, https://www.brennancenter.org/our-work/research-reports/case-against-filibuster.

285 legislation to strengthen background checks: Waldman, *The Second Amendment*, 156.

285 "cloture" motions: Data from United States Senate, "Senate Action on Cloture Motions," https://www.senate.gov/legislative/cloture/clotureCounts.htm (last accessed July 2019).

285 "Let's honor him": "Barack Obama's Eulogy of Rep. John Lewis," *Atlanta Journal-Constitution*, July 30, 2020.

285 Senators had changed: For a recent highly readable history of the filibuster, see Adam Jentelson, *Kill Switch: The Rise of the Modern Senate and the Crippling of American Democracy* (New York: Liveright, 2021).

286 Exceptions already were carved out: Molly E. Reynolds, *Exceptions to the Rule: The Politics of Filibuster Limitation* (Washington, D.C.: Brookings Institution Press, 2017), 2–3.

286 New version of the legislation: U.S. Congress, Senate, *Freedom To Vote Act*, S. 2747, 117th Cong., 1st Sess., https://www.congress.gov/bill/117th-congress/senate-bill/2747/all-actions-without-amendments.

287 "This is election subversion": President Joseph Biden, "Remarks by President Biden on Protecting the Sacred, Constitutional Right to Vote," Philadelphia, PA, July 13, 2021, https://www.whitehouse.gov/briefing-room/speeches-remarks/2021/07/13/remarks-by-president-biden-on-protecting-the-sacred-constitutional-right-to-vote/.

Conclusion

290 what we see in Hungary: See John B. Judis, *The Populist Explosion: How the Great Recession Transformed American and European Politics* (New York: Columbia Global Reports, 2016) and *The Nationalist Revival: Trade, Immigration, and the Revolt Against Globalization* (New York: Columbia Global Reports, 2018).

291 "Build the Wall": Michael Wolff, making this point, calls it Trump's "unique selling proposition." Michael Wolff, "Why I'm Sure Trump Will Run for President in 2024," *New York Times*, July 23, 2021.

291 state party committees: Bill Barrow, "Georgia GOP committees vote to censure Kemp, Raffensperger," Associated Press, April 19, 2021.

291 pushed out Liz Cheney: Alayna Treene, Shawna Chen, "House Republicans vote to remove Liz Cheney from leadership," Axios, May 12, 2021, https://www.axios.com/liz-cheney-republican-leadership-vote-9274d8ad-50b9-4442-af54-6225d277cbe0.html.

291 "bamboo fibers": Sam Levine, "Arizona Republicans hunt for bamboo-laced China ballots in 2020 'audit' effort," *The Guardian*, May 6, 2021.

291 Biden won Arizona by an even bigger margin: Jen Fifield and Robert Anglen, "Hand Count in audit affirms Biden beat Trump, as Maricopa County said in November," *Arizona Republic*, September 23, 2021.

291 They know the Big Lie is a lie: See Jane Mayer, "The Big Money Behind the Big Lie," *New Yorker*, August 2, 2021. Mayer quotes Republican officials in states such as Arizona as knowing the voter fraud charges are false, but facing pressure from Republican Party officials and a well-funded conservative legal network to push it anyway. Further evidence: a leader of the Republican state senate in Michigan investigated charges of election fraud, and found only lies. Tim Alberta, "The Senator Who Told the Truth," *Atlantic*, June 30, 2021.

291 Republican candidates for secretary of state: Tim Reid, Nathan Layne, and Jason Lange, "Backers of Trump's false fraud claims seek to control next elections," Reuters, September 24, 2021.

292 "what the United States did not have": David Frum, "There's a Word For What Trumpism is Becoming," *Atlantic*, July 13, 2021.

292 data from the 2020 election: See Pew Research Center, *Behind Biden's Victory*.

292 since Grover Cleveland: Woodrow Wilson fought for women's suffrage. Franklin D. Roosevelt and Harry Truman urged an end to the poll tax, and Truman brought that fight to the Senate floor. John F. Kennedy and Lyndon Johnson supported expanded voting rights, and Johnson won passage of the Voting Rights Act and campaign finance laws. Jimmy Carter unsuccessfully pushed multiple reforms on voter registration and campaign finance. Bill Clinton signed the National Voter Registration Act and proposed a system of public financing for congressional campaigns (the author was his principal policy aide on that legislation).

292 some Democratic pollsters: Stanley Greenberg, Bill Clinton's original pollster, long believed that political reform has become a gateway issue. Voters will not listen to new policy ideas unless a candidate shows she or he understands the need for profound political reform. Stanley Greenberg, "The Average Joe's Proviso," *Washington Monthly*, June/July/August 2015. Joel Benenson, Obama's pollster, published a study in late 2014 reporting "a clear disconnect between the Beltway and Main Street on campaign finance. Curbing the influence of money on electoral politics was one of the strongest policy initiatives tested." The research found that 88 percent of voters—obviously including those from all parties—wanted to end unlimited campaign spending by corporations, unions, and outside groups. Benenson then joined Hillary Clinton's campaign as chief strategist. Benenson Strategy Group, "Beyond the Beltway," December 2014, http://www.beyondthebeltwayinsights.com/content/read-the-beyond-the-beltway-report?submissionGuid=0b1bedce-5346-48fe-a68d-37af93459c29.

293 "identity politics": Stacey Abrams, "E Pluribus Unum: The Fight Over Identity Politics," *Foreign Affairs*, March/April 2019.

294 seven in ten voters still are white: Yair Ghitza and Jonathan Robinson, *What Happened in 2020*, Catalist, https://catalist.us/wh-national/#pp-toc-608eee40d2225-anchor-1; Andrew Prokop, "A new report complicates simplistic narratives about race and the 2020 election," Vox, May 10, 2021, https://www.vox.com/2021/5/10/22425178/catalist-report-2020-election-biden-trump-demographics.

295 At times there has been a hygienic aspect: For a critique of prior reform efforts, see Bruce E. Cain, *Democracy More or Less: America's Political Reform Quandary* (New York: Cambridge University Press, 2014).

295 Political realists are right to see: See, for example, ibid.; Pildes, "Democratic Romanticism"; Jonathan Rauch, "The Case for Corruption," *Atlantic*, March 2014. A young scholar recently noted how reformers' attacks on corruption (and New

Deal liberalism) in the 1970s had weakened public support for government, clearing a path for Reaganism. Paul Sabin, *Public Citizens: The Attack on Big Government and the Remaking of American Liberalism* (New York: W.W. Norton, 2021).

295 National legislative party leaders: Richard Pildes makes this argument when he writes, "Party leaders once had their greatest leverage over their members through the power of committee assignments. These assignments were valuable because they were the means to work on substantive issues a member cared about, ways to raise the member's profile and stature, and ways to raise money for subsequent elections" ("Democratic Romanticism," 833–34). Pildes is broadly right. But for nearly the entire twentieth century, party leaders had only intermittent control over congressional committees. These were run as near-independent fiefdoms by lawmakers who rose through seniority. Typically these were reactionary southerners. Even as president, Lyndon Johnson was forced to work with insurgents to try to evade the power of the House Rules Committee by pushing a "discharge petition" to bring the Civil Rights Act of 1964 to a vote. See Caro, *The Passage of Power*, 484–88. Only when reformers in the mid-1970s allied with national party leaders such as Tip O'Neill did the national Democratic Party gain measurable control. That process was accelerated by Republican Speaker of the House Newt Gingrich. The Contract with America Republicans elected House committee chairs through a caucus vote—again a break with past practice. Nancy Pelosi, when speaker in 2008, wielded tremendous power, deposing John Dingell as chair of the House Energy and Commerce Committee and backing his successor, the environmental leader Henry Waxman.

296 Reformers should swallow hard: Ian Vandewalker and Daniel I. Weiner, *Stronger Parties, Stronger Democracy: Rethinking Reform*, Brennan Center for Justice, September 2015, https//www.brennancenter.org/sites/default/files/publications/Stronger_Parties_Stronger_Democracy.pdf.

297 partisan gerrymandering: *Rucho v. Common Cause* ____.

297 Republicans won the popular vote: Democrats won the popular vote in 1992, 1996, 2000, 2008, 2012, 2016, and 2020, while Republicans won it in 2004. Republican presidents appointed Roberts, Thomas, Alito, Kavanagh, Barrett, and Gorsuch.

297 "almost surgical precision": *North Carolina State Conference of NAACP v. McRory*, 831 F.3d 204, 226 (2016).

297 Texas's harsh ID law: *Veasy v. Abbott*, 830 F.3d 2016 (2016).

297 the Court gave its answer: *Brnovich v. Democratic National Committee*, 594 U. S. ____ (2021). The Supreme Court had interpreted Section 2 as requiring discriminatory *intent*. *Mobile v. Bolden*, 446 U. S. 55 (1980). Congress made clear it wanted discriminatory *impact* to be the standard. "S.1992 - 97th Congress (1981-1982): Voting Rights Act Amendments of 1982." December 2, 1982. https://www.congress.gov/bill/97th-congress/senate-bill/1992.

298 Republican lawyers now eye ways to use the Constitution: The goal is to hinder state courts interpreting state laws and constitutions, as well as election officials, from protecting voting rights. The Elections Clause gives "the legislature" power to set "times, places, and manner" of federal elections. In the Arizona redistricting case described in chapter 13, the Supreme Court rejected this interpretation, and allowed voters to pass redistricting reform. Chief Justice Roberts wrote a dissent in that five-to-four case. In *Rucho*, in 2019, Roberts seemed to have a change of heart, praising state ballot measures (as an alternative to having federal courts police gerrymandering). During the Trump campaign's efforts to bring a case to

the Supreme Court to overturn the election in 2020, three justices indicated some sympathy for the idea of "independent legislatures" unbound by state courts. When the Supreme Court declined to hear the Pennsylvania GOP's challenge to a state court ruling on ballot counting, Justices Alito, Gorsuch, and Thomas wrote, "there is a strong likelihood that the State Supreme Court decision violates the Federal Constitution." *Republican Party of Pennsylvania v. Boockvar*, 592 U.S. ___ (2020). In another case, Justice Kavanaugh veered off the topic (whether a Wisconsin court's ruling on late-arriving absentee ballots would confuse voters) to quote William Rehnquist's assertion, in *Bush v. Gore*, that "'the clearly expressed intent of the legislature must prevail' and that a state court may not depart from the state election code enacted by the legislature." *D.N.C. v. Wisconsin State Legislature*, 592 U.S. ___ (2020), No. 20A66 (Oct. 26, 2020), slip op. at 9 n.1 (Kavanaugh, B., concurring in denial of application to vacate stay).

298 the "right to keep and bear arms": *District of Columbia v. Heller*.

299 That followed decades of advocacy: See Waldman, *The Second Amendment*, 87-137; Reva B. Siegal, "Dead or Alive: Originalism as Popular Constitutionalism in *Heller*," *Harvard Law Review* 122 (2008): 209.

299 "Public sentiment is everything": Fehrenbacher, *Lincoln: Speeches and Writings, 1832–58*, 524–25.

299 Many activists lately have mobilized: See Jeffrey D. Clements, *Corporations Are Not People: Why They Have More Rights Than You Do and What You Can Do About It* (San Francisco: Berrett-Koehler, 2012). The Senate debated an amendment to empower strong campaign finance rules again. S.J. Res. 19, 113th Congress (2013–14). The text reads:

> SECTION 1. To advance democratic self-government and political equality, and to protect the integrity of government and the electoral process, Congress and the States may regulate and set reasonable limits on the raising and spending of money by candidates and others to influence elections.
>
> SECTION 2. Congress and the States shall have power to implement and enforce this article by appropriate legislation, and may distinguish between natural persons and corporations or other artificial entities created by law, including by prohibiting such entities from spending money to influence elections.
>
> SECTION 3. Nothing in this article shall be construed to grant Congress or the States the power to abridge the freedom of the press.

299 "In recurring cycles": John F. Kowal and Wilfred I. Codrington III, *The People's Constitution: 200 Years, 27 Amendments, and the Promise of a More Perfect Union* (New York: The New Press, 2021), 7.

299 "when we consider": Ibid., 6.

300 Look no further: The fight over voting in North Carolina is described in Jim Rutenberg, "A Dream Undone: Inside the 50-Year Campaign to Roll Back the Voting Rights Act," *New York Times*, July 29, 2015.

301 "our Selma": The "Moral Mondays" movement is described in Berman, *Give Us the Ballot*, 287–93.

301 The protests lifted to prominence: Lisa Rab, "Meet the Preacher Behind Moral Mondays," *Mother Jones*, April 14, 2014. Rev. Barber tells the story of the movement in a powerful book, Rev. Dr. William J. Barber III with Jonathan

Wilson-Hartgrove, *The Third Reconstruction: Moral Mondays, Fusion Politics, and the Rise of a New Justice Movement* (New York: Beacon Press, 2016).

301 A bookshelf's worth of bestselling titles: See Steven Levitsky and Daniel Ziblatt, *How Democracies Die* (New York: Crown, 2018); Timothy Snyder, *On Tyranny: Twenty Lessons from the Twentieth Century* (New York: Crown, 2017); Anne Applebaum, *The Twilight of Democracy: The Seductive Lure of Authoritarianism* (New York: Doubleday, 2020: David Frum, *Trumpocracy: The Corruption of the American Republic* (New York: Harper Collins, 2018).

301 "the constitutional crisis": Robert Kagan, "The Constitutional Crisis is Already Here," *Washington Post,* September 23, 2021.

302 The Roman Republic: See Edward Watts, *Mortal Republic: How Rome Fell Into Tyranny* (New York: Basic Books, 2018); Yascha Mounck, "What the Fall of the Roman Republic Can Teach Us About America," *New York Times*, December 24, 2018. But see Mary Beard, *SPQR: A History of Ancient Rome* (New York: W. W. Norton & Co., 2016), 216, arguing that Gracchus was not the first to break the nonviolent political norms of the Roman republic—and that what the Senate really feared from him was his assault on their economic privilege.

302 The 2020 census: Nicholas Jones, Rachel Marks, Roberto Ramirez, and Merarys Rios-Vargas, "2020 Census Illuminates Racial and Ethnic Composition of the Country," United States Census Bureau, August 12, 2021, https://www.census.gov/library/stories/2021/08/improved-race-ethnicity-measures-reveal-united-states-population-much-more-multiracial.html.

The explosive statistic about the declining number of white Americans means less than it appeared in early media reports. Those who identify as white—whether solely or along with another identity—actually increased by over four million people from 2010 to 2020. See Hansi Lo Wang, "This Is How The White Population Is Actually Changing Based On New Census Data," NPR, August 22, 2021, https://www.npr.org/2021/08/22/1029609786/2020-census-data-results-white-population-shrinking-decline-non-hispanic-race.

302 "bowling alone": The phrase comes from Robert Putnam, *Bowling Alone: The Collapse and Revival of American Community*, paperback ed. (New York: Simon & Schuster, 2001).

INDEX

Page numbers beginning with 331 refer to notes.

ABOUT THE AUTHOR

Michael Waldman is president of the Brennan Center for Justice at NYU School of Law, a leading nonpartisan law and policy institute that focuses on improving the systems of democracy and justice. He was director of speechwriting for President Bill Clinton from 1995 to 1999, responsible for writing or editing nearly two thousand speeches, including four State of the Union and two Inaugural Addresses. He was special assistant to the president for policy coordination from 1993 to 1995. He has been a lecturer at Harvard's Kennedy School of Government and an attorney in private practice. His books include *The Second Amendment: A Biography*, *My Fellow Americans* and *POTUS Speaks*. He appears frequently on television and radio to discuss the presidency, democracy, and the Constitution. Waldman is a graduate of Columbia College and NYU School of Law. He lives with his family in Brooklyn, New York.